MAKING TORONTO MODERN

McGill-Queen's/Beaverbrook Canadian Foundation Studies in Art History

Martha Langford and Sandra Paikowsky, series editors

Recognizing the need for a better understanding of Canada's artistic culture both at home and abroad, the Beaverbrook Canadian Foundation, through its generous support, makes possible the publication of innovative books that advance our understanding of Canadian art and Canada's visual and material culture. This series supports and stimulates such scholarship through the publication of original and rigorous peer-reviewed books that make significant contributions to the subject. We welcome submissions from Canadian and international scholars for book-length projects on historical and contemporary Canadian art and visual and material culture, including Native and Inuit art, architecture, photography, craft, design, and museum studies. Studies by Canadian scholars on non-Canadian themes will also be considered.

The Practice of Her Profession
Florence Carlyle, Canadian Painter in the Age of Impressionism
Susan Butlin

Bringing Art to Life
A Biography of Alan Jarvis
Andrew Horrall

Picturing the Land
Narrating Territories in Canadian Landscape Art, 1500 to 1950
Marylin J. McKay

The Cultural Work of Photography in Canada
Edited by Carol Payne and Andrea Kunard

Newfoundland Modern
Architecture in the Smallwood Years, 1949–1972
Robert Mellin

The Codex Canadensis *and the Writings of Louis Nicolas*
The Natural History of the New World, Histoire Naturelle des Indes Occidentales
Edited and with an Introduction by Francois-Marc Gagnon,
Translation by Nancy Senior,
Modernization by Réal Ouellet

Museum Pieces
Toward the Indigenization of Canadian Museums
Ruth B. Phillips

The Allied Arts
Architecture and Craft in Postwar Canada
Sandra Alfoldy

Rethinking Professionalism
Essays on Women and Art in Canada, 1850–1970
Edited by Kristina Huneault and Janice Anderson

The Official Picture
The National Film Board of Canada's Still Photography Division and the Image of Canada, 1941–1971
Carol Payne

Paul-Émile Borduas
A Critical Biography
François-Marc Gagnon
Translated by Peter Feldstein

On Architecture
Melvin Charney: A Critical Anthology
Edited by Louis Martin

Making Toronto Modern
Architecture and Design, 1895–1975
Christopher Armstrong

watts

MAKING TORONTO MODERN

ARCHITECTURE AND DESIGN 1895–1975

CHRISTOPHER ARMSTRONG

McGill-Queen's University Press
Montreal & Kingston • London • Ithaca

ISBN 978-0-7735-4349-2

Legal deposit second quarter 2014
Bibliothèque nationale du Québec

Printed in Canada on acid-free paper

This book has been published with the help of a grant from the Canadian Federation for the Humanities and Social Sciences, through the Awards to Scholarly Publications Program, using funds provided by the Social Sciences and Humanities Research Council of Canada.

McGill-Queen's University Press acknowledges the support of the Canada Council for the Arts for our publishing program. We also acknowledge the financial support of the Government of Canada through the Canada Book Fund for our publishing activities.

Library and Archives Canada Cataloguing in Publication

Armstrong, Christopher, 1942–, author
Making Toronto modern : architecture and design, 1895–1975 / Christopher Armstrong.

(McGill-Queen's/Beaverbrook Canadian Foundation studies in art history)
Includes bibliographical references and index.
ISBN 978-0-7735-4349-2 (bound)

1. Architecture–Ontario–Toronto–History–20th century. 2. Architecture–Ontario–Toronto–History–20th century–Pictorial works. 3. Modern movement (Architecture)–Ontario–Toronto–History–20th century. 4. Modern movement (Architecture)–Ontario–Toronto–History–20th century–Pictorial works. 5. Toronto (Ont.)–Buildings, structures, etc.–History–20th century. 6. Toronto (Ont.)–Buildings, structures, etc.–History–20th century–Pictorial works. I. Title. II. Series: McGill-Queen's/Beaverbrook Canadian Foundation studies in art history

NA747.T6A75 2014 720.9713'5410904 C2014-900654-3

CONTENTS

ACKNOWLEDGMENTS

Many people have helped me in the preparation of this book. One who has contributed greatly to its appearance is Mark Fram, who I retained as a consultant on the selection of the illustrations; as a trained architect, student of Toronto history, book editor, and designer, Mark provided a vast fount of knowledge about sources for pictures and sought out some very fine images. Other friends and colleagues who read early drafts of the manuscript were Professors George Baird, Ramsay Cook, and the late James Lemon, each of whom brought a different perspective to bear with valuable results.

The staffs of various repositories provided access to important sources, in particular the City of Toronto Archives, York University Library, the Baldwin Room at the Toronto Reference Library, and the Thomas Fisher collection at the University of Toronto Library. At the Canadian Architectural Archives at the University of Calgary, Linda Fraser guided me to a treasure trove of photographs in the records of Panda Associates, once Canada's premier firm of architectural photographers, and these photos account for about one-third of the pictures reproduced here. Other people who held copyright to pictures were also cooperative in agreeing to have them included; I thank them and have included their names in the list of illustrations.

York University provided financial support that was crucial to the preparation of the photographs for inclusion in the book. I was also the recipient of a grant from the Aid to Scholarly Publications Program of the Social Science Federation of Canada, and I had the benefit of the assessments from their two anonymous reviewers. Philip Cercone took on supervision of the production of the book at McGill-Queen's University Press, and Joanne Muzak did the copyediting with a keen eye. Errors and infelicities in the text are, of course, my own responsibility.

MAKING TORONTO MODERN

Star Building | Guarantee Trust Building | Canada Permanent Building | Concourse Building | Northern Ontario Building | Bell Telephone Building | National Building

Toronto's New Skyline: Looking West from Yonge Street

INTRODUCTION

How does a provincial society respond to ideas and influences from outside? This book attempts to answer that question by looking at the reception of new ideas about architecture and design in Toronto from the turn of the twentieth century through the 1970s. This era saw repeated pressure to replace the old with the modern. Local boosters felt that modernization was of great significance: their city could be considered on a par with larger metropolises such as London, New York, Chicago, and, within Canada, Montreal. They tirelessly devised monikers intended to convey the message that Toronto had already arrived at that point: "The Queen City of the West" (in the 1890s), "the city that works" (in the 1970s), and "a world-class city" (circa 2000). More than anything, Torontonians wanted to avoid the kind of condescension handed out by the world-weary sophisticate Rupert Brooke who visited in 1912:

0.1 (Opposite) "Toronto's New Skyline," *Construction*, March 1930.

> But Toronto – Toronto is the subject. One must say something – *what* must one say about Toronto? What can one? What has anybody ever said? It is impossible to give it anything but commendation. It is not squalid like Birmingham, or cramped like Canton, or scattered like Edmonton, or sham like Berlin, or hellish like New York, or tiresome like Nice. It is all right. The only depressing thing is that it will always be what it is, only larger, and no Canadian city can ever be anything better or different. If they are good they may become Toronto.[1]

Architecture and design seem like a good lens through which to view the process of cultural transmission and adaptation. Words, pictures, and people arrived in Toronto from elsewhere. The question was what effect new ideas would have. If they were taken up by local professionals, they might seek to persuade a client to commission something à la mode. If funds could be found, a structure might go up that reflected the new thinking. Buildings, after all, are frozen ideas that speak to their heredity so such influences can be discerned.

Yet the obstacles that stand between the first conception of a building design and the ribbon cutting at an official opening are many. Toronto's New City Hall, which opened in 1965 (and is analyzed in considerable detail in

Chapter 6), clearly reveals the interplay of ideas and influences that stand between the conception and completion of a project. Almost from the opening of the city hall and courthouse at Bay and Queen Streets in 1899, municipal officials began pressing for more office space. The question was where would a new building go and what would it look like. Above all, how much would it cost? In the case of an important public building like a city hall, of course, the debate soon became bound up in local politics. (Such questions enter into any discussion about new construction, even of the smallest bungalow, where zoning, design, cost, builder, and the views of neighbours must all be considered.) And in the background of such planning lay broader economic and social concerns. An initial plan for a new municipal building foundered at the time of the First World War. The discussion resumed at the end of the prosperous 1920s but soon died owing to the prolonged economic depression and the outbreak of war again in 1939. Only in the 1950s, during a period of prosperity, did municipal politicians finally agree that something must be done.

Even after voters gave their approval for the funding, a fierce debate broke out about the design of the new city hall. Established architectural firms favoured a staid Neoclassical design. Soon the press, other interested architects (students as well as practitioners), and local politicians all offered their own ideas. Only gradually was the notion of an international design competition accepted. In 1958 Viljo Revell's striking layout won the day, but several years of wrangling followed owing to the concerns of city council about the form and the cost. Seven years elapsed before the new building finally opened to general acclaim. Every architectural project passed through a version of this same gauntlet regarding location, design, and cost en route from conception to completion. In Toronto, however, the process was made more complex by the strength of an aesthetic conservatism not only among many architects but particularly among homebuyers who continued to reject newfangled notions like flat, unornamented walls, and corner windows that they associated with modernism in architecture. An enthusiasm for experimentation with architectural and urban design, which seemed to exist in other cities such as Chicago, was much more muted amongst Torontonians.

What did it mean to make Toronto modern? This book concerns the rather halting impact of modern architecture on Toronto, but it is not a comprehensive study of the various meanings and connotations of that term, especially in the wider world. Particularly after the events of 1968, architectural theorists commenced a long period of debate about the meaning of modernism and when and where it might have died, producing an extremely lengthy shelf of literature.[2] This study is not part of that discussion. Rather, it is an analysis of the buildings that were actually proposed and constructed in the city over the eighty years from 1895 to 1975.

In architecture and design the connotations of the term *modern* have displayed a remarkable plasticity during the twentieth century. In the period covered by this book, the term took on a succession of meanings, sometimes signalled by variations in spelling: "modern, moderne, Modern." Many of the most celebrated practitioners of the modern in Toronto, such as Viljo Revell, Mies van der Rohe, John C. Parkin, and Peter Dickinson, came from elsewhere, bringing their intellectual baggage and skills with them. In time,

0.2
Mayor Nathan Phillips presenting the New City Hall, 1958: "Coming up ... one of the world's finest city halls." Phillips is pictured in an advertisement for Atlas Steels, a major construction supplier.

however, homegrown talent developed, even if Toronto was never recognized elsewhere as a site of avant-garde design to the extent that the most ardent promoters of modernism had hoped.[3] The speed with which new notions gained currency depended, of course, upon external factors. Was there enthusiasm among architects for the ideas that they were reading about in journals, hearing of in speeches, or discussing in classrooms? And what did clients think about the new designs? For instance, it remained largely a losing battle to gain acceptance for houses with flat rather than gabled roofs, whatever might be thought best by the Bauhaus.

Governing the reception of change lay wider economic and social conditions. The First and Second World Wars produced a redirection in priorities whether due to shortages of labour, wage and price inflation, or physical controls on certain supplies like iron or steel. Likewise, the worldwide economic depression of the 1930s led to the evaporation of building contracts and the shelving of planning schemes, not to speak of the unemployment or even bankruptcy of architects and builders. Talk of modernizing might continue but not much was accomplished on the ground during such times. By contrast, the boom years before 1914 and during much of the post-1945 era saw opportunities multiply for the replacement of the old and the addition of new structures. Around the turn of the twentieth century, as Toronto's population shot upward, the city emerged as a regional metropolis. By the close of the period covered in this book, when Toronto had supplanted Montreal as Canada's national metropolis, there was plenty of architectural work to go around. At such times, clients seemed more prepared to listen to proposals for novel projects.

Notions about the best route to social progress also abounded. Was the city of Toronto going to replan its physical infrastructure or was it to make merely incremental changes to what had developed out of market forces during the nineteenth century? On the whole, the answer was that change was desirable, but the parsimony of the ratepayers (municipal property taxpayers) produced a long list of schemes that were rejected outright or proceeded with only after lengthy bouts of public debate and aldermanic cheeseparing.[4] And some notions imported from outside found only grudging favour: apartment living, for instance, was slow to gain acceptance because those who could afford single-family houses continued to prefer them, especially for families with young children.

This narrative begins at a moment when urban planning emerged as an independent discipline. In the 1890s a coalition of local leaders, headed by architects, adopted the tenets of what soon came to be called the "City Beautiful" movement. They sought to improve the street system and, in the process, to create broad ceremonial boulevards lined with monumental structures and preferably framing vistas where important public buildings could be located. Spacious parks and impressive intersections with traffic circles beautified by statuary: that was what the modern city should look like. Proper water and sewage systems were required to make urban living healthier. Up until the eve of the First World War, a great deal of energy was spent on trying to persuade Toronto's politicians and taxpayers to support these changes.

These proposals demonstrated that the term *modern* would possess a significantly different meaning than in later times. From the 1890s, the hallmark of the up-to-date in building design was almost entirely a matter of using new materials and providing new amenities. Iron, steel, glass, and concrete provided architects with the possibility of new construction methods. In 1896 S.H. Capper was imported from Scotland to head up the new department of architecture at McGill University, the first institution in Canada intended to train students in theory and design rather than just the more mundane technical architectural training at the University of Toronto's engineering School of Practical Science. Two years later, Capper produced an article for the periodical *Canadian Architect and Builder* called "The American Tall Building" in which he attacked those who dismissed New York's skyscrapers with their iron and steel frames encased in brick or stone as "a quite illegitimate method of architectural construction, being a sham of the most flagrant kind." He argued that, "The problem asking for a solution is an eminently modern one … We must … put definitely aside the criticism so often heard: 'These tall monstrosities are not architecture at all; they are only engineering with a stone veneer.' They are the buildings of our modern city streets; and if these be not architecture, where indeed is modern architecture to find her place … It is essentially in responding to the needs of modern complex life, in interpreting and meeting them, that the art itself is modern and living."[5]

Not only did the new materials permit taller, safer structures, more fireproof than their predecessors, but they also permitted amenities like elevators, central heating, and ventilation. This message was clearly conveyed by a brief article immediately following Capper's piece in the *Canadian Architect and Builder* that described the private electrical plant recently installed in the new Temple Building at the corner of Bay and Richmond Streets in Toronto, one of the city's first skyscrapers. Three generators would provide direct current power, one to run the elevators and the ventilating fans, the other two to supply up to 2,800 electric lights. These engines and dynamos were described as being "practically noiseless … perfectly dry, and persons can place their hands on any part without feeling the least current."[6] Here was the epitome of up-to-date convenience.

This brand of modernity applauded by Capper in the 1890s was, then, a functional one intended to improve physical and mental comfort in daily life. The irony was that well into the twentieth century this kind of modernity did not entail any radical alterations in the external appearance of buildings. As Capper noted in his article about New York's skyscrapers, "It is one of the misfortunes of their steel-skeleton construction that it must all be, perforce, concealed. The material, unless buried in a fire and weather resisting shell, is extremely ephemeral and unenduring."[7]

As in New York, modern buildings in Toronto remained cloaked within traditional historical styles. Victorian eclecticism, and particularly Richardsonian Romanesque, remained the style of choice for the public buildings up until the mid-1890s, when, again like their American neighbours, those fashions were replaced by the Neoclassicism and Renaissance Revivalism favoured by the Beaux Arts. Impressive temples and miniature palaces lined the streets of Toronto by the First World War. Even the new skyscrapers of ten or a dozen storeys downtown were constructed in the form of classical pillars with traditional base, shaft, and capital. Neo-Gothic structures, which remained attractive to churchmen and university educators, had their hammer-beamed ceilings supported by steel girders and iron tie rods.

Modern conveniences had the same appeal in the field of housing. Indoor plumbing, central heating, artificial lighting, and gas stoves became the hallmarks of the modern house, desired by all who could afford them. Yet the new cookers and electric chandeliers were to be found amongst the inglenooks and panelling that studded Toronto's English cottages and Tudorbethan retreats. The modern was called into service to improve the traditional, to make the familiar more comfortable and efficient.

During the first decade of the twentieth century, a coalition of architects and businessmen expended much energy on plans to redesign and improve Toronto's street system and to secure better access to the waterfront of Lake Ontario. But such schemes were going to cost a great deal of money, and local politicians proved more interested in keeping municipal taxes down while settling for a few more mundane projects like the improvement of the water and sewage systems. So when recession and then the First World War put these proposals on hold, the physical layout of the city remained little changed.

When peace and prosperity returned in the 1920s, however, modernism gained another meaning. New ideas about interior design, developed in Europe, eschewed gloomy, highly intricate Victorian and Edwardian décor. Rather than the sinuous, naturalistic lines characteristic of Art Nouveau, there was now an emphasis on clarity of line and sharpness of edge in products that appeared machine-made. These designs were intended to reflect new inventions and technological developments such as airplanes and motorcars. L'exposition internationale des arts décoratifs et industriels modernes, which opened in Paris in 1925, provided a showcase for these new ideas and products. Toronto interior decorators and architects quickly became aware that these notions merited their attention. Before long, fabrics and furniture began to sport the bright colours and dynamic shapes that came to be called *moderne*. (Here I have avoided the use of the now more common term *Art Deco* on the grounds that it is anachronistic, having only come into common usage in the later 1960s, and, since then, has been stretched to cover so many diverse objects that its precise meaning has largely been drained away.)[8] These ideas were reflected in interior design as well as exteriors. New skyscrapers on Toronto's Bay Street now glistened with colourful ornamentation. By the 1930s so-called *Streamline moderne* was supposed to make cinemas and automobile dealerships look like ocean liners, and sharply incised patterns, sunbursts, and radio waves came to adorn all sorts of products.

However eye-catching, these shapes and colours did not reflect the kind of dramatic changes in framing, heating, lighting, and ventilation that the earlier wave of modernism had entailed. Though new materials such as plastics and aluminum were sometimes involved, the moderne was mainly a decorative movement rather than one of fundamental transformation in architecture or design. Perhaps for that reason it was quite readily accepted in many quarters, even in conservative Toronto, partly thanks to the promotional skill of firms like the T. Eaton Company Limited, whose new department store on College Street, which opened in 1930, was a kind of monument to the moderne. And such fashions demonstrated remarkable staying power as products such as automobiles with ostensibly aerodynamic fenders, fins, and rooflines continued to be manufactured for a generation after the Second World War (and, in many places, retain their popularity to the present day).

At the same time during the 1920s, however, a much more radical shift in ideas, which came to be called the Modern Movement, also developed in Europe. Le Corbusier's provocative manifesto, *Vers une architecture*, was published in 1923 but not translated into English until 1927 and only reviewed in the *Journal of the Royal Architectural Institute of Canada* in 1929. Le Corbusier represented Modernists who were committed to functionalism not merely in services but in external design, which was expected to reflect the internal uses of buildings. Such architects demanded the elimination of ornamentation and the use of flat wall planes and clear expression of framing.

Those notions acquired a creed in 1932 when Henry-Russell Hitchcock and Philip Johnson published *The International Style: Architecture Since 1922* in which they attempted to codify an "International Style" derived from the works of Europeans like Le Corbusier, Mies van der Rohe, Walter Gropius, and J.J.P. Oud. From this book and the attendant show at New York's Museum of Modern Art, the word *modern* acquired its upper case *M* to characterize certain types and forms of building.[9] Proponents of this "Modern Movement" demanded that exterior appearance and internal layout should be determined by the functions that a structure was intended to accommodate. Materials like steel and concrete would continue to have significance – even crucial importance – but now their presence was to be emphasized and celebrated rather than concealed. The canonical work on the development of Modern architecture, Sigfried Giedion's 1941 *Space, Time and Architecture*, declared that there were "three generations of men concerned with building up the architecture of this century. There are differences between these generations, but what is significant is that, while being true to itself, none has felt it necessary to renounce its forebears, and each has thus been able to carry forward what the earlier generation had begun."[10] The assumption was that these people formed part of a "Movement" that sought to transform the social role of buildings and their surroundings so that future cities and neighbourhoods might function in ways quite different from the past.

This version of Modernism, however, made little impact upon Toronto in the thirty years after Le Corbusier first issued his manifesto. Even when these new ideas began to penetrate, the Depression of the 1930s pretty much halted major new construction in the city, and what building was completed (particularly by the federal government) hewed to a fairly conservative path, blending some elements of the Beaux Arts and the moderne in what has been described as Stripped Classicism. During the Second World War, other priorities and shortages of key materials kept civilian building largely dormant. Only in the early 1950s did architects and, equally important, their clients begin to be persuaded to consider designs that were based upon the principles propounded by the Modern Movement. Two major projects, Viljo Revell's New City Hall (opened in 1965), which drew upon the naturalistic forms favoured by Scandinavian architects like Alvar Aalto, and the severe abstraction of Mies van der Rohe's black towers for the Toronto-Dominion Centre (first occupied at the end of 1966), showed that attitudes were undergoing a shift.

Torontonians did not, however, embrace the Modern with enthusiasm in residential design, particularly in the case of single-family housing. Flat roofs, plain white walls, and exposed steel or concrete made little headway against the longstanding preference for brick-faced Georgian revivals or bungalows and split-levels in the city's rapidly expanding suburbs. As they had since the turn of the twentieth century, homebuyers proved themselves open to the conveniences of the functionalist brand of modernism (to which were now added picture windows, air conditioning, and oil furnaces), but remained quite content to cloak them in traditional exteriors.

Thus, between the late nineteenth century and the 1970s, Torontonians were presented with three developments in architecture and design, which I have called "modern/moderne/Modern." The first two were much more readily accepted than the last, whose reception was delayed not only on account of the impact of economic depression and war between 1930 and 1945 but also because it was much more radical. Only the prolonged era of postwar prosperity in the 1950s and 1960s allowed the Modern Movement to gain a firm foothold in Toronto, though it never penetrated deeply into the field of low-rise housing.

Where had these ideas about modern architecture and design come from? The answer, of course, was abroad. News about Chicago's 1893 Columbian Exhibition was quick to reach Toronto and helped to spark demands for improvement of its urban plan. Outside consultants and new immigrants also arrived in the city to add to the mix. A lucky few Canadians were even able to study the methods of the Beaux Arts in France or to apprentice in the United States, though most aspiring architects could not afford to do so. They had to rely upon print and pictures to keep up with trends elsewhere, though a steady flow of information continued to arrive, even if persuading local clients to accept some of the more radical notions was another matter.

The first architect in the city who could claim a direct personal association with the giants of the Modern Movement was John C. Parkin, who came originally from Manitoba and studied at Harvard with European émigrés Walter Gropius and Marcel Breuer before arriving in Toronto at the end of the Second World War. Parkin became the local architect whose designs most closely resembled the severe abstraction of the International Style represented by Mies van der Rohe.

Parkin was only one of a number of arrivals after 1945 who brought with them and developed divergent interpretations of Modern architecture. Despite Sigfried Giedion's claim that successive "generations" of Modernists did not renounce the ideas of their predecessors, these newcomers represented a number of different streams and crosscurrents. One important group were the men who had trained in Great Britain and assimilated their avant-garde ideas from academies like the Architectural Association. The most notable of these was Peter Dickinson who demonstrated an extraordinary energy and versatility before his career was tragically cut short by illness. In addition there were people like Ronald (always called "Ron") Thom from British Columbia, who blended together elements of a West Coast style (which reflected influences from California) with the more naturalistic designs of Scandinavians like Alvar Aalto. The most dramatic building in twentieth century Toronto sprang, of course, from the Finn Viljo Revell (much influenced by Aalto), who won the international competition for a new city hall in 1958. But that competition also brought to the city men like Australian John Andrews (by way of Harvard), who awakened the local citizenry to currents like Brutalism, however hard many of them found it to share his enthusiasm for the rough textures of concrete, *béton brut*.

In addition to the newcomers, by the 1950s, the local scene displayed much more intellectual breadth and vigour than it had earlier. The education offered at the School of Architecture at the University of Toronto, from which the majority of local practitioners graduated, had undergone changes as it gradually squirmed free of the grip of engineers and tradition-minded teachers. Professor Eric Arthur, who joined the faculty in the early 1920s, came to have greater sympathy and understanding of Modern trends over the following decades. Arthur invited eminent visitors to the school, including Frank Lloyd Wright, and students were set to reading works like Giedion's to become familiar with developments in the wider world. As the Canadian economy picked up steam after the Second World War firms were ready to hire new staff. Some clients began to appreciate that their businesses might project a more positive image with an up-to-date office or factory, even if homebuyers remained distinctly cool to design innovations.

Technological change also continued to exert an influence on workplace design. Most important were steel framing with glass or brick infill and artificial lighting. In the suburbs this meant plants with large open floor spaces, which allowed more flexible placement of materials and machinery. In fact, a number of factory buildings like the Ford Motor Company's assembly plant, completed in 1923, bore many of the hallmarks of modernism but attracted little attention from Torontonians who did not think of such industrial structures as "real architecture." By the 1960s the curtain walls of the International Style proved an economical blueprint for creating the office towers that developers erected in Toronto's drive to overtake Montreal as Canada's national economic metropolis, particularly in fields like banking. Mies van der Rohe's complex of skyscrapers for the Toronto-Dominion Bank, following immediately upon Revell's New City Hall, finally seemed to sustain the claim that Toronto was becoming a modern place like New York or Chicago.

Critics have said that in Canada architects did not show much interest in the solution of broader social problems. Yet some practitioners did demonstrate such concerns. In the 1950s Don Mills, which has been represented as the epitome of the suburb created by a large profit-seeking corporation, was laid out to reflect advanced urban planning ideas such as those that had given birth to Britain's "new towns." The problem of providing decent housing and improved amenities for less well-off Torontonians was not approached in precisely the same way as the Bauhaus had done. Yet architects such as Irving Grossman began to lay out large-scale apartment and townhouse projects that aimed to push the automobile away to the periphery and to create pedestrian walkways and common green spaces to improve quality of life. Among some members of the profession, there also remained vestiges of the interest that the original Modernists had displayed in the machine aesthetic, particularly as displayed by the use of prefabrication in order to reduce construction costs without compromising improved design.

The 1970s, where this book ends, saw several important shifts. The Modern Movement in architecture marked its half-century. Ideas that had once seemed radical were now becoming workaday. New challengers, such as Postmodernism, were arising, which argued for the reincorporation of traditional elements into current designs. In the city of Toronto a political reform movement arose, fuelled largely by concerns about overdevelopment of the central business district, suburban sprawl, and the construction of expressways primarily designed to serve commuters. At the same time, the incursion of high-density construction into traditional residential neighbourhoods composed of detached or semi-detached family houses created concerns, particularly among those who were familiar with Jane Jacobs's 1961 book, *The Death and Life of Great American Cities*.[11]

Following the approval of a formal city land use plan in 1969, city council, which had been elected in 1972, imposed a holding bylaw that limited downtown high-rise construction to forty-five feet pending the development of a central area plan. The eventual result was a set of policies and regulations that encouraged ideas like the combination of commercial and residential uses within a single development. So in intellectual terms, the 1970s proved to be not unlike the 1890s with the revival of interest in a detailed land use plan that had eluded Toronto for so long.[12]

During the eighty years chronicled in this book, the champions of making Toronto modern meant different things. At the start, modernity was a matter of functionalism, providing more pleasant living conditions whether by innovations in plumbing or heating or by making the urban landscape more attractive by adding amenities like parks. The moderne was intended to add decorative flourishes but did not entail fundamental change. Slower to gain acceptance was Modern architecture, though in the end it did much to change the face of the city through office buildings and apartment towers. Private houses were much less affected by the Modern Movement so that large areas of Toronto did not look all that different from the previous incarnation, even after acres of new developments sprawled into the suburbs for miles around. Yet the combined influence of ideas from abroad, practitioners who moved to the city, and changes in architectural education did do much to transform the local scene.

This book is ordered roughly chronologically in chapters that deal with the transformations of the idea of the "modern/moderne/Modern" into concrete form through architecture and design. The first chapter deals with the period from the 1890s to the end of the First World War. Chapter 2 focuses on the arrival of moderne ideas in the mid-1920s. As the third chapter shows, the Depression snuffed out most building so that the radical doctrines of the Modern Movement were slow to gain traction. The Second World War pushed other priorities to the forefront as the fourth chapter shows, and thus it was not until around 1950 that these new notions began to gain prominence. Chapter 5 focuses on a time of rapid change up to 1955, and the sixth chapter looks at new varieties of Modernism that entered city building by examining several notable projects, such as the New City Hall. Chapter 7 carries the story forward from the mid-1950s through the 1970s as the logic of Modernism gradually began to be challenged, though its monuments and its influential ideas would remain even after alternative models began to emerge.

The illustrations are such an important element of this book that something should be said about them. A conscious effort has been made to choose a variety of types of pictures. There are a few maps, a few portraits, a few plans and drawings, and not just shots of the fronts of buildings. The photographs were taken around the time that the projects were undertaken and are, therefore, intended to show readers what structures looked like around the time of their completion. I decided to use only contemporary photographs since the narrative concentrates upon the responses that these buildings elicited when they were first erected.[13] There are no present-day rephotographs, which would most likely require retouching or manipulation to remove alterations or additions (such as room air conditioners or signage) that are the inevitable fate of almost all buildings.

General questions arise about the dating of the photographs and of the buildings they depict. It is virtually impossible to date precisely the creation of most of the photographs used here.[14] In many cases all that is known is the year in which a particular picture was taken (which the cameramen from Panda Associates, the source of about one-third of the images, were careful to note), or the date of the publication in which an image was reproduced. In fact, it is not always easy to know what date to give to a building, even a well-known one. The exact date when construction began is usually unknown; nor is it clear on what date work was finished or when occupancy commenced. For instance, the first tower of the Toronto-Dominion Centre, one of Toronto's most famous buildings, seems to have welcomed its first tenants at the end of 1966, though the formal opening ceremonies were held on 1 July 1967, the centennial of Canadian Confederation. Thus, the dates given for buildings in the text and in the list of illustrations are the ones usually assigned by the sources, normally the date when publication of the pictures occurred.

Given that the book covers a period from the late nineteenth century to the late twentieth, marked variations in the quality of the images reproduced are obvious. Often, the only available pictures come from printed publications, and, though efforts have been made to remedy their most obvious deficiencies, they cannot be the equal of pictures scanned directly from large, glossy prints. Every effort has been made to render the older images as faithfully and clearly as possible.

Finally, something should be said about the reasons that various pictures were taken, which often affected what the photographer chose to focus upon. Much of the architectural literature in this period was aimed at self-promotion. Architects, builders, and owners supplied the pictures and often the accompanying text with the intent of making their work look appealing and dramatic. In the case of Figures 2.20 and 2.21, for instance, the interiors of the T. Eaton Company's College Street department store were published in *Construction* to draw customers into its dramatic new premises. Publicity was the avowed purpose of retaining Panda Associates (Canada's leading architectural photographer in the post-1945 period), but Panda pictures share a highly recognizable style that is in some measure responsible for the way in which certain buildings are still perceived today. Some of the illustrations include bits of written text to show the kind of commentary that appeared alongside pictures.

View of Toronto in 1920. Twelve miles of waterfront boulevard, parks and driveways.

Channel to be 6,800 feet long, wide, and 24 feet deep, and v minate in a basin 1,000 feet

1

PRESSURE FOR CHANGE 1895-1919

In 1895 Toronto was just recovering from a nasty recession that had severely dampened economic growth and slowed the increase of population. Moreover, a judicial inquiry had confirmed charges that bribery and corruption of city councillors in connection with the street railway franchise and the electric street lighting contract were all too well-founded. The citizenry were deeply divided over whether the new electric trolleys should run on Sundays, the ratepayers having turned the idea down in plebiscites in both 1891 and 1893 with another vote likely pending before long. As if to signal divine displeasure with the "City of Churches" the worst fire in its history broke out on 7 January 1895, destroying all the principal buildings along King Street, the main east–west commercial artery. In September the intake pipe on the bottom of the harbour, which delivered water for drinking, sanitation, and firefighting, blocked up, filled with air, and bobbed to the surface, forcing residents to take deliveries from watercarts.[1]

1.1 (Opposite) Waterfront ambitions, 1912. "View of Toronto in 1920," as anticipated by the Harbour Commissioners.

A change in the structure of municipal government seemed long overdue. How else to deal with crackpot schemes like a hugely expensive aqueduct running southward along Yonge Street from Lake Simcoe to supply fresh water and generate electricity at its bottom end? The "aqueductors" and their aldermanic friends proved irrepressible, despite repeated defeats in votes at city council. In the spring of 1896 Toronto got a new executive Board of Control, composed of the mayor and three aldermen, that prepared the financial estimates and administered the municipal civil service. Their recommendations could only be overturned by a two-thirds vote of the whole council.[2]

At long last, the city seemed equipped with a government that might be able to deal with a number of increasingly pressing urban problems. Like other North American cities, Toronto had been allowed to grow during the nineteenth century under the influence of private decision making expressed through market forces and modulated only intermittently by governmental intervention and philanthropy. By 1890 the city was a gritty, somewhat higgledy-piggledy place, crisscrossed by railway tracks that cut off the downtown from the shores of Lake Ontario and created annoying level-crossings on the main streets. Alongside the tracks ran a strip of factory buildings with their tall chimneys belching dark smoke, extending right across the waterfront from the distillery in the east, past the gasworks and the railway station with its huge yards to the vast farm implement plant where the tracks bent northward to "the Junction" between the two main railway systems, surrounded by another heavy concentration of industry.[3]

As the pace of urban development speeded up once the recession ended concerns focused on health and sanitary issues and the need for urban green spaces, but such matters were dealt with in isolation from one another. Dismay over the ugliness and pollution of much of the modern industrial cityscape aroused alarm, but only in the 1890s did some people begin to become convinced that such problems required coordinated action in the form of comprehensive urban planning.[4]

From that time onward, a number of leading citizens pressed for changes that would improve the look of Toronto and offer residents greater health and happiness. To make the city "modern" had several meanings in this period before the First World War. Efficiency was one objective, to be achieved through the improvement of the flow of traffic with street straightenings and widenings. Hand in hand might come new parks and especially better access to the shores of Lake Ontario. Construction could begin on new buildings, particularly monumental structures like a railway station and new government offices. And this drive for modernity was to be facilitated by the use of modern materials like steel, glass, and reinforced concrete, which would permit buildings higher than about four storeys. Housing should now include creature comforts like indoor plumbing and central heating. The difference between these objectives and the eras of the "moderne" and the "Modern Movement," which were to follow, was that these materials and techniques were not to be used to create distinctive forms of architecture and design but rather to permit the continuation of older traditions while the new conveniences were largely hidden from view.

In pursuit of these objectives, the modernizers gave speeches, experts were consulted, and ambitious plans were published. Parts of the city did acquire a changed appearance as new buildings went up. Victorian excess began to be shunned for the more austere Neoclassicism of the Beaux Arts, which was becoming popular in the United States. Banks and other businesses, even the University of Toronto, saw a burst of construction that lasted up until another recession hit the country on the eve of the First World War. When a serious fire destroyed a large area of the downtown in 1904, the result was a wave of reconstruction that included the city's earliest skyscrapers. The biggest project of all was the creation of a monumental new railway station along a widened Front Street, just the kind of building that civic beautifiers were especially enthusiastic about. To the dismay of the keenest activists, however, the results in the public sphere, such as new street layouts and expanded parklands, proved few and far between.

I

By the mid-1890s Torontonians had an image for their modernized city to aspire to: Chicago. That city had hosted the 1893 Columbian Exhibition with its dazzling "White City" on the lakefront, the design of the buildings coordinated by architect Daniel Burnham and the open space laid out by landscaper Frederick Law Olmsted, the person behind New York's Central Park, who had also been retained by Montreal to redesign the park on Mount Royal in the 1870s.[5] The city's growing community of architects was the first to take up the cause of civic improvement.[6] At the January 1895 convention of the Ontario Association of Architects (OAA), W.A. Langton told the members that, "beginning in Chicago and taken up in Montreal," a widespread movement was already afoot to create "societies to have supervision of the ornamentation and laying out of those cities." Langton proposed that the Ontario association create a similar body to oversee Toronto's redesign. The seconder of Langton's motion emphasized the "very great importance that some standard of good taste should be established." Another architect added that quick action was needed to prevent a hotel from being erected on the former grounds of the boys' private school, Upper Canada College (which had recently moved to a new building in the north end of the city). He claimed that the site on King Street at Simcoe had as much potential for development as an open space as the Champs-Élysées in Paris, but that "The tendency in Toronto seemed to be towards covering every open spot of ground with buildings." W.R. Gregg contended, however, that it would be more effective to try and get an influential group of local citizens to lobby for more modest projects like the clearance of the lands on the south side of Queen Street opposite the new City Hall for a public square. Some OAA members argued that such issues were a matter of concern only to Torontonians rather than the profession province-wide, but, in the end, a Civic Adornment Committee was created. The committee was composed of two Toronto architects, along with one each from Ottawa, Hamilton, Kingston, and Stratford.[7]

In January 1896 the chair of this committee, M.B. Aylesworth, reported to the next OAA convention about the duty to take to "heart the aesthetic education of the Canadian people and recognition of the beneficial influence of artistic surroundings." The members had identified a number of "practical questions for Toronto" that needed attention: the extension of College (later University) Avenue (which ran south from the new legislative building at

Queen's Park only as far as Queen Street) right down to the railway station on Front Street;[8] increasing the open space at major street intersections and their embellishment with sculptures and fountains; "regulating the erection of buildings"; the laying out of parks and driveways; the erection of statues commemorating notable Canadians; the establishment of museums and art galleries; the improvement of the Toronto Island; and the reservation of certain streets for "better class residences only."[9]

Around the same time, a group of local artists sought support for creating history paintings for the new city hall, which was under construction on Queen Street at the head of Bay. In the spring of 1897 a new organization called the Toronto Guild of Civic Art was created. Its board was composed of artists, architects, and interested "laymen," and the organization aimed "to promote and encourage civic art."[10] Led by Bank of Commerce executive B.E. Walker, a delegation from the Guild appeared before the city's Board of Control to urge the city to put up $8,000 to finance the murals at city hall. The politicians declined to give the money, but city council did agree to consult the Guild about all aspects of public art in the city to ensure a high standard of excellence.[11]

The Ontario Association of Architects therefore dissolved its committee,[12] leaving it to the Guild to promote such amenities in Toronto. One of its board members, artist George Reid, offered to undertake the first mural in the city hall at his own expense to be followed by a series of other similar pictures, an offer accepted by the city. The Guild then successfully sought to have a large number of historical pictures executed for the recently completed legislative building in Queen's Park.[13] Once these paintings had been agreed to, however, the first blush of enthusiasm faded away; by 1900, the Guild had declined to just eleven members, and it was not clear what future the organization had.[14]

Still, the prosperous times encouraged some Torontonians to believe that their city could afford ambitious improvement schemes. Between 1901 and 1911, the city's population increased from 208,000 to 376,000, and the value of building permits issued annually during that decade rose from about $3.5 million in 1901 to more than $24 million. As new buildings spread across the landscape, the value of the city's real estate assessment went from about $130 million in 1901 to more than $309 million in 1911. Between 1905 and 1912, the city embarked on a great expansion in area, annexing a ring of suburbs to the north that created the inverted T-shape that the municipality would retain until 1998.[15]

By the turn of the century the idea of relying upon professional experts such as architects and landscape designers to draw up integrated schemes for city planning was gaining supporters in the United States. The term *City*

Beautiful was coined in 1899 to stand for the remodelling of urban spaces to reflect beauty, order, system, and harmony in place of slums and sweatshops. Grand schemes were devised for vistas down broad tree-lined avenues framing monumental Neoclassical buildings such as railway stations and civic centres. Plans began to take shape in Washington, DC in 1902 to remove the railway sheds on the Mall and restore Pierre L'Enfant's eighteenth-century layout with a grand vista from the Potomac River past the Washington Monument towards the Capitol building.[16] The parks designed by the firm that continued Frederick Law Olmsted's practice provided examples of green spaces as a restorative for debilitated residents.[17] Such ideas went hand in hand with proposals for more modest street improvements and the establishment of local playgrounds. At the same time, attention was paid to the solution of functional problems like garbage collection, sewage disposal, and public transit. The objective was to improve the physical environment of the gritty, crowded metropolises of North America so as to make the lives of ordinary city dwellers more rewarding. Great interest was created by the revamping of Washington, and urban planners began to organize themselves, culminating in the creation of the American Civic Association in 1904.[18]

In 1901 a group of young Toronto architects persuaded the Guild of Civic Art to create a series of committees to gather information on projects such as city parks and public squares, new driveways and boulevards, and the improvement of the waterfront.[19] The Guild (now usually known simply as the Civic Guild) then reached out to other organizations, such as the Engineers' Club and the Board of Trade, and organized a meeting at which a motion was passed that urged city council to take action on planning. In June 1901 W.A. Langton, representing the Guild and backed up by architect Edmund Burke, chair of the recently created Toronto chapter of the OAA, led a delegation to the city's Board of Control to insist that "some systematic plan" was urgently required. The architects requested the city to set aside $1,000 for expert advice from somebody like Frederick Law Olmsted Jr, who was carrying on his father's practice.[20] They argued that leaving such planning to a group of voluntary "enthusiasts" would militate against the results being taken seriously in future. The mayor and the Board of Control expressed interest in the idea but failed to come up with any funds.[21]

Toronto architects continued to press this issue. In the spring of 1902 W.A. Langton gave an address on "City Planning" to the Central Ontario School of Art, which showed that he was thoroughly familiar with recent developments. German cities, he observed, were especially progressive in imposing overall plans that specified permitted land uses so that homeowners need not be concerned about their neighbourhoods losing their existing character or being encroached upon by factories or apartment blocks.

Among the scores of lantern slides he showed his audience were pictures of the Ringstrasse in Vienna, with the medieval city walls demolished and replaced by a grand boulevard carrying electric trams past monumental buildings.

Langton's talk made clear that, in his mind, the ideal urban place was like one of Ebenezer Howard's "garden cities" in Britain.[22] The ideal city should have a compact residential district for the better-off citizens, "in touch" with offices and business premises downtown so as to limit the amount of travel through the centre. Factories should be located around the periphery where land was cheaper and nuisances like noise and smoke less evident; the workers who toiled there could live nearby so that they need not take lengthy streetcar rides to and from their jobs. Railways could serve these factories more efficiently with only a small number of spur lines entering the downtown to deliver passengers and goods to retail outlets. These objectives necessitated strict land use bylaws to protect the better residential districts, the foundation of sound municipal planning.

Toronto must aim to eliminate the jumble of residential, commercial, and industrial activities that gave the city its nondescript air. Langton even criticized Jarvis Street, one of the city's finest wide tree-shaded boulevards lined with grand houses. Ornamental it might be, but this layout should not be imitated elsewhere: "These suburban streets and suburban residences in the heart of the city are misplaced." The houses were so close together that they could not have windows on all sides, a "distressing" situation, which created a monotonous and characterless streetscape. Better to build blocks of three or four row houses extending right to the sidewalk broken up by large grounds for grand mansions that would provide a "contrast of solidity and openness and gives a varied picturesqueness." Elsewhere, the finest sites must be reserved for the highest purposes, public ones, as "I think we have passed the time when power and wealth can absorb the best there is in the city."[23]

Toronto's street network would have to be extensively modified. Langton argued that the rectangular street grid made the trip from the northeast and northwest to downtown unnecessarily time-consuming; his solution was to cut wide diagonal thoroughfares across the grid. L'Enfant's original plan for Washington, now being implemented, had provided for such a layout, creating more varied and interesting intersections. "This is the sort of thing," he claimed, "which might be superimposed upon Toronto for the benefit of our children." To those who complained of the expense and disruption, Langton pointed out that London was already undertaking such schemes and had discovered the cost to be less than expected as the new streets created building lots with prime frontages that could be sold off to developers. "In order to

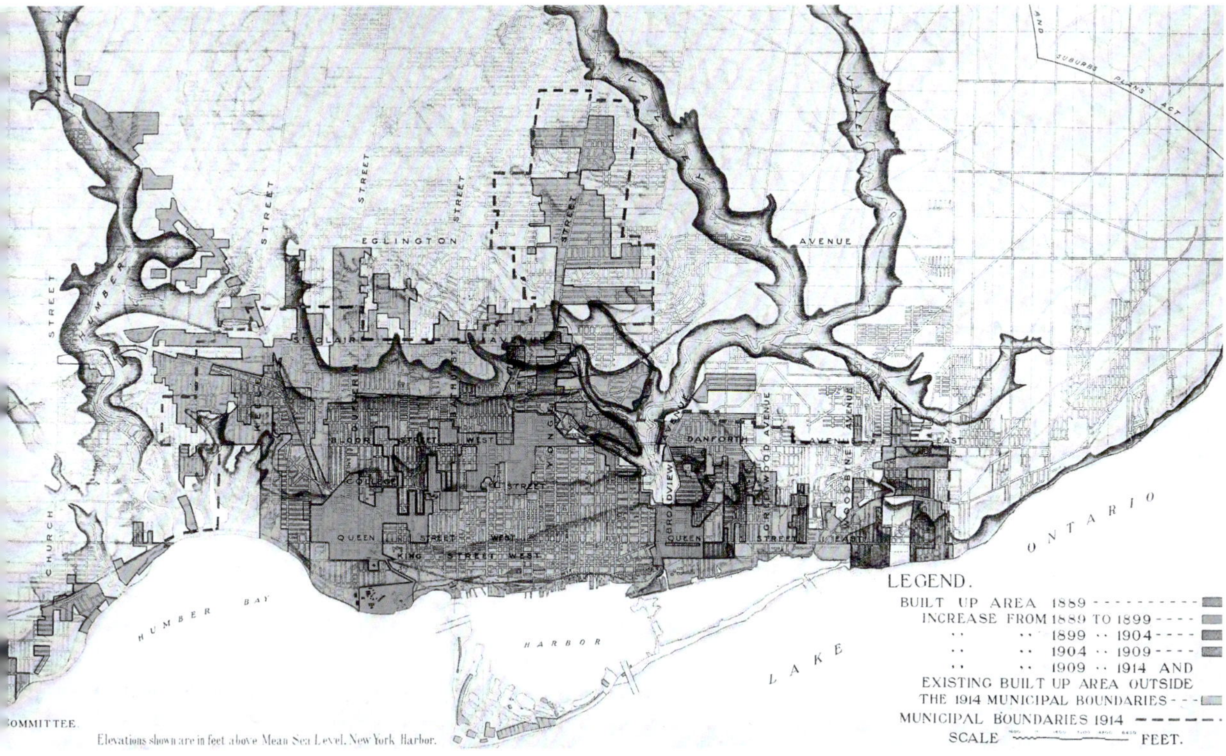

1.2
Civic topography, 1915. Most of the ravines and glacial beaches that defined the nineteenth-century city and environs were obscured during the twentieth century.

make a city beautiful," he advised, "you have to attend in the first place to a plan. As far as convenience goes ... the nearer we can make our plan approach to that of a spider's web the better."[24]

Langton's analysis of Toronto's street layout highlighted certain problems that stemmed from decisions taken very early in the city's history. At first glance, the city appeared to have been plunked down on a fairly level plain on the north shore of Lake Ontario, acreage across which it might spread without much hindrance like some prairie railway town. The site had originally attracted British imperial officials in the 1790s because it lay behind an arc of sandbars (called "The Island"), which provided a large, protected harbour. From the shoreline a fairly flat plateau sloped gently back for a couple of miles, cut only by the beds of some creeks. To the north lay a continuous escarpment about fifty to seventy-five feet high that marked the ancient shoreline of Lake Iroquois, whose waters had receded in the Pleistocene era. The eastern and western edges of the Victorian townsite were delimited by the wide deep valleys of the Don and Humber Rivers; these valleys and the escarpment created obstacles for road and railway builders.[25]

The first town plan was a small grid laid out by British military engineers at the eastern end of the harbour between Parliament and Jarvis Streets. To the west of this "Old Town" was added the "New Town," which stretched as far as Peter Street, and the east–west streets of the first two grids matched up fairly accurately though with some dead ends.[26] Outside the tiny townsite, surveyors marked out a pattern of concession lines and side roads in squares approximately one mile and a quarter per side. Queen Street formed the baseline north of the broken front created by the angled shoreline of Lake Ontario, and the nine concession lines (Queen, Bloor, St Clair, Eglinton, Lawrence, Wilson-York Mills, Sheppard, Finch, and Steeles) became and remained the major east–west thoroughfares. Yonge Street was the principal north–south route with Bathurst and Dufferin to the west and Bayview to the east. Along these roads, the surveyors laid out farm lots as long, narrow, two hundred-acre rectangles, twenty surveyor's chains (1,320 feet) wide by one hundred chains (1.25 miles) deep. North of Queen (once Lot Street) between Parliament and Lansdowne, the original layout was halved into slender hundred-acre "park lots" (only ten chains wide) stretching up to Bloor. These lots were handed out to the town's elite before 1800. In other areas of the city, the long axis of the lots ran east and west rather than north and south.

Unlike many American cities, Toronto never had a grid pattern of streets superimposed on its original survey (like Manhattan as early as 1807 or Boston as late as 1890). When owners eventually subdivided their large lots into building sites during the nineteenth century, the minor streets were laid out in an irregular pattern. Where the long axis of the original lots was oriented north–south, streets running in that direction were often long and straight (though not necessarily connected across the concession lines), while the east–west cross streets were often not aligned with those on the neighbouring lots. Likewise, where the lots were laid out east and west the shorter north–south streets often did not link together across the lot lines. Thus, Toronto's overall street pattern was rectangular but often discontinuous outside of the few main routes. In 1891 the *Canadian Architect and Builder* complained that a look at a map of the city left one "disgusted by the piecemeal method which has characterized the extensions and growth of the metropolis of Ontario – streets stopping abruptly, jumping a block and then continued, … streets beginning and ending nowhere, lots having an abnormal depth and others too shallow." The result, as one geographer has noted, was a layout that almost resembled the complexity of a medieval town, even if most street corners were ninety degrees.[27]

The road allowances for the concession lines were only one surveyor's chain (sixty-six feet) wide. Downtown commercial establishments and some row housing were quickly constructed flush with the property line. In the

1860s horsecars appeared on the main streets, replaced by electric trolleys in the 1890s. Horse-drawn carriages and wagons competed for space until the twentieth century when automobiles and trucks were added to the mix. The narrow sidewalks were overhung by signs and encumbered with poles for streetlights, trolley cables, telephones, and electric service. Traffic thickened then clogged on the major streets. The only wide avenues running north and south were Spadina, which terminated at the escarpment, University, which started at Queen and ran only the short distance up to Queen's Park, and Jarvis Street, which did not extend across the ravine just north of Bloor.

Outside the core lay some steep hills and broad ravines, but the concession road allowances paid little heed to topography. Yonge Street was the main route north to the interior along which settlement began to spread from an early date, but it crossed the wide valley of the west branch of the Don River at Hogg's Hollow where the roadway meandered up and down sharp grades. To the east, Bayview could not be put through owing to the barrier created by the lower Don valley. Among the east–west thoroughfares, Bloor Street simply ended a few blocks east of Yonge where it encountered the Rosedale Ravine running down to the Don, leaving the growing subdivisions east of the river along Danforth Avenue isolated from the rest of the city except by roundabout routes lying far to the south. Further north, roads like Lawrence and Eglinton Avenues simply ended at the Don in the east and the Humber River in the west (though they resumed in the outlying rural areas). Thus, getting about the city and its surrounding areas often involved irritating detours.

Despite W.A. Langton's call to arms, municipal officials showed no inclination to commit funds to drawing up a master plan, much less embark upon improving the street layout by selective widenings, jog eliminations, and the construction of bridges. In 1904, however, fate seemed to offer an opportunity for a thoroughgoing revamp of the central business district. On 19 April fire broke out in a factory near the corner of Wellington and Bay Streets and quickly spread owing to high winds. Low water pressure in the hydrants and below-freezing temperatures hampered the efforts of firefighters. Before the blaze was brought under control after about eight hours, it had consumed approximately one hundred buildings located on nearly twenty acres on both sides of Bay as far south as the Esplanade along the waterfront railway tracks.[28] Here, surely, was an opportunity to begin a full-scale remake along modern lines.[29]

In the spring of 1905 the Civic Guild created a new Plan Committee chaired by W.A. Langton that, by the end of the year, produced the first comprehensive plan for reordering the city. A "small provincial town with no idea as to its future growth" had suddenly developed into a city lacking

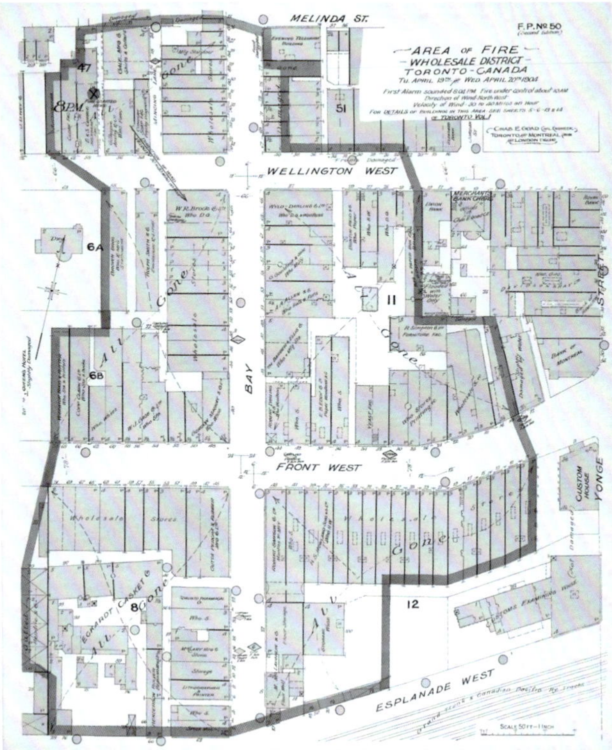

1.3 (Left)
The extent of the damage from the 1904 fire.

1.4 (Above)
After the fire.

1.5 (Below)
After the fire, panorama of damage looking west from Front and Bay.

A FAIR ILLUSTRATION OF WHAT IT COSTS TO BUILD OF "SHODDY" CONSTRUCTION, IN A PANORAMIC VIEW OF TORONTO'S WAREHOUSE DISTRICT AFTER THE MEMORABLE FIRE OF APRIL, 1904, WHICH SWEPT AWAY OVER SIXTEEN MILLIONS OF DOLLARS OF PROPERTY, BROUGHT ALMOST TO A STANDSTILL THE BUSINESS OF CANADA'S SECOND LARGEST CITY AND LAID RUIN CLOSE TO THE DOORS OF MANY LARGE PROSPERING BUSINESS INSTITUTIONS. SUCH A DISASTROUS CONFLAGRATION WOULD HAVE BEEN IMPOSSIBLE IN A DISTRICT OF WELL BUILT, PROPERLY PROTECTED WAREHOUSES. Photo by ' Galbraith," Copyrighted.

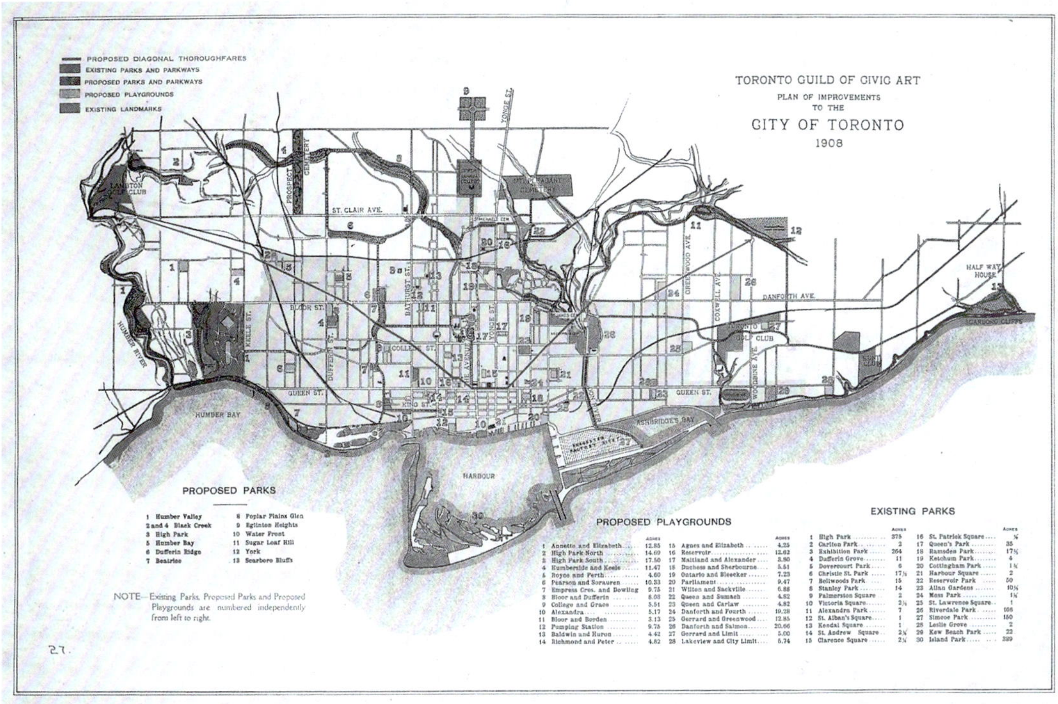

1.6
Guild of Civic Art, proposed improvements: "Plan of Improvements to the City of Toronto, 1908."

satisfactory thoroughfares – its narrow, cramped streets often short and "blind." In the built up area, parks and playgrounds were scarce or neglected, while access to the lakefront and the valleys of the Humber and the Don with their wooded side ravines, which could provide "great recreation grounds," was lacking.

The Civic Guild produced a map that envisaged a burst of road construction. A system of parkways would form a continuous route westward along the waterfront and north up the Humber valley, before turning easterly along one of its tributaries north of the city, crossing over into the watershed of the Don and running back down that valley to the lake. An eastern extension along the waterfront would lead to a large park atop the three hundred-foot high Scarborough Bluffs, so the entire route "practically girdles the city and takes in all the best vantage points." The central element of the plan included two brand new roads, the diagonals so much prized by Langton, running northeast and northwest from Queen Street near Yonge towards the distant suburbs. Several lanes of traffic would flank rapid transit lines on the central medians with new city services laid down well in advance of immediate need.[30]

1.7 (Above)
Bird's-eye view of the Guild's plan for the central waterfront, 1905.

1.8 (Right)
John Lyle, c. 1926.

A bird's-eye view of the city centre looking north from the harbourfront showed a dramatic new entry into the downtown, along the line of a much-widened York Street, stretching from a large park built on reclaimed land projecting out into Lake Ontario. This roadway passed between two towering pylons at the Esplanade, which would be broadened and planted with trees to connect with the "circumambient" parkway system. To the west of York would lie the railway freight sheds and the shipping docks with their warehouses, and, to the east, several piers for passenger ships and the ferries that plied to and from the Island. Bridges on York, Bay, and Yonge Streets would carry traffic to the waterfront overtop the rail lines. The accompanying map showed York Street terminating at a large square south of Queen Street in front of Osgoode Hall (from which the northwesterly diagonal would branch out).[31]

Here was a classic City Beautiful layout for Toronto. Other urban plans that followed at intervals incorporated similar ideas. In 1909 a glossy pamphlet entitled *Report on a Comprehensive Plan for Systematic Civic Improvements in Toronto* was issued.[32] Unfortunately, local politicians showed little interest in funding the kind of urban planning being promoted by the Civic Guild. That autumn, the city council finally agreed to create a Civic Improvement Committee (CIC) consisting of the mayor, two city controllers, and six aldermen, along with six private individuals. In August 1910 the CIC was given $2,000 in city funds to draw up a formal plan. At its first meeting in 1911, council reappointed the CIC, which delivered its report at the end of the year.[33]

The only important addition to the Civic Guild's previous recommendations came from the CIC's consulting architect, John Lyle, who proposed to lay out an entirely new hundred foot wide ceremonial avenue running due north from the centre of the facade of a new Union Station on Front Street. This grand entrance to the downtown would create 3,600 feet of prime commercial frontage in the area devastated by the 1904 fire and terminate in a huge square north of Queen to be surrounded by new buildings not only for the municipality but the federal government, including a large central post office. In acknowledgment of Ottawa's participation the new street was to be called Federal Avenue.[34]

In 1912, however, the city council refused to provide funds for the CIC to continue its activities. Meanwhile, the federal government's newly created Toronto Harbour Commission came up with its own scheme to use its control of the city's port lands to reshape the waterfront, for which Frederick Law Olmsted Jr acted as consultant.[35] The commission proposed to fill in the marshlands of Ashbridge's Bay east of the mouth of the Don River and create a huge industrial park. Their plans also included the construction of a parkway along the lakefront, crossing a lift bridge over the harbour entrance at the Eastern Gap to reach the Island, with a fixed bridge over the Western Gap to join up with the parkway running through the Canadian National Exhibition grounds and along the Sunnyside Beach to the Humber. The landfill at Ashbridge's Bay and on the western waterfront did eventually go ahead, though neither bridge was ever built. (See also Figure 1.1.)[36]

To relieve traffic congestion downtown, the city also began to consider a subway system and, in 1910, retained a New York consulting firm that reported favourably upon the idea.[37] The CIC incorporated into its plan the idea of a line from Front Street running under Bay Street up to Bloor then continuing under Yonge Street to St Clair Avenue, but, in 1912, the ratepayers, who had to approve such large capital spending projects, voted the idea down.[38]

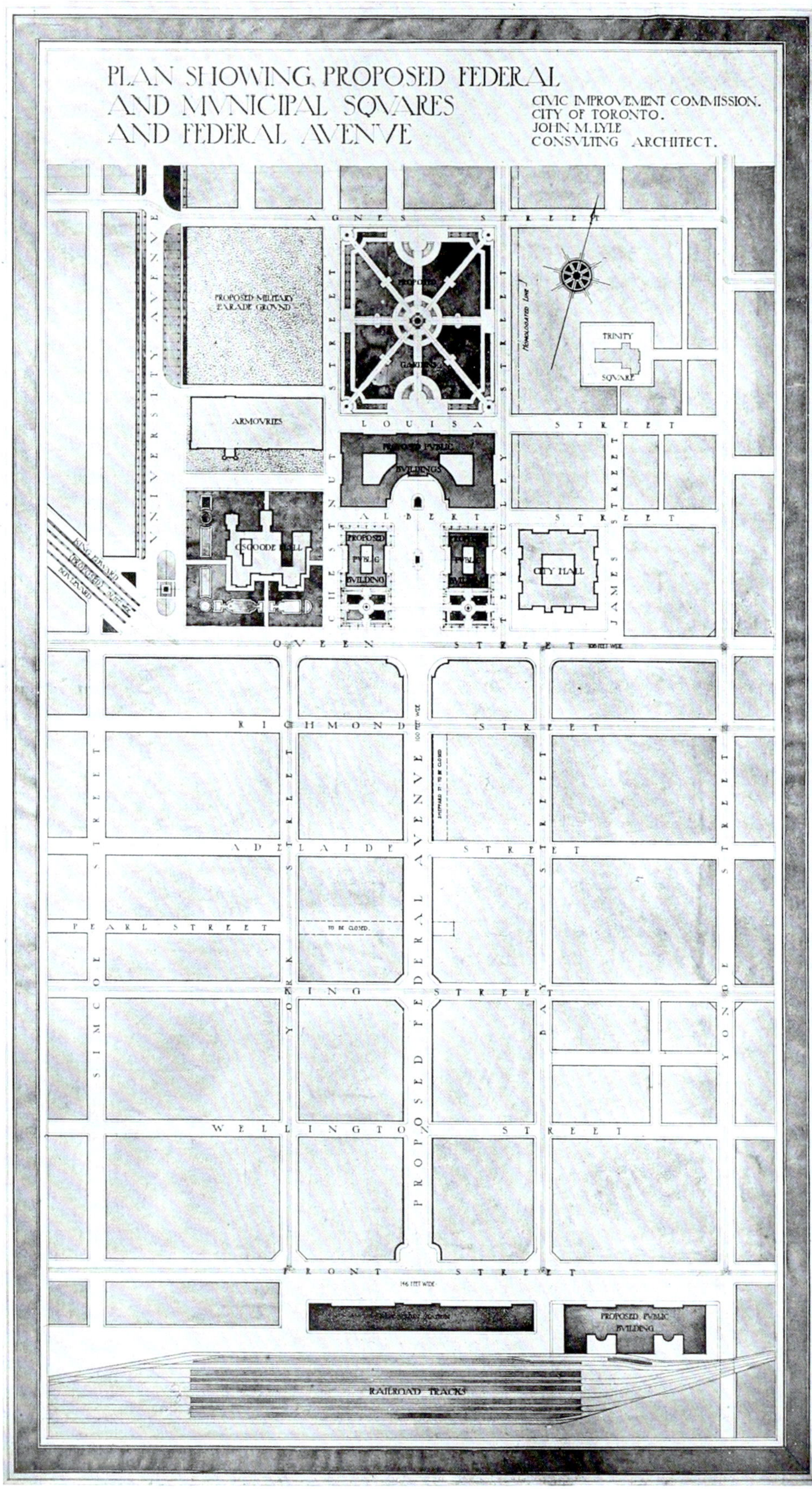

1.9
Civic Improvement Commission, "Plan Showing Proposed Federal and Municipal Squares and Federal Avenue," 1911, which continued to be part of the civic vision for decades.

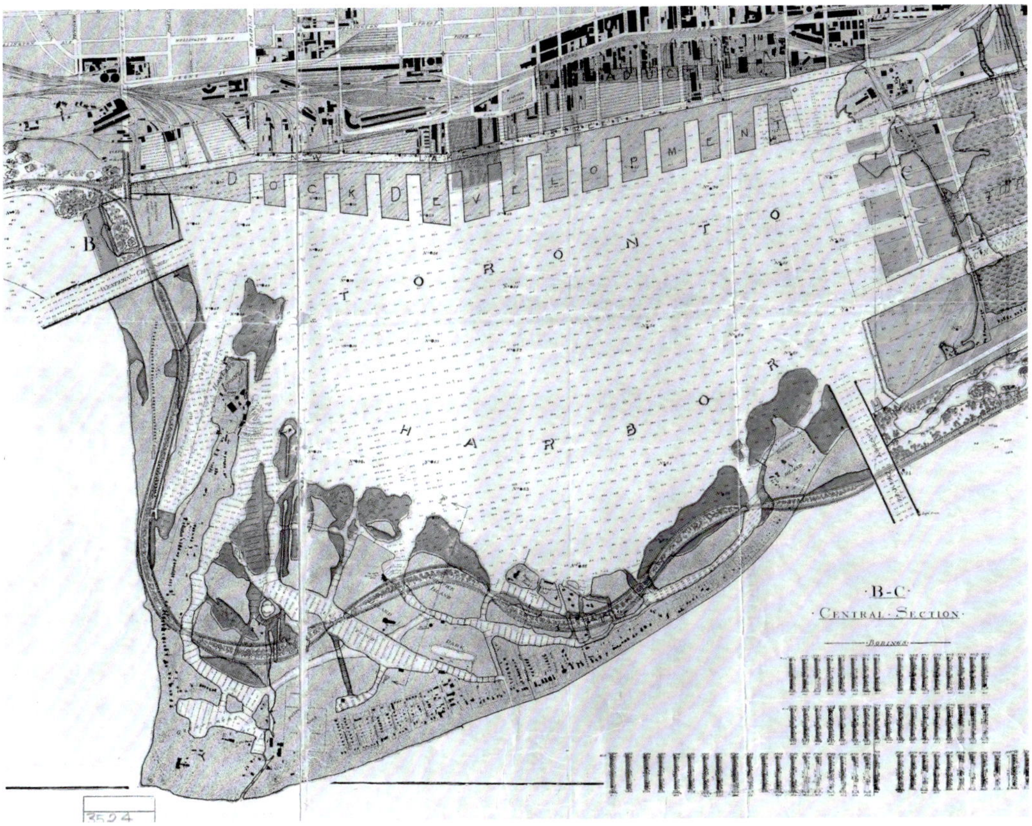

1.10
Toronto Harbour Commissioners' plan, 1912, the central portion of an ambitious scheme for the entire city, from the mouth of the Humber River to the bluffs of Scarborough. (See also Figure 1.1.)

By 1913 the Canadian economy was slipping into a pronounced recession that undercut support for heavy spending. The government in Ottawa had already refused to build a new post office on the proposed square at the head of Federal Avenue, arguing that every other large city in the country would then demand similar treatment. Claims that such plans were not merely cosmetic "fads and extravagances" but "good business and good economy" needed to speed the movement of people and goods fell upon increasingly deaf ears. Parks might be the "lungs" of a city, necessary for the well-being of residents, but thrifty politicians and hard-pressed ratepayers proved increasingly resistant to big expenditures.[39] These grand ideas simply faded away under the impact of hard times, their demise confirmed by the outbreak of the First World War in 1914.

The only concrete result of the pressure for an urban plan was the construction of the Bloor Street viaduct, which linked the central city directly to the growing eastern suburbs across the wide, deep valley of the Don River. Various schemes were proposed in the early twentieth century, but the municipal ratepayers voted the project down in both 1910 and 1912. Finally, John Lyle suggested that Bloor Street be extended eastward from Sherbourne along the southern lip of the Rosedale ravine where a short bridge would connect to Castle Frank, from which a massive structure would cross the Don valley. The ratepayers finally approved the proposal in January 1913. The city engineers even had the foresight to include in the plans openings in the piers below the traffic deck so that a subway might eventually run underneath. Work began in 1915 and was completed by 1919.[40] For all the talk about urban planning after 1895, the viaduct was the only major infrastructure project promoted by the planners that was completed by the end of the First World War.[41]

II

The architectural look of Toronto began to change around the turn of the twentieth century. During the 1880s, the city limits had expanded by the annexation of a whole ring of suburban areas to the east, west, and north, so there was plenty of land available for new housing as well as commercial and institutional use.[42] Even during the recession of the 1890s, a number of important new buildings rose, followed by a rush of construction once the good times returned after 1897. Romanesque Revival, popularized in the United States by H.H. Richardson, was the city's style of choice in the early 1890s.[43] Notable public buildings included Victoria College at the University

1.11
Prince Edward viaduct over the Don valley. The photo shows the lower deck ready for a transit line, eventually installed in 1966.

1.12 (Above)
Victoria College, W.G. Storm, 1892.

1.13 (Right)
City Hall, E.J. Lennox, 1899. The building is completed here but the clock is not yet installed.

of Toronto (1892), the Ontario legislative building nearby at Queen's Park (1893), and the new city hall at Queen and Bay Streets (commenced 1889 and finally opened in 1899), along with businesses like the Confederation Life (1891). Toronto's first really tall structure, the nine-storey Temple Building, erected at the corner of Bay and Richmond Streets in 1895 for the insurers of the Independent Order of Foresters, opted for a similar look. Architect G.W. Gouinlock's lingering distrust of the load-bearing capacity of its steel framework led him to specify masonry walls that tapered from four feet at grade to eighteen inches at the top floor. Meanwhile, in the prosperous residential districts of Rosedale and the Annex to the northeast and northwest of Yonge and Bloor Streets, large houses of the same Romanesque ilk were sprouting.[44]

At the same time, more modern designs began to appear, such as the new department store for the Robert Simpson Company at the southwest corner of Queen and Yonge, begun in 1894. Architect Edmund Burke was obviously

1.14 (Left) Confederation Life Building, Knox, Elliot, and Jarvis, 1891.

1.15 Temple Building, George W. Gouinlock, 1895.

paying attention to the skyscrapers going up in Chicago, for the load-bearing frame of the building was a cage of cast iron and steel. A stern reminder that those materials required careful fireproofing with brick, stone, or terracotta was delivered when the store burnt to the first floor in the spring of 1895, just after opening. Simpson immediately commissioned a replacement from Burke whose design filled almost the entire space between the vertical and horizontal framing with glass, particularly for the ground floor show windows. In the Chicago fashion the external decoration was restrained with terracotta mouldings and Classical-style capitals.[45]

By the time the city hall finally opened on Queen Street in 1899, the day of Romanesque Revival had passed. New buildings now reflected the Beaux Arts, utilizing features from Classical and Renaissance design and made popular in the United States by architectural firms like McKim, Mead, and White and its offshoot, Carrère and Hastings. Here was a way to make Toronto look as modern and up-to-date as New York. The city had long needed a central public library, and, in 1903, the Carnegie Corporation offered $350,000 to support construction. College Street, which ran just south of the provincial legislature at Queen's Park along the edge of the campus of the University of Toronto, was one of those thoroughfares that civic boosters wanted to see widened to one hundred feet and lined with monumental buildings.[46] In 1905 the city held a competition to design a new library at the northwest corner of College and St George Streets. The winning entry was by Alfred H. Chapman whose Beaux Arts layout clearly reflected the influence of Carrère and Hastings's design for the New York Public Library, which had been started in 1897.

The building, intended to house both a circulating and a reference library, stretched along College Street clad in stone and yellow brick. The wall was pierced by a long row of two-storey-high windows separated by Corinthian pilasters, which lit the reading room. The entrance to the reference library at the east end was up a broad flight of steps crowned by a semi-circular pediment and inside lay an interior staircase rising three storeys between a double row of arches. Architectural historians Dendy and Kilbourn call this ensemble, which opened in 1909, "easily the most effective demonstration in Toronto of the Beaux Arts emphasis on an innately formal, processional sequence of entrance spaces that gradually introduces the visitor to the functions of a major building."[47]

The adaptability of Beaux Arts designs for commercial purposes was displayed by the head office for the Bank of Toronto. To get the newest thing, the bank went right to the source and retained Carrère and Hastings for a design for the highly prominent site at the southwest corner of King and Bay Streets, 120 by 134 feet, which necessitated the largest land assembly in the city to date. As with most of their work, the New Yorkers drew upon French Renaissance Revival forms, in particular the Paris Bourse of 1808–26, because they could be utilized for many different purposes. Completed in 1913, the building emphasized the bank's stability by its smooth stone plinth, above which Corinthian columns covered the steel framework in between large windows that allowed light to flood into the main banking hall along with a skylight overhead. No expense was spared for the marble and bronze fittings.[48]

1.16
Central Public Library, College and St George Streets, Wickson and Gregg and A.H. Chapman, 1909.

1.17
Bank of Toronto, King and Bay Streets, Carrère and Hastings, 1913.

1.18
Chorley Park, the Lieutenant-Governor's residence, F.R. Heakes, 1915.

Sometimes the adaptation of historical forms was less successful, as in the case of the residence for the Lieutenant-Governor of Ontario at Chorley Park, off Roxborough Drive in the northeast corner of Rosedale. Here, too, there was a competition, but, in 1909, the chief architect of the provincial Department of Public Works, F.R. Heakes, pronounced all the entries too expensive. He simply appropriated the design for a French Renaissance chateau by the winner G.W. King and plopped it down on the isolated fourteen-acre site overlooking the Don River to the east. To create the ambience of the Loire Valley, the property was elaborately landscaped, including a bridge (spanning nothing) leading to a vast forecourt. On various corners of the building were

1.19
View northwest from the City Hall clock tower, 1925. In the distance, the vast roof is the Armouries; closer in to the left is Osgoode Hall, and to the right is the Registry Office.

installed tiny pointed turrets that looked much like firecrackers ready to go off. Inside was a huge three-storey hallway with a skylight and elaborate furnishing, which helped to push the cost up to $1 million by the time the project was completed in 1915.[49]

Many public buildings showed a more restrained Neoclassicism. In 1911 as part of the Civic Improvement Commission's plan, John Lyle had suggested a civic square surrounded by impressive public buildings on the north side of Queen Street west of Bay, presently occupied by the rundown tenements of St John's Ward. The only new structure to be completed was the Registry Office of Deeds and Land Titles on Albert Street between Chestnut and Louisa at the northwest corner of the proposed square. Charles S. Cobb, who had come to the city from the United States, won the city's design competition. Later, it was reported that he had arrived at "a time of crisis in Toronto architectural circles. The older school of practitioners had well-nigh outlived its usefulness when, within a comparatively short period, an influx of new life revivified the Mother Art and set Architecture agoing in the channels of the Renaissance."[50] His design for the Registry Office was squarely in the Beaux Arts tradition and followed the Roman Classicism favoured by C.F. McKim of McKim, Mead, and White with a stern colonnade of eight fluted Doric columns supporting an entablature below a recessed attic. Started in 1914 and completed in 1917, the Registry Office was never given any grand companions but instead left to look out upon a decaying slum until the building was demolished in the 1960s.[51]

At the turn of the twentieth century, the University of Toronto had few buildings of architectural distinction. After the interior of the original

University College building (1859) was destroyed by fire in 1890, it was restored by architect David B. Dick, who was also given the job of designing the new university library. Both buildings were ready in 1892, but by 1901 the university was in dire financial straits with total income being only about $125,000 and the province's contribution amounting to only $7,000, leaving a deficit of more than $30,000. Under pressure from the recently formed alumni association, the government agreed to grant about $25,000 a year to support the science departments. A fund of $200,000 was also provided for new construction, including a Chemistry and Mining Building on the north side of College Street, since graduates were expected to find ready employment in the newly opened mineral deposits in northern Ontario. F.R. Heakes, architect of Public Works, produced a layout for a large red brick building in the Beaux Arts style with pilasters supporting a pediment at the centre.[52]

Having succeeded in persuading the government to put up more money for the university, the alumni association then offered to raise $50,000 towards the cost of a new auditorium, which could hold a large crowd for ceremonies like graduations, provided that the province would match the sum. Darling and Pearson was an up-and-coming firm; Frank Darling displayed great versatility in utilizing the Beaux Arts style. The architects created a two-thousand-seat amphitheatre modelled upon the Sorbonne in Paris with a semi-circular colonnade supporting a massive cornice topped off by an attic storey and a huge dome. Convocation Hall was designed to face southeastward down Taddle Creek Road, which was then the main entrance to the campus.[53]

1.20
Convocation Hall, University of Toronto, c. 1930, Darling and Pearson, 1906.

Having succeeded so effectively in influencing the provincial government, the university's alumni association then turned its attention to securing a building devoted to the study of physics. A deputation waited upon Premier George Ross in the spring of 1904, just before the cornerstone of Convocation Hall was laid, and reminded him that, with an election coming soon, he should pay heed to their wishes. Within months, the government agreed to put up $180,000 for the new physics building, standing just south of Convocation Hall and also designed by Darling and Pearson. The result was another Beaux Arts structure of yellow brick and limestone whose most notable feature was a semi-circular apse projecting eastward with a stone foundation and a cornice supported by pairs of Ionic columns.[54]

Just to show that university architecture in the pre-First World War years had not been entirely captured by the Beaux Arts, some of the institutions connected to the university opted for something very old that was becoming new again – Collegiate Gothic.[55] Knox College, the Presbyterian theological establishment, chose this style when it moved to a new building on the west side of the front campus next to Convocation Hall in 1915.[56]

When the Methodist church decided to move Victoria College from Cobourg and federate with the University of Toronto in the 1890s, the college had approved a Romanesque Revival building. In 1906 Victoria approached Andrew Carnegie to finance a new library, and he agreed to donate $50,000, provided that matching funds were found as an endowment for maintenance. Cyrus Birge, a wealthy alumnus, agreed to contribute, and, in 1908, the college held a design competition, which was won by Sproatt and Rolph. Located on Charles Street West at the northeast corner of Queen's Park, the Birge-Carnegie Library was an up-to-date Collegiate Gothic building, a cruciform layout of gray ashlar from the Credit valley that opened in 1910.[57]

In the same year Vincent Massey graduated from the University of Toronto and became involved in the philanthropic affairs of his grandfather's estate, funded by the fortune garnered from the Massey-Harris farm implement company. The Massey family, faithful Methodists,[58] decided to fund a men's residence at Victoria. Young Vincent, who had contemplated becoming an architect, was not enthusiastic about the heavy red and white stonework of the 1892 structure, so he took a hand in the design of the new building. In his memoirs, published a half-century later, he recorded, somewhat defensively,

> As a trustee I had been able in the academic year 1910–11 to influence its plans. It resembled an Oxford or Cambridge college; the undergraduate rooms were divided into houses and the building possessed a

dining hall, a senior and a junior common room and so on. The architectural style of the building was collegiate Gothic – what the current generation of architects would not call architecture at all but archeology; but for all that, in the hands of an architect with the requisite feeling and skill, it was an agreeable form for academic structures so long as the necessary craftsmen could be found. We were fortunate in having Henry Sproatt as the architect.[59]

Sproatt and his partner, Ernest Rolph, born in Toronto in 1866 and 1871, respectively, produced a most satisfactory L-shaped design for Burwash Hall with the towering hall running along Charles Street and the residential staircases attached at right angles to the east, neatly matching the adjacent library.[60]

While Vincent Massey was still an undergraduate, his father agreed that the Massey estate should contribute a large sum of money for the construction of a student centre for men (only) at the University of Toronto, to be called Hart House after his grandfather, the farm equipment tycoon, Hart A. Massey. Vincent wrote,

> It was of great importance that someone who understood the idea behind the project, which in many ways was novel, should work with the architect in the early critical period. To do this I postponed my arrival in Oxford for a year to collaborate as a layman with him. Henry Sproatt was a man of real genius and a master of the Gothic form – the last of his kind in Canada. Gothic to him was not a language to be acquired – it was his own vernacular. He was unfamiliar with university life and the purpose to be served by Hart House, but he and I worked together – very happily – and the plans of the building grew under our joint efforts ... I travelled a good deal, visiting students' unions in Great Britain and the United States, the study of which had a bearing on the plans of Hart House.[61]

1.21
Hart House, University of Toronto, Sproatt and Rolph, 1919.

1.22
Flavelle House, Darling and Pearson, 1902.

In 1911 Vincent Massey departed for England to take a second undergraduate degree at Oxford, but when he returned to Toronto in 1913 to become Dean of Men at Burwash Hall in Victoria College, he watched carefully over the construction of Hart House. Begun in 1911, it was by far the most elaborate university building in the country and "perhaps the finest example of Beaux Arts Gothic Revival in Canada."[62] Located at the northeast corner of the original University College, its long southward front contained most of the main rooms between projecting entrance porches at either end. To the east was the Great Hall with its stained glass windows and panelled walls decorated with the crests of other universities, and painted around the top of the panels a passage from Milton's *Areopagitica* enjoining freedom in the pursuit of learning. Sproatt also provided a virtuoso demonstration on the way in which Collegiate Gothic could be manipulated to encompass a variety of functions. Like other architects, he showed how the ancient forms could be improved by using modern materials. (Ralph Adams Cram, the most prominent Gothic Revivalist in the United States, who designed many of the buildings at Princeton University, often declared his faith in load-bearing members that truly performed their apparent functions but sometimes inserted steel tie rods into his hammer-beamed roofs.)[63] The north wing of Hart House contained the athletic facilities, and Sproatt, not wishing to erect an enormous gabled roof over the gymnasium, used historically correct

1.23
Ardwold, Wickson and Gregg, 1911.

1.24
Casa Loma, E.J. Lennox, 1913.

masonry arches and buttresses to support the steel truss framing of a flat roof. Squash courts, a rifle range, and a theatre whose roof was formed by the central quadrangle were also provided to meet the needs of the modern student.

Construction slowed owing to shortage of materials during the First World War, inflated costs, and a decline in the income from the Massey endowment as company factories were converted to war work. The formal opening of Hart House did not take place until 11 November 1919, exactly one year after the Armistice. On that same day, the cornerstone was laid for the Soldiers' Tower at the west end of the building as a memorial for all members of the university killed during the war. Once again, Sproatt and Rolph were commissioned to produce a soaring Gothic tower modelled upon Magdalen College, Oxford with a memorial carillon of bells and an archway on which the names of the dead could be carved. Soldiers' Tower was finished in 1924. Together, these buildings formed the finest assemblage of Collegiate Gothic in Canada.[64]

While these commercial and institutional buildings were going up in the years after 1900, some of the city's richest businessmen were also erecting fancy homes, each with its own name, in the various Beaux Arts styles that broke away from Victorian eclecticism and evoked different historical models. In 1901 Joseph Flavelle, the meat-packing baron who shipped bacon by the ton to Britain, commissioned a highly visible house for himself right across the street from Victoria College at the northwest corner of Queen's Park called Holwood, or by the less deferential "Porker's Palace." Darling and Pearson produced a design for a very grand Georgian Revival house of the sort that had recently become popular in England. The main entrance faced northeast through a portico with Corinthian columns supporting a triangular pediment, behind which lay two storeys of formal reception rooms and spacious family quarters.[65] Set at an oblique angle was a three-storey service wing, the two parts linked together by another tall pedimented pavilion, which contained the main staircase, together making a harmonious ensemble.[66]

Once John Eaton had succeeded his father as head of the family's department store empire he began to plan a new house for his family. In 1908 he purchased a ten-acre piece of property off Walmer Road south of St Clair on the brow of the escarpment. Eaton retained Wickson and Gregg whose 1911 design was modelled upon less monumental Georgian country houses in Britain. Twelve bays wide of brick with a steeply pitched roof pierced by dormer windows and topped by an octagonal lantern, Ardwold had two-storey porches at the east and west ends and a bay window to the south facing the elaborate gardens overlooking the city. The double-height great hall had a huge organ whose pipes filled the space over the fireplace.[67]

At the same time, stockbroker Henry Pellatt was building Toronto's most idiosyncratic house, Casa Loma, just to the west and south of the Eaton house, harking back more to the excesses of Victorianism. Pellatt wanted a real castle with an elaborate stable for his horses in proper medieval fashion. Architect E.J. Lennox, who had designed the city hall and would later build his own house to the west of Pellatt's, produced a plan for a vast building that drew eclectically upon various European castles of all ages. The most spectacular of the main rooms (all framed in steel with concrete floors overlaid by parquet) was the great hall with a sixty-foot-high hammer-beamed ceiling and a forty-five-foot-high oriel window looking down upon the gardens to the south. Whatever may be said about the jumble of towers of contrasting styles on the outside, Casa Loma was equipped inside with all sorts of the most modern conveniences like a built-in vacuuming system, 150,000 feet of electrical wiring to light its ninety-eight rooms, and refrigeration to cool the wine cellar.[68] Here was the summit of Toronto's pre-First World War modern architecture in which up-to-date materials and technology were cloaked in pseudo-medieval garb.

For those Torontonians who lacked the golden means to create such elaborate advertisements for themselves there were the houses of the architect Eden Smith. Between the mid-1890s and his retirement in the 1920s, he designed 2,500 of them in all. According to Dendy and Kilbourn, his comfortable homes, sometimes called the English Cottage style, "dominated middle-class housing design in Toronto from the late 1890s until the 1930s (replacing the Romanesque Revival in popular esteem)." Smith showed a willingness to break away from Victorian layouts that positioned the principal rooms around the entrance hall and main staircase. What was particularly notable was the way that he produced designs that were "turned about" with the kitchen facing onto the street and the living and dining room at the rear, an especially suitable layout for sites in Toronto when the rear of the house faced south.[69]

Curiously, this architect, who was well-known for his pleasant family homes and could even be relied upon when needed to produce Tudorbethan designs with fake half-timbering setting off light-coloured stucco infilling,[70] also created one remarkable work that seemed to carry clear hints of modernism of a kind unknown in Canada before the First World War. In 1913 artist Lawren Harris (who was another heir to the Massey-Harris fortune) joined with Dr James MacCallum, a keen patron of the visual arts, in financing a building with spaces to be let to practising artists with rents geared to recover expenses. For them, Eden Smith designed what was called the Studio Building at 25 Severn Street off Rosedale Valley Road, northeast of Yonge and Church Streets; the building was a three-storey concrete-framed structure faced in brick that looked like a warehouse. What was particularly noticeable were the six very large north-facing windows designed to let light into the twelve-foot high studios. Smith produced something that looked as though it were modelled on the very modern looking factory designs that Albert Kahn was turning out for companies like Packard and Pierce-Arrow just across Lake Ontario in Buffalo.[71] There, however, leading businessmen also commissioned houses from Frank Lloyd Wright in a clearly avant-garde style; Toronto had nothing similar.

III

As new fashions in architecture were beginning to make headway in Toronto, the great fire in the spring of 1904 seemed to offer a unique opportunity to rebuild much of the centre of the downtown. Having watched scores of warehouses constructed with load-bearing brick walls and wooden beams consumed in the inferno, Toronto officials were aware of the need for more fire-resistant construction methods. Iron and steel framing could bear greater loads but for safety required casing in stone, brick, or terracotta. Reinforced concrete, poured over metal bars often in the form of patented systems of reinforcement like that devised by the Kahn brothers, permitted beams and posts to span longer distances and to carry much heavier loads.[72] This material seemed an obvious choice for rebuilding on account of its high fire resistance, and, in 1904, Toronto's building code was rewritten to allow for its use.[73]

A few structures did utilize reinforced concrete like the six-storey warehouse erected in 1905–06 at 60 Front Street West, right in the centre of the burnt-over area; the framing permitted the entire area between the structural members to be glazed. However, the new city architect, Robert McCallum, appointed in 1905, was highly conservative and refused to approve some buildings framed in concrete, considering it a flimsy and unproven material. He sometimes required buildings to be up to 25 percent over-strength in construction, which discouraged the use of concrete. Much of the area devastated by the fire was rebuilt in nineteenth-century style.

Not until McCallum was forced to resign in 1913 after a judicial inquiry did innovative designs in reinforced concrete, such as the Methodist Book Publishing warehouse at Queen and John Streets (1913) and a new mail order warehouse for the Robert Simpson Company on Mutual Street (1916), begin to appear.[74]

Yet the revision of Toronto's building code in 1904 also permitted office towers more than one hundred feet tall to be constructed, provided that auxiliary pumps and other special fire extinguishing devices were installed.

1.25
Bay Street, 1905: reconstructed warehouses in nineteenth-century form.

In a city where structures of more than four storeys had once been unusual, new office towers with load-bearing steel frameworks and curtain walls began to appear. In 1905 work began on a new fifteen-storey building for the Traders' Bank on the east side of Yonge Street south of King, designed by the well-known New York architects Carrère and Hastings. For a time the tallest commercial building in the British Empire, this skyscraper featured a classical base two storeys high, above which rose eight floors of rental office space topped by a heavy overhanging cornice containing several attic floors, the whole resembling a huge classical column.[75]

While the nation and region prospered up until the First World War, the city's downtown took on a new appearance as other skyscrapers appeared. During this period, the Canadian Pacific Railway Company and both the Royal Bank and the Dominion Bank built office towers on three corners of King and Yonge Streets, each of which mirrored the form adopted by the Traders' Bank of an oversized classical column with base, tall shaft, and capital in the form of a distinct attic section and an overhanging cornice.

1.26
Robert Simpson Company's Mail Order Building, Mutual Street frontage, N. Max Dunning and Burke, Horwood and White, 1916.

1.27
Conveyor and parcel chute, Robert Simpson Mail Order Building.

1.28
Yonge Street, when it was the office district. (*Left to right*) Dominion Bank (Darling and Pearson, 1913–14), Royal Bank (Carrère and Hastings with Eustace G. Bird, 1913–15), CPR (Darling and Pearson, 1911–13), Traders' Bank (Carrère and Hastings, 1905).

Buildings like these had to be granted special exemptions because they breached the city's bylaw limiting the maximum height of buildings to 124 feet. The twelve-storey Dominion Bank building, designed by Darling and Pearson and costing over $1 million, was described by the building trade periodical *Construction* as "the culmination of all the study which has been centred for years on our American-evolved skyscraper."[76] The Royal Bank, also produced by Carrère and Hastings, succeeded as the tallest building in the British Empire when completed.[77]

Some Torontonians began to worry about the bulk of these huge towers. In the spring of 1913 the Board of Trade demanded that a ten-storey height limit should be enforced, since "the steadily-increasing height of skyscrapers constitutes a serious menace to the public health, especially of those whose work must be done in the lower storeys away from the sunlight; it also adds unnecessarily to the already great congestion in the narrow downtown streets and unduly concentrates land values at or near a few leading corners, this concentration, in turn making necessary still higher structures to meet the increasing ground rents." The Municipal Improvement Conference of Toronto, consisting of three representatives from each local ratepayer group, held a special meeting and voted for a limit on the main portion of any tower at twice the width of the adjoining street (132 feet on an ordinary 66-foot right of way), though setbacks on top might rise higher. But local boosters were having none of this: all but one of the newspapers favoured skyscrapers, which would make the city look like a real metropolis such as New York or Chicago. The city council's Property Committee shared those views, endorsing a 250-foot height limit in districts served by the high pressure water system to permit firefighting.[78]

Far and way the most ambitious project resulting from the fire of 1904 linked the desires of the propagandists in the Civic Guild, who believed that a City Beautiful ought to have wide streets, sweeping vistas and monumental structures, with their architectural allies who favoured the fashionable Neoclassical designs of the Beaux Arts. Everywhere railway stations were seen as key buildings, whose function as the transportation gateway to a city should be announced by the grandest possible structures like Pennsylvania Station in New York City. When travel by water had been vital the lakeside Esplanade in Toronto had been envisaged as a promenade, but instead it gradually became a broad rail corridor with more and more land to the south being reclaimed from Lake Ontario by infilling. A visitor from Britain sent to the city in 1907 to help the Civic Guild in drawing up its urban plan reported that the shoreline did not have a single building of any architectural merit to draw attention amidst the docks, warehouses, freight-sheds and railway sidings.[79]

In 1873 the Grand Trunk Railway had constructed a station on the Esplanade west of York Street consisting of a triple train shed with administration and services in an attached block topped by three towers along its south facade. The Canadian Pacific Railway gained access to southern Ontario in the 1880s and built a line running down the Don valley into the downtown. Before long, the station became overcrowded, and, in 1893, the two railway companies agreed to build a second three-track train shed to the south. A Romanesque Revival office building and waiting rooms with

1.29
The old Union Station, Thomas Seaton Scott, 1873, and Strickland and Symons, 1895.

a huge arched entrance, modelled upon Chicago's just-completed Illinois Central Station, stood on Front Street just west of York. Because the land sloped southward towards Lake Ontario this building was linked to the platforms by a long elevated concourse that bridged over Station Street.[80]

From the point of view of many local citizens, the railway tracks were a nuisance because they cut across every north–south street at a level crossing. The amount of locomotive traffic created great backups for pedestrians and wagons coming and going to the many businesses and the docks to the south. In 1892 the city signed the "Esplanade Agreement," by which it was agreed that the city would share with the railways the cost of building a very long bridge over tracks on York Street from Front all the way to the lakeshore. The bridge was completed five years later. The fire of 1904 consumed all the buildings as far south as the Esplanade from Yonge to just east of York Street. The city decided that this was the time to build a new station and quickly moved to expropriate the lands along the entire 850 feet of frontage on the south side of Front Street between Bay and York as far down as the Esplanade. In 1906 the railways created the Toronto Terminal Railway Company to lease these lands and build and operate a new station there.[81]

Almost at once, wrangling broke out. City officials had two main objectives. First, they desired an impressive and commodious building (the headhouse in railroad parlance) to provide services like ticketing, waiting rooms, baggage handling, and office space. Second, local politicians wanted an earth-fill viaduct about twenty feet high stretching from the Parliament Street westward as far as York Street to carry the tracks. All the main north–south streets would cross below these tracks in underpasses ("subways"), which would end the annoying traffic jams. The city agreed to pay about one-third of the projected $6 million cost, but Canadian Pacific objected strenuously to the plan, claiming that it would seriously disrupt the operations of its railyard. The company wanted to let passengers walk at ground level to board trains (and so avoid paying for its share of the viaduct). In 1909 the federal Board of Railway Commissioners, which regulated railway companies, sided with the city and ordered the construction of the viaduct with the platforms under a train shed to be reached from the headhouse by tunnels and stairs. After more foot-dragging, the board refused a request from the Canadian Pacific in 1912 to close off York Street and ordered the viaduct built.[82]

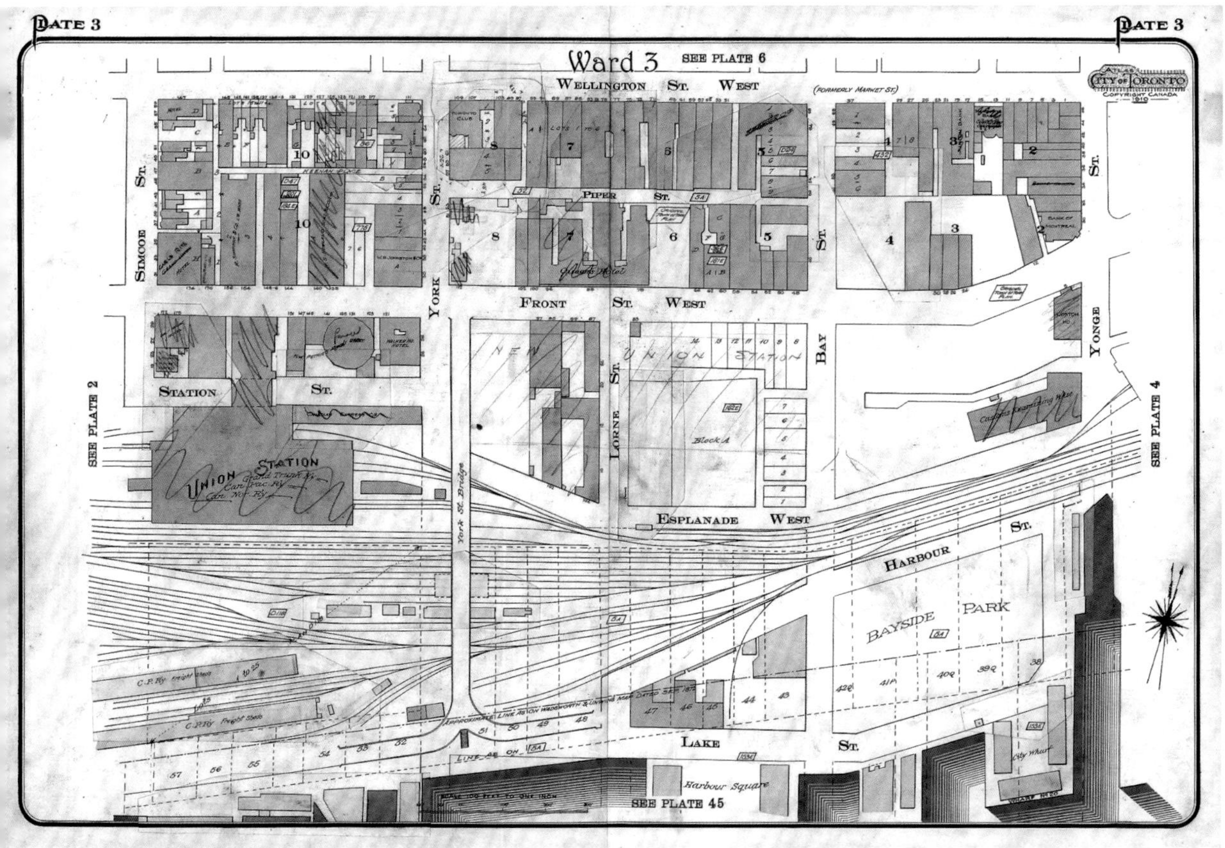

1.30
A city atlas plate, annotated with anticipated demolitions and the location for a new Union Station, 1910.

1.31
CPR's North Toronto Station, Darling and Pearson, 1916.

Canadian Pacific was so annoyed that it shifted as much traffic as possible to its midtown line that crossed Yonge Street at Summerhill Avenue just below the escarpment. When their existing North Toronto station became overcrowded, the railway company decided to build a new depot there for its trains to Montreal and Ottawa. Proponents of the City Beautiful were particularly concerned that important buildings like railway stations should display a monumental presence. Darling and Pearson produced a suitable design for a three-storey block with lower wings on each side that would stand south of the elevated tracks. A relatively small station for passengers, only the main waiting room occupied the central space, rising to the building's full height and lit by three large arched windows. Yet to make the building a landmark in the approved Beaux Arts fashion, the architects placed a tall slender clock tower at the northwest corner just off Yonge, visible from all directions when the station opened in 1916.[83]

In 1913 the Board of Railway Commissioners finally approved an agreement between the city and the railways to build the new Union Station on Front Street at a cost of $14 million. In 1911 John Lyle, as consulting architect to the Civic Improvement Committee, had sketched a design for the station centering its facade upon the new Federal Avenue to lead north from Front to the proposed civic square on the north side of Queen Street, making a suitably ceremonial entrance into the city. Working with Ross and Macdonald of Montreal for the Grand Trunk and Hugh G. Jones for

1.32
The proposed Union Station, Ross and Macdonald, Hugh G. Jones and John Lyle, 1914.

the Canadian Pacific, Lyle came up with a design for a station with ten platforms serving twenty tracks. The layout was approved by the board in the spring of 1914 and tenders called for $4 million worth of work to begin in the autumn.

Lyle's design for the headhouse was in the most advanced international idiom of the Beaux Arts, "a monumental centre for the City Beautiful," reflecting Toronto's soaring ambitions even at a time when its population was only about four hundred thousand. If not avant-garde, the layout was at least as up-to-date as anything that New York could boast, such as McKim, Mead, and White's Pennsylvania Station, which had opened in 1910. Front Street was to be widened so that the building could be set back more than seventy feet from the original street line to make it fully visible. Seven bays wide with a continuous cornice line, there were separate pavilions for a post office at the east end and for office space to the west. The middle third of the frontage had a colonnade of eighteen huge Doric columns, four of which were stepped forward at each side to provide two entrances into the space where departing passengers would purchase tickets and check baggage. Arrivals would come in at a lower level and make their way up ramps behind the ten central pillars to reach the street level.

The soaring Great Hall, modelled upon the Roman baths of Caracalla, had an arched coffered ceiling and was flooded with light, particularly by the towering four-storey windows at the east and west ends. Ticket booths lined the north wall, with baggage and parcel rooms along the south. In the centre of that wall was a ramp down to the main waiting room, which would be at the same level as the tracks until the viaduct had finally been constructed, after which travellers would climb stairs to the elevated platforms. Lyle was immensely proud of his Beaux Arts design, which he believed reflected the concern of the modern age with functionalism and efficiency yet utilized historical forms – the kind of work produced by architects who were "inspired traditionalists." Around the cornice line of the vast room Lyle inscribed the names of all the Canadian cities served by the two railways, running from east to west, for he believed that this building showed the superiority of the Canadian Beaux Arts (with its British influences) over the American version.[84]

Work commenced on the station just after the First World War broke out; the foundations were poured by 1916, and stone was delivered to the site to be cut. The scarcity of steel and stone due to the war delayed progress somewhat, but the exterior walls were completed by 1918, though strikes and shortages meant that the post office and the office space in the east and west wings were only occupied two years later. However, an application from the Toronto Terminal Railways to begin using the main building for passengers was rejected by the Board of Railway Commissioners. Meanwhile, the dispute over the viaduct dragged on and on as the railways squirmed to evade their commitments. The concourse building leading to the tracks, which was a reinforced concrete structure 1,200 feet long and 250 feet wide, had not yet been started. As a result, the Great Hall, 260 feet long and 88 feet to the ceiling, stood empty and unused until the northern part of the concourse was finally finished in 1927. The Prince of Wales presided over a formal opening, but another three years went by while the railways carted in thousands of yards of fill from the city's suburbs until the viaduct was finished along with the southern half of the concourse and underpasses were constructed over all the main north–south streets. The final transfer of all passenger traffic from the old tracks to the new raised ones was only completed at the end of 1930.[85]

During the long process of construction, certain changes were made to the main block, largely in the interests of saving money. The height of the roof over the hall was reduced, but the huge room remained the grandest interior space in the country. The pediments over the entry porches were simplified, and the groups of sculptures prescribed by Lyle to stand on their roofs were dropped. These simplifications actually emphasized the monumentality of the street frontage; the pavilions at either end were altered so that they appeared like the Stripped Classicism of a later time. The results fitted well with the federal Customs and Excise Building erected along the south side of the curve of Front Street to the east between Bay and Yonge Streets during the 1930s, creating Toronto's most impressive and unified streetscape in the very manner that the proponents of the City Beautiful had advocated so many years before.[86]

Between 1895 and 1919, there were important pressures for change in design and architecture in Toronto. The activists in the Civic Guild who were eager to see the city redesigned along City Beautiful lines devoted themselves to drawing up elaborate plans, but the unwillingness of local politicians to provide the necessary funds to bring about these changes meant that little actually got done. In the end there were few concrete achievements to show for all this agitation beyond the construction of the Bloor Street viaduct by 1919.[87]

At the same time, however, new architectural styles replaced the Victorian eclecticism and the Romanesque Revival that were so popular up to the mid-1890s. Looking abroad to places like New York, Torontonians began to appreciate the way in which the Beaux Arts adapted historical motifs for contemporary uses. Businesses, institutions, and the builders of private houses gradually accepted such new ideas in the years leading up to the First World War. After the fire of 1904, the downtown was transformed by the construction of a number of steel-framed skyscrapers to accommodate the growth of office space that reflected Toronto's increasing importance in the economic life of the nation.[88]

The fire of 1904 also provided an opportunity to undertake one project that linked together the proponents of the City Beautiful with enthusiasts for the architecture of the Beaux Arts: the construction of the new Union Station on Front Street. Architect John Lyle stood at the centre of this undertaking from the outset. Despite the delays that plagued this project, the walls of the new building were complete by 1918 and its first occupants moved in two years later, even though the great station would not be fully operational for another decade. The first stage in modernizing architecture and design in Toronto had taken only a few, hesitant steps.

Street Elevation

Central Motor Apartments, Toronto

By H. A. Babcock, B. A. Sc.

THE continually increasing use of the automobile, together with the growth of urban centres in both the United States and Canada, have brought with them the necessity of providing modern parking facilities. The business man, who drives his car to the office day after day is coming to realize the distinct advantages of having convenient accommodation for parking his car during the daytime, accommodation suitable for all kinds of weather and such that there will be a minimum loss of time in placing the car in and out of storage. Many organizations carrying on business in the centre of the city have felt the need of securing space for parking trucks and delivery vehicles during the night where they are conveniently situated and obtained without delay each morning. It was to meet these demands, together with the demand for temporary storage space created by the tourist, that the Central Motor Apartments, Limited, constructed their modern parking garage in practically the centre of the business district of Toronto.

In the past, many automobile owners have declined to secure space for the parking of their cars during the daytime, owing to the delays and loss of time in placing them, and in obtaining them from storage. These delays and loss of time have been due to the facts that there is relatively short interval each day during which many of the cars in storage are wanted, and that buildings designed to permit the removal of many cars in a short time have not, therefore, been very numerous. The Central Motor Apartments building has been planned to make all cars in storage readily accessible, so

CONSTRUCTION, MARCH, 1925 91

2

“MODERNE” ARRIVES THE 1920s

In the 1920s prosperous times gradually returned in Canada once the post-war recession evaporated. The last years of the decade saw particularly strong economic growth in which Toronto participated. Though still very much playing second fiddle to Montreal as a national metropolis, the Ontario city strengthened its claim to predominance in certain fields like mining finance, symbolized by the rapid growth of the Standard Stock and Mining Exchange.[1] That prosperity was expressed in a building boom, centred upon the skyscrapers filled with mining promoters, brokers, and lawyers that came to line Toronto's Bay Street near the stock exchange during the latter part of the decade. New construction created opportunities for architects and builders to offer designs that reflected the latest ideas.

2.1 (Opposite) Central Motor Apartments, Temperance Street, Wickson and Gregg, 1925. These apartments were "first building of this type to be built in Ontario."

New publications appeared that spread the word about developments at home and abroad. In 1924 the Royal Architectural Institute of Canada (founded in 1907) began publication of a quarterly periodical (*Royal Architectural Institute of Canada Journal*) directed at its members. An editorial in the first issue promised to draw its subjects from "Canadian work of national importance," but warned that it would only publicize outstanding examples of the art of architecture "in order to avoid any appearance of discriminating amongst the works of members of the Institute."[2] The result was that the periodical (which eventually became a monthly) was severely hampered in supplying critical analysis by the conviction that it was unprofessional (and perhaps even libelous) for one architect to engage in public criticism of the work of another. Many articles consisted of little but anodyne generalities about selected buildings mixed up with a considerable quantity of self-congratulation. Still the journal did provide a vehicle by which its readers could inform themselves of developments in their field.

A similar function was also performed by the appearance in the following year of a new magazine called *Canadian Homes and Gardens*, which was aimed at a broader audience. Originally the brainchild of newspaperman W. Rupert Davies and emanating from the unlikely location of Renfrew, Ontario, it was acquired after just two issues by the empire of the Maclean Publishing Company of Toronto. With J. Herbert Hodgins installed as editor, the magazine became a monthly in 1926. Thick with advertisements for automobiles, furniture, rugs, and building hardware, it touted the virtues of up-to-date products such as Crittall's weather-tight steel casement windows (just then available for residential use). Hodgins chose well-known artists to produce many of the glossy covers. Black-and-white photographs along with small plans accompanied the descriptions of houses designed by architects for socially prominent people, overwhelmingly Toronto residents. From the outset Hodgins declared it to be a matter of national pride to develop and publicize Canadian home styles as well as the kind of gardens that the local climate dictated. Canada was, after all, a nation of home lovers as evidenced by such upscale districts as Toronto's Rosedale, Moore Park, Forest Hill, and Lawrence Park, whose houses formed the staple of the magazine throughout its existence.[3]

When L'exposition internationale des arts décoratifs et industriels modernes opened in Paris in 1925 architects were promptly alerted by a communiqué from the secretary of the Royal Architectural Institute of Canada who reported that the displays there were "not only artistic but of an entirely modern character," which showed that the "most simple objects" were "capable of as much beauty as the most precious works of art."[4] *Canadian Homes and Gardens* also gave extensive publicity to what was occurring in France. From such bulletins Canadians learned that something was afoot in Europe, a new style that came to be called "*l'art moderne*" or "moderne." These developments were not, of course, the radical experiments of European architects like Le Corbusier or the Bauhaus but more decorative. Some architects and designers did take up the new forms for exteriors and interiors, while a great deal of attention was also focused upon the question of the development of a distinctive Canadian style.

In Toronto some new commercial buildings downtown displayed the motifs of the moderne, but both architects and clients resisted such innovations for housing. Well-off Torontonians preferred to live in Georgian Revival houses with historically appropriate detailing, though the more adventuresome did adopt furnishings and interior designs that reflected the new ideas. An earlier modernizing impulse also reappeared when right at the end of the 1920s some civic leaders revived the plans for improving the road layout that had been promoted in the decade before the First World War, including the proposal for a grand civic square on Queen Street. In the end, however, this movement again produced few concrete results. Where the tenets of European modern architecture in which innovative materials were used for the open expression of functional requirements, factory buildings were more likely candidates but these developments attracted little attention from architectural commentators.

I

Had Torontonians wished to inform themselves about developments in avant-garde architecture in Europe it would have been no easy task in the immediate postwar years. A good number of architects and draftsmen had served overseas with the Canadian Expeditionary Force, but that experience was hardly a route to leisurely study and contemplation. In the summer of 1919 the Royal Architectural Institute of Canada and the Ontario Association of Architects (OAA) held a joint meeting: along with a display of drawing of recent work by Canadians was a special exhibition of photographs of cathedrals in France but nothing that contained any reference to the work of people like Peter Behrens and Walter Gropius.[5] An analysis of the impact of the Bauhaus in the United States indicates that it was only in the late 1920s and early 1930s that much discussion of the European avant-garde began to appear even in specialized periodicals.[6]

In fact ideas tended to flow in the opposite direction. In the early 1920s progressive architects in Europe became interested in certain developments in North America. Reyner Banham argues that in addition to a knowledge of and admiration for the work of Americans like Louis Sullivan and Frank Lloyd Wright, dating back before the First World War, the European avant-garde took careful note of certain industrial buildings, such as factories and grain elevators, in the United States. Relying upon a series of photographs of such buildings published by Walter Gropius in 1913, Le Corbusier in his 1923 book, *Vers une architecture*, became, in Bantham's words, "the ultimate propagandist for American industrial buildings as the models of modern architecture." (The only Canadian structures pictured in the book were the Government [Grain] Elevator at Calgary and the Port of Montreal's Grain Elevator No. 2.) Banham contends that such buildings were "the most internationally influential structures ever put up in North America because of their effect on the architectural vocabulary of the founders of modern architecture."[7]

Currents of thought did not emanate from Europe. Many of architecture's most innovative practitioners were Germans or Austrians; any acceptance of their ideas in Canada collided with continuing antagonism towards the wartime enemy. Even people who might have noted developments in Berlin or Vienna before 1914 were wary of falling into a similar trap again. In 1922 J.H.R. Webster observed, "It is so regrettable that in the late years that the influence of a German alliance with our own monarchy should have been the means of such a debauch in architecture and interior work, which makes even the veriest tyro blush with shame to know that we were slaves to a regime of monkeyish mimicry to customs that have left their baneful influence upon a world only just emerging from the throes of such passion, which was dominated by the bastard trend of art." Webster was all for "abolishing the interior whimsicalities of the early and mid-Victorian era, and reverting (with the desirability of modernity) to the glorious traditions of the English XVII and XVIII centuries, which were founded upon the indescribable beauty of the classics of the early Grecians."[8]

In 1921 Canadian architect G.H. Macdonald delivered a fairly comprehensive condemnation of recent stylistic innovations: "The art nouveau had a brief popularity, distinctly unsound, violating many canons of art, lacking in significance, and was short-lived." He regretted that the California bungalow "lacking in unity, generally atrocious in detail, still maintains some measure of popularity." Industrial buildings sporting bands and vast triangles of brickwork sought to replace the "functional and significant" ornament of the past, but such invented decoration violated fundamental principles of design. The only modern construction technique to escape Macdonald's condemnation was the skyscraper framed with steel or concrete like Louis Sullivan's Prudential Building in Buffalo, but even these structures were deemed deficient in their sparseness of ornament. Would a genuinely new architecture emerge from such experiments? Probably not. "Better then to continue to express the historical traditions of the past than momentary phases, never reaching the point of sustained development."[9]

Awareness about the latest trends in European design during the 1920s was also hampered by the state of formal architectural education in Canada. University training in the discipline was confined to a few places like McGill and Toronto. At the University of Toronto, architecture had been taught in the engineering school since 1890 with a heavy emphasis upon technical and structural issues. Years later architect A.S. Mathers recollected that, in his time as a student in 1919, the head of the architectural faculty was still "lecturing on water closets."[10] The place of education of the city's architects, the University of Toronto did import some junior faculty members, but they came from Britain, not then a place sympathetic to the avant-garde. In 1920 Adrian Berrington arrived as part of the plan of the dean of engineering to improve the course in architecture, and in 1922 the university began to award its students the bachelor of architecture rather than an engineering degree. Berrington had graduated from the University of Liverpool in 1904 and undertaken further study at the Royal Academy in London. After visiting the continent he taught with Patrick Geddes at the University of London until he joined the army during the war. Wounded and shell-shocked, his health was permanently affected, though he continued his work on urban planning and taught that subject in Toronto, but he died suddenly in 1923, aged only thirty-five.[11]

2.2
Eric Arthur, upon arrival in Canada, 1923.

His successor at the University of Toronto, Eric Arthur, was to enjoy a long and influential career in Canada.[12] Born in New Zealand in 1898, he was apprenticed to an architect there before joining the army and being shipped to Britain in 1918. Once discharged he took his architecture degree at the University of Liverpool where he studied under Professor Charles H. Reilly who had adopted a curriculum based upon that at the École des Beaux-Arts. Arthur himself studied briefly at the Beaux Arts in Paris. After a short sojourn in the office of Edwin Lutyens, he joined the faculty of the University of Toronto for a salary of $2,500 after Berrington's untimely death. With senior professors H.H. Madill and C.H.C. Wright he became mainly responsible for teaching design. From his arrival in Toronto, Arthur was a frequent commentator on exhibitions of work by Canadian architects but during the 1920s he remained conventional in his ideas. He favoured historically accurate Georgian reproductions, an interest reflected in his scheme to produce measured drawings of pre-Confederation Upper Canada's significant buildings. By 1933 he had recorded more than three hundred such structures, and he took the leading role in the incorporation of the Architectural Conservancy of Ontario, which aimed to preserve such buildings on the model of the National Trust in Britain.[13]

Published commentary on the state of new architectural projects elsewhere was not sophisticated in Canada during the 1920s. When the Chicago *Tribune* held its celebrated competition for the design of a new head office in 1922, *Construction* merely observed that the four entries submitted by Canadians were of good quality: "Where they differed essentially in this competition was on the style of design. In nearly every instance they adhered to the Renaissance type, while the first, second and third prize designs catered to the Gothic." The author completely failed to grasp how different the winning historicist design by John Mead Howells was from the second place entry by Finnish expatriate Eliel Saarinen, which later attracted so much acclaim.

To Canadian architects or design commentators during the 1920s the term *modern* continued to mean contemporary or up-to-date. Canadian houses were described as modern if they were supplied with advanced plumbing and electrical wiring. Modernity was associated with new colours and textures that entered home décor in the form of fabrics, wallpapers, high gloss enamels along with new chrome and ceramic fixtures for kitchens and bathrooms.[14] A member of the architectural staff of the Bell Telephone Company of Canada, which was responsible for scores of exchange buildings in Ontario and Quebec, argued in 1930 that "A design that has been logically developed is modern. The term 'modern' has been misinterpreted frequently, and the unhappy and negative aspects of modernity are brought to mind when that misunderstood expression is used. In its proper sense the word 'modern' means characteristic of today. The principal object of modern design is not to do something different or radical." He drew the following contrast with now-unfashionable Victorianism: "At its best modernism in architecture is based on sound principles of construction, on reality, directness, honesty, and simplicity. This is the very opposite of what we so often find in the Victorian age, a period characterized by pretense, architectural or otherwise."[15]

Adapting to new inventions like the automobile constituted the epitome of modernity. (See Figure 2.1.) A stable for horses had to be located some distance from a house on account of fire risk, odours, and so forth, but on small city lots it was impractical to surrender a sizable portion of the frontage to a detached garage. In 1924 one author suggested putting a garage right in the front of a new house as a focal point: "Modern requirements impose numerous conditions that a few years ago were absolutely non-existent. The growth of the motor car and the consequent demand for suitable garages for housing them has undoubtedly influenced the design of modern residences."[16]

Visitors to Toronto in the early 1920s did not find much innovative design. On a 1924 trip Charles Reilly, who had trained Eric Arthur at Liverpool University, reserved his greatest enthusiasm for the recently completed Bloor viaduct, an "excellent road bridge of steel and concrete and a thing of beauty." Trees and ravines provided pleasant grace notes, but Reilly found it "curious" that the city should be so thoroughly cut off from the shores of Lake Ontario by railways and warehouses. He could only express restrained but tactful hopes for the future: "One left Toronto with the feeling that it was not only a city of singular achievement, but one which with its wealth and energy and freedom from racial difficulties, held immense and unlimited possibilities, not only for the Empire of which it is so naively proud, but for the world at large."[17]

A good index of how far advanced were architectural tastes in Toronto in the early 1920s was provided by the fact that the most discussed and praised structure at that time remained Hart House, the men's student centre at the University of Toronto, which opened in 1919. In a 1925 appreciation of the work of the architects Sproatt and Rolph, John Lyle declared Hart House their "masterpiece." He noted how much they loved stonework, sticking loyally to the Gothic in their other works, such as Bishop Strachan School for girls in north Toronto. The partners not only valued the symbolism of the Gothic but had discovered its adaptability for institutional purposes.[18]

Vincent Massey, who had commissioned Hart House as a memorial to his ancestor, recorded in an assessment of local architecture that great strides were being made in Toronto without succumbing to the "bizarre, jazzy" structures popping up in London, the ornate and debased in France, or the tiresome straining after originality in Germany. When the Royal Institute of British Architects recognized Sproatt and Rolph's achievements in 1926 by making them Fellows, Eric Arthur declared that in most hands Gothic might be a dead letter but the partners had kept it alive in Hart House by avoiding too many pinnacles and turrets, producing one of the "best College works, ancient or modern."[19]

Content to stick with tried-and-true historical styles of the Beaux Arts, leading architects of the mid-1920s spent much time fretting about when, where, and how a distinctively Canadian school of design might emerge. Percy Nobbs of McGill told the Royal Institute of British Architects in 1924 that popular writers had been stymied in the effort to identify a genuine Canadian building type. A good deal of the blame could be laid at the doorstep of the Americans whose models were being shamelessly aped. As a result Canada's cities were filling up with "standard features such as useless but elegantly designed columnar porticos to banks and useless and ill-designed Gothic towers upon churches." Legislative buildings were being created in "the recognized [American] state Capitol type with pedimented porticos and central lantern domes," while educational institutions sprouted "mullions, buttresses and parapets all turned out by the yard with a singular lack of … the Gothic spirit." Even though formal architectural education in Canadian universities dated back more than two decades, so that a score of new Canadian graduates were yearly joining some nine hundred trained men (immigrants and native-born), there was still too strong a pull from the American Beaux Arts tradition with its "elegant insincerities." "Enough has surely been shown and said," sputtered Nobbs, "to maintain the thesis that, beyond the practicalities of the window and roof making, at the moment Canadian architecture is a polite fiction."[20]

Citing the maxim that "Architecture mirrors the soul of a nation," S. Lewis Milligan wondered, "How does the soul of Canada appear in the mirror of architecture?" His conclusion was gloomy: the new Union Station under construction on Toronto's Front Street seemed more suitable as a museum or a mausoleum than a gateway to the city. Could the "severe and heavy" front with its massive columns and entablature not be enlivened with some carved decoration memorializing the achievements of business enterprise?[21] Or perhaps a dome might be added to the roof so that the building looked less like a morgue? He could only conclude that Ontario needed a distinctive style of architecture to reflect both its pioneer past and its progressive present and suggested it might combine the Gothic with the Italian and the Arabian.[22]

John Lyle was the most prominent Torontonian to spend a great deal of time worrying about whether a distinctive national style of architecture would develop in Canada. Surveying the scene in 1926 he expressed the hope that perhaps "a subconscious architectural taste" was developing in Canada, which might be on the "eve of an architectural renaissance." To him Hart House and his own Union Station seemed to be the product of "a phase of architecture characterized by a certain restraint, a certain Anglo-French character that stamps it as personal."[23]

The following year Lyle and a group of other members of the Toronto chapter of the Ontario Association of Architects organized an exhibition at the Art Gallery of Toronto on *Architecture and the Allied Arts* to showcase the work of their colleagues as well as craftsmen in glass, metalwork, and the like. In an effort to drum up publicity, the organizers styled themselves the "Diet Kitchen Group" after the local restaurant where they gathered for lunch. In an address entitled "Canadian Architecture" delivered at the gallery, Lyle lamented that "in Canada we still attach too much importance to the purely utilitarian. Typical of our attitude is our indifference to the work of men who in Europe would be acclaimed as master-craftsmen, engineers and architects." He cited as notable buildings the chateau-style railway hotels, the Sun Life tower in Montreal, the *Herald* building in Calgary, the legislative buildings in Regina as well as his own Union Station: "I say the Canadian architect has demonstrated by such works that he is worthy to be accounted among the best – and he is frequently so accounted – abroad." This exercise in self-congratulation was sufficiently successful that 29,000 people visited the Art Gallery of Toronto during the two weeks that the show ran.[24]

Not everybody was equally impressed. One of the architects pictured in *Saturday Night* as part of the Diet Kitchen Group told the *Toronto Daily Star* that some of the architects named might eat lunch at the restaurant, but he personally had never done so and "The Group is a fiction."[25] Lyle seemed to want to "head a ginger group who aim to emphasize Canadian architecture. No one has said so much about this in public as Mr. Lyle." The *Star* observed that these architects did not share a common style, and anyway, "Radicals in architecture are not wanted. Futurize, impressionize architecture and we shall all go crazy. Jazz our buildings and we shall go to the bow-wows ... The nearest thing Toronto has to a jazz note in public buildings is Convocation Hall,[26] which jangles out of harmony of those older academic buildings like a Stravinsky eleven-note chord stuck into a Bach fugue." The paper's view was that Sproatt and Rolph's Gothic Hart House showed the right way to adapt tradition to present needs.[27]

Yet John Lyle continued to fret because there was no "distinctly national note" to design in a country where Victorian eclecticism still had "architectural Canada by the throat." He concluded that the only solution was to develop ornamental motifs unique to Canada, and in the late 1920s his office began to produce such models. Soon the numerous branch banks that Lyle designed sprouted wheat tassels and balsam buds.[28] A particularly notable example was the Dominion Bank at the corner of Yonge and Gerrard Streets in Toronto. On the north facade were pairs of swans and pigeons, back to back, along with eight urns filled with Ontario sunflowers plus two octagonal reliefs representing industry in Toronto and a harbour scene. Lillies and sunflowers formed the capitals of the quarter-columns flanking the main entrance with ox heads as the capitals of the bronze doorjambs.[29]

Before long Lyle's enthusiasms became so well known in the profession that Eric Arthur teased that he must fantasize about Noah leaving the ark with pairs of skunks, gophers, and Canada geese:[30] "A dream of bliss for Mr. Lyle who prefers skunks ... to Corinthians or anyone else."[31] Another critic noted that he had become as renowned for his use of Canadian animal forms as was the totem pole. One of Lyle's buildings, wrote William Fleury, "has quite a little zoo up by the cornice." Yet muskrats and yellow-bellied sapsuckers were as strange to most people as panda bears: "To us a frieze of fur-hatted policemen trying to keep their ears warm would be much more typical [sic] Canadian than a whole clutch of muskrats." The claim that "Lyle's espousal of a new spirit of design led others to original sources of Canadian inspiration" seemed to ignore the fact that the direction of this leadership was backwards towards the Victorian encrustations of the past.[32]

After visiting the biennial exhibition of work by members of the Ontario Association of Architects in 1931, the correspondent for *Construction*

March, 1932 THE JOURNAL, ROYAL ARCHITECTURAL INSTITUTE OF CANADA 67

BRONZE ENTRANCE DOORS
DOMINION BANK, YONGE & GERRARD BRANCH, TORONTO
John M. Lyle, Architect
(Balsam Root of British Columbia in full bloom and in bud used as decorative motifs)

2.3
John Lyle's bronze doors, Dominion Bank, Yonge and Gerrard Streets, 1929.

observed how many native plants and animals had been recruited to "provide ornamentation for truly modern work and essentially Canadian buildings." Not only were such flora and fauna being carved as decoration but were now incorporated into metal grillwork. At the same time another writer concerned about the development of a recognizably national movement in the arts recorded with pride that these motifs had crept indoors. Mr and Mrs W. Gordon Mills (she being the well-known artist Doris Huestis Mills who exhibited with the Group of Seven) had apparently filled their home in north Toronto with light fixtures, firescreens, and firedogs embellished with trilliums, pine needles, squirrels, and chickadees. Conscious of their national identity, Canadians were no longer afraid to substitute milkweed for acanthus. The Mills were applauded as "people in tune with the modern movement, whose house is a shrine of things Canadian."[33]

At least one person disagreed strongly about this kind of fixation, saying that it made much more sense to look across the Atlantic in search of motifs. Was the "polecat" any more intrinsically decorative than some medieval or mythological beast? Why "build our ornament on the crude hatchet work of illiterate tribes whose influence on the development of our civilization has been practically nil"?[34] But concerned Canadians seemed to agree with the notion that native motifs were the route to follow to establish a modern and distinctive architectural style for the country.

II

L'exposition internationale des arts décoratifs et industriels modernes in Paris showcased what came to be known as the moderne. Canada was invited but, like the United States, did not participate. The new styles rejected the organic, naturalistic figures like the vines and blossoms of Art Nouveau for hard edges, straight lines, and sharp angles that could be applied or incised into furniture, walls, or building exteriors. Low-relief carving for wood or masonry using repetitive machine-like forms was combined with the use of new materials like polished aluminum, Monell metal (nickel plate), or "artificial stone." Along with flames, urns (standing for accumulation), rising suns (health and rebirth), and waterfalls (eternal hope), decorative symbols like Egyptian pyramids became particularly popular as a result of the discovery of Tutankhamun's tomb in 1922. Later during the 1930s the moderne often featured references to advanced technology showing radio towers or winged tires that blended well with the vogue for streamlining products like airplanes and automobiles. In the case of Canada these international symbols could be mixed and adapted to include maple leaves, wheat sheaves, beavers, all intended to signal national distinctiveness.[35] John Lyle, the great proponent of specifically Canadian motifs, was enthusiastic about the way in which Beaux Arts designs could be embellished in the moderne manner: "Its characteristics are a simplicity of wall surface, both of exterior and interior, a use of parallel lines or concentric curves, a use of incised relief ornament with semi-flat surface, a daring use of modern materials such as the combination of metal and glass, wood and metal, and an altogether charming use of what might be called sunshine colours."[36]

In *Canadian Homes and Gardens* Herbert Hodgins offered his readers information about the moderne. He recruited a number of journalists and designers, many of them women, to contribute to the profusely illustrated articles. In 1926 associate editor Anne Elizabeth Wilson was quick to respond to the innovations, advising her readers about "the amusing, amazing and sometimes almost overpowering creations of the new art, those fabrics of cubist and symbolic portent, which at once fascinated and took away the breath of buyers who a short time ago were irresistibly drawn to a certain fifty-seven acres in the very heart of Paris ... It was remarked that if the modernistic fabrics were to persist they would require modernistic furniture to carry them. This was brought to pass at the Exposition, not only in furniture but in architecture."[37] In an issue devoted to current design in 1928 Mary-Etta Macpherson observed that modernism was a natural development of the go-ahead age like the airplane. The jagged outlines and harsh colours

2.4
Breay-Nash automobile showroom, Earle E. Sheppard, 1927.

of early experiments had now been smoothed out and toned down, and the new forms were sincere, simple, and well-made. She expressed only the wish for a better descriptive term than the purely relative "modernism," which had originated back in the last century and now lumped together everything developed since the war.[38]

Yet critics of the new style also had their say. Well-known Toronto decorator Minerva Wilson asked, "Will modernity last?" and responded with a resounding *no*. The objects displayed at the continuation of the Paris exposition in 1927 were "actually distressing to the sensitive eye. They seemed to have found their inspiration in the crippled, the deformed, the hunch-backed ... A petulant egotism is discernible in most examples of the *art modern*."[39] Herbert Hodgins waffled. He noted that debate on this subject seemed to produce no compromise: "You either like it or your don't; you are ready to be martyred to the cause, or you are eager to assist in such a demonstration against it." He claimed it was his duty to keep his readers informed about new products and styles from abroad, but admitted that he didn't want to alienate his subscribers.[40] Even Mary-Etta Macpherson observed at Christmas 1930 that change could go too far; the violet-painted chairs with their white leather seats might be arrayed around a mirror-topped table but the turkey and plum pudding would be just as good as ever: "Thank heaven there is nothing modernistic about Christmas."[41]

All of these commentators discussed modernism as a matter of interior decoration. Some local architects were obviously aware of more radical developments in Europe, but they seem to have had little luck in selling unfamiliar notions. Designs incorporating moderne motifs were slow to appear in Toronto, at least in residential settings.[42] In a critique of the 1926 exhibition of photographs of the best works designed by members of the Ontario Association of Architects, Eric Arthur observed that little displayed there was truly in keeping with the European avant-garde: "One rather timid triangular-headed doorway on a small house would scarcely suggest that Toronto was being swept by the vogue for the modern German, Finnish or French."[43] The most receptive clients were commercial undertakings keen to associate themselves with the up-to-date and the fashionable. For instance, in 1927 Earle E. Sheppard created an automobile showroom for Breay-Nash on Bay Street that included a vast three-paned plate glass window stretching across fifty feet below a polychrome mosaic frieze featuring motifs like an Egyptian lion.[44] The new premises of the Gorrie Chevrolet dealership on Gerrard Street, designed by Scottish immigrant Murray Brown, also showed an awareness of the moderne; Eric Arthur praised this outstanding design as "simple in its composition, ornament is sparingly used and the lettering is excellent."[45]

2.5
Automotive Building, CNE, D.E. Kertland, 1929.

In 1928 the directors of the Canadian National Exhibition decided to construct a building exclusively devoted to the automobile. A competition was announced to create 120,000 square feet of display space, the cost not to exceed $1 million. For the Automotive Building the jury chose a moderne design by Douglas E. Kertland over a kind of Renaissance palace from Charles B. Dolphin and Mathers and Haldenby's traditional Neoclassicism.[46] A commentator in the RAIC *Journal* applauded the design for the "modernity" of the fusion of "Classical dignity and almost Grecian restraint," which did a much better job of blending the two than previous "modern" buildings. The stone carving did not reflect historical precedents and harmonized well with the green metal grilles, railings, and the cast iron spandrels. The sharply cut window openings towards Lake Ontario to the south created a pleasing play of light and the building looked well when floodlit. Inside, Kertland adapted "classical forms to modern requirements and the decoration is of a successful modern character." In a survey of recent Toronto buildings *Construction* praised Kertland's work as "a masterpiece of modernism."[47]

Like the automobile industry, moving picture chains were interested in presenting a contemporary image, and Murray Brown designed a number of cinemas in Toronto and elsewhere that were praised for their striking look.[48] The Toronto cosmetics salon of "Madame Helena Rubinstein" on Bloor Street, designed by Martin Baldwin and his partner, Gerald Greene, aimed to resemble the newest shops in Paris: "The simplicity of the interior architecture is a foil to the richness of the ultra-modern furnishings and decorations." To the commentator in *Construction* such work was proof that the well-informed architect need no longer copy from or plagiarize historical styles but could create something that was "a spontaneous outpouring of his own age."[49] Yet the same author also noted around that time that there were plenty of new commercial buildings that faithfully reproduced tried-

and-true models like Ridpath's new store on Yonge Street north of Davenport. Appropriately, this heavily half-timbered Tudor job housed one of the largest sellers of reproduction furniture in the city, where conservative Torontonians could acquire fake Sheraton or Chippendale to fill up their living and dining rooms.[50]

Moderne was as far as Torontonians were prepared to venture towards the avant-garde during the 1920s. In the spring of 1929 John Lyle, back from a summer in France, told the Royal Architectural Institute of Canada that, "This modern movement has in my opinion much to commend it. It might be described as a revolt against archeology in architecture, and while much that has been done in this manner is thoroughly bad, there is also much that is sound and beautiful." If there were reservations about the new styles, they had arisen because "unfortunately much of the modern work has been executed by untrained men and not by the great designers. The former have, in many cases, substituted sensation for taste." Furniture designers were particularly guilty of turning out products "the most of which [sic] is obese, bulbous and lacking beauty of line and form." Yet modernistic ideas were making strong headway in Europe (even in Britain) and "great strides" in the United States. Canada needed to pay attention: "It is a movement that we Canadian architects might study to our advantage, and if we are to develop a Canadian note along modern lines, I should be inclined to follow the Swedish." Architecture here at home was "too archeological," and practitioners had to stop "pandering to the picturesque – especially in our domestic work." "When one drives about Toronto and sees the endless mongrel combinations of shooting roofs, gabbing gables and strutting bow windows, that jostle each other on a twenty-five foot front, he is almost moved to tears." "The architect is the great arbiter of taste," said Lyle, praising such moderne designs as the *Toronto Star* and Canada Permanent buildings and calling upon other RAIC members to take up the challenge.[51]

From the Massachusetts Institute of Technology, where he was said to be "the presiding genius in design," Jacques Carlu came to Toronto to preach the gospel of the moderne. For a display of drawings at the RAIC Convention in Montreal in 1930, Carlu and his students submitted the most futuristic designs, including one for a restaurant flying through the air like a rocket ship.[52] In the spring of 1931 Carlu gave a speech to the Toronto chapter of the Ontario Association of Architects where he argued that sound design involved logical solutions to problems depending on the state of current knowledge, customs, and materials. It made no sense to look to the past in an age of steel and concrete because new buildings should suffer "no fake skin-like treatments unrelated to the structure." Modernism was already well past its experimental phase in Europe, said Carlu, after thirty years during which Auguste Perret had moved decisively away from the Gothic with works like his reinforced concrete church at Le Raincy in France.

Yet many Torontonians were not prepared to agree. Carlu's address provoked an impassioned response from E.H. Blake, who complained in a speech at the Art Gallery of Toronto that modernists were trying to dismiss all of their critics as retrograde provincials. Ordinary men could judge the quality of buildings, and merely looking at photographs of the most radical work, said Blake, was enough to show that nobody would wish to live in a moderne house because of its starkness. Those who saw the use of historical styles as mere copying were victims of false and misleading theories, and Canadians should be thankful for the native Georgian tradition now reemerging from under Victorian Gothic or Rosedale Tudor.[53]

In residential architecture the taste of wealthy Torontonians remained unchanged after the First World War. In mid-1918 *Construction*, the monthly periodical devoted to the building trades that focused almost all its attention upon the Toronto area, reported that some residential work was reviving as the fighting drew to a close; the houses pictured showed lots of dark panelling and beamed ceilings.[54] When peace returned the richest Torontonians continued to want spacious estates, each with its own name. Beyond the northeasterly limits of the city architects Wickson and Gregg produced an imitation of a Norman country house for lawyer David Dunlap in 1919. Donalda Farms (named after Dunlap's wife) spread out wide eaves with dormer windows above, and inside the dining room had a beamed ceiling and a vast stone fireplace, including a bake oven in the manorial fashion. Even the Guernsey cows and Clydesdale horses enjoyed a life of luxury in white-tiled stalls cleaned with specially designed brass pitchforks.

2.6
Donalda Farms, Wickson and Gregg, 1919.

The following year Dr Herbert Bruce, founder of the city's Wellesley Hospital, got Eden Smith, designer of so many "English Cottage" style houses, to create Annandale standing in extensive grounds at the end of a tree-lined driveway, a mock Tudor with beamed ceilings and a huge fireplace. Nearby across Bayview Avenue (then a rural road broken by the valley of the Don River) Sir Clifford Sifton, newspaper and property magnate, began in 1923 to build three huge brick houses for himself and his sons on Lawrence Avenue in a blend of Tudor and Dutch styles with stables and a covered riding ring to the rear.[55]

During the 1920s there was little call for advanced designs in residential architecture. Murray Brown tried to introduce small playful touches into some of his plans but does not appear to have built houses anything as radical as his cinema designs.[56] Typical of many Toronto practitioners was W.L. Somerville, who became president of the Ontario Association of Architects in 1927 and was a frequent contributor to both the RAIC *Journal* and *Canadian Homes and Gardens*. In numerous articles he reiterated the view that Georgian was best suited to Canadian taste and climate and that brick was the best facing material. Other acceptable alternatives included American Federal or Quebec vernacular, both part of Ontario's "rightful heritage." He warned sternly against falling for ridiculous fads like the Spanish look imported from Miami or Hollywood. Part of the job of the architect was to prevent clients from going on a "jag" after reading foreign books or American magazines. Torontonians need not suffer "the freakish styles of the moving picture scenario artists or be carried away by the bizarre extremes of our more temperamental cousins."[57]

Few of Somerville's fellow citizens fell prey to such temptations, but there were a very few outliers. As early as 1922 the proprietors of a well-known photographic studio, C.G. Ashley and J.B. Crippen, commissioned a most unusual house at 110 Inglewood Drive in Moore Park. The pebble dash exterior with flat roof and irregular window placement (including even a small porthole) had a broad flagged forecourt outside the front door overlooking a garage entrance below grade. As an article in *Construction* noted, "The style of the window treatment presents continuity of line and lends itself to the design." In the large front hall a broad arched opening (closed by a curtain on an iron rod rather than a door) gave onto a sun room atop the garage flooded with light through three round-headed windows to both front and rear and four on the side, giving sweeping views over the city below the escarpment. Across the hallway a similar entrance led to the living room with a large fireplace. The ceilings were supported by heavy axe-hewn beams stained to appear weathered, the outside doors made of heavy planks with prominent iron hinges. The ground-floor layout featured an unusual open plan with "a dining room which is practically part of the living room although partly shut off by the fireplace" and beyond "a white enamel-finished kitchen with built-in cupboards." The stair tower ascended from just inside the front door, the first flight lit by a window whose stepped lower sill emphasized it on the exterior with a tall narrow window on the landing overlooking the front lawn.

The article in *Construction* in which the Ashley-Crippen house was featured was actually devoted to the virtues of hollow tiles each the size of a dozen bricks to which a stucco finish could be applied. The air-filled cavities in the tiles were claimed to make the walls almost as good insulators as traditional materials like brick and plaster. *Construction* argued that "Its varying heights, flat roof and plain surfaces belong to the southern clime where the Spanish Mission style of architecture predominates. To our northern climate it is unusual, but the moderate winters of recent years seem to warrant us in perhaps being a little less exacting and allowing ourselves a little more latitude for variety in design." Where did this mixture of the Moorish with a dash of moderne originate? The "associate architects" of the house were named as one B. Kelly (about whom no other information has been found)

and A.E. LePage, not recognized elsewhere as an architect but as a man whose fame in Toronto would subsequently rest upon his success as a realtor. Perhaps the photographers had come upon something like their remarkable home in their travels or seen an enticing picture, but its precise intellectual origins remain elusive.[58]

Just in case too many people might yield to the temptations of Hollywood glitz, interior decorator Minerva Elliott reported in 1935 on what she had learned during a visit there to advise on period English room settings for a film. Having toured many houses, she warned that the glamour was little more than a facade: the star often ate out at cheap restaurants rather than dining in a sad imitation of a Spanish or French villa, which she "furnishes ... with a noxious claptrap of ill-assorted fads and lounges about at parties in slatternly pajamas." The living was far more gracious in a well-to-do Canadian home.[59]

In 1927 *Canadian Homes and Gardens* published a feature on "small" houses recently completed by Toronto architects at a cost of $20,000 or less. The photographs and plans ran under the following headings: "A Dutch Colonial of Charming Simplicity," "A Small House in the Georgian Manner," "An Architect's Studio Home," "The Well-Proportioned [Tudorbethan] Small House," "[Georgian] Home of Dr. John C. Maynard, St. Clair Avenue West, Toronto."[60] Out near the western city limits R. Home Smith continued to develop the lands centred round the ruined Old Mill on the Humber River, where his company had created a tea garden in imitation of Olde Englande. Home Smith's company constructed numerous houses in the

2.7 (Opposite) Ashley-Crippen house, 110 Inglewood Drive, North Toronto, A.E. LePage and B. Kelly, 1922.

2.8 (Left) Ashley-Crippen house, interior.

same heavily timbered style, designed either by his company's architects or by A. Colpoys Wood (formerly of Sproatt and Rolph), faux cottages that were considered "well-mannered" but included practical conveniences.[61]

Those people who could afford to build their own houses chose to stick with the traditional. Though they shunned imitation of the heavily ornamented Victorian and Edwardian piles of the prewar era, well-to-do Torontonians now filled up the streets of Rosedale, Forest Hill, and Lawrence Park with Georgian Revival houses. None of these was more elaborate and careful in its period details than the building at 8 Castle Frank Road in Rosedale that George, Moorhouse, and King designed for Gerald Larkin in 1926. Heir to the founder of the Salada Tea Company, Larkin chose a firm of architects that included Allan George, son of Sir Ernest George who had been a leader of the Georgian Revival in Britain. A brick house seven bays wide, the centre three stepped forward under a sculpted pediment with an overhanging lantern; it was a gentleman's residence. Concealed by a parapet lay a flat roof, the only radical innovation in the snow-heavy Canadian climate. The main rooms faced to the rear and were filled with Larkin's extensive collection of English and European furniture and art. The results won a medal of honour for the architects from the Royal Architectural Institute as well as first prize for an exterior design costing more than $50,000. Eric Arthur applauded the house as an "exceedingly competent and scholarly design," "charming in every detail."[62]

Mary-Etta Macpherson of *Canadian Homes and Gardens* observed that three-quarters of the designs in the 1929 RAIC show were similarly Georgian. Arthur's only reservation was that too many of these designs "had a bookish look that indicated a lack of sympathy with the style on the part of the designer." Still, he praised F. Hilton Wilkes's plan for a house for C.A. Withers in Forest Hill, which included a two-car garage, for showing "a breadth of wall and a lightness to the cornice that is missing in many of the Georgian facades shown. Too often one can picture Banister Fletcher[63] or 'the [Classical] orders' brought out and diligently studied in modules, a message that may produce a Field Museum [in Chicago] but not a house under $20,000." He waxed sarcastic about the shrunken parapet on Dr E.A. Morgan's house on Oriole Parkway, which had cost over $20,000, as "with all its simplicity a daring piece of design for this country. I don't know Mr. Dyce Saunders, or whether he hears the rumours which emanate from the clubs and kitchens (architects meet in kitchens in Toronto rather than in taverns) of this city, but certain members of the profession are but biding their time, and then, if the parapet has not been knocked over by the ice they will themselves break forth in the corniceless period of the 18th century."[64]

2.9 (Left)
Gerald Larkin house, George, Moorhouse and King, 1926.

2.10 (Right)
University Club, Mathers and Haldenby and F. Hilton Wilkes, 1928.

Some architects grumbled about the lack of boldness shown by clients. At the 1929 RAIC annual meeting there was discussion about the future of its journal, which now went to eight hundred members, with another 325 for libraries, advertisers, and so forth. Popular magazines (like *Canadian Homes and Gardens*) had demonstrated the market for articles devoted to the homes of the socially prominent. One architect suggested that perhaps it would be better to divide the journal into two, one part for sale on the newstands devoted entirely to such grand homes, even though they might be "the most unsightly thing ever created." A couple of years later Eric Arthur was complaining that the typical client wanted nothing more than a four-car garage, a glass-enclosed shower, and a built-in bar.[65]

Like the socially and financially prominent people who made up their membership, Toronto institutions demonstrated similar conservatism about their premises. In 1928 the city's University Club proposed a new building on University Avenue across from Osgoode Hall. A design competition was announced. Each of the four entries proved to be a variation on the three-storey London club or townhouse on the Regency model adorned with Classical details like swags, balustrades, and so forth. The jurors, Eric Arthur and W.L. Somerville, chose Mathers and Haldenby as winners with a design that includes a large Palladian window over the central doorway. But because of the very strong similarity to the entry from F. Hilton Wilkes, they suggested that he be made associate architect.[66]

III

During the 1920s Toronto did sprout a modest thicket (not really a forest) of skyscrapers along the Bay Street corridor north of Front as the city continued to develop from a regional metropolis towards national prominence. Yet many citizens, even architects, had serious doubts about erecting so many high-rise office towers. In 1924 the announcement of plans for a twenty-one-storey tower at the corner of Adelaide and Victoria Streets led the Toronto chapter of the Ontario Association of Architects to create a committee to consider the question of height limitations on buildings, since the city council never seemed to feel constrained by the recommended maximum of 130 feet (or roughly twice the width of the main streets). The committee report concluded that while the public might think of ever more skyscrapers as a civic asset, the reality was different. Isolated office towers of up to twenty storeys built on high-cost land might generate maximum rents, yet too many closely grouped high-rises actually depressed average real estate values throughout the entire downtown. Two separate ten-storey buildings might benefit the city more than one twenty-storey tower where internal travel times would be equal to walking a city block. Rush hour traffic created by skyscrapers would require costly solutions paid for by the ratepayers. In addition to purely economic considerations there were the effects of high-rise construction upon the circulation of light and air, along with fire safety concerns. The report argued that such problems had led both New York and Chicago to impose building height limitations, and recommended that the association lobby the city council to restrict skyscrapers to about one hundred feet on the sixty-six foot wide streets.[67]

In the autumn of 1924 Toronto chapter chair Walter Moorhouse gave a speech to a joint meeting of the OAA and the Royal Architectural Institute of Canada condemning "land pirates" from New York who were determined to put up a building taller than any in Toronto at present. He pointed out that more and more cities were imposing height limitations all the time, "as the disadvantages of the skyscraper were every day becoming more apparent," and proposed that a 130-foot maximum be strictly adhered to. Otherwise there should be size controls such as one foot of setback for every two vertical feet above that limit, with 10 percent of any lot left vacant along with an additional 1 percent for every added storey. S.G. Curry also condemned high building densities as the cause of traffic congestion, which was becoming increasingly serious because car owners believed that they had a right to park anywhere they chose downtown. The RAIC voted to approve a draft bylaw that no structure should be higher than twice the width of the adjoining street.[68]

2.11 Metropolitan Building, William F. Sparling, 1925.

The following year *Construction* observed that critics had both aesthetic and economic reservations about more skyscrapers, wanting to spread new development more evenly across the downtown. A proposal from architect F.H. Marani for a civic skyscraper commission to pronounce upon such designs in advance was cited approvingly. The Metropolitan Building had shot upward at the corner of Adelaide and Victoria in a mere four months. Using innovative technology such as the steel floor joists, which were now becoming common in the United States, the Metropolitan, at 316 feet, replaced its near neighbour the prewar Royal Bank headquarters at King and Yonge as the tallest building in the British Empire. The top seventy-eight feet of the building were, however, set back as a more slender tower. The *Toronto Star* complained "that the reactionaries who object to all skyscrapers, and who want Toronto to look as it did fifty years ago, would be better occupied if they were to launch a crusade against the unsightly old buildings only a storey or two high which are to be found on valuable land along some of the main streets of the city."[69] Over the next few years the debate about skyscrapers rumbled on. As late as 1928 the *RAIC Journal* still continued to fret about the skyscraper "problem," though most civic boosters celebrated this building boom as a sign of Toronto's emergence as a major metropolitan centre.[70]

Toronto's prewar skyscrapers along Yonge Street, beginning with the work of New York's Carrère and Hastings for the Traders' Bank in 1905, had all assumed the form of a Classical column with an imposing base topped by a plainer shaft enclosing leasable office space and capped off by a sizable overhanging cornice. Designers of newer structures seemed to be learning some lessons from Eliel Saarinen's losing 1922 entry in the Chicago *Tribune* tower competition. As "Sinaiticus" later put it in *Construction*, "The most remarkable feature of Saarinen's design was the emphasis upon verticality and the fact that the vertical masses, great and small, of the shaft of the building were not terminated by any heavy, brutal, depressing horizontal cornice line. Like the pointed arches of Medievalism, these soaring lines seemed to be aspiring toward infinity."[71]

Certainly the developers of high-rise office buildings and their architects did pay attention to the fact that striking structures like New York's Chrysler Building (which opened in 1930) were prestige addresses, which made space easily rentable. Adapting to the decorative features of the moderne might increase appeal to tenants. The firm of Chapman and Oxley was responsible for several Toronto towers, starting in 1925–26 with the Northern Ontario Building at Bay and Adelaide, a simple, smooth yellow brick structure that still retained a wide cornice in artificial stone. When completed its sixteen storeys formed the largest building in Canada framed with reinforced concrete. Easy to plan and construct and profitable to lease, it covered its entire lot and cut off much light and air, so beginning the transformation of Bay Street into a canyon. Chapman and Oxley followed up in 1928 with the twenty-two storey Sterling Tower, a block to the north, which rose straight up from its Classical base in pinkish artificial stone for thirteen storeys and included setbacks at the top on the New York zoning rules.[72] Romanesque details decorated the upper levels with the final five floors scalloped at the corners into a central tower crowned by a row of arched windows surmounted by a parapet. This building succeeded as the tallest concrete framed structure in the British Empire, but concrete, while fireproof, created such a heavy framework that it was ultimately to be replaced by steel in tall buildings, even though that material required careful fireproofing of the structural members.[73]

More notable still was Chapman and Oxley's new office for the *Toronto Star*, which was designed in 1928–29 to sit upon the corner of the ceremonial avenue proposed to link up the new Union Station on Front Street with a grand civic plaza on Queen Street. The RAIC *Journal* received the *Star* building with over-the-top enthusiasm, claiming that it was "so different to most of the buildings erected in this country during recent years, … a complete departure from precedent and tradition": "Although it follows to some extent the modern American trend of office building design with its vertical lines and corona fading into the sky, the design is nonetheless original even to the details of ornament and decoration … The carving and architectural details are modern in treatment and design, the carving being executed in bold relief and carried out identically on all sides. Bronze has been used extensively." In *Construction* "Sinaiticus" got even more overheated

2.12
Sterling Tower, Chapman and Oxley, 1928.

2.13
Toronto Star Building, Chapman and Oxley, 1929.

claiming that both the Sterling Tower and the *Star* building were "exquisite essays in the harmony of line and form, the melody of light and shade."[74]

Exuberant decoration characterized the 1929 Concourse Building on Adelaide by Baldwin and Greene; some critics complained that it was too nearly a copy of the Bush Terminal Building in New York but it brought a burst of colour to Toronto's downtown. The sixteen-storey tower rose straight from the street line in order to maximize floor space with vertical piers between the windows crowned with abstract flames. Artist J.E.H.

(Clockwise)
2.14
Concourse Building, Baldwin and Greene, 1929.

2.15
Concourse Building, entrance.

2.16
Victory Building, Baldwin and Greene, nearing completion, 1936.

MacDonald of the Group of Seven was retained to create the Canadian-themed decorations. The arched entryway featured a brightly coloured facing of entwined foliage while the coffers contained mosaics of airplanes and ships, and the panel above the door had a riotous semi-abstract landscape with a sun blazing down upon birds and fish. The following year the same firm undertook the twenty-storey Victory Building one block to the north, which mixed coloured brick, marble, and artificial stone into streamlined patterns. Across the shop fronts at street level were alternating wide and narrow bands of polished black marble, with a broad band of brick above carrying the building name in stylish sans serif metal letters under more horizontal stripes of red-brown and yellow brick that were repeated at the flat top of the building. Height was emphasized by tall strip windows between yellow brick piers. Owing to the Depression, however, the Victory Building was not completed for several years and stood empty of tenants until 1938.[75]

In 1929 F. Hilton Wilkes and Mackenzie Waters provided the Canada Permanent Trust Company with the most exuberant of these moderne towers, a New York-style limestone building at Bay and Adelaide featuring setbacks, even though these were not required by Toronto's zoning rules. Vertical thrust was emphasized by recessing the windows between projecting piers as the tower narrowed towards a sculptured roofline. The impressive arched entranceway was framed with Classical stonework leading to the banking hall, which was decorated in bronze with floral and leaf patterns adapted in the moderne mode from the tomb of Tutankhamun. "Sinaiticus" pronounced the result "one of the greatest monuments to Canadian skill in both architecture and engineering erected to date."[76]

2.17
Canada Permanent Building, F. Hilton Wilkes and Mackenzie Waters, 1930.

The Bank of Commerce tower, opened on King Street east of Bay in 1930, aimed to capture public attention by its sheer size. The design was by York and Sawyer of New York, chosen because of their experience in combining historical decorative features with up-to-date building techniques. The seven floors in the base provided the banking hall and corporate offices topped with twenty-seven storeys of rental space above, so that at 434 feet the building became the tallest in the British

2.18
Bank of Commerce, York and Sawyer with Darling and Pearson, 1930. This tower was the "tallest building in the Commonwealth," even into the 1960s.

Empire. The arched entrance was adorned with a garland of carved bears, squirrels, roosters, bees and their hives, chosen as symbols of thrift, while above the door were female figures of Industry and Commerce with Mercury, god of bankers, and in the background a grain elevator and the building itself with a flight of Canada geese. The huge banking hall, loosely modelled on the baths of Caracalla, had plum-coloured stone walls and a blue vault with gilt mouldings. The top of the building had tall arched windows above a stone terrace, with each of the main piers on the four sides crowned with the projecting stone heads of enormous deities representing Courage, Observation, Foresight, and Enterprise.[77] Visible from miles away this towering structure dominated the skyline of downtown Toronto until well after the Second World War.

Finally, several blocks north of the downtown on Yonge Street there was the new building planned for Eaton's department store, which had concluded that the city's main east–west commercial thoroughfare would soon shift up to College Street. The design by Ross and Macdonald of Montreal, "along classical lines" yet "modern in every respect," was to spread over an entire city block stretching from Yonge along College west to Bay and south to Hayter.[78] A seven-storey podium to house the department store would form the base

2.19 (Above)
Eaton's College Street store, Ross and Macdonald, 1930.

2.20 (Left)
Eaton's College Street, elevator arcade, interiors by Jacques and Natasha Carlu, 1930.

for a vast 670-foot tower with setbacks, containing 4.2 million square feet of rentable space. Construction on the store building began at the corner of Yonge and College in 1928 using Tyndall limestone from Manitoba with metal and granite highlights. The interior was done in the highest moderne style with the pièce de résistance being the seventh-floor auditorium and restaurant executed by Jacques Carlu. The Round Room restaurant was a domed circle contained in a square, and Carlu used shades of fashionable beige, grey, and black. His wife, Natasha Carlu, executed the murals on the curving walls with a lighted fountain in the centre, above which hung a great fixture with built-in radio speakers. Torontonians professed amazement at this mixture of worldly sophistication with advanced technology, and Eaton's hoped that female shoppers would flock to the store. Said "Sinaiticus" in *Construction*, "Here is classic simplicity in smart, ultra-modern design of refinement."[79]

2.21
Eaton's College Street, dining room.

The Eaton's College Street store and the work of the Carlus did have the result management had hoped for in creating a favourable buzz for such moderne interior design. "How does the smart young person today like to have her house furnished?" asked Mary-Etta Macpherson. "Does she take her Gertrude Stein and her Bartok into an 'Elsie Dinsmore' and 'Blue Danube' atmosphere or does she demand consistency and chairs of bent steel tubing? Is she sufficiently dexterous to use the old traditional forms and blend them into an individual setting, expressive of herself and her times, and thus marked by the most subtle kinds of modernism?" When Eaton's asked well-to-do "young matrons and debutantes" from the Junior League of Toronto to furnish rooms for a "House of Today," with no limitations as to cost or style, most of the women stuck to panelled libraries and Georgian dining rooms, but a few opted for modernistic designs like a bookcase and writing desk painted a taffy colour or a bedroom set painted blue and silver.[80]

IV

The skyscrapers along Bay Street gave Toronto's business district a more progressive look, which accorded with the desire to challenge Montreal for metropolitan dominance in Canada and to be viewed like New York. Prosperity also revived support for replanning the downtown core along the lines unsuccessfully promoted before the First World War. Broad new avenues would make the city more impressive, and widenings and jog eliminations would allow traffic to flow more smoothly. If the citizens would not pay for a City Beautiful, perhaps they could be persuaded to support a City Efficient. In 1921 John Lyle, who had been consulting architect to the Civic Improvement Committee a decade earlier, gave a lecture to the Toronto chapter of the Ontario Association of Architects in which he argued that, "If the idea of a beautiful and monumental city does not appeal to the imagination of our citizens, perhaps it might appeal to them when considered from a 'cash' point of view." Yet the only significant alteration made to the street layout in this period was the city council's vote to widen Bloor Street between Bathurst and Sherbourne Streets.[81]

In 1927, however, the Canadian National Railway (CNR) proposed to build a vast hotel on Queen Street right at the foot of University Avenue.[82] In a speech to the RAIC, Ontario Premier Howard Ferguson denounced the ideas as a "crime," since it would prevent the extension of the city's grandest thoroughfare all the way south from the legislative buildings at Queen's Park down to the lakefront. Toronto, he said, needed such a ceremonial avenue, like Washington.[83] The provincial legislature therefore passed a University Avenue Extension Act in 1928 to permit the street to be extended due south from Queen and gave the city power to expropriate property if required. However, the city refused to move immediately to register any of the proposed acquisitions on the land titles in order to prevent price inflation; council members objected that such action might make the municipality liable for damages if the plans were not ultimately carried out.

A number of organizations now began to express interest in a new comprehensive plan.[84] James Blomfield wrote several articles in *Construction* about the need to beautify the city, suggesting a volunteer committee of architects and engineers to draw up a plan like Chicago's. In 1928 architect S.G. Curry proposed to add a whole new street layout to the existing grid, including several arteries running north and south as well as reviving the notion of two diagonals leading out of the downtown to the northeast and the northwest with round "circuses" at major intersections.[85]

The Toronto Real Estate Board endorsed the idea of a formal planning body created by the city council.[86] The aldermen responded by empowering Mayor Samuel McBride to appoint an Advisory City Planning Commission to be composed of prominent local businessmen.[87] The RAIC welcomed the creation of this body to take over shaping the process of growth that had hitherto been allowed to proceed haphazardly while other progressive cities planned for the future. The organization's only reservation was that no architects or engineers had been included.[88] S.G. Curry expressed the hope that this body would take a broad look at the city's problems. For instance, he wanted to see a site reserved for a new city hall and other civic buildings like police headquarters in the southeastern part of the downtown, which would reverse the westward drift of the central business district that had begun in the mid-nineteenth century and intensified with the opening of the present city hall at Queen and Bay Streets in 1899. Curry thought such a change could be promoted by extending Jarvis Street north of Bloor across the ravines in Rosedale to north Toronto (a scheme of which much more would be heard over the next two decades). Donning the hat of a futurist, James Blomfield proposed that facilities for mooring dirigibles should be required on the roofs of the tallest buildings, now that Britain had announced its intention to introduce airship service throughout its empire.[89]

The Planning Commission decided that its aims should be less ambitious: simply to recommend street improvements to facilitate the movement of traffic. The idea of a broad ceremonial street leading north from newly opened Union Station (as in John Lyle's 1911 plan) was, however, revived by the committee. Cambrai Avenue (like the other proposed new streets to be named after a First World War battle involving Canadian troops) would run north from Front alongside the newly opened Royal York Hotel to King, where it would also flank the just-completed *Star* building. North of that, the roadway would split on either side of a monumental public building on an island and so bypass the Concourse Building (1928) on Adelaide and the Federal Building (1922) on Richmond, which now stood in the line of Lyle's original Federal Avenue. North of Queen Street would be a civic square (St Julien Place) with a new municipal building adjoining the existing Neoclassical Registry Office. In addition, University Avenue would be pushed south from Queen as far as Richmond Street to a roundpoint called Vimy Circle, from where a new street (called Queen's Park Avenue) would cut across the existing grid to join Front at York Street, permitting access to the railway underpass to the lakefront just west of the new station. It was hoped that buildings for North American Life, the Canadian Pacific Railway, and the *Mail and Empire* newspaper would all front on that new avenue.[90]

To improve the flow of traffic in and out of downtown the Planning Commission also recommended a new diagonal thoroughfare (called Passchendaele Road after another battle) leading southwest from Vimy Circle to Spadina and Front, linking up via Richmond Street to a northeasterly diagonal (to be named Arras Road after one more battle), and running up to Dundas Street to permit access to the eastern suburbs across the Don River. Out beyond the city limits the commission also envisaged improving traffic flows through a whole series of diagonal routes running northeasterly and northwesterly across the grid lines of the original concession surveys as in the original City Beautiful layout.[91]

The extension of University Avenue southward to Front Street at York became a hot issue in the municipal election of January 1929, when the *Globe* attacked Mayor McBride for supporting this "crooked lane," owing to his supposed conflict of interest in accepting endorsements by both the *Star* and the *Mail and Empire* whose buildings would stand alongside the new thoroughfares. Safely reelected, the mayor struck back in a speech, expressing a preference for "straight men on a crooked street to crooked men on a straight street."[92]

The Planning Commission's final report on "The Improvement of the Central Business Section of the City of Toronto" was delivered in March 1929. This document was then referred to a committee of civic department heads for analysis, and in the autumn the civil servants reported that land acquisition costs for the new streets would total \$37.75 million, of which \$22.75 million would be recouped by the resale of surplus property. In addition to the net capital cost of \$13 million there would be \$6 million in carrying charges to be paid by the taxpayers. Council eventually approved a draft money bylaw to be submitted to the ratepaying property owners at the next election and voted for \$5,000 to finance publicity designed to drum up support for the plan.[93]

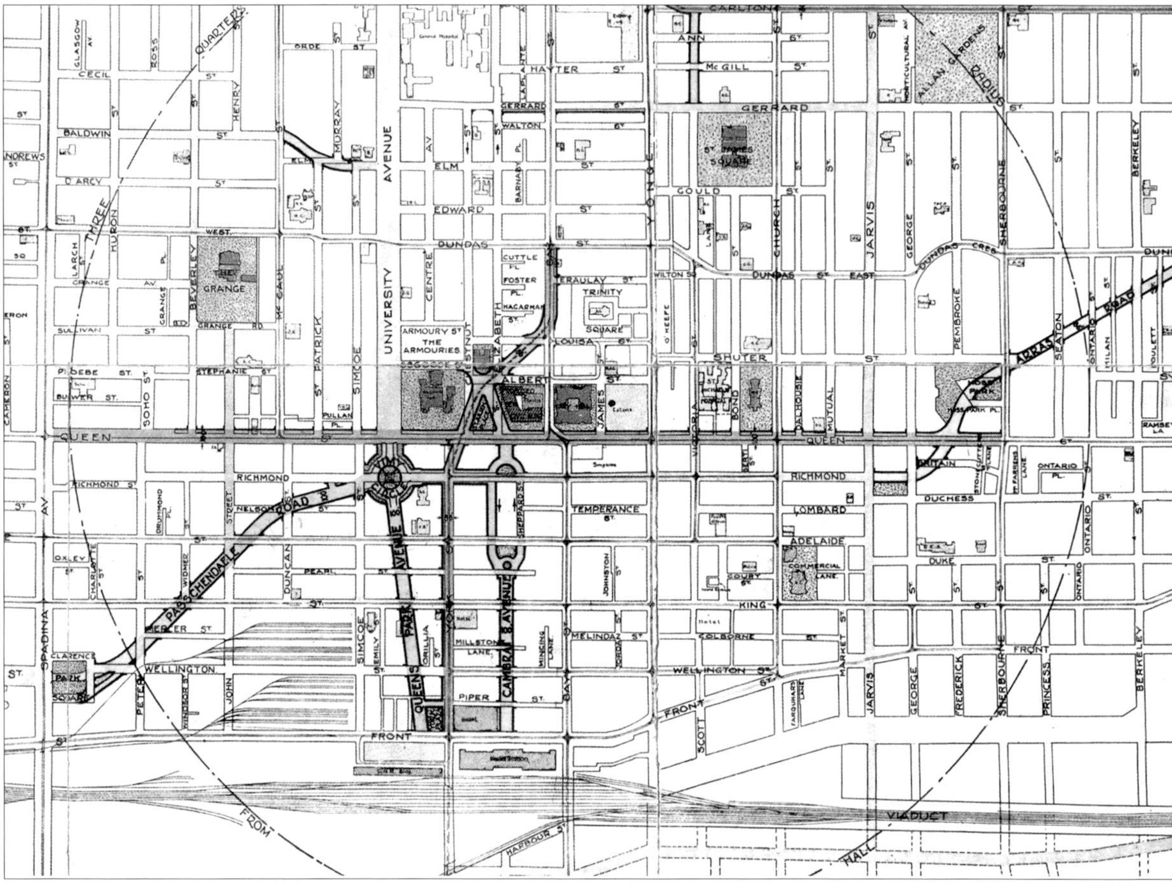

Initial enthusiasm was strong. At a meeting of some thirty civic organizations at the Board of Trade in December 1929, A.E.K. Bunnell of the Town Planning Institute predicted that for every public dollar spent there would be five times as much private money going for construction so that the city would benefit mightily. There was general consensus that Toronto needed this kind of redevelopment, and a citizens' committee was set up to campaign in favour of the bylaw. Using the city funds this committee got down to work despite suffering a setback when its chair, Anglican Canon H.J. Cody, felt compelled to retire after a fortnight, after it became known that he owned some property on the route of the proposed Cambrai Avenue. The *Globe* was not to be swayed from its opposition, insisting that the principal beneficiaries of the scheme to get the traffic moving would be corporations and wealthy individuals with interests downtown: nothing was proposed to relieve congestion for the ratepayers of north end of the city.

The controversy really heated up after architect J.P. Hynes told the reporters that opponents of the scheme were "jellyfish." When Controller Bert Wemp announced his candidacy for mayor in opposition to McBride, the bylaw vote became the central election issue. Wemp said that he had supported the plan unanimously endorsed by city council two years earlier to extend University Avenue due south to Front Street, but like the *Globe* thought that the "crooked lane" favoured a few big shots at the expense of the majority of ratepayers. When the votes were counted in January, Wemp had won the mayoralty by more than 4,700 votes, and the bylaw was turned down by 29,524 to 26,006, effectively killing the plan.[94]

2.22 (Opposite) Advisory City Planning Commission's 1929 "Suggested Improvements to the Street System."

In the autumn of 1930 Toronto did move to create a professional planning staff. The responsibilities of city surveyor, located in the Assessment Department, a post occupied since 1911 by Tracy leMay, were moved to a new department where he became commissioner of city planning and surveying.[95] LeMay saw his task as "utilitarian" rather than concerned with aesthetic objectives like the City Beautiful's ambition to create vistas or special sites for monumental buildings. He would focus upon arterial road construction to ensure that congestion caused by overlong journeys to work should not bind the city, and "force an ever-narrowing circle of multiple family dwellings with its inevitable depressing effect on the physical and moral status of the citizens." LeMay occupied himself by laying out diagonal roads extending far into the suburbs, yet he was severely hampered because the city lacked provincial enabling legislation to permit the necessary road construction and city council showed no disposition to move ahead without such authority in hand.[96]

2.23 (Below) Beginning of demolition south of Queen Street (1930) for the University Avenue extension, with the new Canada Life building.

As the increasing severity of the economic depression made any sizable civic spending programs less and less politically viable, piecemeal planning measures became the order of the day. City council did accept the Planning Commission's recommendation to extend University Avenue at an angle southeast from Richmond Street to the corner of Front and York, but the plan was shorn of its grand Vimy Circle at the northern end and a broad open space at the southern end. The only vestiges of the City Beautiful plan for wide ceremonial avenues that had originated before the First World War saw the city council establish architectural controls on buildings to be constructed along University Avenue in 1931. Height and setback requirements were imposed upon designs that must be approved by the Property Committee after being submitted to an advisory committee composed of civic officials and nominees of the Toronto chapter of the Ontario Association of Architects. The first building on each block would establish horizontal planes for succeeding structures, all of them situated upon bases of grey or buff stone. Other building materials were to be regulated and signage strictly controlled. Similarly, the uses of the structures were also highly regulated. But the impact of the Depression meant that the only sizable building built under these controls was for Canada Life on the west side of University just north of Queen, a Neoclassical confection that looked like a wedding cake.[97]

V

Contrary to impressions there was some construction going on during the 1920s that was demonstrably "modern," but architects and designers failed to notice. If modernism entailed design of a structure not according to some preconceived historical model but with a focus upon the space to be enclosed and the flexibility of the internal plan, a few such structures were being erected in the city at that time. But these were industrial buildings created for manufacturing operations, often planned and laid out by engineers rather than architects, so that the principal objective was functional efficiency without much regard for applied ornamentation or decoration beyond a kind of regularity and repetition of elements that sent a message of technical perfection.

These structures, of course, were by no means the first built according to functional principles. Factories erected during the nineteenth century often required the enclosure of large areas. After the fire of 1904, reinforced concrete began to be used for framing, once experience demonstrated that reinforcing bars could be placed in precise positions before the cement was poured over them, giving rise to various patented systems of "rebar" design for different purposes. Steel beams were lighter than concrete ones and could span long reaches but had to be carefully coated to be fireproof – hollow terracotta tiles being particularly effective against fire. Eventually, the availability of large amounts of high quality structural steel, which could be riveted together, led to its widespread use, particularly for very tall structures like skyscrapers. Either concrete or steel framing carried the weight of the building, which permitted the use of new kinds of applied exterior cladding. This meant that almost an entire opening could be filled with glass, increasing the glazed area by up to 80 percent, which admitted much more daylight at a time before full interior electric lighting became commonplace. These new-fangled factory buildings gradually replaced their predecessors, though they were usually still ornamented externally with historically derived details like arched window openings, decorated spandrels, pilasters, and parapets.

Eventually production experts concluded that for many manufacturing activities large single-storey structures with big open bays between the columns supporting higher ceilings were most efficient. Such layouts became more desirable when machinery no longer needed to be linked to a central powerhouse by intricate overhead shafting and belt drives. As time went on electric motors replaced such arrangements, first for groups of machines then for individual units. Adventuresome designers discovered that new materials like steel and reinforced concrete permitted previously impossible feats of construction such as wide long-span truss roofs without interior support columns.[98]

The advantages of such modern productive facilities were first evident in very heavy industry such as foundries, which needed large open spaces to shift massive castings using overhead craneways slung from the ceiling above. In 1918 the *Contract Record and Engineering Review*, which covered the activities of the Canadian construction industry, reported on the expansion of the Reid and Brown Structural Steel and Iron Works on the shores of Toronto's harbour. "Steel is the all-important material today. Munitions requirements have strained to the limit the capacity of every firm engaged in the steel industry in Canada ... Many plants have been expanded more than once to cope with conditions, until they have assumed proportions undreamed of in the pre-war days." By more than doubling the size of its plant, the company aimed to fabricate four thousand tons of steel annually, mainly for the munitions industry. The steel-framed building would be 150 feet long with a clear width of forty-six feet beneath a flat truss roof twenty-two feet above the floor. Down the unobstructed length of the plant's ceiling would run a ten-ton electric travelling crane, which would extend outside the building to the harbourside and permit products to be loaded and unloaded from ships as well as freight cars on a rail siding connected to the building. The steel I-beams, which framed the side walls and supported the roof and the crane, were bolted to reinforced concrete footings sunk five feet below grade. The forty-two foot spaces between these columns would be completely filled with wood sash windows "as large as it is possible to make them." To admit even more light, a central skylight of heavy wired glass ran the length of the roof, topped with ventilators to enhance air circulation.[99]

The rapid expansion of the automobile industry during the 1920s caused carmakers to build large new plants that reflected current ideas. In 1922 Durant Motors of Canada built a complex of half a dozen buildings in the Toronto suburb of Leaside. The design was entrusted to the general contracting firm of Norman McLeod Limited, "the only requirement being that the designs meet with the approval of the owners and conform to the general plan laid down by them." With speed being of the essence, once the contract was let the layout was allegedly completed between noon on a Thursday and the following Monday morning; and the whole project was finished in just four months. The principal structures were two parallel three-storey reinforced concrete framed buildings over four hundred feet long, the larger of which was one hundred feet wide, the smaller about eighty feet, between which ran a three-track railway siding with loading docks on either side. Inside, the concrete slab floors were spaced into twenty by twenty foot bays and supported by round columns with mushroom caps (which permitted them to carry heavier loads) below a flat roof. External towers contained electric-powered elevators, the stairs, and the toilets. Between the concrete framing members, the entire external openings were filled with low brick spandrels topped by glazing. In addition there was a steel-framed structure five hundred feet long by 130 feet wide with two railway tracks running through the centre.

Some components were very up-to-date like the steel-framed windows that had been developed in Britain with hinged panels that swung outward to promote air circulation. The loading docks had large numbers of electrical outlets so that extension cords could be used to light the interior of boxcars being loaded and unloaded.[100] Yet, as a car plant, the Durant layout was already somewhat dated by its multistorey buildings; these were being supplanted elsewhere in North America by large single-storey structures that permitted greater freedom to locate machinery and ease of interior movement, particularly after the development of the electrically powered forklift truck near the end of the First World War, which could manoeuvre in confined spaces to deliver parts and shift completed assemblies.

Henry Ford always prided himself as being an innovator as demonstrated by his adoption of the moving assembly line for car components like magnetos before the First World War and later for the bodywork itself. Ford and his minions spent significant time preparing the layout of his automobile plants as production of the famous Model T spiraled upward. The Highland

Park plant in Detroit developed around the First World War as a set of multi-storey buildings arranged around a rail siding and a craneway. Demand for the Model T was so strong, however, that Ford also created regional plants across North America to assemble knocked-down components. Ford of Canada opened such a building in Toronto early in 1915, a five-storey concrete-framed, brick-faced structure at Christie and Dupont Streets, right alongside the crosstown railway tracks and served by a siding along its north wall.[101]

Before long, Ford and his plant designer, Detroit-based architect Albert Kahn, concluded that a single-storey layout through which components flowed continuously would be more efficient. In 1917 Kahn began work on the River Rouge plant near Detroit, the first of a series of one-storey steel-framed, glass-walled structures that would make him the most famous industrial architect in the United States by the time of the Second World War. After the First World War, with demand for the Model T skyrocketing and the River Rouge plant expanding as Ford reduced prices through economies of scale on a single model, Ford of Canada concluded that its Toronto operation should be extended. In 1922 Albert Kahn (who had also designed the earlier building in the city) produced a plan for a much larger assembly plant for Ford just outside the eastern limits of the city. Rather than following the pattern of the Durant factory, which was going up at the same time, the architect decided to create a structure more like that at River Rouge. In its combination of elements of design and construction this was a truly "modern" building, erected in Toronto in 1923, the very year that Le Corbusier published *Vers une architecture*.

Ford of Canada had acquired an entire city block at the corner of Danforth and Victoria Park Avenues for $100,000. The land lay just to the north of the main east–west railway line that would permit connection to a siding. To the east of the building would remain a large open space that could be used as a parking lot for finished vehicles (since Henry Ford required local dealers to drive them away to their own premises) while still providing ample room for future expansion if required. The Danforth trolleys of the Toronto Transportation Commission ended their line at a loop just to the west of the site, which allowed workers easy access by public transit. The location seemed ideal.

Like other designers working for industry Kahn obeyed a functionalist imperative, laying out the building in accordance with the needs of efficient production. He therefore planned a vast steel-framed shed stretching about four hundred feet along Danforth Avenue and running south about five hundred feet.[102] Using steel for the framing did not require the expense or expertise demanded by concrete forming and curing and so permitted quicker completion.[103] With continuous reinforced concrete footings for the walls and individual bases for the structural girders, the 182,000 square feet of enclosed area would consist of 144 bays, thirty-two by forty feet, for the assembly work. The height from the floor to the roof trusses supporting the flat roof was fourteen feet. The five bays along the street at the northwest corner could be partitioned off for a company showroom plus the offices of the district manager and support staff. Along the south side of the plant one entire bay was devoted to a railway siding running right through the building and sunken to a depth of four feet to permit unloading boxcars directly onto the factory floor. To the west stood a freestanding powerhouse for the factory containing three oil-fired boilers to provide the hot water for the heating system.[104] Alongside that was a hundred-foot high tower topped by a one hundred thousand gallon water tank ready to supply the fire suppression sprinklers in the paint shop[105] (where Ford's mandatory shiny black finish would be applied).[106]

A series of photographs, ordered by the architects and taken about every fortnight by a local photographer, documented the state-of-the-art construction process.[107] The earliest ones from April 1923 show the site with railway sidings from which a steam crane is unloading flatcars of prefabricated steel trusswork. Once the powerhouse framework was finished and was starting to be clad in brick, the girders of the plant began to be assembled working from north to south with steel being unloaded from railcars right inside the still-open centre of the building by two cranes travelling along the same rails with a compressor car to provide air for the rivet guns. With that framework complete by July, the building was roofed with cement tiles covered by asphalt. Some of the most complex framing was situated atop the roof as Kahn's design included an elaborate system of sawtooth skylights and ventilators integrated into the "Pond" truss roof, similar to the ones he used on several buildings at Ford's River Rouge plant. Running east and west along the roof stuck up three ranges of "butterfly" or *M* shapes, whose large internal slopes were glazed to admit natural light while the outer sides were composed of shutters that could be opened to allow air circulation. Between the M's were three smaller ranges of A-shaped ventilators whose shutters could be opened to permit fresh air to enter the building.[108] The Lupton glazing and shutter systems, including the ten-foot-high, twenty-four paned steel-framed windows on the side walls, all had horizontally pivoting panels that could be opened and closed by electric motors.[109] Once roofed the factory had its piping installed running above the lowest members of the roof truss, and electric lights were hung near the corners of each bay. Then the entire interior was spray-painted by machine with one layer of primer and two coats of enamel.[110]

2.24
Ford Motor Company, Danforth assembly plant, c. 1933, Albert Kahn, 1923.

Albert Kahn included a few decorative touches on the exterior brickwork along the street side; each vertical column was treated on the surface as a pilaster rising from an Indiana limestone base course, and there were stone window sills, lintels, and a coping for each pilaster.[111] Above the windows and below the stone-edged roofline were several dentilated courses of header bricks designed to emphasize the horizontal. At the northwest corner of the building, where the showroom and offices were located, a diamond pattern of polychrome brickwork was inserted over the windows, and the public entrance had a higher triangular pediment above. Ever conscious of the value of advertising, even before the completion of the building the company had the powerhouse smokestack labeled "FORD," while the water tower and the showroom both had horizontal signs for Ford in the familiar cursive script.[112]

Here was a truly modern building, its shape and layout dictated by internal activities. Construction was of the most up-to-date materials: reinforced concrete foundations, structural steel framing, and metal-framed windows. There was access to heavy goods transportation with a railway siding running right through the factory. The ceiling was supported by trusswork high above the floor and supplied with natural light and good ventilation through its rooftop monitors. The vast level assembly floor consisted of large bays uncluttered with ramps or staircases, heated by oil-fired hot water radiators and protected by a sprinkler system. Electricity was available to power machinery and operate windows and ventilators. The exterior was plain and workmanlike with only a few touches of decorative brickwork that were not

2.25
Ford Motor Company, Danforth assembly plant, interior, 1923.

functionally necessary. Some people regarded sawtooth roofs as "lacking in aesthetic outline" and argued that they ought to be concealed behind a decent parapet, but Albert Kahn resisted this form of cover-up here and in several other Ford buildings.[113] If, as Le Corbusier opined in his 1923 book, *Vers une architecture*, houses should be "machines for living," this Ford plant was a machine for making other machines in which form carefully followed function.

Even mounting such a construction project as the Ford factory would have been a challenge to most Toronto architects in the mid-1920s. Looking back thirty years later, A.S. Mathers recalled that prior to 1925 there had been no such thing as a general contractor in the city, which meant that, for a project, separate agreements had to be reached with each of the different trades. Materials like reinforced concrete were relatively uncommon, and few architectural firms retained the services of structural or mechanical engineers to make the complex calculations required to check specifications. Though general contracting had become common in large American cities and in Montreal, the construction industry in Toronto proved difficult to convince of the merits of such arrangements. As a result large projects like the new Union Station were handled by firms from outside the city.[114]

Why did most Torontonians fail to recognize the arrival of a modern building such as the Ford plant in their midst? Some people were certainly excited about the undertaking as a spur to economic growth in the city's east end. When construction was just beginning in April 1923, a local real estate agency started advertising for buyers for lots in its nearby Eastbourne Park subdivision at the corner of Danforth Road and St Clair Avenue East: "By September next Toronto will be producing Ford automobiles. That means tremendous things for East Toronto. Hundreds and hundreds of highly-paid workmen getting fat checks regularly every week. These men have got to eat, sleep and be clothed and have recreation, but first of all they must have homes close to their work. You have an opportunity now – September will be too late." Ten dollars down and five dollars a month would secure one of the hundred lots left. Everybody knew what had happened in Detroit and Windsor: "As soon as Ford factories were established these cities grew at an enormous rate. Prosperity follows Ford factories ... Double the population and you will double the value of your land. Buy now – Ford will double its value for you."[115]

But architects and designers appeared to pay no attention to Kahn's work. Industrial building was largely ignored, the focus being upon new private homes and commercial buildings downtown. And Kahn had no contemporary reputation as a modern architect whose designs merited study. W. Hawkins Ferry points out that for domestic designs Kahn was keenly interested in the Arts and Crafts movement, and relied upon Tudor or Georgian stereotypes such as the beamed and panelled interiors he had created for his own house in 1907. During the 1920s he became more archeological as in the Cotswold-style stone house he designed for Edsel Ford in 1926. He criticized the European avant-garde for glorifying glass and steel and throwing out all precedents and abandoning the tried-and-true.[116] One recent commentator has concluded somewhat unconvincingly that, though he repudiated European modernism, Kahn developed a uniquely American Modernism (without the element of social reform); another claims that "by the early 1920s the production sheds designed by Kahn's firm exhibited a mature industrial modernism."[117] But without the advantage of hindsight nobody in Toronto, besides the *Contract Record*, appears to have taken notice of the design innovations of this Ford factory or other industrial buildings.

Nevertheless, the later years of the 1920s saw architects and designers become familiar with the moderne, a decorative style first popularized by the Paris exposition. And these features came to be displayed both on the newer skyscrapers downtown and in the domestic interiors of bolder householders. And the prewar ideas of the City Beautiful movement about modernism with its broad avenues and monumental buildings enjoyed a brief renaissance, though the practical results were minimal. The more radical ideas about architectural designs being developed in Europe made little headway in Toronto.

3

COPING WITH MODERNISM 1930–1939

During the 1930s ideas concerning the "Modern movement" in architecture made their first impact in Canada. At least these radical notions began to be debated. A few practitioners indicated cautious interest in promoting the innovations, and architectural students began to show themselves receptive. Montreal seemed a bit more attuned to such progressive tastes, but it proved hard to persuade clients in Toronto to approve advanced designs. In particular, housing remained firmly stuck in the mould of Georgian Revival and other traditional styles. Though Torontonians began to worry about the deterioration of certain districts of the city, and questions were raised about whether new land use and zoning regulations ought to be imposed to promote redevelopment, little change occurred. By the time Canada went to war in 1939 there was scant evidence that avant-garde ideas had gained any wide acceptance with the public.

3.1 (Opposite) Toronto Hydro-Electric Commission, 1933. In the very midst of the Great Depression, a showroom space to rival the department stores – and pay your electrical bill.

One fundamental problem was the prolonged economic depression. Little construction of any kind was undertaken, and many architects found themselves on the brink of insolvency or worse for lack of work. Only a few major projects were completed, such as Maple Leaf Gardens to house the city's professional hockey team, a plain and functional barn put up at great speed with only a few moderne touches of decoration. The federal government funded some new public buildings but clung to a simplified or Stripped Classicism in design. Thus talk about Modernism greatly outpaced action.

I

Only around 1930 did the radical ideas of the European avant-garde begin to filter across the Atlantic.[1] Le Corbusier's highly influential *Vers une architecture* appeared in 1923 but was not translated into English for another four years.[2] The *Royal Architectural Institute of Canada Journal* finally ran a review of this translation at the end of 1929, the first notice taken of a book dealing with the European avant-garde six years after the periodical's foundation. Toronto architect Martin Baldwin (whose work had shown him to be sympathetic to the moderne) did his best to approach Le Corbusier's work on its own terms; Le Corbusier, Baldwin suggested, was not simply advocating the rejection of all that had gone before in architecture but contending that key underlying concepts about design had become obscured over time by superficial forms of decoration. Now new materials like reinforced concrete had made possible radical architectural solutions. Le Corbusier, using a series of provocative axioms, aimed to blow away an accretion of cobwebs, and so, said Baldwin, "The effect of the book is the same as that of a walk across hilly country on a windy day."[3]

More typical of the generally cool reception accorded European Modernism was Philip J. Turner's review of Bruno Taut's *Modern Architecture* (1929) that appeared a few months later. Turner admitted that new materials like the reinforced concrete used for Eugene Freyssinet's parabolic airship hangers at Orly, France (dating from 1916) did represent an interesting and logical solution to a design problem. Yet he thought Taut was pressing the case for "practical efficiency" too far by urging the elimination of all decoration. Long, horizontal, flat-roofed buildings, "bare to the bone as far as architectural features are concerned, cannot be said to look anything but out of place or to fit well in a charming or undulating country district, for nothing in nature has such cold hard lines." Economic factors might account for the disappearance of "architectural details and ornamental trappings" on new European buildings, but aesthetic considerations should not be swept away altogether. Interesting and stimulating as Taut's notions might be, Turner thought their practical application doubtful.[4]

The ideas of the European avant-garde received a kind of codification in 1932, when Henry-Russell Hitchcock and Philip Johnson published their book *The International Style: Architecture Since 1922*. The appearance of the book coincided with a show at the Museum of Modern Art in New York organized by the same two men along with Alfred H. Barr, and accompanied by a catalogue entitled *Modern Architects*.[5] These two publications and the show defined what the authors called the International Style in the works of the Europeans like Le Corbusier, Mies van der Rohe, Walter Gropius, and J.J.P. Oud. The aesthetic principles uniting these men included conceiving of the space occupied by a building in terms not of mass or solidity but by the volume enclosed, the flexibility of a building's plan, and the regularity of vertical or horizontal repetition as the basis for composition rather than an artificial emphasis on a central axis or a base and cornice. Taken together, argued Hitchcock and Johnson, the use of modern materials and structure would create technical perfection and a fineness of proportion that in previous times might have been supplied by applied ornament.[6]

The opportunity for interested Canadians to see firsthand something like an International Style house came in 1929, though ironically this specimen was merely a model erected indoors. Always eager to keep up with marketing trends, the T. Eaton Company commissioned its staff designer, René

Right: The exterior of la maison d'aujourd'hui is simple, yet dramatic. Door and window frames are painted scarlet, and the body of the house is developed in gray-white T. Eaton Co., Calgary

Below: The breakfast nook is a 20th Century invention — why not treat it as such? The colors here are green, pink and blue; the chairs will not tip over, and the table is designed for convenience

THE CANADIAN HOUSE OF TODAY

An exponent of the new school of interior decoration lays down the broad principles of Canadian moderne

By MARY-ETTA MACPHERSON

PICTURE a house of gray-white stucco with scarlet bandings, a house with inverted bay windows and a detached, uncompromising air; try to imagine an entire interior of sweeping and dramatic force, where walls are plain and lights glow from concealed troughs or niches, where only the furniture and accessories of the 20th Century have been given a place, and where the fine arts of this age are welcomed and made much of—and you will have some inkling of *la maison d'aujourd'hui*, as it is conceived by a leading European designer and architect. And not, mind, merely "a house of today," but, more significant still, "a Canadian house of today." We shall see!

Last year M. Rene Cera, a sincere exponent of modern decoration, and well known in France, was invited by one of the large Canadian firms to come to this country. One of his first undertakings was to design and furnish a house that would meet all the requirements of the household of average size, that would be modern in the best sense of the word, that would be entirely Canadian not only in materials and furnishings, but in spirit and conception as well. It was, in short, to be the first concrete example of "Canadian moderne."

The experiment was made in the new store of the T. Eaton Co., at Calgary, Alberta, and the finished house proved of tremendous interest in the West, where, so far, there had been little opportunity to study contemporary styles, imported or domestic.

To eyes unaccustomed to the eliminative lines, dimensions and ensemble effects of the new art, the results of M. Cera's months of observation and effort, glimpsed on this and the following pages, may seem strange and sudden. There is a possible bareness in the plain, flat walls, bereft of door or window frames; the old-fashioned "cosiness" is missing, although most of the furniture is undeniably comfortable and usable. The ensemble idea, i.e., the planning and assembling of all details to make a perfect unit in color and line and proportion, produces an odd formality, different entirely from the old effect of rooms that, like Topsy, "just growed." But there is a certain reasonableness and directness in these new forms, and, for those who delight in the contemporary, who find older styles more irksome and less simple, and to whom the romantic past has little personal appeal, there is bound to be tremendous interest and stimulus.

The architect-designer in this case was handicapped, to begin with, by the limitations of a department store floor space, where standing pillars and beams had to be considered and allowed for. In spite of this, however, M. Cera achieved notable success with his design, and the rooms flow naturally and easily in the one-story square building.

The exterior is worthy of note. It is of gray-white stucco, with splashes of scarlet at the door and around the small windows. The usual frames for doors and windows have been dispensed [*See also page 51*]

3.2
René Cera house, 1929. This was a model house and rooms that travelled the country as an exhibition of modern domestic design for Eaton's.

Cera, to create *La maison d'aujourd'hui* as a display to launch its new store in Calgary. Grey-white stucco walls, plain and flat, were accented by scarlet door and window frames; the interior, illuminated by concealed lighting, was filled with moderne products made in Canada. Mary-Etta Macpherson of *Canadian Homes and Gardens* found the ensemble stimulating and expressed hope that it would lead to the development of a truly Canadian modernism.[7] When the display reached Eaton's in Toronto in the autumn of 1929, however, her editor at CHG, Herbert Hodgins, was far less enthusiastic. Cera's designs might set people thinking about the Modern movement, but Hodgins didn't believe that he could live with furniture, which was "too lacking in grace." From time to time he'd almost convinced himself he liked it, but moderne pieces were "too squat, too stolid, too square, too awkward." People might trick themselves into accepting the unfamiliar colour combinations, but the new-fangled would never replace the classic styles. Demand for antiques and fine reproductions would not cease, though he conceded that indirect lighting might hold its own through time.[8]

Torontonians would soon have their first opportunity to see a real International Style house. The building was commissioned in 1930 by an unusual patron: painter Lawren Harris, a member of the Group of Seven, who had by then turned to semi-abstraction in his rendering of Canada's northland. Harris, heir to the fortune of the farm implement makers Massey-Harris, was wealthy enough to commission a brand new home, and he had visited Stuttgart in 1930 where he would have seen other examples of Modern architecture. He, in turn, seems to have chosen a most untypical designer: Alexandra Biriukova was an emigré from post-revolutionary Russia where Modern architecture had enjoyed considerable sway. After passing through Paris she joined her sister, Yulia, who was an artist in Toronto.

3.3
Drawing of Lawren Harris house, Alexandra Biriukova, 1931.

The Harris house in Forest Hill clearly reflected the tenets of the avant-garde. The southwest-facing facade emphasized its verticality with a central entrance topped by a tall arched window over a semi-circular portico; the lower wings, extending to either side at a forty-five degree angle, had French doors under second-storey windows all let into recessed panels. Recognizably Canadian motifs included pine needles in the cast spandrels between the windows, over the front door, and in the terrace railings across the tall metal-framed windows with their chrome balustrades. The influence of the moderne was evident in the room design, which featured an octagonal living room (within a rectangular space) and a similar octagonal dining room (within a square), an elongated oval front hall (with a curving staircase), and a five-sided library. The broad expanses of wall space painted in neutral tones were well-suited to display Harris's large paintings. *Canadian Homes and Gardens* declared the result "an essentially modern design, depending on its simple statement of mass proportion and the quality of the materials themselves for its beauty and effect."[9]

The combination of client and designer for this house was thus highly unusual. Though Biriukova formally registered in 1931 as an architect in Ontario, she received no further commissions and terminated her registration in 1934. In fact, she withdrew from design work altogether and later became a nurse in a tuberculosis sanatorium.[10] This house was unique for its time in Toronto, a complete outlier amongst other contemporary works until well after the Second World War.[11] Instead Torontonians continued to erect buildings large and small that faithfully reflected the historical styles with which they felt comfortable.

Even such a sophisticated observer as Eric Arthur had his doubts about Modern design. In 1931 architect Ernest Cormier created a house for himself facing onto Montreal's Pine Avenue and sloping down two storeys in the rear, a design "quite different and radically experimental."[12] Seeing photographs of Cormier's house at the Royal Architectural Institute's annual exhibition in 1932, Arthur was not much impressed. The front view seemed "thin and mechanical," though he did concede that the "masculine" treatment of garden and studio (including its furnishings) was splendid. He had to admit that when it came to innovative design Montreal seemed well ahead of Toronto, where clients and designers remained strongly attached to Georgian Revivals such as the University Club.

The following year, 1933, when Arthur went to Montreal for the RAIC meeting and actually visited Cormier's house, he changed his tune somewhat. Seeing it in person made all the difference, and he now judged it "the strongest case on this continent, if not abroad, for a return to the masculine qualities which make great architecture."[13] As an architect himself Arthur

3.4
J.S. McLean house: Eric Arthur's pre-modernism, 1933.

remained faithful to his training in the Beaux Arts. Having obtained his architect's license in Ontario in 1929 he set to work designing a mansion for J.S. McLean of Canada Packers. The result in 1932 was an early Georgian Revival house with correct historical ornament applied in a formal and predictable way that fitted comfortably with the other estates along the stretch of Bayview Avenue south of Lawrence. Arthur admitted that Torontonians seemed well-satisfied with the Georgian, though "unenlightened" modernists might try to trick out their décor with machine-made terracotta lightning bolts and "rams horns caught in stellar thickets."[14]

Such conservatism suited most of Arthur's fellow architects quite well, particularly for residential work. When Eaton's ran a juried contest to design the "Ideal Ontario Home" in 1930, only one of the ten prizewinners (out of 239 entries from across Canada) was a modernist effort. Ian Forbes won fifth place for a design with a flat roof and concrete walls to be formed on-site, with steel sash windows and cornices and spandrels of cast aluminum. The interior woodwork was to be painted in bright colours with all the hardware in stainless steel. Though rather a tepid layout, the publication of these plans was the first time that such a modernist effort had been featured in *Canadian Homes and Gardens*, five years after it was founded.[15] Four more of the prize designs later pictured in the magazine included a sixteenth-century French house, an American Federal, a Tudor, and an English cottage.[16]

A member of the architectural staff of the Bell Telephone Company, responsible for scores of exchange buildings, complained that he considered it "distinctly bad form to carry a window (as had been done recently on the Continent and also in America) to the very corner of a building with no obvious support for the masonry above. It is hard to see beauty of form where the successive storeys of a building step back at regular intervals like a gigantic flight of steps."[17] Radical experimental building methods were treated as little more than curiosities. A note in *Construction* about a display by Buckminster Fuller of his revolutionary hexagonal Dymaxion House, strung from a central pillar with translucent walls, did not even merit an illustration and only drew the heading "Some House?"[18]

In a three-part article in 1930, RAIC president Percy Nobbs of McGill reflected the prevailing caution when he lectured the members on "Present Tendencies Affecting Architecture in Canada." In the past ornamental details for buildings had been adopted from the Georgian, Classical, and Gothic, even though such things as crockets and stone spires tended to fare poorly in strong winds and cold nights followed by warm days. He identified "Modernity" as a blend of the Vienna Secession and Art Nouveau that had coalesced after the First World War to create a growing interest in the architecture of "reality" versus "make-believe." Nobbs warned against a loss of moorings in abandoning the traditional vocabulary entirely as had occurred in Europe, Holland in particular. He condemned the "host of architectural farceurs of the independent maniac type," amongst whom were only few real masters who might ignore the past and seek novel solutions. Absolute or engineering realists trusted the solution of a design problem to explain itself while architectural realists tried to make their buildings an organic whole. What were the worst influences? German architects, he claimed, were fond of horizontal panels separating glazing, which Nobbs, entirely wrong-headedly, conceived as having something to do with advertising. In true Canadian fashion, however, he concluded that the most malign influences on domestic architecture came from the United States, especially as a result of employing American architects. Keeping cool and not being rushed into trendiness would ensure that the masterpieces of the past outlasted any fads.[19]

As the economic depression worsened during the 1930s architects had fewer commissions, which gave them more time to stage debates about the comparative value of modernism versus tradition. Before the American Institute of Architects, George Howe (with whom William Lescaze would soon complete one of the first truly International Style skyscrapers for the Pennsylvania Savings Fund Society in Philadelphia) dismissed previous designs as "incoherent" and "formless." Many older buildings, he said, were "ramshackle, pretentious, dishonest and ugly," and the Modern would "win hands down on the score of soundness, reality, simplicity, and honesty." In reply C. Howard Walker of Boston rejected the claim of Modernists to have escaped the past: they were simply ignoring tranquility and adored "excess in every direction, to be shapeless, explosive in detail to chaos, and to create sensationalism with the slapstick and the bludgeon." The editor of the *RAIC Journal*, I. Markus, suggested that both sides might have a point. Design was changing along with new construction methods, so clients wanted entirely different buildings from the past. Couldn't people agree that, "Modernism in architecture should not be an attempt to do something that has never been done before, but rather something made necessary through the use of modern materials, new methods of construction and the practical and economic requirements of the present age?"[20]

Herbert Hodgins of *Canadian Homes and Gardens* remained a skeptic. In November 1931 he announced that the interior design promoted by 1920s modernists already appeared passé. Tables that looked like something else and chairs that made good posture impossible had failed; attempting to persuade people that towering bookcases should look like stepped-back New York skyscrapers had proved to be "so much wasted breath." The public went on buying Queen Anne dining room sets and Sheraton sideboards, and "For once the vast majority was right." Later Hodgins claimed that one Canadian manufacturer estimated that 30 percent of bedroom furnishings sold in 1934 would be modern, but only a quarter of that was destined for the living room. Rushing headlong into faddishness was foolish, and the home was the last place for such experiments.[21] Another of his contributors agreed: "From the relative failure of *art modern* in Canada and the rising popularity of decorative styles, it is obvious that severity in furnishings is giving way before richness and variety." People were weary of the sensible and the utilitarian, eager to return to "the champagne type of furniture" of the traditional French styles.[22]

3.5 William Lyon Somerville, 1936.

Eventually Hodgins had to admit that there was another serious problem facing the construction industry. At the end of 1931, in his first reference to what he archly called the "Repression," he urged Canadians not to just sit back and suffer; now that the building trades had hit rock-bottom, it was time to start constructing and furnishing houses. W.L. Somerville agreed. A three-bedroom house on a forty-five foot lot with built in garage and maid's room above could easily be produced fully furnished for $10,000, since costs were 10 to 20 percent lower than in the booming twenties. Brick-faced Georgian Revival was the obvious style to combine "architectural beauty and comfort at reasonable cost." After all a house should not be too exciting but soothing and restful on account of its simplicity, regularity, and sound proportions. Georgian was not open to the "facetious criticism" leveled at the "pseudo-Tudor or other picturesque styles." "A modernist would scorn it and a Georgian archeologist hoot with derision, but nevertheless, that is what it is. If it isn't either it must just be Canadian."[23]

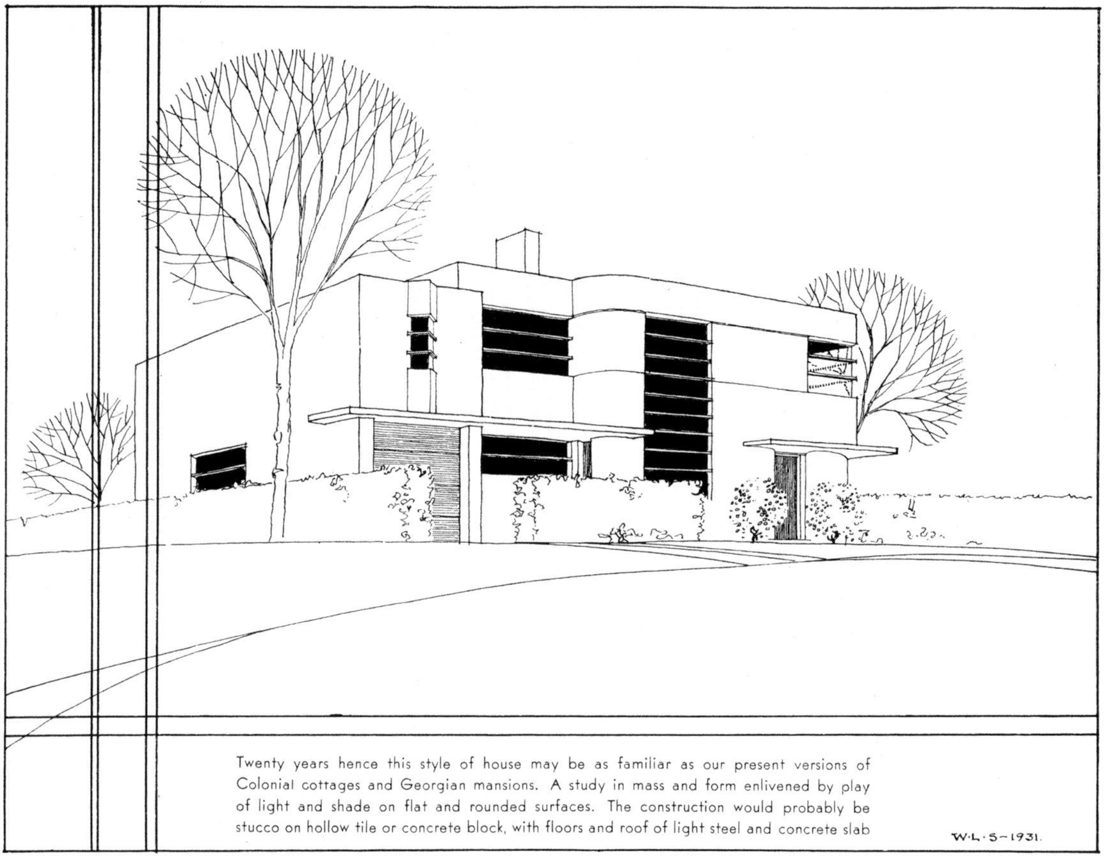

3.6
W.L. Somerville's "Small House of Tomorrow." Until very late Somerville remained a resolute champion of traditional styling, so this was a surprising prediction for *Canadian Homes and Gardens* in 1931 of what might be common "twenty years hence."

John Lyle also warned his fellow architects against quack remedies: "This new medicine is called 'Modernism,' and it seems to make the old young and the young frantic." For one thing everybody seemed to have a different definition of the new style: geometric, functional, mechanical. Some Modernists shunned all ornamentation, which would only make all buildings look like "the slab-sided box outlines of Germany and France."[24]

Reviewing the Ontario Association of Architects show in 1933 the correspondent for *Canadian Homes and Gardens* observed that the Georgians still had a firm hold on institutional work such as Mathers and Haldenby's new building for Upper Canada College. Brick remained the material of choice: "Concrete blocks, extolled by the modernists, have little appeal in Canada." Hugh Allward's design for a French provincial chateau, featuring a round tower of whitewashed brick with a fake thatched roof, won a prize from the OAA as the best exterior costing over $50,000 and was adjudged "refreshing," "a novelty" by *Canadian Homes and Gardens*.[25] This award was too much for Eric Arthur: in the sharpest piece of criticism by one architect of another during the RAIC *Journal's* first decade of existence, he condemned the "architectural romanticism" of a well with a bucket and a candlelit staircase in the midst of Rosedale. He pointed out that George Howe had once specialized in wavy rooflines and duck ponds but had given all that up, and suggested that Hugh Allward should follow Howe into "a world in which architecture stands on its own feet and is admired for its own sake."[26]

John Lyle seized upon Arthur's endorsement of Ernest Cormier's house to suggest that he was simply adopting a new fad. Lyle alleged that Arthur was "going modern" and that other architects should be sent to Montreal to test some of the same champagne, vintage "Cormier, 1933." But Lyle was annoyed by Arthur's criticism of the lion-bolstered pylons of the bridge he had just designed in Hamilton, Ontario. Lyle praised the freedom of his new designs, which covered everything with sculpted skunks and squirrels. Architects could now break away from "historical and stuffy styles of the past." "Don't be so academic, Professor, lean out of your modern window a little further and throw away your book of rules."[27]

Unfortunately for architects and interior decorators alike, the Depression's bite was worsening. By 1932 issues of *Canadian Homes and Gardens* began to shrink from about one hundred pages to seventy as advertising dried up. Two years later falling revenues forced the publishers to combine many monthly issues into double numbers and cut the cover price from thirty-five cents to a quarter. By mid-1934 the editor insisted "that the late Depression has been duly interred," but the practice of periodically doubling up issues continued. Even the celebrations for the city of Toronto's centennial failed to provide a boost. *Construction* noted that after four and one half years of bad times there was much renovation in the city that needed doing.[28] By the end of that year that periodical had ceased publication altogether.

Some people hoped that an appealing brand of modern architecture might spring from the use of new materials and techniques. Chicago's Century of Progress fair in 1933 featured eleven model houses that seemed to be the "machines for living" advocated by radical European designers, eschewing all ornament and traditional layouts for functional principles. One was constructed of sheet steel coated in porcelain; another had a steel frame to which wooden members could be attached. Many were single-storey without basements but with flat roofs and long bands of windows stretching around corners. American manufacturers were beginning to promote prefabricated elements to be assembled on-site. But *Canadian Homes and Gardens* predicted that most people, particularly of Anglo-Saxon origins, would find such innovations dismaying or loathsome even if construction costs were cut by two-thirds. Instead the magazine presented sketches of alternative designs for three small houses by architect John G. Roper, all variations on the English cottage, "a tradition to which we are historically entitled and which is readily adaptable."[29]

A pilot project for a steel-framed house designed by architects Hutton and Souter drew an equally mixed response. Piggott Construction of Hamilton, Ontario claimed that "entirely modern building practice brings it to a place of great significance in the movement towards better housing in Canada," by fastening three inches of cork insulation with wire mesh to the metal frame and using stucco on the outside and plaster on the inside. For a mere $13,000 one could have an exterior that "shows no revolutionary departure from traditional, well-balanced design" with pink brick framing the window openings. The completed model had a few moderne touches such as a cantilevered balcony and a freestanding curved staircase to descend into the garden.[30]

Architect B. Evan Parry was dismissive of these new-fangled ideas. Steel framing was more expensive than wood, and insulation was required to avoid condensation from cool outside air. Concrete blocks were not desirable for masonry work; glass blocks being used in Europe were still too expensive. Metal windows might suit modern houses but had to be very carefully fitted and caulked to avoid leaks and condensation, which made wooden ones more practical.[31]

Percy Nobbs still could not bring himself to accept the new trend. Admitting that little had been built in recent times, he praised the Neoclassical headquarters for North American Life in Toronto as "refined." He declared Mathers and Haldenby's Georgian Revival women's residence at the University of Toronto accomplished, if not up to their best work; at least the "affectation of mullioned windows has been avoided." This rather aimless piece of commentary provoked an angry letter from Robin Montgomery that complained, "architecture is an almost scholarly branch of dressmaking, specializing in period costumes." How else to account for Nobbs's views, entirely preoccupied with the "modish exterior coverings" of buildings and with assessing whether or not "the stiff ruff about the neck is historically apt or the unavoidable marriage of old Roman toga with modern plus-fours is handled suavely?"[32]

Every so often during the late 1930s some architect, usually a professor familiar with recent trends, would take to the pages of the RAIC *Journal* and try to persuade his colleagues to stop designing the Georgian brick boxes that their few clients wanted and to convince practitioners of the virtues of the International Style. Housing starts had reached a low point in the spring of 1933 and three years later still had not yet returned to 1926 levels, so "Build Now!" should be the watchword.[33] In 1935 Professor Eric Venne of the École des Beaux-Arts in Montreal described works by Peter Behrens in Germany and Sven Markelius of Sweden. "Logical and rational" domestic architecture without superficial decoration or ornament was evolving. Markelius, in particular, had showed how new designs were made possible by new materials like reinforced concrete along with the elimination of peaked roofs for flat ones. Inside, rooms flowed together, one opening off another, and the garden was drawn into the living room.[34]

The following year Milton Osborne of the University of Manitoba was preaching the gospel according to Frank Lloyd Wright and Walter Gropius. (This appears to have been the first reference in the *Journal* to Gropius, who had dissolved the Bauhaus and fled Germany following Hitler's takeover and was to join the faculty at Harvard in 1937.) Horizontals were the order of the day with the ceiling lines emphasized by bands of windows. The effort was to find building forms that showed what would go on inside, and because this new style had been recognized across the world it had properly been dubbed "International." Osborne observed that the Canadian climate posed special challenges to keep in heat and clear snow and ice off roofs so that low buildings might be necessary to ensure proper insulation, but he urged the search for a happy medium between the traditional and ultra-Modern geometric forms.[35]

Professor H.H. Madill of the University of Toronto told the readers of *Canadian Homes and Gardens* in 1937 that "If I Were Building a House of My Own This Year, I'd Choose the Modern Style." When cars and airplanes were being redesigned for grace and efficiency, there was no reason why buildings should not follow suit. In the booming twenties clients had showed up asking for copies of California bungalows or Tudor mansions. Traditional Ontario designs had served their times well enough, but picture windows were quite feasible nowadays. New materials and methods were available, and rooms need not be closed off for differing functions so spaces could flow flexibly one from another. Even flat roofs might be tolerated if they suited the purpose. "Modern architecture is like a breath of fresh air in a stagnant atmosphere of medieval revivals, and with the elimination of stunts I look for a development and evolution such as has characterized all the great periods of architectural history."[36]

Toronto architect Mackenzie Waters (who began his studies at the University of Toronto just before the First World War and graduated afterwards) underwent something of a conversion and took the cause of modernism directly to the public in a series of radio broadcasts. He cited Frank Lloyd Wright for taking up "functional principles" as early as 1895, and Charles

Rennie MacIntosh for showing the way from across the Atlantic. He told his listeners that the new designs were sensible because they did not tie themselves to outdated forms but used new materials and methods. Simplicity had now replaced the over-ornamentation that had characterized the Victorian era. Still, he admitted that these changes had found few exponents in the United States, and it was necessary to cite European examples since the "new architecture is practically non-existent in Canada." The only comfort to be drawn from this fact was that Canadians had avoided some of the monstrosities of the previous decade, but there was still work to be done to convince a businessman, who would never travel in a horse-drawn wagon nowadays, not to build himself a pseudo-fifteenth-century dwelling.[37]

Journalistic cheerleaders took up the cry. A 1936 article in *Canadian Homes and Gardens* declared, "Just a few years ago the very word 'modern' uttered at a dinner or tea party had as great an effect as an announcement of policy at a political meeting. If it didn't evoke boos and hisses it was because listeners were too well bred. It invariably provoked wordy warfare. Now it can't be depended on for a ripple of excitement. Because, of course, those who once reviled have begun to admire." There may have been excesses in the early days after 1925, "crudities" of colour and form, tubular chairs designed like bicycles, but now the work of the pioneers of Modernism had created a "simple and exquisite style" called "20th Century." Eleanor Stephens declared, "Modern design has made a very complete conquest."[38]

Even a traditionalist like W.L. Somerville suggested in *Canadian Homes and Gardens* in 1938 that Modern architects in Europe might have demonstrated that it was no longer necessary to build houses to seventeenth- or eighteenth-century designs even if that was what mortgage lenders still favoured. Yet he hastened to add that "modern" was a confusing term characterized by boxlike structures on stilts with corner windows and flat roofs. Somerville dismissed a design by Serge Chermayeff for a living room opening completely onto a terrace, which had been photographed for a recent display at the Art Gallery of Toronto, as of "the extremist school" and compared it unfavourably to simplified Georgian designs from England. It turned out that it wasn't the modernist concrete walls, strip windows or flat roofs that Somerville approved of, but only Scandinavian chairs with four solid legs made from birch. He did admit that contemporary Europeans were capable of some sound urban planning but this hardly constituted a ringing endorsement of modernism.[39]

Flat roofs, which many Canadian architects considered the signature of the Modern movement, remained a vexed question for Canadian architects. In 1938 *Canadian Homes and Gardens* included an article by Toronto practitioner R.S. Morris claiming that flat roofs had developed following the First

World War because European designers were keen to economize and made a virtue out of necessity by eliminating gables as so much waste space. Yet Canadians had rightly been suspicious of structures from which rain and snow failed to drain properly. Only recently, said Morris, had effective insulation made them satisfactory even in summer. A flat roof might be acceptable in certain circumstances but it required much care in construction to be certain that moisture did not build up.[40]

Not surprisingly, though, advanced ideas about design aroused the greatest enthusiasm amongst architectural students. In 1937 recent University of Toronto graduate Kent Barker (who had moved on to study with Eliel Saarinen at Cranbrook Academy in Michigan) noted of an RAIC exhibition of student work, "There is a definite impression in the mind of the average layman that flat roofs, corner windows, and glass-brick stairwells are the inevitable hallmark of modernism in house design. It is perhaps natural that many student drawings in the junior class should show the effects of similar beliefs." When Eaton's department store ran a juried contest for house designs, Barker shared first prize in the small house category costing under $7,500 with an entry that showed Modernist influences. A commentator in the *RAIC Journal* observed that "an interesting fact showing a trend of architectural taste in Canada is the large preponderance of designs in the modern manner. There were very few competitors who adopted the traditional styles. This is particularly noteworthy as the program of requirements left the competitors free to choose any style they wished." Where living space was limited architects seemed to agree upon the virtues of allowing rooms to flow into one another rather than continuing to ape a mansion.[41]

By the mid-1930s Eric Arthur became increasingly prominent as a proponent of Modernism as evidenced by invitations to Chermayeff, Wright, Gropius, and Marcel Breuer to visit his students at the University of Toronto.[42] The design that Arthur and his partner Anthony Adamson prepared for the Edmonton plant of J.S. McLean's Canada Packers resembled the stripped-down reinforced concrete structures that American Albert Kahn had created for firms like the Ford Motor Company, and it won a gold medal from the Ontario Association of Architects in 1937. That same year Arthur secured a ready pulpit from which to preach when he assumed the editorship of the *RAIC Journal*.[43] In his review of the annual OAA exhibition Arthur grouched that "the exteriors contained the usual number of conservative designs, ranging from the bloody Tudors to the psalm-singing [American] Colonials."[44]

In his column Arthur took up a critique of "Art in Canada" by Graham Campbell McInnes, which had recently appeared in *The Studio* (London). McInnes suggested that, aside from Ontario farmhouses and Doukhbour

[Ukrainian] sod houses on the Prairies, Canada had no "distinctive native architecture." The grain elevator and the Ontario barn represented solutions to uniquely Canadian requirements, but McInnes bemoaned the fact that the power of the Gothic Revival, the influence of American models, and the recent vogue for the International Style had diverted Canadian architects from searching for solutions to local problems such as climatic extremes. Arthur dismissed these concerns: "We have never attached much importance to this business of a 'distinctive national architecture.'"[45]

Arthur suggested to his architectural colleagues that they needed to cast a wider net for solutions to the "problem of monumental architecture in the modern manner." Buildings of civic importance should not be treated in the same way as low-cost housing. "We have been afraid that someone would do a federal government building in reinforced concrete, black glass and balconies. It would be functional, light, airy, expressive of its age, economical, and all those things, but it would lack dignity and permanence, both of which we realize (too late) are outmoded bourgeois terms." The Stockholm Town Hall, for instance, despite all the plaudits it had attracted, "always looked expensive to us, and the Golden Hall incomplete without Chu Chin Chow." Perhaps it was worth considering the House of Arms in Mussolini's new Roman Forum, which seemed to be monumental architecture in the modern style at its best.[46] Arthur also solicited an article from Richard Neutra on the grounds that some younger architects had expressed an interest in his designs such as a school in Bell, California. Though accompanied by photographs, the resulting piece was mostly generalities, but its interest lies in the fact that it was the first contribution to the RAIC's *Journal* from a recognized proponent of the International Style.[47]

Arthur also gave some prominence to the views of Humphrey Carver, a fellow British immigrant who was establishing a reputation as an urban planner and wanted to shake the dust off design in Canada. In mid-1938 Carver complained that "the glass blocks being used in Europe were still too expensive." *Modernistic* was a term that ought to be dropped for lack of any precision, since he had heard a member of the Ontario Association of Architects (probably Mackenzie Waters) declare in a recent radio broadcast that it applied to contemporary uses of various historical styles. The ideas of Le Corbusier and Walter Gropius had become well-known but had little to do with what Canadian architects meant when they talked about *modernistic* designs, a view with which Arthur concurred.[48]

Conservative resistance remained deep-laid. In *Canadian Homes and Gardens* A.H. Gregg commented that the "war" between modernists and traditionalists was by no means over. Popular belief persisted that all moderne buildings were white concrete and floodlit at night; magazines might be full of such illustrations but houses of this sort represented a tiny proportion of new homes in Canadian cities. The average person still found such designs hard to accept. Modern buildings needed modern furnishings and people still preferred the traditional. Only gradually would adaptations of these older designs come to be accepted.[49]

Even the prophets of change were sometimes hard to bear. Under the heading "Lion Among Sheep," Arthur's partner, Anthony Adamson, reported on Frank Lloyd Wright's visit to Toronto, during which Wright told those assembled in Convocation Hall that true architecture grew from the inside out. Classical orders applied to buildings were simply wrong. Sympathetic as he might be to such views, Adamson found Wright's self-importance difficult to tolerate.[50]

When the Toronto chapter of the Ontario Association of Architects staged a humourous debate on modernism in 1938, Gladstone Evans concluded his defence of traditionalism with this bit of doggerel:

"QUO VADIS"

In days gone by it was the vogue
To build a house to live in;
With windows that were straight and square,
And playful touches here and there
A pleasant aspect givin'.
The column and the cornice then,
The label-mould and gable
Were not banished out of court,
Or viewed with wonder as a sort
Of prehistoric fable ...
The multi-purpose living room,
The slick and stream-lined kitchen,
May only to the world foretell
The roads to architectural hell
For which our youth is itchin' ...
Throw out this yen for crazy tricks –
This nauseating hokum,
And if those hare-brained modernists
Begin to double up their fists,
We'll know just where to poke 'em.[51]

As the 1930s drew to a close Europe tottered towards the brink of war, and Britain's position made it certain that Canada would not escape involvement in the fighting. Canada's declaration of war in September 1939 started the final stages of recovery from the decade of depression, but it also meant that non-military-related building would soon be sharply curtailed. Humphrey Carver could only provide architects with lessons for the future by recommending they read J.M. Richards's *An Introduction to Modern Architecture* (1939). "More neatly and comprehensively" than anyone before, Richards had explained the tenets of the Modern movement, unlike those who delighted in "intellectual snobbery and dialectic obscurity." But the chance to rebuild the world (or even Toronto) in this image would have to wait until the war was over.[52]

II

As the economic depression of the 1930s dragged on and on, concerns about Toronto's dilapidated areas increased. Residential neighbourhoods on the fringe of downtown suffered from the unwillingness or inability of property owners to undertake renovation or redevelopment, and the situation was an invitation to penetration by new uses like shops or factories, which would only spread the decay amongst the houses. Toronto did have zoning bylaws governing land use, but they were ill-suited to remedying the problem.

In 1901 prosperous homeowners on Sherbourne Street near Queen had petitioned the city council to block the establishment of a bakery near their large, well-kept houses. The local aldermen, keen to protect the property values of their electors, took up the question but discovered that the city would require the grant of additional authority from the provincial legislature. Three years later power was secured to prohibit specified land uses in particular neighbourhoods. The first such bylaw passed under this authority in 1904 covered a stretch of Sherbourne and blocked the bakery. Another measure permitted the city property commissioner to take the initiative in imposing land use controls even in the absence of ratepayer pressure, power that was then used to ban the establishment of Chinese laundries on Parliament Street. At its final meeting the 1904 council approved general restrictions upon commercial penetration into southwest Rosedale and the Annex even though no new developments were proposed there at that time.

Over the succeeding decades scores of such "Restricted Area" bylaws were passed, prohibiting various kinds of businesses, factories, and "noxious" activities like stables, junkyards, and dancehalls from locating in specified neighbourhooods. In addition the city council approved numerous "spot" re-zonings forbidding certain land uses in particular locations. Within twenty years most residential districts in the centre of the city south of Bloor Street between Dufferin Street and the Don River were subject to such bylaws, often passed on the initiative of local aldermen. These rules protected residential neighbourhoods by banning the incursion of "nuisances." Nevertheless, sizable areas south of Dundas Street and along railway rights-of-way, as well as in working class districts adjacent to industrial zones and in the inner city's east end, were left unprotected against the incursion of industrial and commercial activities.[53]

Thus plenty of downtown land remained uncontrolled for new uses, and even near Restricted Areas there were often strips along major arteries that could be used for commercial activities or were not subject to any restrictions. Purpose-built apartment houses began to appear about 1905, and in 1912 two bylaws imposed controls on them in most residential districts, though such buildings were permitted in areas south of Bloor and along other major routes.[54] In 1921 the city successfully sought authority from the province to create exclusively residential districts and was also given power to regulate the height, size, spacing, and location of structures. North of Bloor Street a number of streets with high real estate values were explicitly restricted to detached houses. Some bylaws specified the value and size of new houses and their construction materials as well as lot sizes, building envelopes, and setbacks. The first such rules were applied in 1927 to the Lawrence Park district in the north end in order to continue the restrictive covenants imposed by the original developer when the lots were laid out in 1909.[55] The Lawrence Park Protective Association clearly stated its desire to exclude semi-detached, duplex, or apartment houses, and many other areas north of Eglinton Avenue subsequently enjoyed similar protection.

By 1929 most of the area north of Bloor except along major streets was restricted to residential use, though property owners were permitted to take in up to three boarders or roomers, and medical offices, churches, and playgrounds were exempted from the controls. The controls were rooted in the desires of neighbourhood residents. When amendments were proposed, the Property Department was directed to poll the surrounding area, the survey results playing an important role in shaping regulations. However, a proposal to enact a comprehensive zoning law setting out permitted land uses everywhere was rejected by the city council in 1927, which left the aldermen with a good deal of discretion.[56]

As part of the city's centennial celebrations in March 1934 Ontario's Lieutenant-Governor, Dr Herbert Bruce, delivered a speech in which he observed there were seriously rundown districts that exerted "an unhappy environmental influence" upon residents. The mayor and Board of Control therefore asked Bruce to head an advisory committee to inquire into housing conditions and suggest remedies. Volunteers conducted surveys to make an inventory that led to more intensive studies of two inner city districts. The two inner city districts were "Moss Park" and "The Ward." Moss Park ran from the Don River to Sherbourne and the waterfront to Carlton Street and The Ward ran from University Avenue to Bathurst and the waterfront to College Street. House-to-house studies revealed no large contiguous districts of "decayed" structures inhabited by numerous families, "herded together, overcrowded, shiftless, perhaps criminals or semicriminal." Nevertheless Bruce's report concluded that the inner city did contain areas composed of "small and scattered groups of dwellings in which the conditions of slum life are in full evidence."[57]

Detailed examination of 1,332 dwellings inhabited by 1,421 families determined that 96 percent of them lacked a minimum standard of amenities (complete inside plumbing, cooking facilities for the private use of each household, freedom from vermin, central heating, artificial light in all rooms and cement cellars). Nearly three-fifths of these buildings had no bath, one-fifth had no inside toilets, and more than half were infested with vermin. Overcrowding (more than one person per room) affected two-fifths of the buildings. Overall, Bruce's committee reported that there were between 2,000 and 3,000 substandard houses in the city, with nearly 18,000 families forced to double up. The most serious problems were found in the "Bad Area" located in the southeastern corner of the inner city.[58]

Studies of slum housing concluded that severe overcrowding was associated with physical and health problems like tuberculosis, polio, measles, and higher than average death rates, especially among infants. Living quarters with fewer than forty square feet per person not only led to the spread of infectious diseases such as measles but caused a deterioration of family life, which in turn spawned criminal and anti-social behaviour. Not surprisingly such analysis also translated into concerns about juvenile delinquency and street gangs, which were publicized around the same time.[59] In the absence of any funds flowing from either the provincial or federal government, however, the city did not feel in a position to take any positive action to construct new housing.

In 1936 the city did pass a new housing standards bylaw, which permitted the demolition of substandard structures. Over the next six years 1,100 dwellings and more than 1,600 sheds were removed, but only 164 new buildings were constructed on the sites cleared by demolitions. City council created another advisory committee on housing problems in 1936 that recommended the replacement of 4,000 "obsolete" units. However, the lack of low-income housing was attributed to nationwide economic problems, and in the continuing absence of any federal remedial program, nothing occurred. Another report by civic officials in mid-1939 suggested that a block of land in the distressed Moss Park area could be redeveloped with 444 units of new housing at a cost of $1.6 million. Once again the city, faced with reduced tax revenues stemming from lower real estate assessments, took no action.[60]

Tracy leMay was made the city's commissioner of planning in 1930.[61] He soon became concerned that the existing system of prohibiting particular land uses did not remove anxieties amongst property owners who wanted to be able to prevent incursions by other undesirable (but not proscribed) activities. The problems were aggravated by the Depression because local politicians were inclined to countenance lax enforcement of the bylaws in order to avoid inflicting additional pressure upon already hard-pressed ratepayers. Yet leMay believed that the penetration of industrial and commercial activities into residential neighbourhoods was destabilizing, leading to an irreversible decline of standards with the danger of creating "slums" in the inner city. Without the city having large, clearly delineated areas devoted to residential uses, there was little to encourage orderly redevelopment. What was needed, in leMay's mind, was a comprehensive zoning bylaw prepared by professionals like himself to replace the patchwork of hundreds of bylaws stemming from neighbourhood pressure upon the aldermen over the previous three decades. Such a framework seemed to him essential to preventing the spread of urban blight and ensuring orderly redevelopment of residential and commercial areas.[62]

In 1934 leMay and a committee of other civic officials officially endorsed the desirability of a comprehensive zoning bylaw to replace the estimated eight hundred Restricted Area bylaws along with some three thousand spot rezoning measures. Nothing resulted, but as concerns about blight in the inner city increased Alderman J.D. McNish was able to persuade city council to reconsider the idea in 1936. Planning Commissioner leMay and Property Commissioner Graham Bland were directed to establish current land uses as revealed by the tax assessment rolls, the city directory, and the telephone directory. This data revealed that about half of the land in the city was currently in residential use with about 20 percent occupied by business activities, while streets covered about 30 percent of the area and parks represented less than 5 percent of the land use. With this information in hand the two municipal officials devised a scheme to categorize land uses into four residential zones: R.1 for areas limited to detached single family houses; R.2 for areas that might also include semi-detached or duplex dwellings; R.3 for rooming house districts; and R.4 for apartment buildings, located mainly in midtown. Business premises were categorized separately: C.1 for the office district; C.2 for light industry; C.3 for heavy manufacturing; and C.4 for unrestricted uses. City council officially endorsed these definitions in June 1937.[63]

The officials then spent the next two years transforming the data into maps to delineate the eight zones. LeMay's aim was to create areas of particular land uses as large as possible and clearly separated by boundaries such as railways, ravines, and major thoroughfares. Non-conforming uses would not be eliminated since business people could not be prevented from earning a livelihood, particularly in the absence of any program of compensation for their displacement. Maps would be prepared showing zone boundaries, and a comprehensive zoning bylaw could then replace the present confusing and complicated restrictions (which covered about four-fifths of residential areas) and prevent future incursions by unauthorized uses.[64]

This analysis revealed that the absence of Restricted Area bylaws for working-class residential areas in and around the downtown core meant that a much larger space was potentially available for industrial expansion than was currently being used or even deemed necessary in future. Almost all of the unrestricted area downtown was currently occupied by dwelling houses, which were beginning to deteriorate, but developers were unwilling to renovate or replace owing to fears that industry might move in nearby. What was needed, leMay believed, was a regimen that would promote investor confidence about the future of property values in the residential areas that were threatened with encroachment by industry in order to prevent an exodus to the suburbs in search of "fresh air and low taxes."[65] Civic officials therefore proposed zoning rules that would increase the area in the downtown available solely for residential use by some 1,800 acres, leaving 48 percent of the land area of the city for housing, 24 percent for business activities, 21.5 percent for streets, and 6.5 percent for parks.[66]

LeMay and Bland submitted their report to council in July 1939 noting that there had been serious complaints about "wholesale and indiscriminate infiltration of non-conforming uses in the middle and lower value residential districts, bringing with them speculative values and residential depreciation which are the forerunners of blight or slum conditions." What was needed to protect property values against such incursions was a comprehensive zoning bylaw, which was impossible to amend "except where it can be shown to be in the general public interest." The way to devise such a law, free from the influence of turf-proud local politicians, was to recruit a panel of highly qualified citizen volunteers to review the evidence collected by the civil servants, undertake further consultations, and produce a draft that could then be opened for comment to interested taxpayers.[67]

In February 1940 the city council created the Independent Committee on Zoning (ICZ) – the name was intended to emphasize its freedom from the meddling of politicians. Composed of realtor W.H. Bosley as chair with civil engineers S.R. Frost and J.S. Galbraith and architects F.H. Marani and W.L.

Somerville, the ICZ had the city commissioners of assessment, buildings, property and planning as official advisors. Over the next eighteen months the ICZ worked away, hearing individually from a large number of experts and holding more than eighty meetings to study the experience of other North American cities.

The ICZ delivered a draft report in mid-1941. The aim was to "correct a very undesirable situation, remove doubt, establish confidence." As a first principle the committee accepted that zoning should "of necessity closely follow existing uses." "Proposals embodying drastic changes in the use of land, in the opinion of the committee, would be doomed to failure. The character of a district cannot be changed by legislation alone." That meant that even though some residential districts had suffered from incursions by industrial and other non-conforming uses, removing these enterprises, however desirable in theory, would be an "arbitrary exercise of police power" that could not be justified. Lacking funds to compensate owners for the expense of relocation, such non-conforming uses must be permitted to continue subject to conditions regarding their future expansion.[68]

The draft zoning bylaw and its maps sought to segregate certain types of land uses, particularly industries, which emitted noise, dust, smoke, or fumes to the detriment of their neighbours, as well as other objectionable undertakings like junkyards. No longer should Restricted Area bylaws be framed to prohibit certain activities but rather to specify permitted uses. Residential districts would thus be guaranteed protection against the intrusion of activities that might undermine land values.

The *Report of the Independent Committee on Zoning* contained other proposals. Not only land uses (defined according to the categories of R.1 to R.4 and C.1 to C.4), but the height and size of certain building types as well as lot coverage and the provision of setbacks should be governed by new regulations designated V.1 through V.3. These density rules were intended to control the impact of new buildings, like the amount of traffic congestion that might be generated. Echoing proposals made during the 1920s to restrict the number and height of downtown office towers, the committee reached the somewhat surprising conclusion that "the day of the skyscraper is over, and all authorities agree that limitation of height is essential and in the public interest." For that reason the height of new office towers rising from the sidewalks in the downtown was to be limited to seventy feet, though total height might extend up to one hundred feet by using setbacks for the topmost floors. New regulations were suggested to cope with parking problems created by apartment houses, theatres, and auditoriums as well as the curbside loading and unloading of trucks. A series of public meetings was announced for the autumn of 1941 to allow property owners to express their views on the proposed bylaw.[69] Changes in zoning laws to promote redevelopment in the blighted areas of downtown Toronto did not, however, come into force before mobilization for the Second World War started to revive the local economy.

III

For the well-to-do people who could afford to commission new houses even during the depressed 1930s, familiarity with Georgian Revival only bred popularity. In 1932 George, Moorhouse, and King, were called in to produce a Rosedale house for Mrs Peter C. Larkin. *Canadian Homes and Gardens* thought it should "rank high among the important houses of the year": "The superb fitness of the Georgian style for the formal city house is again demonstrated, and in a manner to prove, in addition, the skill and resourcefulness of Canadian architects." Going the Larkins more than one better was Mrs J.S. Burnside, whose Clarendon Avenue house by Burden and Gouinlock cost more than $75,000 in 1931 and won a prize in that category from the RAIC. Grey brick and cut stone were used throughout without any concrete ("artificial stone") detailing. Inside, the cornice of the entrance hall was copied from eighteenth-century work by Sir William Chambers, the dining room sported a mantel made by the Adam brothers, a Sheraton table, and pictures by Romney, Reynolds, and Raeburn hung in various rooms.[70]

3·7
Mrs Peter Larkin's house, George, Moorhouse, and King, 1932.

Elsewhere in the northeastern suburbs fancy new houses in a variety of historical styles had begun to sprout up during the later 1920s for people rich enough to leave the central city behind. Ownership of a named "estate" was still desirable as a sign of the social prominence the owners were seeking. In 1925 E.R. Wood (founder of the Wood, Gundy brokerage firm) gave his city house to Victoria College at the University of Toronto and moved to Bayview Avenue and Lawrence East. "Glendon Hall," designed by Molesworth, West, and Secord, was sufficiently elaborate to set a kind of fashion for later emulators. A winding driveway, entered through an imposing stone gate, led to a country house of Italian Renaissance inspiration with a sunken garden and views across the Don valley to the rear from the living room. To the south, J.J. Vaughan, an Eaton's executive, commissioned Donningvale from Burden and Gouinlock in 1930, another Elizabethan country house with lofty gables and a vast park.[71]

By joining the Siftons and Dr Herbert Bruce in that area, Wood and Vaughan attracted others to build northward along Bayview Avenue, one of the original concession lines laid out to the east of Yonge Street. Once little

3.8
Glendon Hall (E.R. Wood house), Molesworth, West, and Secord, 1927.

3.9
Penryn, Mathers, and Haldenby, 1934.

more than a gravel road interrupted by the wide, deep valley of the Don, upper Bayview north of Lawrence was transformed as the automobile made the area more easily accessible to downtown. Low taxes in suburban York County encouraged the laying out of large properties with grand houses. When a bridge over the river was finally built on Bayview at Lawrence East in 1930, Frank Wood immediately began construction of a vast new estate across the ravine from his brother E.R. The New York firm of Delano and Aldrich (who had worked for the Astors and the Rockefellers) designed a French country house of smooth-cut limestone topped with a slender cupola and adjoining stables at a cost of $400,000. Norman D. Perry left his Rosedale home in 1932 to move further north to Penryn, a Georgian Revival design by Mathers and Haldenby. Red brick with seven bays across including projecting wings, it stood beside a sunken rose garden.[72]

The economic depression of the 1930s severely cut into the demand for architect designed houses, but even during the darkest days of the depression stockbroking remained fairly lucrative thanks to the appeal of gold mining shares. Those who chose to relocate northward in the 1930s and fortify their social standing by joining the horsey set had conservative architectural tastes. H. Rupert Bain used the fortune he gained from promoting stocks like Pickle Crow Gold Mines to buy one hundred acres northeast of Leslie Street and Don Mills Road. For $250,000 George and Moorhouse created Graydon Hall, a twenty-nine room Georgian Revival mansion with a broken pediment over the door sporting the date, 1936. To the rear lay a sunken garden with a fountain draining to a waterfall in the woods along with a nine-hole golf course and stables and kennels.

The same year, E.P. Taylor used his profits from creating the Brewing Company of Ontario through a series of mergers to commission Windfields, not far north of Frank Wood's house. An American Federal design in stone,

3.10 (Right)
Graydon Hall, George and Moorhouse, 1936.

3.11 (Below)
Toronto Stock Exchange, George and Moorhouse, 1938.

the house sported a pineapple (symbol of hospitality) on the pediment above the front door beneath a Palladian window. Modernity was celebrated with a private movie theatre in the basement. The extensive grounds stretching eastward down to a tributary of the Don included stables in which Taylor housed the first racehorse that he purchased in 1936, the beginning of a long and illustrious history for his Windfields Farm racing stable.[73]

New commercial and industrial buildings were scarce in Toronto during the 1930s, though there were signs of the influence of moderne ideas as some construction was undertaken after the economy began to improve late in the decade. When the Toronto Stock Exchange expanded into new quarters in 1937, George and Moorhouse, who had made their names as students of Georgian Revival, produced quite an up-to-date design. The building rose sheer from the street line to maximize floor space on a small property on the west side of Bay Street just south of King. The facade was Stripped Classical, gesturing to the past but abandoning the elaborate columns and entablature so often favoured previously by financial institutions. Two low recessed doors were topped by a jazzy, zigzag

(Clockwise)

3.12
Toronto Stock Exchange, east wall of trading floor, Charles Comfort's murals at left.

3.13
Toronto Stock Exchange, members' dining room, interior by S.H. Maw.

3.14
Toronto Stock Exchange, management committee room, interior by S.H. Maw.

frieze designed by artist Charles Comfort consisting of low relief figures representing various occupations (in which the businessman appeared to be picking the pocket of the overalled working man). Above that, Classical features were hinted at by large smooth vertical piers between the tall windows and a small cornice below an attic. Inside, the large trading floor showed broad bands of backlit opal glass running up between the windows and across the ceiling along with Cubist-style murals by Comfort, which provided a futuristic appearance. The interiors by associate architect S.H. Maw showed an interesting contrast between the contemporary members' dining room and the boardroom on the third floor, which was intended to speak of the "sound traditions of British finance," and "to signal that at long last the exchange had achieved respectability as a key Canadian financial institution and had put behind it the sleazy reputation that had attracted so much criticism during the early 1930s."[74]

3.15 (Above)
Customs House (Dominion Public Building), first phase, Department of Public Works, Chief Architect's Branch, 1931.

3.16 (Left)
Postal Station K, Yonge Street, Murray Brown, 1937.

3.17 (Opposite)
City Delivery Building, York Street, Charles B. Dolphin, 1939–40.

The federal government also constructed a couple of buildings in Toronto that showed that it had finally abandoned its previous commitment to the Beaux Arts. The Toronto Customs House on Front Street, completed in 1935 to echo the Union Station across Bay Street to the west, was the last of the older breed.[75] Now the federal Department of Public Works adopted a kind of Stripped Classicism in which historically accurate decoration was replaced by simplified detailing. The change also reflected the department's shift from its reliance upon the centralized Chief Architect's Branch to a policy of commissioning some designs from local architects. Postal Station K on Yonge Street north of Eglinton at Montgomery was the work of Murray Brown, who had already established a reputation for his sympathies to the moderne. The building had a seven-bay front with symmetrical windows but was almost unadorned except for two freestanding pillars on either side of the main doorway topped by a lion and a unicorn, which gave it a more up-to-date look.[76]

At Queen's Quay on the waterfront the Post Office also constructed its central City Delivery Building in 1939–40. Charles B. Dolphin designed the four facades with Stripped Classical pilasters at the centre. On each of the corners of the building, however, he included wraparound windows without any visible supports adopted from the Modern. In this case "the architect simply borrowed a motif associated with the movement and applied it to a modern classical design." Following the moderne, Dolphin included relief panels beside each window and at the roofline a carved frieze (like Comfort's for the stock exchange) that depicted the various ways that the mail was transported and delivered.[77]

When the *Globe* merged with the *Mail and Empire* the new owner of the *Globe and Mail*, William H. Wright, celebrated the event by constructing a new building at the corner of King and York Streets in 1937. The moderne design by Mathers and Haldenby showed off some of the possibilities that new technology permitted. The long bands of windows on the York Street facade appeared to exist without the need to support the curtain walls, and at the street corner there were smaller windows, which turned the corner without requiring a column. On the ground floor there was even a circular display window whose glazing spanned a ninety-degree angle.[78]

Out in suburban Leaside the same firm of architects produced a factory for the Staunton Wallpaper Company, which looked like the industrial buildings that Albert Kahn was creating. Long strips of glazing were set flush with the plane of the wall, which was unbroken by visible columns, some of the glass panels hinging outward for ventilation. On the flat roof of the two-storey building were A-shaped monitors of the kind used by Kahn for his Ford plant in Toronto in the early 1920s to admit more light and air. Like Kahn the architects did not conceal these monitors with a parapet but merely placed on the cornice outside a jaunty railing of piping that would have done credit to an ocean liner.[79]

As prosperity returned in the later 1930s, changing social morays were heralded by the fact that some prosperous Torontonians were prepared to consider living in the apartment buildings now common in many other cities. The Jackson-Lewis Company purchased a large property in the northeast corner of the city three and a half miles from downtown on the edge of the suburban town of Leaside. Instead of adding to the stock of detached homes nearby selling for between $8,000 and $11,000, the company decided upon multiple housing. Apparently convinced that middle-class tenants would still not be interested in renting in a conventional block of flats, Robert Jackson decided to produce a layout then novel to Torontonians. Familiar with "garden court" apartments in Britain, he commissioned Forsey Page and Harland Steele, who formed one of Canada's most successful firms in the field of

3.18 (Top)
William Wright Building, home of the Toronto *Globe and Mail*, Mathers and Haldenby, 1937.

3.19 (Bottom)
Staunton Wallpaper Factory, Leaside, Mathers and Haldenby, 1937.

domestic architecture, to produce a layout that drew not upon Modernism but owed more to Ebenezer Howard's 1902 book, *Garden Cities of Tomorrow*, and to Clarence Stein and Henry Wright's 1927 plan for Radburn, New Jersey.

The five and a half acre site stretched 350 feet along the east side of Bayview Avenue north of Moore, for which Page and Steele designed a cluster of yellow brick buildings, none of them more than three storeys high and occupying less than one-quarter of the area. Commenced in 1939 and finished in 1941 the Garden Court apartments surrounded a long rectangular green space. Most units were entered from this court where the buildings blocked off noise and traffic from the surrounding streets. Separate entrances to every four or six units were by staircases, which eliminated the need for internal corridors. To make them more like conventional houses, each apartment extended the full width of the building, creating cross-drafts and avoiding overlooking windows. The architects bowed to the moderne with curving balconies, metal grillwork, and steel-framed windows, but were careful to respect tradition with sloping roofs and corner quoins in a simplified Georgian manner.

This effort to strike a balance between house and apartment living to make the Garden Court appealing to middle-class tenants proved highly successful with the units quickly leased at rents between fifty dollars and eighty dollars per month.[80] Not only the residents but architects were impressed with the design. It attracted sufficient acclaim that in 1950, when the Massey Foundation first established its awards for the best of various Canadian building types, the Garden Court won the medal for the apartment category. The prize, intended to be awarded triennially, thus went to a project completed almost a decade earlier. In 1958 the newly founded periodical *Canadian Architect* applauded the building as unique for its time and still noteworthy for its innovations.[81]

The 1930s saw the ideas of the Modern movement slowly begin to percolate into the consciousness of architects and designers in Canada but, owing to the Depression, tangible results were few. In Toronto Lawren Harris's house stood alone in its radicalism. Moderne motifs were more widely seen in such structures as movie theatres. But many homebuyers still considered flat roofs and strip windows the spawn of European longhairs, to be avoided if possible for comforting red brick of a Georgian Revival, even though it might now include a built-in garage.

CANADIAN HOMES & GARDENS, JANUARY-FEBRUARY, 1944 25

New concepts of urban living deal with satisfaction of various residential needs within a single area. Accordingly, Garden Court provides accommodation suitable for many different family types. There are both houses and apartments

Garden Court

GARDEN COURT is dedicated to the ideal of better living. It recognizes that the large group of citizens who, for one reason or another, do not wish to own homes of their own should not have to put up with inferior accommodation on that account.

Dwellings, in the form of semi-detached residences as well as apartments, have been designed to satisfy the needs of a wide range of family types. Recreational facilities and green open spaces are provided for enjoyment of tenants.

Located on Bayview Avenue in Leaside, Garden Court is about 3½ miles from downtown Toronto. The property is level, about 5½ acres in extent. Less than one quarter of the total area is occupied by buildings. The surroundings are of residential character, free from industrial encroachments.

The layout developed by the architects embodies a departure from conventional apartment house design. By well-studied grouping of buildings, large court areas were created to ensure plenty of light and air for every dwelling. The large central court was treated in a formal, park-like manner, while tennis courts and play-yards are incorporated in adjacent courts of secondary importance. Garage accommodation is provided on north and south boundaries of the property.

Durable materials—concrete, masonry, steel sash, streamline piping and fittings—have been used throughout. The automatic oil heating system is by Trane. All bathrooms are finished in vitrolite and hardwood flooring is of the block type. In the basement complete laundry and drying-room facilities are installed. The erection of Garden Court was financed under the National Housing Act.

Forsey Page & Steele, Architects

3.20
Drawing of Garden Court, Bayview Avenue, Page and Steele, 1941. This is a good example of the self-promotion that filled publications about architecture and décor.

4

MODERN ARCHITECTURE DELAYED 1940–1950

4.1 (Opposite) Toronto Waterfront, 1957. The view from the Island ferries hardly changed from the 1930s to the 1960s.

The Second World War wrought significant changes in Canada. The federal government originally intended the country to play a relatively restricted military role and to concentrate upon supplying the Anglo-French alliance with food, raw materials, and munitions, but the fall of France in the summer of 1940 left Canada second only to Britain in importance among the Allied belligerents.[1] Mobilization for war intensified rapidly. The lingering vestiges of the economic depression of the 1930s evaporated, and before long fears about inflation led to the imposition of wage and price controls. Commodities like steel and timber were reserved for strategically important purposes, and the construction industry concentrated upon military needs like barracks, munitions plants, and airports. Civilian projects were sharply restricted. Only when the victory of the Allies seemed assured could planning for peacetime reconstruction get under way.

At that point Canadians could consider how to deal with a severe shortage of housing, a problem rendered all the more acute by the onset of a "baby boom," which made families eager to secure new accommodation. When peace returned in 1945 and the fear of a postwar recession evaporated, a prolonged burst of economic growth occurred. Attention could turn to producing houses, shops, offices, and factories designed to serve a rapidly growing population. Yet these buildings did not reflect any widespread acceptance of Modern architecture and design but continued the historical traditions that had always dominated.

I

Opportunities for Canadian architects to exercise their skills were severely restricted during the war. A few voices continued to be heard singing the praises of Modernism. During the late 1930s some young practitioners had set out to emulate the Modern Architectural Research Group (MARG) in Britain by establishing Architectural Research Groups (ARGs) in various cities.[2] In 1941 the Toronto branch of the ARG produced a manifesto that pronounced the "dead hulks" along Yonge Street "more pathetic" than acres of bombed-out ruins. The group promised a "complete rebirth" of understanding about the design and construction of buildings and announced its ability to solve contemporary social problems using the so-called "IDEA-WEAPON" of "Creative Planning," but this gust of hot air dissipated without any concrete achievements.[3]

The rationing of scarce construction materials posed a serious problem for the profession. In 1942 one person complained that the steel shortage was becoming so acute that architects would soon find themselves out of business altogether unless planning and allocation were improved. In the *Royal Architectural Institute of Canada Journal* the editor Eric Arthur published repeated complaints that the federal government was ignoring architects much more than other professionals in the organization of the war effort.[4]

A photomontage prepared for a display at the United Nations soon after the war telegraphed the grim tale of the architect's-eye view of the recent past in Canada. The headings for the six panels of pictures were: (1) "1938–40: Building was as yet unaffected by wartime shortages" (illustrated by Ernest Cormier's Supreme Court building in Ottawa); (2) "1940–45: Wood construction is mass-produced for war purposes" (barracks and temporary

4.2
Postwar architecture exhibition for UNESCO, 1947. Panel 5 shows four John B. Parkin projects: two TTC buildings and two schools (see Figures 4.7, 4.8, and 4.14).

office buildings); (3) "Expanding war production also required permanent buildings" (airports and the Shipshaw generating station on the Saguenay); (4) "The war only allowed a small amount of normal building" (Montreal's Bonaventure Station and some residences in British Columbia); (5): "Post-war conditions encourage a search for new focus" (veterans hospitals, schools, and transit depots); (6) "Architects are now assuming wider social responsibilities" (town planning).[5]

"Forecasting Things to Come" in 1943, A. Leslie Perry insisted in *Canadian Homes and Gardens* that architecture had reached a transition point by 1939 with events like the New York World's Fair presenting examples of the avant-garde on the way to gaining public acceptance. He predicted new materials like plywood, plastics, and glass blocks would gain a firm foothold using advanced production methods like extrusion machines. In the same issue, "Prefabrication Contributes to Progress" noted that Canada would require half a million new houses after the war, and prefabrication might permit their construction by relatively unskilled labour. Already the American designer Norman Bel Geddes was experimenting with a "House of Tomorrow," which could be produced in dozens of models out of twenty-seven basic components.[6]

The practical obstacles standing in the way of prefabrication were revealed, however, by a symposium of experts in 1944. O.J. Firestone, the senior research associate at the federal government's Reconstruction Committee, contended that prefabrication might cut in half the 5,300 hours needed to build an average prewar house. But the president of the National Construction Council, Toronto architect A.S. Mathers, pointed out that precise prefabrication of parts like that achieved by the automobile industry was impossible and would remain so until agreement on a whole range of standard dimensions had been reached. The manager of Aeroparts Limited, Frank Smith, concurred that however desirable prefabrication might be it would be a long time before it was achieved, and in any case the cost of transporting large units to building sites would limit its usefulness. C.J. Woolsey, president of the Toronto and District Labour Council, reminded people that prefabrication might cut into the hours worked by skilled tradesmen who would strongly oppose any moves to make the construction industry resemble the automobile production line.[7]

Canadian Homes and Gardens gamely continued to celebrate the innovations in home building expected once the war ended. In November 1944 "Looking Forward" listed the discoveries and developments during the war with great potential once industry had been converted back to peacetime operation. Products like aluminum and synthetic rubber would transform living inside prefabricated houses equipped with air conditioning. Yet two

4.3
"Home in Bayview," Hawke House, Park Lane Circle, 1944. Eric Arthur bends to modernism *very* slowly.

feature articles on new upscale houses in the same issue of the magazine revealed the strong grip of traditional styles. J.F.C. Smith had designed an "Urban Modern" home in Toronto's Lawrence Park, which turned out to be a brick and clapboard American Colonial with a conventional hip roof; in a timid bow to novelty, the garage had a flat roof and inside an archway linked the southward-facing living and dining rooms. Eric Arthur meanwhile produced a plan for a stripped-down Georgian mansion nearby across Bayview Avenue on upscale Park Lane Circle that made only a couple of bows towards modernism like the ill-advised outward-sloping railing on the balcony over the front door.[8]

Perhaps the technological advance that would ultimately do the most to alter house design in postwar Canada was the bonding of two separate sheets of glass to metal framing. The inner pane could remain warm without condensation forming on the outer one due to the insulating layer of air trapped between them. University scientists in Chicago estimated that heating costs might be cut by up to one-third depending on the amount of sunlight. In 1944 *Canadian Homes and Gardens* reported on one early experiment with the new material. The "Sun House" in Rosedale designed by Gordon S. Adamson was a one-storey pavilion with a combined living-dining room looking south to the garden through picture windows and a glass door. Patented Thermopane windows (only recently available in Toronto) were sealed, requiring mechanical air circulation inside the building along with wide eaves to cut off direct sunlight.[9]

Picture windows aroused considerable interest. In a 1945 response to letters from readers, architect W.L. Somerville, long-time contributor to *Canadian Homes and Gardens*, presented a design for a flat-roofed house with an open-plan living-dining room having double-glazed windows giving onto the garden. A two-storey section contained bedrooms for a family of four, though Somerville showed that he was not quite abreast of current social trends by describing the building as a "help-less" house – meaning that there was no accommodation for a live-in maid. The magazine's gardening editor applauded the glass wall with door opening onto the terrace, which brought the outdoors inside, one of the distinguishing features of up-to-date home design, adding that "modern architecture is so fundamentally honest in its functioning that it demands similar honesty in its enframement."[10] Yet many questions remained about whether Canadian homebuyers would accept such innovations.

4.4
"Sun House," Rosedale, Gordon S. Adamson, 1944.

II

When Canadians began to think about what they could expect in the postwar era many of them concluded planning was what had made mobilization for war so effective. Similar careful preparation would be required to reap the full benefits of renewed peace. The idea that Toronto required a comprehensive urban plan to regulate the city's growth regained its popularity.

In mid-1941, after working for almost a year and a half, Toronto's Independent Committee on Zoning delivered the draft of a comprehensive zoning bylaw. City council decided property owners should be allowed to express their views at a series of nine public meetings held that autumn. These gatherings often became heated, particularly in neighbourhoods like south Rosedale and the Annex where large Victorian and Edwardian houses were undergoing conversion into flats. These conversions had begun in earnest during the Depression, as owners struggled to make ends meet and accelerated due to a severe housing shortage during the war. Single-family homeowners protested vehemently that rezoning their neighbourhoods to legalize these changes would seriously depress property values and ultimately create slums.

City planning commissioner Tracy leMay, the official most closely involved in drafting the new bylaw, was well-aware that the popularity of zoning rested upon the perception that it was the best way to protect residential neighbourhoods against incursion by undesirable uses and so preserve property values. Like other professional planners, however, leMay believed that regulation could also have a positive effect. The hundreds of Restrictive Area bylaws covering most residential areas in Toronto simply prohibited the establishment of various enterprises that could be deemed "nuisances."[11]

He argued that downzoning to permit a wider range of land uses could not only be beneficial if it encouraged new investment to redevelop the lands for semi-detached homes, single or double duplexes, and multiple units but would also protect property values. LeMay told one meeting that "some of the most satisfactory modern types of housing in the big cities of the United States are groups of houses, grouped around perhaps a little courtyard or garden. They have been found to be very satisfactory and well liked by the people living in them." Relaxing restrictions on some neighbourhoods now limited to detached single-family homes might also permit other desirable uses like art galleries, libraries, and museums that improved the quality of urban life.[12]

LeMay pointed out that outside of areas like south Rosedale and the Annex the proposed bylaw would hardly alter permitted land use in Toronto. Though he almost certainly exaggerated the positive effects of rezoning, his views carried the day. The Independent Committee on Zoning retired to study the comments made at the public meetings, but, in September 1942, forwarded the comprehensive zoning bylaw to city council unchanged.[13]

By that time the local newspapers and the Board of Trade were also pressing for the creation of a proper urban plan. Supporters of planning argued this was long overdue if Toronto was not to become an impoverished slum. Efforts at planning during the interwar years had "failed miserably." Even before the war people had been leaving the city owing to high living costs and lack of employment, and in the absence of action the return of peace would only add to this flow.[14] In June 1942 council appointed an advisory City Planning Board. In an effort to ensure a broad consensus, the six citizen members of the new board were drawn from the business community, organized labour, academic life, and the Toronto Transportation Commission, joined by one member of city council and by leMay. To assist them an Advisory Technical Committee of engineers, architects, and planners was also created.[15] LeMay was instructed to consult with his counterparts in the American Society of Planning Officials to discover which American cities already had master plans that might guide Toronto.[16]

In December 1943 the Planning Board delivered its "Master Plan" for the development of the Toronto region over the next thirty years.[17] The challenge identified was to create a modern city on the framework of the "old pre-machine-age town" and stop the decay eating away at the heart of the downtown and its strangulation by traffic congestion. The plan covered about one hundred square miles in the city and in its surrounding suburbs, not just the current built-up area of some fifty-five square miles. Admitting that earlier planning efforts had simply been pigeon-holed when initial enthusiasm dissipated, the board insisted that this must not be permitted to

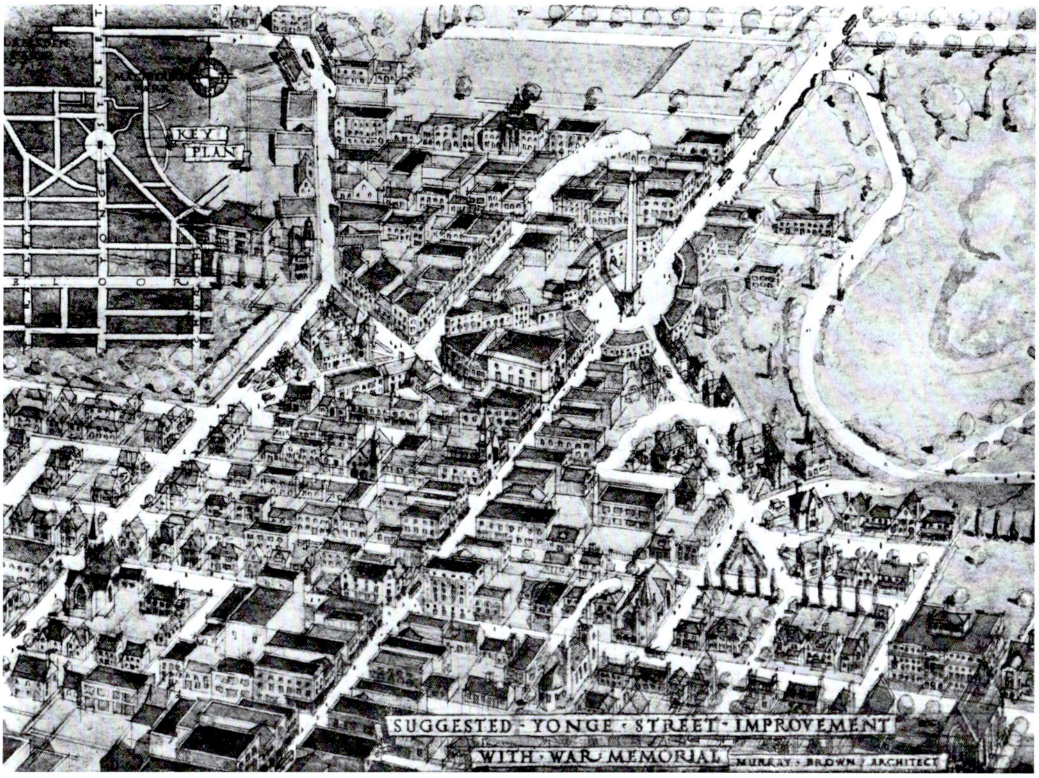

occur again if the citizenry was to have congenial living conditions and their children a proper place to grow up. While large ambitious projects would have to be undertaken, the total cost would be lower than if each local area municipality formulated separate plans over three decades during which total population was expected to grow from about 900,000 to between 1.25 and 1.5 million.

4.5
New roadways for the new motorcar: Suggested Improvement to Yonge Street, Murray Brown, 1922.

Inside the city there should be an extensive program of road construction to push existing arterial roads across ravines and river valleys. For instance, Eglinton Avenue would be extended east and west across both the Don and Humber Rivers, while north–south circulation would be improved by linking Jarvis Street across the Rosedale ravine to Mount Pleasant Road in north Toronto. Such ideas echoed much earlier proposals like Murray Brown's 1922 proposal to improve traffic flow by linking Bay and Church Streets to Yonge at a traffic circle several blocks north of Bloor.

In January 1942 the Toronto Transportation Commission (TTC) proposed to relieve congestion downtown caused by the streetcars by constructing a subway line south from Eglinton Avenue under Yonge Street, then looping north from Union Station up University Avenue and west along Bloor Street to Dundas. The Planning Board endorsed this idea along with the TTC's scheme for another east–west subway under Queen Street from Pape Avenue to Ossington where it would curve northward to St Clair Avenue.

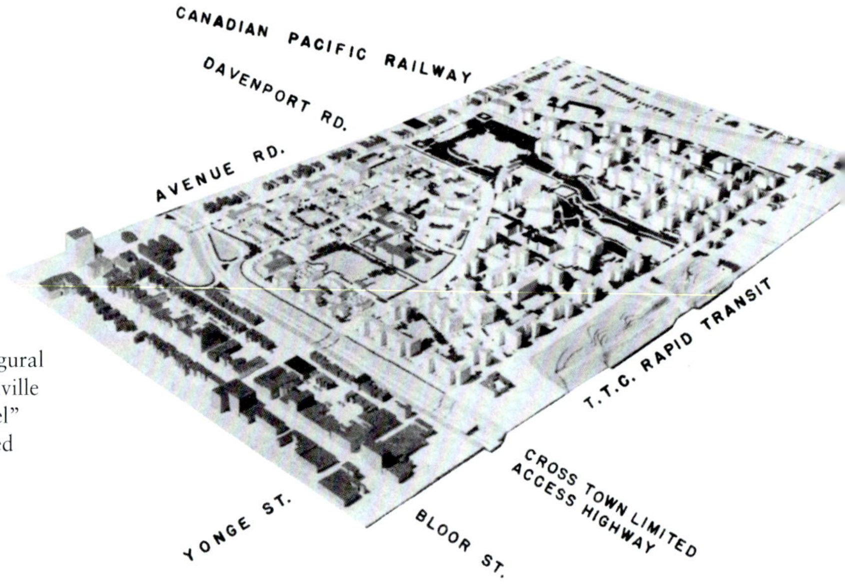

4.6
City Planning Board's inaugural Master Plan, 1944 – "Yorkville Area Redevelopment Model" with a "Cross Town Limited Access Highway."

In addition the plan provided for a network of "superhighways" or limited access expressways to speed automobiles through and around the city. These projects, each delineated by letter, proved to be the most lasting legacy of the plan, and most of them would ultimately be built. Superhighway A would cross the waterfront to link up the Queen Elizabeth Way from Niagara and Hamilton to the Kingston Road and the lakeshore in the city's eastern suburbs (eventually the Gardiner Expressway and the unbuilt Scarborough Expressway). Route B would run north from A near the grounds of the Canadian National Exhibition to connect with a new provincial roadway (Highway 400) stretching towards Barrie (the unbuilt Christie-Grace Expressway), while C would run through the east end to link up with another new provincial route northeast to Peterborough and Ottawa (the Don Valley Parkway). Bypass D would cross through the city's northern suburbs from Highland Creek on the eastern lakeshore to join at the west with a new provincial highway running down through southwestern Ontario through Guelph to Galt and Kitchener (Highway 401). Most disruptive to the existing urban fabric would be a roadway cutting through dense neighbourhoods like Yorkville along a line just north Bloor Street (the unbuilt Crosstown Expressway). The result would be a central city enclosed within a box of high speed, limited access roads.

Proposals for beautification of the city included in earlier plans were also repeated, in particular for a civic square surrounded by government buildings located northwest of Queen and Bay Streets. Stemming from the 1934 Bruce Report came the idea of acquiring the blighted area between Parliament and

River Streets south of Gerrard for demolition and redevelopment as a major public housing complex. The Civic Guild's 1911 plan of a ribbon of parkland around the perimeter of the old city, linking up lands in the valleys of the Humber along Black Creek and the Don, was revived. Through these ravine lands, reserved from building to the tops of their slopes, could flow a parkway, designed not as an expressway but to permit visitors access to green space and to the smaller intersecting ravines as well. Outside the built-up area a broad band of agricultural land surrounding the one hundred square mile core should be reserved as a permanent greenbelt, so that subdividers did not create something "little better than a desert of weeds" in the suburbs as they waited for the moment to develop their lands.

The Planning Board also recommended that the comprehensive zoning bylaw be adopted as a necessary basis for future development (though suggesting some fifty minor amendments). The planners observed that historically in central Toronto neighbourhoods had begun to decline once they were about three-quarters built up. Thereafter, as buildings outlived their original uses or were permitted to deteriorate, land values began to drop. Without zoning, a mixture of uses proliferated with unfavourable results as industrial activities penetrated into residential neighbourhoods. South of College Street, in the central city, mortgage lenders had proven unwilling to provide funds for house construction. Careful zoning and planning could encourage redevelopment at the same standard as in the newer suburbs, which would also maintain tax revenues for the city. That did not mean eliminating industrial activities downtown and might even see some expansion so that workers need not travel long distances to their jobs.

The RAIC *Journal* devoted an entire issue to "Toronto and Its Master Plan, 1943," prepared by architect Anthony Adamson and planner Eugene Faludi.[18] After describing the history of attempts at planning in the city, the authors explained the "Chief Reasons Why Toronto Was Convinced of Need for Planning." The downtown area was in decline as municipal assessments had fallen significantly during the depressed 1930s. Only along Front Street near the new Union Station were there buildings of architectural importance; elsewhere "ugliness is a symptom of decay." Existing traffic problems were being exacerbated by the lack of good north–south arterial roads, and the presence of trolleys on many major thoroughfares was slowing travel to a crawl and driving motorists to seek alternative routes. Construction of a subway under Yonge Street was therefore of prime importance.

Planning was seen as essential to peacetime reconstruction. Civilian economic growth would resume, bringing with it a shift in population, as "Toronto citizens are deserting considerable areas within their city to live in outlying municipalities." While the suburbs were growing rapidly, the inner city was already in decline with 13 percent of houses needing external repair and 12.5 percent being overcrowded. Yet suburban developments were going ahead unplanned, leap-frogging one another into surrounding rural areas without any coordination, leaving gaps in the countryside and creating "serious public concern."

In "A Criticism" of the master plan Anthony Adamson applauded the work undertaken, though expressed fears that the lack of public participation in the process might hamper it from gaining wide acceptance. His principal concern was that the planners had been too conservative in their estimates of postwar population growth. The plan, he said, seemed to echo many local architects who shared the views of people like the prominent American critic Lewis Mumford that the quality of life inevitably declined as cities grew ever larger. But nothing could stop the rise in population and employment that Adamson believed was likely to occur once peace and prosperity returned. The idea of a greenbelt was highly desirable, and within it there was still plenty of undeveloped land. He noted presciently that the network of expressways proposed would make travel so quick and easy that commuters would prefer to locate as far away as Oakville (near where Adamson himself lived). On balance, however, he applauded the "wonderful possibilities" of the plan for which the Planning Board was to be highly praised.

As the members of the Civic Guild had learned, making plans was one thing, seeing them implemented quite another. After all this bureaucratic activity the city solicitor reported that it was doubtful that Toronto possessed the legal authority to enact a comprehensive zoning bylaw. Though council went ahead and passed such a measure in December 1944, no steps were taken to bring it into force. Provincial legislation would be required to impose the zoning code and to give the master plan the force of law, and this was not forthcoming until 1946.

Once peace returned the city began to take action where it possessed legal authority. The Toronto Transportation Commission was eager to begin construction of the Yonge Street subway, since it had a large reserve fund on hand and expected that the federal government would meet 20 percent of the capital cost. At the municipal election in January 1946, the ratepayers approved funding for the subway by a majority of almost ten to one. Ground was broken in 1949 and the line opened with great fanfare in 1954.[19]

Meanwhile, the TTC tried to improve its service by establishing improved bus service, sometimes through its wholly owned subsidiary, Gray Coach Lines. As early as 1944 a new downtown bus terminal for commuters was planned near the corner of Adelaide and Yonge Streets. When it opened in 1947 this building featured a striking Modern design with a glass cube for

4.7 (Left)
TTC Adelaide Coach Terminal, John B. Parkin Associates, 1947.

4.8 (Right)
TTC Adelaide Coach Terminal.

a waiting room and a wide, flat, cantilevered concrete roof overhanging the platform from which the letters TTC were suspended in dramatic form. This structure offered downtown office workers express service to various outlying points where similar (though less dramatic) terminals were also constructed. The Adelaide bus station was far-and-away the most avant-garde structure in Toronto in the immediate postwar era, its Modern lines making it look twenty years ahead of its time, though it was soon demolished and thoroughly forgotten. This building was commissioned by an otherwise fairly conservative municipal agency, but the designer chosen, John B. Parkin, was one of the very small number of Canadian architects who had studied Modern ideas in Europe before the war. After taking his architectural degree at the University of Toronto in 1935 he went to London to work in the office of Howard and Souster. With his bus terminal design Parkin certainly lived up to his Modernist pedigree.[20]

Parkin's firm also received the commission to design the stations on the new Yonge Street subway line. When they opened in 1954, these stations were of more utilitarian design than the bus terminal, their walls clad in glazed porcelain tiles in the muted pastel shades like green and yellow (that were to become the height of fashion in kitchen appliances during the 1950s) highly durable, easy to clean, and graffiti-resistant. Careful experiments were carried out, including the creation of full-scale mockups of a station and its newsstand. More striking in a Modernist vein were some of the ground-level entrance pavilions like the one at Davisville Avenue where the TTC also located its much more sober-sided headquarters building. Yet the transit commission received little notice for its rather advanced design ideas as the public preferred to focus upon the novelty of riding the new red cars intended to reduce severe traffic congestion along the tram line on Yonge Street.

After peacetime returned, attention also began to be paid to the severe shortage of low-cost housing. The Citizens' Housing and Planning Association, founded by representatives of a number of social welfare organizations, began lobbying strongly for action. Moss Park, a six-block area of over forty acres bounded by Parliament, Gerrard, Dundas, and River Streets, was identified in the master plan as an area for "slum clearance." Tracy leMay thought that acquiring and demolishing all the dilapidated structures in area was "in line with what appears to be the best planning policy for both the city and its suburbs, namely the limitation of further urbanization of rural lands outside the city and better economic and social use of the older residential areas within the city."[21] In the autumn of 1946 the mayor and Board of Control somewhat reluctantly agreed to endorse the construction of new housing in Regent Park at a cost of $5.9 million. The ratepayers gave their approval in January 1947 by a vote of 29,677 to 18,028, and the Housing Authority of Toronto was created to undertake the task. The buildings, however, were rather plain low-rise brick boxes, which had little claim to architectural distinction, although the interior streets in the redevelopment were erased and replaced with communal open space in keeping with Modernist dogmas concerning urban planning.[22]

4.9 (Top)
TTC subway, full-scale station mock-up, John B. Parkin Associates, 1954.

4.10 (Bottom)
TTC subway, mock-up of newsstand. The leftmost figures are mirror images of the men in front.

In 1946 the provincial legislature finally passed a new Planning Act that granted statutory authority for municipalities wishing to establish local planning boards composed of residents and elected officials. An official plan could then be submitted to the Community

4.11
TTC subway, Davisville Station, John B. Parkin Associates, 1954.

Planning Branch of the Ministry of Planning for approval as legally binding. The legislation did not, however, specify the purposes for which planning should be undertaken, and there was little detail about the contents of official plans beyond general references to land use, municipal services, communications, and drainage. Municipalities were permitted to freeze lands for future development by designating properties as urban development areas and referring a plan to the ministry. Such lands could later be released from these controls bit by bit as applications for subdivision were received. Section 23 of the act therefore became a key tool in planning greater Toronto in the postwar era by preventing piecemeal development in the suburbs.[23] LeMay made an effort to include the authority under official plans to impose formal design controls on new buildings, but he was not successful.[24]

The Municipal Act was also amended in 1946 to establish the authority of local governments to impose comprehensive zoning. The planners had hoped that all land use regulations would be included in the Official Plan, but the city solicitor, obedient to the wish of councillors to retain control over zoning, concluded that detailed zoning bylaws could be kept separate. The provincial government (well-stocked with former municipal politicians) accepted this division of responsibilities. Zoning bylaws could even be amended without requiring the endorsement of the Planning Board, though changes required the approval of the Ontario Municipal Board, which was mandated to hold hearings unless there were no objections.

By that time the need for regional planning in the greater Toronto area was already clearly evident. Eugene Faludi, a European-trained architect and planner who had fled from fascist Italy to Canada before the Second World War, was a keen promoter of such ideas, and he pointed out a number of important assumptions that underlay the 1943 plan. A decision had been

24 CANADIAN HOMES & GARDENS, JANUARY-FEBRUARY, 1944

PLANNING

The Community

by E. G. Faludi, Manager, Toronto Planning Board

Many signs encourage us to hope for a bright tomorrow. Because in the past living conditions did not keep pace with social and scientific progress, nearly all Canadian cities and towns have problems that now call for urgent solution.

Residential districts have gradually deteriorated. Downtown properties are often depressed because revenue from them is barely enough to pay taxes. New construction has been discouraged. Blighted areas, slums, lack of open space, traffic congestion are other problems.

Outgrowing their compact character, cities sprawl out in all directions at the expense of beauty and efficiency. Suburbs have haphazardly evolved on the circumference in natural reaction to overcrowding of central areas. But they reproduce the bad features of urban life.

Shall we abandon existing cities and build new communities elsewhere? This proposal is not always practical. We must first consider rebuilding our cities in such a way that they will supply the fundamentals for a healthy community life.

What are these fundamentals? For the people there must be work with adequate pay. Their houses must be comfortable, soundly designed and situated in pleasant residential areas, properly located in relation to shops, schools, cultural and recreational centres.

Commercial and industrial districts should be separated from residential neighborhoods by playing grounds and green spaces available to both residential dwellers and workers in offices and factories. Speedy, inexpensive transportation must be provided between work and home.

The Neighborhood

by G. S. Mooney, Director, Montreal Economic Bureau

Most Canadians are street and number dwellers. We live in wards and districts: few live in neighborhoods.

A neighborhood connotes a social community. It is an area set aside for living; where dwellings of the people are grouped so that necessary adjuncts of family functional life—schools, churches, play-parks, shopping marts and the like—form an integral part of the whole.

To most of us our neighborhood begins and ends with the distance between our doorstep and the tram line.

It is not that we will it that way. But the gridiron pattern in which most cities and towns are laid out negates neighborhood planning. It forces us to regiment housing, row-on-row, and to crowd it on the land.

To make neighborhood living the rule rather than the exception we must begin with the site. Dirt, smoke, noise; smell from nearby factories or railway lines are incipient causes of most urban blight. Likewise, a busy trafficway or converging network of arterial roads is a poor location for a residential neighborhood.

Within the neighborhood, each dwelling should be orientated to obtain maximum sunlight. Dwellings should be well spaced and have ample front lawns. Sun porches and living rooms should have access to view and open space.

The route to school, playground and local stores should be so planned as to eliminate crossing street traffic.

Compact neighborhood planning of this description will facilitate commercial deliveries to homes, enable central heating, reduce local street paving, effect economy of services and maintenance, permit community landscaping, and generally add to the dignity and efficiency of living.

The Dwelling

by E. R. Arthur, Professor of Architecture, Toronto

The modern movement in domestic architecture has hardly touched Canada. In the past, through carefully organized campaigns the public has been sold Tudor, Cape Cod and Georgian dwellings.

Elsewhere a different sort of house has been evolving. It is a house designed to be lived in and enjoyed. Each of the historic periods produced a fine domestic architecture, but represented a mode of life as different from each other as ours is from theirs. The one point they had in common was the employment of numerous servants. On the other hand, we see today the gradual replacement of numerous servants by robots of one kind or another. The modern plan must be simplified, not only for the housewife, but for construction. On the building industry nearly all our plans for reconstruction rest. Former methods must of necessity give way to prefabrication of cottages and apartment houses alike. In the small and medium house class, living and dining rooms will undoubtedly become one. Laundry rooms will come upstairs; only a fraction of the basement will be excavated.

One of our great postwar problems will be to halt the creeping barrage of cottages and bungalows on the fringes of our cities. We shall, I hope, build houses in groups of three, five or even more in the interests of economy and decent street design. The lure of heating from central plants, which will govern all our postwar housing, may break down that "rugged individualism" which makes a hodge-podge of every Canadian residential area. Where lures fail, there will be mandatory town-planning requirements and a rising tide of informed public opinion.

4.12
"Planning": a one-page, three-part, three-expert promotion of modern planning in a 1944 issue of *Canadian Homes and Gardens*, including the views of Eugene Faludi and Eric Arthur.

taken about the optimal size for the city, and beyond those limits a greenbelt would be set aside to contain urban sprawl. Additional population would be accommodated beyond this barrier in largely self-contained suburban communities with their own commercial and industrial establishments to provide employment. In the absence of such planning, Faludi complained, residential suburbs had already sprung up far beyond the city limits, in "dismal rows of unsightly, identical little box-like houses … like Eskimo villages unconnected

4.13
Model of Thorncrest Village, Planning Consultants (Eugene Faludi), 1945.

with the rest of the world," where dreary layouts faced onto streets leading from "nowhere to nowhere."[25]

In 1945 Faludi was offered the chance to put some of his theories into practice by laying out the planned community of Thorncrest Village on one hundred acres of farmland between Islington and Kipling Avenues in suburban Etobicoke. Fifteen percent of the area was left as open space, 4 percent for a small shopping centre at the southeast corner, the remainder laid out as 180 three-quarter acre lots on winding streets, which permitted the houses to be sited in desirable locations such as knolls with views southward to Lake Ontario. Frontages between seventy-five and one hundred feet (versus about forty feet in the city) would suit homes of modern design. Every homeowner would possess a car, a major selling point being that residents would be a mere twenty minute drive from downtown Toronto. Off-street parking would be provided in every block for delivery trucks and visitors' automobiles so as not to clutter up the streetscape. With a recreation centre in its midst, this "country-club-type of community," with all commercial activities pushed to the outer perimeters, was presented by Faludi not as the product of "snobbism" or a "class-conscious effort to be exclusive" but an attempt to prevent the future declines in property values common to ordinary suburban developments.[26]

Five years later Faludi confessed to his fellow planners that Thorncrest Village had not been as successful as anticipated. The development "looked too radical to make it acceptable to realtors, mortgage investors, municipal engineers, councillors." Real estate agents disliked the houses constructed on pads without basements, while mortgage lenders thought the development charges would make houses too costly. The engineers opposed the curving streets and dead-ends, while local politicians feared that the residents might be "morally unstable." Prospective buyers complained about south-facing living rooms that turned their backs on the streets as well as the upkeep costs of frills like the community centre. By 1950 only half the houses had been built and sold mainly to relatively prosperous people whose incomes averaged between $6,000 and $10,000. Faludi complained that without the kind of backing from government that new towns were receiving in Britain, municipalities seemed to prefer "ordinary" subdivisions where lots or houses were disposed of one-by-one. Rather disingenuously, Faludi admitted that, "We obviously failed in assuming and undertaking to build a community of all income classes. We succeeded in building one for a privileged group."[27]

Toronto city council moved quickly to appoint a Planning Board. In its first annual report issued in December 1947 the board declared that land use planning was now critical because most of the residential areas in the southern part of downtown were declining or blighted if not already slums. In an effort to create a sense of urgency the report made the far-fetched suggestion that even the most desirable parts of the north centre of town were now showing themselves vulnerable to deterioration, so that the need to encourage redevelopment was becoming more and more urgent.[28]

The city planning staff set to work developing an Official Plan. LeMay remained optimistic: "Generally speaking planning is on the upsurge in this area."[29] When the Planning Board published its report in mid-1949, chair J.P. Maher was careful to emphasize that the objectives were not too ambitious to be acceptable to the public. The document aimed at the "practical rather than ideal" because "arbitrary adherence to planning ideals would, in the opinion of the board, almost inevitably add to the list of the many plans in this and other cities that have failed." The recommendations were largely a "compilation" of earlier Planning Board reports.[30]

Thirteen land use maps delineated residential, commercial, and industrial areas. The planners concluded that the downtown south of Queen Street between the Don River and Dufferin Street already contained enterprises that required too many employees for all of them to be housed inside the city proper, though it opposed the expansion of industrial activities north of Queen. As a result some workers would have to commute to their jobs from the suburbs. Toronto was expected to mirror other North American cities where traffic volumes were predicted to double over the next decade (with particularly large increases in truck registrations), so the highest priority must be given to new north–south arterial roads that served the entire metropolitan area. The report ticked off the key projects required: the "superhighways" of the 1943 plan, a waterfront expressway from the Humber eastward to the mouth of the Don, a road up the Don valley to provide better access to the northeast and northwest. A new idea (which was to prove very long-lived) was the extension of Spadina Avenue north beyond St Clair through the Nordheimer Ravine to link with the provincial bypass road (Highway 401). These projects were carefully costed along with road widenings and railway underpasses on existing north–south routes, as well as new parks and squares.

The local Bureau of Municipal Research received the Official Plan's publication with muted enthusiasm, noting that of the half dozen plans produced over the previous forty-odd years this document was far from the boldest or most original. Yet for that reason it might stand a better chance of adoption. Too much time had already been wasted on piecemeal projects. Surely, said the bureau, city council would hesitate to refuse approval to this modest blueprint that included so much that had been previously recommended.[31]

That prediction proved accurate. In November 1949 city council approved the plan with only minor amendments. The Planning Board accepted these changes, and the Official Plan was endorsed by the aldermen on 1 May 1950. With the formal approval of Ontario's Planning Minister William Griesinger, the plan took effect in August. In future, amendments to the Official Plan made by council required the consent of the minister and would involve hearings before the Ontario Municipal Board.[32] Though the Official Plan was complete by 1950, it would take four more years before its provisions took full effect.

Unless paired with a comprehensive zoning code, the Official Plan remained largely toothless. Tracy leMay insisted that the objective remained simply to stabilize existing conditions and prevent deterioration while promoting a few desirable changes. By mid-1951 the Planning Board had prepared a draft bylaw. Zoning was declared "simply a more detailed treatment of the general land use policy established by the Official Plan." The planners contended that, "It needs no argument to prove that selfish or speculative interests in individual parcels of land can destroy the amenities of residential areas, and produce a heterogeneous mixture of conflicting uses that not only depresses land values but also paves the way for the destruction of moral and social values through the depreciation of the home. Security is the right of every property owner against a devaluating effect of some use of adjoining property which is inconsistent with the character of the area." The bylaw would not provide for "drastic changes in existing land use based upon an idealistic land use pattern," because in a fully built-up city such "theoretical" zoning would annoy many property owners. Rather it should be a catalogue of existing uses to create "the best possible living conditions" by preventing the incursion of non-conforming uses causing the deterioration of neighbourhoods. In addition, regulations would be imposed regarding the height, size, and setback of new buildings in order to control density and make them compatible with existing structures.[33]

The new law divided the city into the eight zones originally proposed in 1937, four residential and four commercial. R.1 areas would be restricted to single-family detached houses, while R.2 zones might also have semi-detached and duplex buildings. R.3 areas could include rooming houses and R.4 apartment buildings.[34] Offices and commercial outlets were to be zoned C.1, while C.2 could contain light industry, C.3 accommodated heavy industry, and C.4 was unrestricted. Streets, parks, and railway lands were classified as "other."

Opposition to concentrated clusters of skyscrapers downtown continued because leMay remained convinced that closely packed office towers contributed heavily to traffic congestion. Rather than fixed height or setback rules, the new zoning law established a new Floor Space Index (FSI), which proposed to limit total floor area in such high-rises to a maximum of nine times their lot area. Thus an eighteen-storey building could occupy only one-half its property, and as leMay told the press, "then we will have space on the ground for parking."[35]

The Board of Trade endorsed zoning in principle as an "integral part of civic planning" but insisted that greater density in downtown office towers was essential. Objections were also raised to the "unrealistic" requirement that off-street parking be required within five hundred feet of new commercial buildings downtown. City council proved sympathetic to this demand for greater density downtown and raised the maximum FSI from nine to twelve.[36]

Council passed bylaw 18642 in June 1952 with the proviso that it not come into force for one year. A series of twenty-one public meetings did not attract a great deal of interest from the public. LeMay was not surprised: "Since a zoning bylaw for a completely built-up city must largely be a classification of existing land uses, many owners are not disturbed by the terms of the bylaw with the result that attendance at the meetings has averaged less than 10% of the owners entitled to be present."[37] The Property Committee of city council also heard further representations, but eventually approved only minor revisions and sent the measure to the full council in the spring of 1953, which passed bylaw 18878.[38]

As required the two bylaws (18642 as amended by 18878) were then submitted jointly to the Ontario Municipal Board (OMB) for approval. Hearings were held in June and July 1953 for each ward in the city. Organized interest groups naturally made certain that their concerns were again presented at the

OMB. The Board of Trade crowd repeated the prediction that limiting the density of downtown office towers too much would spell the "death knell" for new developments. Tracy leMay stuck to his long-held conviction that "zoning, in brief, is the control of the use of land insofar as it affects the general welfare of the community, and I do not know of anything which has a greater or more widespread influence on community life than congestion arising from too great a density of occupation." He pointed out that with the exception of a few small areas even midtown Manhattan limited office building densities to twelve times coverage. Because the cost of street widenings was prohibitive, the only way to control increasing traffic congestion (which would eventually undermine land values) was to limit the size of office developments.[39]

The final OMB decision was rendered in January 1954. The maximum FSI of twelve was approved, and the board ordered only a few changes in the proposed law. Apartment developers had objected vehemently to the fixing of minimum unit sizes in R.1A and R.2 zones at nine hundred square feet, and the board met these complaints by requiring only that units in a building should average nine hundred square feet, which would permit builders to offer a variety of sizes if they wished. Otherwise, the new regulations were approved by the OMB with only minor alterations. City council accepted the changes in March 1954 in bylaw 19093, which finally brought the whole code into force.[40]

The decade-long process of creating and passing Toronto's Official Plan and comprehensive zoning bylaw established ground rules as to what kinds of buildings could be constructed and where. In theory these rules specified precisely what property owners would be permitted to do. Yet builders and developers remained convinced that changes in land uses and density rules ought to be permitted. City politicians were determined to reserve to themselves the power to rezone. Municipal officials also came to see the value of rezoning requests in creating leverage to control site plans and even the external appearance of buildings. Where objections were registered zoning changes and Official Plan amendments required approval from the Ontario Municipal Board, which often meant expensive and time-consuming hearings. By separating zoning from planning and leaving future zoning changes to the elected politicians, the system created enough administrative complexity that both builders and planners soon came to see the advantage in avoiding Official Plan changes in favour of ad hoc responses through rezonings.[41]

The effect of the Official Plan and the attendant zoning code upon the city's built environment proved to be significant. For instance, the system of expressways that was envisaged had an important impact upon the location of commercial concentrations like shopping centres, which would often be located where two such roadways intersected. The zoning code largely excluded high-rise apartment towers from existing residential neighbourhoods so that they were mainly located along arterial roads. The construction of Toronto's subway system also led to nodes of new commercial and apartment development around the principal underground stations, such as the corner of Yonge and Eglinton. The effect of the new zoning regulations upon individual buildings was not so easy to discern, but once architects and builders grasped the density rules and height limitations various kinds of structures came to be favoured. (For instance, the broad slab tower became the favoured layout for high-rise apartment buildings.) Overall, the planning and zoning rules (and the requests for rezonings) became critical as wider urban planning issues were largely overlooked.

III

Architects anticipated that the return of peace in 1945 would mean plenty of work. Canada was estimated to require at least half a million new houses over the next few years. Promoters of Modernism revived the claim that a new age of design had dawned. Canadian universities had incorporated such ideas into their curricula over the past decade. Faculty and students now were expected to be familiar with the ideas of Le Corbusier, Oud, and Gropius, and books like Sigfried Giedion's *Space, Time and Architecture* (1941) came to enjoy great influence. In 1945 Kent Barker, who had won a gold medal at the University of Toronto and gone off to do post-graduate study at the Cranbrook Academy with the distinguished Modernist Eliel Saarinen, opined that it would be hard even to find a young graduate to design a Tudor-style or Georgian house. He admitted that competition entries were always two jumps ahead of finished work, but in time builders would catch up. American Ralph Walker told the 1946 annual meeting of the Ontario Association of Architects that there had been a radical revolution between the wars which had knocked off the "taste-barnacles" of the past; younger people now accepted the new principles so thoroughly that even they risked becoming clichés.[42]

The recently appointed architectural editor of *Canadian Homes and Gardens* laid out "A Case For Modern." John Caulfield Smith expressed wonderment that people who insisted on the most up-to-date design for their automobiles would still accept reproductions of historical styles for homes. Yet many architects were content to continue copying the past, except for the few trying to be truly avant-garde. So far only a few clichés like flat roofs and corner windows had penetrated into domestic architecture. Smith admitted that the early Modern radicals had sometimes created cold and barren surroundings, but there was no reason that present-day homes should not look different to reflect changes in lifestyles. Even Smith's somewhat tepid endorsement was cast into doubt by the next page in the same issue of the magazine that pictured N.A. Armstrong's Colonial Revival layout for a house in Port Credit just west of Toronto.[43]

Even an architect as successful as John B. Parkin had to earn his keep by designing a Georgian house for a wealthy family in the Toronto suburb of Forest Hill. He specified traditional materials but treated the openings in a watered-down moderne manner with a front door made of patterned glass set in a metal frame. Inside, the lighting was indirect or concealed, and the fake beams in the recreation room (a novel appurtenance) were actually air conditioning ducts.[44] As Eric Arthur put it, visitors to Toronto could still be taken to Forest Hill Village "where the authorities discourage houses of other than period design. Tudor, for a time, was de rigueur. For our part, we always take visiting architects to the Royal Ontario Museum, though our technique may change when we can take them for a ride in the underground [subway]."[45]

4.14
Sunnylea School, John B. Parkin Associates, 1946.

In 1947 Arthur concluded that the only region of Canada where "a fully fledged modern movement" had emerged was British Columbia. Far west across the Rocky Mountains that province had always maintained cultural links southward. In California European émigrés like Richard Neutra and Rudolf Schindler had long been working to create a distinctive local variant of Modernism based upon the extensive use of timber framing and glass, and these influences, mixed with ideas brought directly from Britain by a small number of immigrants, eventually coalesced into a "West Coast style."[46] Climate, weather, and topography along with use of native woods produced something distinctive. Local architects, said Arthur, had worked to demonstrate that "the modern house is the only house for a modern family in British Columbia. Nowhere else in Canada has that proof been given."[47] It remained unclear whether these ideas would spread eastward.

Institutional clients sometimes proved more willing than nervous homeowners to accept

4.15 (Top)
Leaside High School, S.B. Coon and Son, 1946.

4.16 (Bottom)
Centennial Road School, Murray Brown and Elton, 1946.

progressive ideas, at least in small doses. During the war architects had begun to anticipate the possibilities of the many jobs that would await them with the return of peace. In the fall of 1942 John B. Parkin predicted in the RAIC *Journal* a vast peacetime school-building program. The following year he demanded that school design be freed from the dead hand of the pseudo-Gothic or the imitation Georgian. He presented a design for Sunnylea School in Toronto. Though less avant-garde than the bus terminal he designed at the same time, the design was intended to show the flexibility of an open-plan layout using new materials like reinforced concrete and steel where few supporting columns were necessary and entire walls could be made of glass.[48]

Once peace did return, new school construction boomed as suburban housing for young families proliferated. In the autumn 1947 issue of the RAIC *Journal* Eric Arthur noted that for generations school design had been bedevilled by boards of education replicating stock plans that confined pupils behind the drab walls and small windows of three- and four-storey fortresses of learning. Such layouts assumed an invariable climate, a level site, and unchanging teaching methods, but with Canada needing scores of new schools the time had come to search for more inspired ideas. Some elements of Modernism like horizontal layouts and large expanses of glass began to

4.17
G.H. Locke Library, Beck and Eadie, 1949.

establish a foothold. Alongside Parkin's Sunnylea School the *Journal* presented photographs and plans for other new Toronto-area schools like Leaside High School by S.B. Coon and Son and Scarborough's Centennial Road School by Murray Brown and Elton. Wrote Arthur, "Probably the greatest victory for modern architecture in Canada has been in the field of school building."[49]

In 1950 John B. Parkin's firm was awarded the overall gold medal in the Massey Foundation's first competition for the excellence of its design for a high school in the city of Oshawa, just east of Toronto. The jury noted that the building evidenced advances in school design in Canada,[50] as the architect "shows the liberation of his art from the stylistic conventions which have prevented in the past the free adaptation of his forms to the many complex activities of the modern school." The result was a building that broke from the traditional mould while remaining both simple and dignified.[51]

Library boards formed another group of institutional clients that might show some sympathy for innovative design. In 1947 Eric Arthur observed that old libraries seemed to him "pretentious, monumental, grimly classical, and forbidding," apparently designed to keep the sunlight away from first editions preserved for bibliophiles. "The past presents little of constructive value, but much in how libraries should not be planned." Yet there were hopeful signs. Young architects, he said, were often discouraged by the slowness with which innovations were accepted by the public, but "in library design the campaign has been in the opposite direction with librarians pleading for modern buildings." As a sign of progress, the RAIC *Journal* presented plans for new libraries such as the George H. Locke branch of the Toronto system at the corner of Yonge Street and Lawrence Avenue by Beck and Eadie with moderne details like a horizontal layout and floor-to-ceiling bay windows with a clerestory lighting the stack area.[52] But library commissions did not prove all that numerous.

Would the University of Toronto become a patron of avant-garde architecture once peace returned and enrollment shot upward? Few buildings at the university had been constructed in the interwar period, and they hewed to the administration's 1920 decision that all structures on the southern and western edges of the campus facing onto College and St George Streets should be "Georgian in character." Mathers and Haldenby, who became the university architects of choice, followed this mandate for the 1926 Hygiene and the 1931 Botany Buildings on College Street and for the Whitney Hall residence (1931) at Harbord and St George Streets. After the Second World War the same firm produced the Georgian Sir Daniel Wilson residence (1954) just to the south of Whitney Hall, while Page and Steele turned out the Wallberg Chemical Building (1949) on College Street, a piece of stripped-down Georgian.[53]

In the classroom Eric Arthur now preached the gospel of Modernism.[54] When architecture students began classes in the autumn of 1940, he declared, "The absence of both modern architecture (at any rate as a movement) and of housing in Canada is clear to every intelligent schoolboy, and he enters his first year [of university] with all the zeal of a missionary. If he finds his view shared by both staff and students, his ardour grows until by his fourth year he becomes quite fanatical ... One did not dare mention it in the pacifist days between one war and another, but the last war opened our eyes to the possibilities of new and exciting materials and the birth of modern architecture was not unconnected with it." A decade later, as the first postwar class of students bolstered in size by returning veterans was about to graduate, Arthur predicted that their effect upon the profession would be like "a high explosive bomb": "They will condemn romanticism in all its forms as anachronistic and timid to a degree, and they will practice it for their employers only under dire economic stress ... They will dilate on the wonders in construction of the twentieth century. They will inwardly burn (and perhaps outwardly rebel) if they are asked to conceal these wonderments in the habiliments of the age of chivalry or of eighteenth century pageantry."[55]

The students were obviously paying attention. In 1948 the annual show of work at the School of Architecture relayed a blunt message summed up by John Beckwith in the student newspaper as follows: "Toronto has no architecture and that the only distinctive aspect of her public buildings is their incomparably hybrid styles." Beckwith thought the photographs of reputed local gems showed they were really eyesores; this message appeared so persuasive that by the time he reached a picture of the Victoria College's Richardsonian Romanesque pile, "it needed no caption to make me guffaw openly that such a monstrosity should have been thought worthy of preservation in any era." The students' manifesto proclaimed that, "The principal object of the School's missionary zeal was an unduly listless university population whose callous indifference to the logic and beauty of modern architecture has long been a source of serious frustration." Their slogan was "MODERN ARCHITECTURE OFFERS AN ENVIRONMENT, HEALTHY, BEAUTIFUL AND STIMULATING. ITS PROGRESS AND ACCEPTANCE DEPENDS UPON YOU." Particular scorn was directed at the university's own buildings with "several volleys at the architectural anachronism of this campus" presented alongside proposals for improvements.[56]

Arthur might be teaching his students about Modern design with the help of younger enthusiasts amongst his instructors like James Murray and Henry Fliess, but the university's central administration was not willing to let any of them actually design buildings for it. Arthur was only allowed to head a 1949 committee on campus expansion; the committee was composed of his erstwhile partner in architectural practice, Anthony Adamson, along with Murray, but to keep things under control A.S. Mathers was also included. Their report concluded that new construction should move west of St George Street towards Spadina Avenue but remain south of Bloor Street because property in that area would be less expensive.[57]

All that Arthur could do was carp about the university's backwardness in his editorials in the RAIC *Journal*. He drew what comfort he could from the fact that at least the buildings featured some diversity of style and did not suffer from the tedious uniformity of Collegiate Gothic (like Yale) or Georgian Revival (like Harvard). Fortunately, he said, there had not been much new construction between the two wars. Arthur was forced to admit that the "one really offensive building" was the School of Practical Science (1878), home of the Engineering Faculty and hence of the School of Architecture since 1890.[58] This structure, he said, reflected the worst excesses of the Industrial Revolution though it lacked even the typical Victorian virtue of solidity. In 1953 Arthur expressed the hope that new buildings might soon explode the notion that the university's physical plant reflected the conservative taste of its board of governors, and that architects could celebrate that no more Neo-Gothic or Romanesque designs would be required.[59]

4.18
University of Toronto Mechanical Engineering Building, Allward and Gouinlock, 1948.

The most venturesome piece of design at the University of Toronto in the immediate postwar years was the Mechanical Engineering Building at the south side of the campus, which opened in 1948. Architect Richard Fisher pointed out that universities everywhere faced problems in deciding upon the design of new buildings as they struggled to outgrow the straitjacket of Gothic or Georgian. The large spaces required to house laboratories, shops, and offices as well as lecture halls for engineering students seemed to demand a functional layout that could be altered or adapted for future needs. Allward and Gouinlock produced a design, which the university's architectural historian claims as "one of Toronto's most significant mid-twentieth century modern buildings, showing influences of both the German Bauhaus school and the Dutch de Stijl movement."[60] In truth, the starkly plain layout with its strip and corner windows let into a smooth limestone facade does not seem much of an advance upon the Stripped Classicism that the federal Post Office Department had adopted in the 1930s for its outlets like the 1936–37 Postal Station K on Yonge Street north of Eglinton or the 1939–40 City Delivery Building on Queen's Quay.[61] Still, for the university, the Mechanical Engineering Building did represent something of a departure.

The only really Modern structure erected by the University of Toronto before the 1960s was very small yet sufficiently unusual to attract attention from as far away as Montreal. In 1948, in a piece in the RAIC *Journal*, Campbell Merrett advised his fellow Quebec architects that while their home turf might not have much to offer enthusiasts for the Modern, there was one bright spot in Toronto, a "refreshing" new bookstore designed by James Murray right in the centre of the University of Toronto campus. It must have taken a bit of salesmanship to persuade university officials to accept the

4.19
University of Toronto Bookstore, James Murray, 1948.

design, said Merrett, but it seemed to suggest some open-mindedness amongst the administrators. He expressed the hope that architects might finally persuade the public to appreciate the virtues of contemporary design and not buckle under so readily to the reactionary tastes of many Canadian clients.[62]

In an editorial in the same issue of the RAIC *Journal* Eric Arthur described the campus as "agog" about the new bookstore, small as it might be. The university's Board of Governors had shown courage in approving it even though it was only intended as a temporary structure. The ancients among the professoriate would doubtless find its horizontal lines and flat roof jarring, but framed against the Norman bulk of University College and the Gothic pinnacles of Hart House it might actually stimulate ideas amongst the undergraduates in the "abbey cum fortress" of the university's main library nearby. Architecture students were bound to be heartened: "There are rumblings in Toronto that presage great things." Later Arthur apparently changed his mind somewhat about the virtues of the little pavilion, noting that while the design was admirable, its siting on a grassy knoll next to the former university observatory, an Italianate building dating from 1855, did not fit well with the vistas east from University College and south from Hart House.[63] Never intended to be permanent and soon long gone and forgotten, it is hard to judge exactly what, if any, impact this bookstore had upon students and administrators.[64] For the next decade the university stuck to its conservative ways in commissioning new buildings.

Industrial clients sometimes showed a willingness to commission buildings that moved away from historical styles in the interests of functional efficiency. In 1940 A.S. Mathers told the convention of the Ontario Association of Real Estate Boards that, "Generally speaking, advances made in building construction techniques have been greatest in the industrial field. There, with no inhibitions regarding architectural styles and precedent, the architect has solved the industrialists' practical problems by a direct application of sound principles to the problem presented. This has resulted in the development of a technique of new material and new ways of using old ones that have been unacceptable rather than impossible in residential buildings." In this regard Mathers spoke from experience, for he had provided the *Globe and Mail* newspaper with a building on King Street, which featured Stripped Classical touches, highly advanced for Toronto in 1937,[65] and his normally conservative firm also produced a wallpaper plant in Leaside that same year along the lines of Albert Kahn's functionalist automobile factories.[66] Mathers told the real estate men that by now people had become familiar with "the spectacular architecture of commerce": "The skyscraper a thousand feet high and the great industrial buildings have ceased to be more than nine-day wonders … We have created an aesthetic that has little to do with the past." Yet house

4.20
Maclean-Hunter Publishing Company, Allward and Gouinlock, 1948.

4.21
CNE Grandstand, Marani and Morris, 1948.

design remained "largely an exercise in archeology," choosing a style from some historical period.[67]

Once private construction resumed after the war a number of companies commissioned buildings that eschewed overt historicism. For instance, in 1948, the Standard Chemical Company constructed a plant of modernistic appearance designed by Earl Morgan, and the following year Allward and Gouinlock laid out a large printing plant for the Maclean-Hunter Publishing Company on Yonge Street north of the future route of Highway 401. The plant was a single-floor structure with strip windows in the Modern manner and large open spaces and few interior columns to permit maximum flexibility in siting the presses.[68]

Even a conservative firm like Marani and Morris came up with quite a dramatic layout for a new grandstand at the Canadian National Exhibition. Its twenty-two thousand seats were sheltered from the weather by a cantilevered roof eight hundred feet long, the 120 foot overhang supported only by eight columns located halfway along the open truss beams overhead. People commented on the slenderness of these supports, which permitted largely unobstructed sightlines to the field used for football and other events.[69] Though more an engineering feat than one of design, the grandstand won a silver Massey Medal in the category of recreational buildings in 1950. John B. Parkin's highly successful firm also won two silver Massey Medals in the same year for a moderne factory for Fabergé Perfumes in the Toronto suburb of Etobicoke and for the offices of the York Township Hydro-Electric System on Yonge Street, north of the city.[70] A number of other companies were prepared to follow in these footsteps.[71] Municipalities and governments showed less readiness to experiment. No Massey Medal was awarded in 1950 for buildings in that category because the jury found that the submissions seemed to indicate a confusion between classical conceptions of plan and form with "an anxiety to express contemporary techniques."[72]

4.22
Bank of Nova Scotia, Mathers and Haldenby, 1951.

IV

Two of the biggest building projects in the city after the end of the Second World War symbolized the failure of the Modern movement to make great headway in Toronto. The Bank of Nova Scotia had planned a new building on the northeast corner of King and Bay Streets in the late 1920s and entered into a contract with the prominent architect John Lyle. The stock market crash of 1929 put an end to the project until 1946 when the bank revived the scheme. Beck and Eadie (the successor firm to the office of the now-deceased Lyle) was made a consultant, but Mathers and Haldenby was given the main commission. Lyle's design had faithfully reflected thinking about skyscrapers like those constructed nearby during the 1920s. He produced a design for a twenty-four-storey moderne tower with pier-like buttresses and picturesque setbacks decorated with his favourite Canadian motifs. The Bay Street facade

4.23
Jacobine Jones with one of her Bank of Nova Scotia murals.

included setbacks totalling twenty-five feet while the King Street frontage was to rise sheer from the sidewalk. Mathers and Haldenby retained Lyle's layout but smoothed away some of the moderne flourishes and added sleek vertical piers on the King Street side. Heating, lighting, air conditioning, and underfloor wiring were all replanned to current standards. The twenty-eight storeys of the new tower contained over five hundred thousand square feet of space, making the building the largest in Toronto in the late 1940s; the architects decided to increase its attraction for tenants by providing old-fashioned single windows to light every room separately rather than using more up-to-date continuous sash, which might interfere with the installation of internal partitions. Exterior ornamentation was limited to sculptured panels above the large ground-floor windows of the banking hall on Bay Street, which depicted classical deities in the muscular heroic realism of the 1930s. The main banking hall was decorated with bas reliefs by Jacobine Jones centring upon a fisherman and a schooner, supposedly reflecting the enterprises financed by the bank.[73]

4.24
Bank of Montreal, Chapman and Oxley and Marani and Morris, 1951.

In the late 1930s the Bank of Montreal planned a new office building designed by Chapman and Oxley right across the street on the northwest corner of King and Bay. The basement was excavated and the steel framework for a sixteen-storey tower was being erected when the war broke out. In view of the shortage of construction material, work was soon suspended, and for six long years the metal skeleton stood forlornly. In 1946 work resumed on cladding the framework. Now in charge, Marani and Morris produced a conventional skyscraper with base, shaft, and corniced top, modified from the original design only the elimination of some of the exterior ornamentation except for twelve panels of bas relief designed by six different sculptors to represent Canada's provinces and territories.[74]

These plum commissions by two of the city's conservative old-line firms did not please everyone. In the RAIC *Journal* Stephen Vickers, who taught art history at the University of Toronto, was highly critical of the Bank of Montreal tower. He argued that true Modern architecture emphasized screen and void, wall and window being deliberately thinned out. The application of the sculptured panels demonstrated a failure by Marani and Morris to grasp this fact by suggesting an inappropriate depth to the surface. The bas reliefs on the lower exterior walls seemed to stand out from the neutral surface of the building creating a weight that dragged down upon the structure. Vickers focused particularly upon the "lamentable figure" by Jacobine Jones representing the province of Nova Scotia at the Bank of Montreal, which featured a low relief unbounded by any moulding with a fishing boat appearing to thrust outward from the wall into space. The architects had also featured the kind of distinctive Canadian motifs so much favoured by John Lyle a decade or more earlier, including two wolves baying at the moon, a beaver, and a resplendent skunk. All in all, said Vickers, the architects had created a thoroughly dated cloak for the steelwork.[75]

Kent Barker, another convert to Modernism, was not impressed with either of the bank towers. The architects had simply worked within the rather dated terms of reference presented to them, so the results would "not be

4.25 (Left)
Bank branches 1: Roya
Bank of Canada, Isling
Avenue, E.C.S. Cox,
1950.

4.26 (Right)
Bank branches 2: Bank
Toronto, Warden Aven
Casewin Ltd., 1954.

notable examples of contemporary architecture ... Only too often the architect's best efforts stops at the exterior wall; the site and its location are imposed by economic factors against which he is powerless. Such appears to be the case in these examples." However, Barker skipped away from criticizing the firms involved directly, arguing that "the city planner will not pass this corner without experiencing resentment and dismay. It is so painfully evident that these huge buildings are Things in the Wrong Place. As architecture we may accept them. As planning they are an utter failure."[76] What was surprising is that in the years after 1950 the chartered banks sometimes proved more adventuresome in the designs commissioned for their small branch offices than they did for their flagship headquarters.

Why was there the reluctance to accept the ideas of Modernism? Here Torontonians simply reflected the views of their fellow-Canadians. Harold Kalman observed,

> From the late 1910s to the 1940s Canadian architects strove to develop a "modern" and a "Canadian" architecture, within an established tradition that was highly dependent on past and imported styles. However, rather than choosing a revolutionary denial of the past, as their contemporaries had done in Europe and the United States, Canadian architects adopted a conservative and evolutionary route to modernism, based on the gentle modification of existing practices. In Canada there was no inexorable march to modernism, nor an inevitable triumph of the moderns over the revivalists ... Canadian architects hardly seemed to notice what was happening at the Bauhaus and other hotbeds of international modernism. While searching for new directions most continued to work with traditional forms as they focused on trying to develop a distinctly Canadian architecture.[77]

In 1987 a group of architects styling themselves the Bureau of Architecture and Urbanism (BAU) who were interested in celebrating and preserving notable Modern buildings produced a book entitled *Toronto Modern: Architecture, 1945–1965*. The text and the accompanying timeline revealed that BAU could find precious little unequivocally Modernist building in the city before the mid-1950s.[78] Precisely the same conclusion may be gleaned from *Winnipeg Modern Architecture, 1945–1974*, where Kelly Crossman argues that "the moment when Winnipeg's architectural culture shifted irrevocably towards the modern can be identified quite precisely. In 1951 the Elizabeth Dafoe Library opened its doors to faculty and students at the University of Manitoba." While it had a modern layout the library seems to have been a transitional work with its steel framework clad in Tyndall limestone so as to blend in with the other buildings on campus. The house that architect James Donahue built for himself in 1950 also had modernist features, but it was only in the middle of that decade that a significant number of Modern buildings began to appear in Winnipeg.[79]

Canadians proved particularly conservative in their tastes when it came to residential design. Writing in 1958, at a time when things Victorian were in deep disrepute, Alan Gowans pointed out that the building styles of that age had long been judged "beautiful" by Canadians because of "certain qualities – 'massiveness,' 'picturesqueness,' and so forth – that clearly in retrospect existed not in the architecture but in their minds. They projected into their buildings and called beautiful a set of emotional responses congenial to the particular climate of the high Victorian age." He added, "Sad but true, the fact remains – that Canada's architectural landscape is still predominantly Late Victorian ... High Victorian ideas lived on in Canada, long after they had ceased to be useful, appropriate, or even very well understood. Like children inhibited by some senile but domineering grandparent, Canadian architects from 1890 until well on into the 1920s continued to take their tastes, attitudes and standards

4.27
Bank branches 3: Bank of Nova Scotia, Yonge Street at St Clair Avenue, Murray Brown and Elton, 1957.

from the High Victorian age." So Toronto remained rather provincial, a follower not a leader that imported its ideas from Great Britain and the United States. Therefore, "intelligent architects could hardly maintain the enthusiasm of their parents' generation for Picturesque Eclecticism, and normally you would have expected them to abandon it and try something new. But they did not, and could not, for one very good reason. No matter how largely the Victorian style had lost its hold upon them, its appeal to their clients and to the public generally was, if anything, stronger than ever."[80]

As the Canadian economy returned to a peacetime footing, sixty thousand new houses were started in 1946 alone, but this burst of construction did not benefit either architects or the cause of advanced design very much. Eighty percent of these homes used no architectural services, as builders and their customers proved content to rely upon stock plans. In the autumn of 1947 Sydney Cooper asked, "Are Canadians Too Conservative to Live in Modern Houses?" He concluded that, "Canadian house architecture is virtually bankrupt," adding that there were not one hundred good Modern buildings in Montreal, Toronto, and Winnipeg combined. People should not be fooled by a few traditional houses disguised with "freakish modernistic designs," including flat roofs, corner windows, and concrete slab walls. Why did Canadian builders not adopt such desirable American innovations as basementless buildings with radiant heating in the floors? The blame could be widely shared: architects and builders were still bound to conventional techniques while buyers resisted change. Building codes were archaic and mortgage lenders clung to outmoded requirements, which urgently needed revision.[81]

Even the RAIC *Journal* sometimes displayed a rather limited vision of what constituted the Modern. In a 1947 issue devoted to interior design, a photo section concentrated on features like floor-to-ceiling glass doors in living-dining rooms, exposed brick walls in entranceways, skylights in the walls of living rooms, built-in dining tables and bedroom cupboards, and exterior decks and terraces. Altogether the impression created was that many Canadian architects still understood modern architecture largely as a series of such features.[82]

In the residential field only a few architects made even timid gestures towards Modernism like Gibson and Pokorny's 1947 design for a house in Oakville, just west of Toronto. The exterior elevation was horizontal with an L-shaped living-dining area lit by large windows, which could not be opened. John Caulfield Smith of *Canadian Homes and Gardens* conceded that the materials used were conventional, but insisted that the layout had been created from the inside out rather than a traditional exterior shaping the floor plan so that the result was less stuffy and more naturalistic.[83]

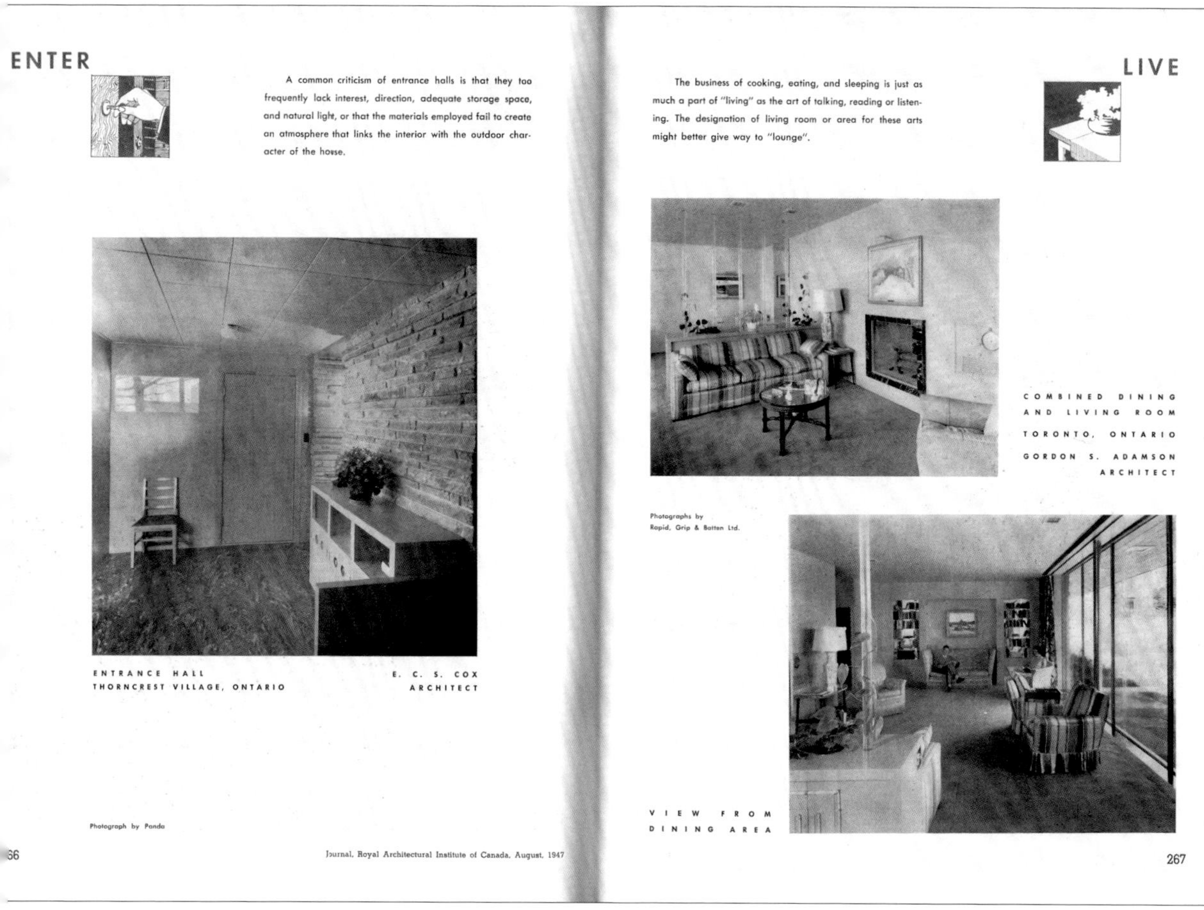
ENTER

A common criticism of entrance halls is that they too frequently lack interest, direction, adequate storage space, and natural light, or that the materials employed fail to create an atmosphere that links the interior with the outdoor character of the house.

ENTRANCE HALL
THORNCREST VILLAGE, ONTARIO

E. C. S. COX
ARCHITECT

Photograph by Panda

66

Journal, Royal Architectural Institute of Canada, August, 1947

LIVE

The business of cooking, eating, and sleeping is just as much a part of "living" as the art of talking, reading or listening. The designation of living room or area for these arts might better give way to "lounge".

COMBINED DINING
AND LIVING ROOM
TORONTO, ONTARIO
GORDON S. ADAMSON
ARCHITECT

Photographs by
Rapid, Grip & Batten Ltd.

VIEW FROM
DINING AREA

267

4.28
Architects E.C.S. Cox and Gordon S. Adamson present "design" to the public in 1947: one of a series of thematic spreads in a postwar issue of the *RAIC's Journal.*

At other times the magazine tried to argue that Modern architecture wasn't really so different from the good design of the past. "How New is Modern?" asked an article in January 1948. The pioneers of the Modern movement had insisted on designing from the inside out using appropriate materials to suit the needs of the structure. In doing so they harked back to the vernacular tradition of building before it had become preoccupied with period styles. What homeowners really wanted was not novelty for its own sake but up-to-date amenities. In the same issue the magazine touted a "splendid example of modern architectural design" by Clare G. MacLean, but this proved to be a rather muted house in North Toronto with a horizontal elevation and a low-pitched roof.[84]

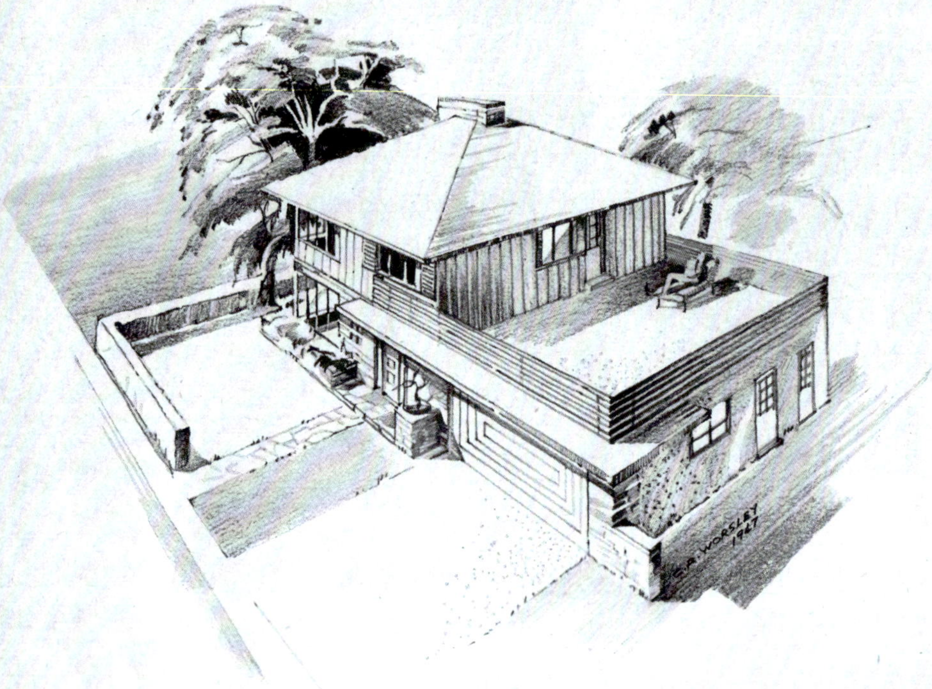

Design possibilities of modern house are endless. Traditional materials and sloped or flat roof may be used in enclosing an efficient 20th century plan.

LET'S GET THE PICTURE STRAIGHT ON . . .

How New is Modern?

Modern is a state of mind. It's the desire to get maximum value and satisfaction in housebuilding by using the best materials and methods available, regardless of period

In a 1947 editorial in the RAIC *Journal* Eric Arthur expressed doubt that any "great building would be commissioned in the contemporary manner, because we have a populace that is aware of fine modern buildings here and abroad but is afraid of what it calls modernistic." He could only hang his hopes upon the belief, "that the royal or noble patron has given way to the industrialist. He builds in the contemporary manner because, however sentimental he may be in his preference for domestic architecture, he sees nothing but efficiency and common sense in the use of modern techniques and materials for his factory." A few years later Arthur recalled the experience of arriving home in Toronto by airplane along with a visiting architect: he was overcome by the feeling that he ought to explain that "the perfectly dreadful architecture" of the airport was not a local product but the work of the national government. He had second-year architecture students at the university who could do better. Perhaps fortunately, he recounted, the airport buildings were in semi-darkness, only dimly lit with oil lamps because the electrical system was undergoing the switch from twenty-five to sixty-cycle power. The following day a visit to University Avenue revealed a central boulevard that looked as though it had just been ploughed: "The horrid truth was that it had looked like that for a year, but that is a long story." All in all Arthur was gloomy about the appearance of his adopted city: "Looking back over a hundred years of building in Toronto, the Roman thermae, the Romanesque skyscrapers and the Beaux-Arts banks appear merely as a reminder of a hypocritical age, which gloried shams and applauded shamsters. They contribute nothing to the sometimes muddy stream that meandered through the flats of Victorian, Edwardian and Georgian tastes." [85]

4.29 (Opposite)
"How New is Modern?" *Canadian Homes and Gardens*, 1948. Like a number of architects after the war, C.R. Worsley produced bungalow designs for both magazines and CMHC publications.

5

TIME OF CHANGE
1950–1955

By the mid-twentieth century Toronto was facing an unprecedented situation: the population of the city proper had almost ceased to grow. In 1941 the census takers found 667,457 residents, but a decade later the number had only risen to 675,754 and by 1961 it had declined to 672,407. Yet these figures were deceptive. Large numbers of additional houses could not be built within the city since there remained little vacant land, but after the war the ring of suburbs beyond began to expand, and during the 1950s population there increased by more than 500,000.[1] Where would these people find employment? Mainly downtown as in the past or in new industrial-commercial complexes in the once-sleepy suburbs? What kinds of housing would be created to accommodate hundreds of families? Would new office towers, factories, apartment buildings, and houses look much like those that had been constructed in the prewar city or would they take on shapes and designs strongly influenced by the ideas of Modern architecture?

5.1 (Opposite) C.B. McLean's Canadian Bank of Commerce, Don Mills Road, in the suburban wilderness of Don Mills, 1954.

The biggest rises in population occurred in the large townships of Scarborough, North York, and Etobicoke immediately to the east, north, and west of the city. To accommodate the 370,000 additional residents who settled in these three municipalities alone during the 1950s, new subdivisions sprang up around existing small towns or villages or spread across what had until recently been farmers' fields. Families, particularly the newly married couples with children who created a "baby boom" in postwar society, flocked to the suburbs in search of more spacious and economical housing – hard to find in the central city. Employment, however, remained heavily concentrated downtown, which created a large body of commuters who travelled to and from work not only by public transit but increasingly by private car, putting more and more strain on arterial roads.

By 1961 it was estimated that about one-quarter of the population of the greater Toronto area was living in residential neighbourhoods less than five years old. In the southerly part of North York, where there were few deep river valleys or other natural obstacles, roads were rapidly extended east–west and north–south, filling in the grid between the original concession lines. Before long these streets began to sprout near-identical bungalows or split-levels, differing only in size due to the income levels of the occupants, accessibility to the city by automobile or public transportation, and the availability of schools for the children. Many of the people living in these houses had just moved from the city, like the middle-class Jews who settled along upper Bathurst Street in North York but continued to use services in the city such as synagogues or food stores.

Outside the city, subdivisions leapfrogged over one another, sometimes leaving large vacant areas between them as builders sought cheaper land in order to keep house prices attractive. Middle-class buyers looked for homes that cost between $11,000 and $20,000, which excluded both the less well-off, who remained behind in the deteriorating housing stock in the inner city, and the more prosperous, who wanted further amenities. In downtown Toronto new buildings began to appear. The gap-toothed look created by vacant lots covered with parked cars where dilapidated buildings had been demolished began to disappear. Office towers rose to provide space for bankers, stockbrokers, lawyers, insurers, and resource developers as the city continued to challenge Montreal to take over as the nation's metropolis. In addition to the hundreds of houses in the outskirts, some factories began to appear there. Both in city and suburbs architects and developers had ample opportunities to promote adventurous new designs if Torontonians proved amenable.

I

Virtually all these new houses were highly traditional in design and materials. In 1954 *Canadian Homes and Gardens* asked a panel of experts, "What Stands Between You and A Better House?" A building inspector from North York maintained that outdated regulations were part of the problem. Toronto (and Montreal) forbade cheap and efficient frame construction, requiring each house to have a first floor of masonry or brickwork. As a result there was no chance of seeing the wood-sided buildings like those found in Vancouver.[2] Suburban developer Harold Shipp put some of the blame on mortgage providers who refused to lend for houses trimmed on the inside with drywall rather than lath and plaster. Architect Michael Bach agreed that lenders were much too conservative because of concerns about the resale value of properties. And all the panelists concurred that the tastes of homebuyers remained highly traditional. Every purchaser seemed to want a basement foundation that extended at least 3.5 feet above grade, which would spoil many Modern elevations. Bach said both buyers and lenders simply failed to see that in twenty years today's brick boxes would look outdated, and new designs would be the norm.[3]

A few months later the magazine returned to the subject of "Why More Canadians Should Have 'Modern' Houses." This time five Toronto architects,

5.2
Applewood Acres, 1954.

including Bach, were asked why buyers still had reservations about new designs. He suggested that a Georgian design sent out a signal that its owner was a success and that well-to-do buyers were often willing to spend extra money on traditional features. People were upset because Modern houses just looked different since their interior layouts determined an unconventional exterior form. Max Roth observed that newer designs were still evolving and didn't all need to look alike. But the panelists agreed that builders were not producing many avant-garde designs since neither owners and lenders seemed to warm to them.[4]

Proof of this proposition was provided by Applewood Acres, developed by Harold Shipp's family in Toronto Township, just west of Etobicoke. Between 1951 and 1954 the Shipps put up eight hundred houses on 250 acres of former orchards. Five different designs were prepared by the architects Hanks and Irwin, costing between $15,900 and $19,400. Most popular was "Breezy Brae," a four-bedroom storey-and-a-half bungalow faced in brick on the ground floor with clapboard above. Architects and planners alike roundly criticized the Applewood Acres designs as "hopelessly behind the times" and also observed that the narrow price range more or less guaranteed that all the buyers would be uniform in socioeconomic characteristics (and presumably taste). Yet the Shipps insisted that their success indicated that they knew what their clientele wanted. Some buyers did ask for more access to the outdoors, but the developers had rejected the idea of a wall of windows overlooking a patio on account of the winter climate. Architects might try to persuade buyers to accept more radical changes, but the Shipps had already found that even replacing the garage with a carport was not a success. With nowhere to store their tools, lawnmowers, skis, and other paraphernalia, homeowners in Applewood Acres complained about being forced to erect garden sheds at their own expense.[5] The scale of the Shipp operation was exceptional at that time, for almost all suburban house building was then still done by small builders who would purchase a few lots in newly subdivided areas and begin erecting a house or two, hoping to finance future construction through sales as they went along – circumstances hardly conducive to innovations in planning and design.

Pressure for development was particularly strong in North York, which wrapped around the north end of the city proper. With about 26,000 residents in 1945 its population rose to 86,000 by 1951 and reached 270,000 by 1961. The municipality prepared an Official Plan in 1948, and Eugene Faludi's firm, Town Planning Consultants Limited, was retained to prepare a comprehensive zoning bylaw, though this did not come into force until 1952.[6] Meanwhile spot rezonings allowed home building to proceed at a feverish pace, but many new arrivals found themselves dependent upon wells and septic tanks, along with unpaved streets. Like other rapidly growing Toronto suburbs, North York faced huge capital costs for roads, water mains, and sewers, despite a relatively limited real estate tax base; assessment was 90 percent residential in 1953 and that had only declined to 70 percent by 1960, while population rose by more than nine times.[7]

During the 1930s E.P. Taylor, one of Canada's leading businessmen, had built himself a grand estate in North York on Bayview Avenue north of Lawrence to accommodate his large racing stable, Windfields Farm (see Chapter 3). In 1947 he and his nearby neighbour and business associate, General Bruce Matthews, joined to retain architect John Layng to lay out an upscale housing development called Wrentham Estates just to the west across Bayview. Though mainly intending to protect their own property values, the developers also included a shopping centre at the corner of Bayview and York Mills Road surrounded by a large parking lot. One of the first such malls in Canada, this proved to be a highly profitable investment.

Then Taylor decided to expand industrial activity in North York by building a plant for Canadian Breweries, which he controlled.[8] His attention became fixed upon a large triangular area cut off by road from rest of the city to the south by the valleys of the East and West Don Rivers and their tributaries but accessible from the north and traversed by two railway lines. Karl Fraser, an executive of Taylor's holding company, Argus Corporation, quickly assembled more than six hundred acres around the intersection of Don Mills Road and Lawrence Avenue East for the new brewery and land to house its workers. In the end, however, Taylor dropped the brewing operation, but he decided to create a fully planned subdivision, including space for both manufacturing enterprises and housing. He established Don Mills Developments Limited, for which Fraser continued to acquire additional land, ultimately securing 2,200 acres altogether.

Karl Fraser's son-in-law, Macklin Hancock, was a landscape architect studying at Harvard's School of Design, where he was influenced by Walter Gropius, the famous Modernist, and by William Holford, the noted British town planner. In the spring of 1952 Hancock was named director of planning for Don Mills Developments Limited; he consulted Holford, who, according to legend, sketched an outline for him on a napkin. Hancock drew up five planning principles to guide the development of this community. There was to be clear spatial separation of various land uses, residential zones being distinct from commercial and industrial areas, while differing housing types such as single-family homes, multiple dwellings, and apartments would be constructed but not intermingled. At the centre would be a shopping centre surrounded by a ring road, beyond which housing would be laid out along winding streets with T-intersections and cul de sacs rather than the familiar grid to discourage through traffic. Lot sizes and shapes would not be rigid rectangles but wider and shallower than normal for a North American suburb, which would provide more space between houses and create a more varied streetscape. Large parks, including the ravines and the mature trees, would make up one-fifth of the site, while internal walkways amongst the houses would allow pedestrians access from periphery to centre without the use of cars.[9]

Hancock's planning principles were not especially radical. Their pedigree extended back at least to Ebenezer Howard's turn-of-the-century ideas about "garden cities" in Britain and contained clear echoes of Clarence Stein's 1927 layout for Radburn, New Jersey. Humphrey Carver's influential 1948 book, *Houses for Canadians*, had emphasized the importance of creating distinct neighbourhoods centred upon institutions like schools. In 1952 the federal government's Central Mortgage and Housing Corporation released an extensive study of "Housing Design." Analyzing the half million houses constructed since the war, it noted that three objectives seemed to govern the layout of large subdivisions: the removal of through auto traffic from residential streets, the provision of schools and shops for surrounding neighbourhoods, and the introduction of a greater diversity of housing types.[10]

Hancock's plan for Don Mills departed markedly from the archetypical North American suburb, Levittown, where endless rows of nearly identical bungalows spread out in lines across the former potato fields on Long Island.

He recruited a team, which included architects with Modernist sympathies like James Murray and Henry Fliess to prepare a detailed plan. The central shopping plaza, surrounded by large parking lots, would be located just southwest of the intersection of Don Mills Road and Lawrence and retained by the development company, which would rent to retailers. The ring road (eventually named the Donway) would encircle the mall, and residential development was to occur in the four quadrants beyond the ring created by the two major arterial roads. The plan provided for a mixture of detached, semi-detached, and row houses, but with apartment units making up one-third of the total, mainly in three-storey blocks given North York's thirty-five foot height limit for residential buildings. Locations were reserved for schools (including a collegiate), churches, a library, and a recreation centre. Industrial lands were to lie both to the south down towards Eglinton Avenue and to the north as far as up as York Mills Road, the next concession north of Lawrence. It was assumed that many of the employees would be Don

5.3
Don Mills underway, 1954.

Mills residents (hence the mix of housing types to attract lower-income earners), so that the community would be largely self-contained like a British new town. The aim was to attract quiet non-polluting producers of goods like electronics and pharmaceuticals, and their properties would be subject to design controls on buildings and to repurchase covenants.[11]

All the planning in the world could not overcome certain practical problems. A 1949 study by engineers Gore and Storrie had identified serious inadequacies in the water and sewage services of the greater Toronto area. The vast R.C. Harris pumping station on Lake Ontario at the eastern edge of the city of Toronto could supply enough water to serve the suburbs if necessary but a major expansion of the mains would be required. One dozen suburban sewage plants were dumping barely treated effluent into the Humber and Don Rivers, turning them into virtual open sewers. Widespread use of septic systems, particularly in North York, was already contaminating the ground water even though wells remained common. New trunk sewers were needed along with several large new treatment plants on the shores of Lake Ontario – the whole program to cost about $35 million.[12]

Moreover, when the idea of the Don Mills project was first unveiled to North York officials in 1951, it was discovered that the zoning bylaw being drafted by Eugene Faludi envisaged delaying development in other parts of the township until the central corridor on both sides of Yonge Street was nearly filled up as far north as Sheppard Avenue. Industries approached to consider relocating to Don Mills showed no inclination to do so in the absence of guarantees about adequate water and sewage services. North York had imposed a system of development charges but Faludi argued that the realty taxes on the predicted assessments would be insufficient to finance the infrastructure required. Nor could the municipality borrow any more money because it had already issued $1.75 million worth of debentures, the maximum allowed by the province's Ontario Municipal Improvement Corporation.

In 1953 Fraser struck a deal with the municipality that Don Mills Developments would finance and build the required water and sewer services. The company would provide a temporary sewage treatment plant to be located on banks of the East Don River near Lawrence (where a dam and scenic lake had originally been planned) until the trunk sewers could be extended to the shores of Lake Ontario. In addition, the developers would purchase debentures issued by the municipality to fund the extension of the water mains and place sufficient funds in escrow in case additional tax revenues proved insufficient to meet the charges on the sinking fund. Thus the company, rather than North York, assumed the risk entailed in providing the necessary services during a period of fifteen years until the municipality had recovered its investment.

Another major issue facing the developers was better road access, particularly for the industrial zones at the north and south ends. Neither Eglinton nor Lawrence, the original concession lines, crossed the wide, deep valleys of the east and west branches of the Don River, permitting direct access from the city or from Scarborough. New bridges would have to be constructed.[13] The major north–south artery, Don Mills Road, descended into the river valley but then climbed up to the east of the Don rather than providing links continuing southwest to downtown.

A scenic parkway had long been envisaged up the valley of the Don to join the city's north end to the waterfront. Planning Commissioner Tracy leMay observed in 1945 that "the ravines of the Don and its tributaries have been recognized as an ideal location for high speed connections to the north and northeast parts of Toronto."[14] But nothing had been done. By the end of the decade this idea had morphed into a plan for a new arterial road extending up the valley to connect, via Don Mills Road, with the province's intercity expressway (Highway 401), but Macklin Hancock complained that the proposed alignment would cut right through the southeastern part of the Don Mills development, ruining a prime residential neighbourhood. He argued that the road should continue along the valley of the East Don beyond Lawrence, bypassing the development to the east and extending right up to Highway 401, a solution that the highway engineers eventually accepted. Construction of an expressway called the Don Valley Parkway ultimately began in 1958.

With these plans in place, building could commence. The capital costs involved in financing the entire development were vast, and no residential developer existed in Canada that could raise sufficient funds at a time when Canadian chartered banks were not permitted to lend for residential mortgages.[15] E.P. Taylor therefore devised a means to get the project under way without delay. Don Mills Developments would offer lots to builders for one-quarter down with the balance payable in eighteen months, a deal appealing to cash-strapped contractors while encouraging speedy construction. In the end, fifty different builders participated, something Macklin Hancock favoured because he believed it would ensure a greater diversity in housing types. To ensure quality and protect resale value, the company required all designs to be approved by its architectural committee, though the architects complained that builders often skimped on quality while some contractors objected to unnecessary requirements, which were likely to reduce profits below the 10 percent margin at which they customarily aimed.[16] Taylor's personal contribution to the aesthetics of the development was to impose a

5.4 (Above)
Don Mills: the builders, c. 1954.

5.5 (Left)
Don Mills: houses under construction, 1953.

ban upon the use of blue roofing, which he believed quickly faded, producing a depressing effect.

The first houses in Don Mills went on the market in 1953 for about $12,500, a level that had increased to $17,000 by 1956. By 1963 population had reached thirty thousand, but the largely self-contained new town failed to materialize. The 320 acres within the industrial zones did prove attractive locations for firms employing 4,500 people in new buildings set in pleasing swathes of green space, but estimates suggested that only about 5 percent of these workers actually lived in the community. The cost of the houses was sufficiently high that about half the buyers had been previous homeowners. Townhouses were included in the housing stock but North York refused to permit two bedroom apartments, and the very success of the suburb pushed up costs so that few blue-collar workers could afford to live there. The completion of the Don Valley Parkway as far north as Highway 401 by 1967, with interchanges at Don Mills Road, Eglinton Avenue, and Lawrence, meant that the suburb was efficiently connected for commuting by automobile to the downtown, making it attractive to white-collar people.

Don Mills was a success as a real estate development, helped along by adroit marketing, but some people argued that Hancock's efforts to promote Modern ideas about planning and architecture were actually detrimental. The decision to include a variety of housing types created controversy. A.L. McClaskey, president of Don Mills Developments, told the convention of the Royal Architectural Institute of Canada in 1957 that "at Don Mills there was a bitter dispute with the purchasers and others over our attempt to provide mixed development of housing. Public resistance to mixed development is very great." Another architect caused a flurry by declaring on a CBC radio program that he thought Don Mills was "the slum of tomorrow."[17]

The row housing designed by architects James Murray and Henry Fliess initially provoked "yowls of protest" from the owners of nearby detached homes because they associated such buildings with overcrowding and poor maintenance, which would undermine their property values. Even the award of a Massey Medal for group housing to Murray and Fliess in 1958 for their design of Southill Village at Don Mills probably did little to change minds.[18] More acceptable were the conventional split-level detached houses that Murray designed, which also won awards.[19]

Critics have pointed out that Macklin Hancock's ambition to create a genuine organic community in Don Mills foundered upon economic realities. The neighbourhood stores planned for each quadrant never came into existence because low population density would have made them unprofitable. Many commentators later asserted that Don Mills became the model for numerous other suburbs across Canada but those claims appear incorrect.

5.6
Southill Village, James Murray and Henry Fliess, 1957.

Other developers did not possess the financial resources that E.P. Taylor was able to mobilize or the imaginative ideas of Macklin Hancock so attempts to create largely self-contained new towns that offered both housing and employment for many of their residents were few and far between. Even Don Mills soon became primarily a bedroom suburb like hundreds of others across North America, despite the existence of a sizable number of industrial jobs within the boundaries of the original development. Perhaps the most lasting legacy of Don Mills was its layout of winding residential streets designed to discourage through traffic, which came to be reproduced from coast to coast over the next half century.[20]

Don Mills was also important, however, for the role that it played in demonstrating the need for the reform of the structure of municipal government in the greater Toronto area. The 1949 report by the engineers Gore and Storrie had recommended the construction of new water mains, trunk sewers, and sewage treatment plants, which would cost at least $35 million. Had the company not been willing to assume part of the risk, the development would probably have been delayed for a considerable time. Similar obstacles existed in other Toronto suburbs to raising the necessary capital to fund new infrastructure. Planners like Tracy leMay were convinced that some form of regional government was required and that the city of Toronto ought to annex its surrounding suburbs to provide a financial base large enough to underpin the necessary borrowing.

Suburban politicians showed little interest in seeing their bailiwicks disappear, and many city politicians were equally suspicious of annexation for fear that their constituents would face large tax increases to pay for services in outlying districts. Nevertheless, after considerable debate the city council voted overwhelmingly to endorse amalgamation in February 1950. Most suburban leaders remained hostile to that idea, and in 1953 the provincial government concluded that the best solution would be the creation of a quasi-federal structure uniting the city and its suburbs in a new Municipality of Metropolitan Toronto. The city and its dozen surrounding suburbs would continue to exercise separate control over local matters such as zoning, police, fire protection, social services, and libraries. "Metro," as it became known, would be responsible for regional planning, arterial roads, major water and sewage facilities, and public transportation with the power to assess real estate for taxation and to issue debentures to finance capital projects.[21]

Beginning in 1954 the new Metro government headed by its dynamic chair, Frederick G. Gardiner, set to work on the construction of an elaborate network of water mains, trunk sewers, and treatment plants along with a waterfront expressway from the Don to the Humber (named after Gardiner himself), which would connect to the Don Valley Parkway. Over the next fifteen years, Toronto was equipped with the infrastructure required by a modern metropolis whose population was undergoing rapid expansion.[22]

II

In the 1950s Toronto architects still had a hard time persuading people to commission Modern houses. James Murray designed one house in Port Credit, west of Toronto, on a southward-facing lot sloping towards Lake Ontario; the Shutte house was a split-level with large areas of glass facing the water. To fit the site the living room was on the ground floor on the lake side with bedrooms above and the dining room and kitchen up half a flight. The lower walls were grey stucco with vertical cedar cladding on top and a shingled roof. Yet the other four Toronto area houses featured in the same 1950 issue of the RAIC *Journal* were much more conventional. The jurors for the first Massey medals in 1950, though eager to recognize innovation, did not make awards of excellence for residences costing either more than $15,000 or less than $15,000 nor for group housing.[23]

A couple of years later Murray prepared an avant-garde layout for a ravine lot in Toronto's Rosedale. Mrs M.H. Spaulding had declared

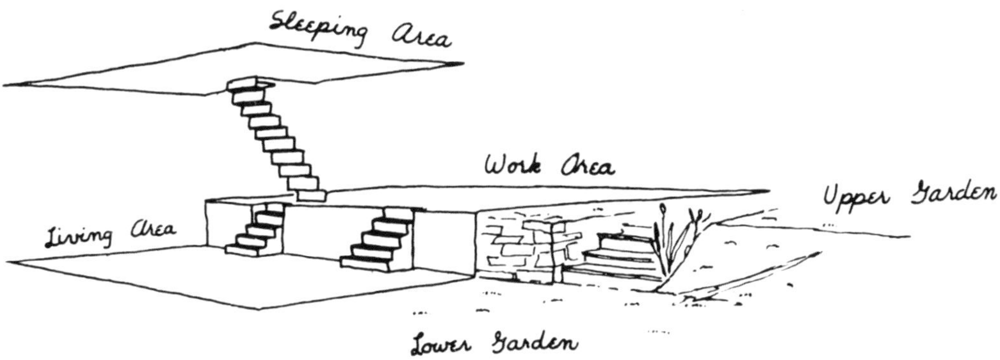

5.7 (Opposite)
Schutte house, Port Credit, south view, James Murray, 1950.

5.8 (Above)
Schutte house: diagram of split levels.

5.9 (Left)
Spaulding house, James Murray, 1952.

5.10 (Below)
Spaulding house, interior.

no stylistic preferences to the architect, and the single-storey structure at 111 Park Road was an L-shape that turned its back to the street frontage with the main rooms facing the ravine in the rear. The roof also sloped from one side of the house to the other, mirroring the landform, which permitted a higher ceiling in the living room, lower ones in the bedrooms, as well as a clerestory that admitted light into the living room and over a front door composed of a single sheet of glass. The walls of the living room were largely of exposed brick with recessed lighting in the ceiling. The results, according to a note in the RAIC *Journal* that was probably written by Murray himself, a form of self-promotion common for architects at the time, were quite out of keeping with the "usual suburban flight."[24]

Toronto homeowners clung to the old ways. If people wanted change but could not bring themselves to plump for a really radical design, *Canadian Homes and Gardens* suggested in 1953 that one way to "Give Yourself Elegance When the Children Grow Up" was to follow in the footsteps of Mrs B.H. Pickard. She had the exterior of her conventional Georgian home in Forest Hill Village converted into a rather ugly moderne design by architect Harry Seidler, who blocked up the casement windows, covered the walls with white stucco pierced by picture windows, and plopped down a carport where the garage had once stood.[25] (Looking at this layout one would hardly predict that Seidler would go on to become one of Australia's most distinguished architects, but Mrs Pickard doubtless knew what she wanted.)

GIVE YOURSELF ELEGANCE WHEN THE CHILDREN GROW UP

These are "Before" and "After" pictures of Pickard house. First it was painted white, an entrance canopy and car port added, plus a setting of terraces and shrubs. Windows on the right have been enlarged and others removed. The garage is now at back of the lot.

Walls and rug in living room are in cafe-au-lait shade and chintz is a quiet combination of greens, grey and cafe-au-lait on off-white. Furniture arrangement is strategic: note how almost every piece is against wall, leaving space in long narrow room for piano.

5.11
Pickard house, Harry Seidler, 1953.

In 1951 Eric Arthur reported that he had attended a meeting of the Toronto chapter of the Ontario Association of Architects and discovered his colleagues were still debating the same old issues. In thirty years nothing really new had been achieved in the field of small house planning. The profession had assumed the problems would be solved by prefabrication but this had proved to be a bust.[26] The following year he noted his amazement that a visit to the RAIC's annual meeting in Vancouver had revealed new houses being put up by speculative builders that cost under $10,000 and showed good taste, enterprise, and an understanding of materials and colours: "All, of course, were modern in design." But Toronto would have nothing similar to show if the visiting architects met there.[27] When Toronto's subway opened in the spring of 1954, Arthur observed sardonically that at least the city now had one thing indubitably modern: no Goths or Classicists had raised critical voices and the stations were "straightforward building," featuring lots of simple brickwork and bright-coloured glazed tile.[28]

5.12 (Top)
Bank of Canada, Marani and Morris, 1958.

5.13 (Bottom)
US Consulate, Mathers and Haldenby, 1951.

The biggest commercial jobs still seemed to go to firms like Marani and Morris and Mathers and Haldenby, who kept proposing variations on the kind of Stripped Classicism common in the interwar years. Their designs exhibited the same features and strove for a kind of elusive monumentality while rejecting the tenets of the Modern Movement. The Bank of Canada building on the west side of University Avenue south of Queen by Marani

5.14 (Above)
Imperial Oil Head Office, Mathers and Haldenby, 1957.

5.15 (Right)
Imperial Oil lobby with York Wilson's mural "The Story of Oil" at left and interior by John B. Parkin Associates, 1957.

and Morris appeared to be a scaled-up version of the United States Consulate by Mathers and Haldenby just up the street and was hard to distinguish from the same firm's Imperial Oil building on St Clair West near Avenue Road. The lobby of the Imperial Oil building, under the influence of John B. Parkin, did have a much more up-to-date look as the setting for York Wilson's mural "The Story of Oil."[29]

This increasingly prominent firm that showed such openness to advanced design was headed by John Burnett Parkin who had acquired some familiarity with Modernism in Europe before the war. In 1944 John Cresswell Parkin (no relation, though often later confused with John B.) graduated from the University of Manitoba and won several fellowships to study at the Harvard Graduate School of Design. While waiting to take up the award, John C.

moved to Toronto and got a job with Marani and Morris. Thirty years later John C. recorded in an interview that thirty-three-year-old John B. had "heard of me as I had been a student at the University of Manitoba" (presumably on account of his brilliant undergraduate record) and invited him to lunch. He persuaded the young man to take a job in his small firm in October 1944 for small raise in salary from thirty-five to forty dollars per week. Within a short time the Parkins had "already won our first private competition (for the TTC Adelaide Coach Terminal)." John C. noted, "We agreed that we would eventually form a partnership. I was only 22, however ... [I]t was jointly acknowledged that I needed design training of the highest calibre and that I should take advantage of the Harvard scholarships."[30]

John C. Parkin arrived at Harvard in January 1946 and studied with those giants of the Modern movement, Walter Gropius and Marcel Breuer, while also auditing the lectures of Alvar Aalto at the Massachusetts Institute of Technology. Among Parkin's fellow-students were I.M. Pei and Paul Rudolph. Parkin recorded,

> We all felt we were participating in terribly exciting days. We were filled with fantastic idealism for we naively felt that we were about to solve most of the problems of the post-war world. Most of us held an unquestioning loyalty to the Bauhaus ethic, to the idea that there was a single universally accepted architecture, which, if disseminated, had a general applicability to all kinds of problems we were about to face. We felt the Bauhaus code or ethic was returning, be it to Thailand, Australia, Canada, or wherever.[31]

5.16
John B. and John C. Parkin in 1947, with Winnipeg architect R.E. Moore.

When John C. returned to Toronto in 1947, the partnership of John B. Parkin Associates was formed, including John B.'s brother, landscape architect Edmund T. Parkin. John C. claimed that

> We had agreed that, as an architectural firm, we would try to do a number of things. Firstly, we would never take a commission that was even in the remotest sense traditional. There were at the time a number of firms who, out of lack of conviction, undertook buildings that were neo-traditional or fully traditional. My namesake [John B.] after all had graduated from the University of Toronto in 1935, and by his own person putdown jokingly had said, "Well, after all, I was a product of the Beaux-Arts, and out the back door before you came along did do mansard roofs and a few things of that nature." When we came together we said, however, that we would only do contemporary design even if we had very little to do. Indeed there were many occasions when we did have very little to do – by that I mean more modest [sums] than that which we might have earned if we worked for someone else.[32]

John C. Parkin was determined to attract public notice to the firm. In the 1947 RAIC *Journal* he published a number of industrial designs for new consumer products like a steam iron and, for the most futuristically inclined, even a "family helicopter" for easy commuting. That same year for a small house design competition sponsored by Central Mortgage and Housing Corporation he prepared an entry showing a Modern one-storey house. The publication that featured the winning entries showed a rendering with two children in the backyard waving as the "family helicopter" banked for a landing.[33]

Soon afterwards, "some very fortunate things happened to intervene" for Parkin Associates. In 1949 the Ontario Association of Architects (OAA) decided to hold a competition for a new headquarters on Park Road just east of Yonge Street in midtown at the edge of the Rosedale Ravine. John C. prepared the firm's entry, and the changes in architectural fashion became evident when 90 percent of the entries received were Modern layouts. In 1950 the jury, composed of Eric Arthur, Murray Brown, and Ferdinand Marani, selected the Parkin firm's design. Parkin claimed that he had been inspired by Mies van der Rohe's Farnsworth house because

> my own attitude to design had changed profoundly from an allegiance to the tenets of the works of Gropius and Breuer to an admiration for the work of Mies ... I doubt if a precise date could be placed on this adjustment in attitude. Certainly I felt much greater personal sympathy

5.17 (Right)
John C. Parkin's "Family Helicopter," 1947.

5.18 (Below)
CMHC offers its own advice on modernism: John C. Parkin's entry for CMHC's first small house design competition, 1947.

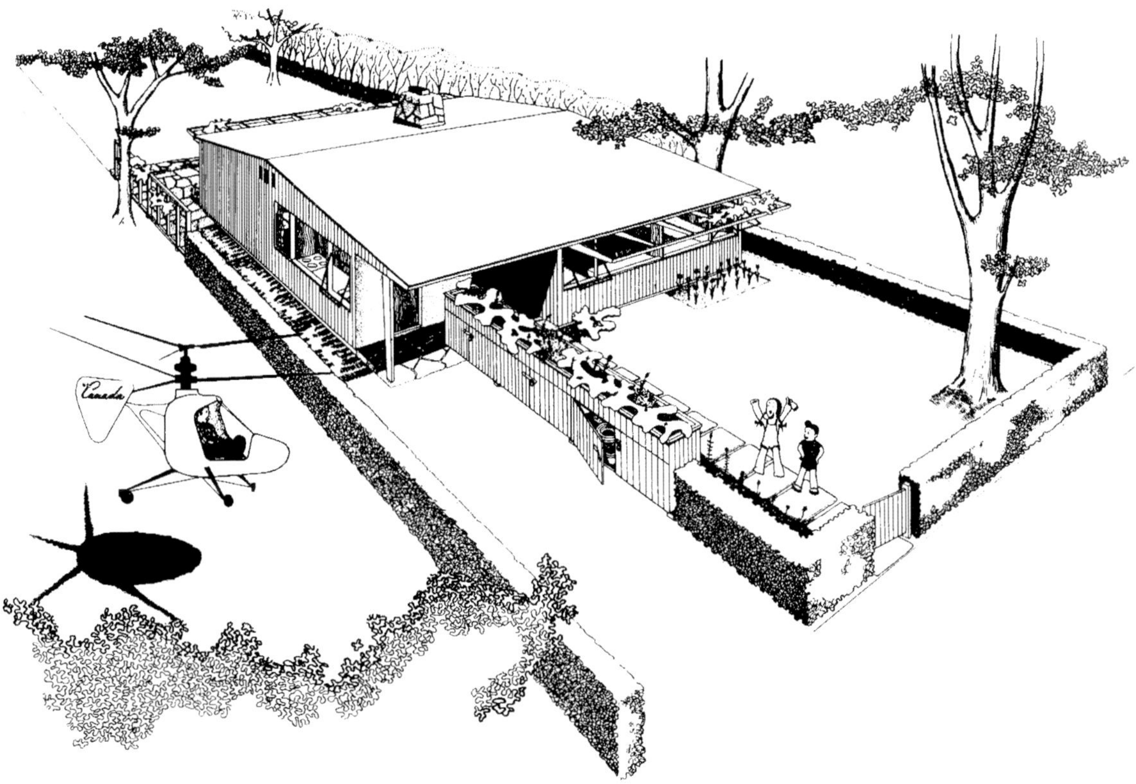

and, much more importantly, philosophic rapport with Mies. For one thing I felt that Mies fit my own belief that there was a degree of universality possible; that there should be a generally accepted design base upon which most architecture could be conceived, and one that would allow buildings built side by side to "fit together" with a sense of harmony.[34]

5.19 (Above)
Ontario Association of Architects building, Park Road, John B. Parkin Associates, 1957.

5.20 (Right)
Ontario Association of Architects building, interior.

The OAA design boasted a white steel frame enclosing brick panels and large windows arranged around an internal ramp, an entire wall of windows overlooking the valley. Parkin claimed, "While the competition was won, it was far from built for there were some very senior and very eminent architects in the city who were determined that what they thought a rather vulgar building, with an excess of glass, should not represent the architectural profession in Toronto. Attempts were made to buy an older building – including one of rather questionable Georgian design on St. Thomas Street." But in the end the job went ahead in good part because another architect, Earle Shepherd, threw his support behind it.[35] The result was described as "a lucidly planned, exquisitely detailed and pristinely finished jewel – a showpiece of International Style design." It was awarded a silver Massey Medal in the 1955 competition for miscellaneous projects, receiving plaudits for the skillful handling of the steeply sloping street frontage on Park Road and the social spaces in a "highly unusual building."[36]

The fledgling Parkin firm's visibility was also raised by the capture of five of the ten medals handed out in the first Massey awards for architectural excellence in 1950. Also important in establishing its reputation as a versatile shop that could turn out all manner of structures with a fashionably up-to-date look was its association with Don Mills. While Macklin Hancock's enthusiasm for Modern architecture was often thwarted by the desires of both homebuilders and buyers for more traditional styles, the innovativeness of the Parkin people became evident in the commercial areas of the subdivision. John C. Parkin was put in charge of designing the shopping centre at

5.21
Don Mills Shopping Centre, John B. Parkin Associates, 1955.

the southeast corner of Lawrence Avenue and Don Mills Road. There the stores were grouped along a pedestrian promenade surrounded by big parking lots, an arrangement that had only recently arrived on the Canadian scene in the early 1950s.[37] By their nature such layouts seemed friendly to Modern hallmarks such as glass walls, flat roofs, and slender supporting columns, and the mall in Don Mills came to be considered a gem of its kind. The individual shops had entrances both from the parking lots and from the covered pedestrian walkway. The developers retained control over all commercial signage, which allowed the architects to control the size and typefaces used, even for the service station that was included.[38]

The two branch banks located nearby on Lawrence Avenue attracted particular attention in view of the conservatism of the chartered banks in choosing designs for most of their hundreds of buildings across Canada. The recently founded journal *Canadian Architect* pointed out in 1957 that these largely transparent glass-walled cubes would have found no favour in the past with bankers determined to project an image of solidity and security. Equally surprising was that the Banks of Montreal and Nova Scotia had consented to almost identical exterior designs side by side with one another, differentiated merely by the blue and the red of their respective signs. Only the vaults and public service areas were clad in concrete with unpolished plate glass set in steel framing for the curtain walls to obscure the staff from view while retaining the transparency of the structures.[39]

In 1955 the Don Mills shopping centre received a silver Massey Medal for commercial buildings with the jury observing, "it is amazing in a way to find this composition so lofty an abstraction, as though Bach were being played at a drive-in movie. With a very limited palette of glass, metal and masonry, the architects have composed in a rectangular style of great finesse, allowing little room for the traditional individuality of the separate shop or the customary anarchy of competitive advertising."[40]

The Parkin firm also designed a number of buildings in the industrial areas of Don Mills, including a much-praised head office for Ortho Pharmaceuticals on Green Belt Drive. The steel structural frame encased in concrete

5.22 (Opposite)
Don Mills Shopping Centre.

5.23 (Left)
Don Mills banks: Bank of Nova Scotia, summer, John B. Parkin Associates, 1957.

5.24 (Below)
Don Mills banks: Bank of Montreal, winter, John B. Parkin Associates, 1957.

was exposed on the section of the building used for offices while the attached plant was clad in glazed white brick. Soon a fan letter from a company official reached *Canadian Architect* observing that recent publicity had led to a flood of requests from outsiders to come and visit Ortho. In the planning stage management had wavered between commissioning a traditional or an "ultra-modern" building but was now convinced of the rightness of the choice as it was "a vitally important part of our public relations and our relations with our clients." The company philosophy had "always been to present the right sort of face. This building has fulfilled our demands overwhelmingly." The "Orthosociates" who worked there were extremely happy with a structure both beautiful and functional, a tribute to the architects.[41]

Perhaps even more striking than the Ortho plant was the structure created on a three-acre site at the corner of Don Mills and York Mills Roads as the new home of John B. Parkin Associates. The offices of architectural firms had differed little in appearance during the first half of the twentieth century even as they grew in size but the new Parkin operation attained industrial scope.

Outside, a white steel frame stood out against blue glass, while the employees inside occupied a vast drafting room with north lighting and a fourteen-foot ceiling. Joist spans forty-five feet long permitted large areas free of support columns, and there was glazing on all sides, which created an extraordinarily transparent structure.[42]

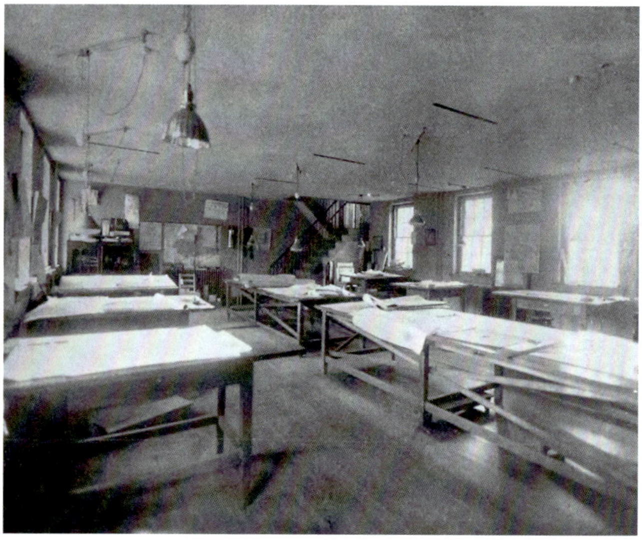

5.25 (Above)
Ortho Pharmaceutical Head Office, John B. Parkin Associates, 1955.

5.26 (Left)
Three twentieth-century architects' offices: Sproatt and Rolph, 1919.

5.27 (Above left)
Mathers and Haldenby's office, 1948.

5.28 (Above right)
John B. Parkin Associates' office, 1966.

5.29 (Left)
Parkin office, Don Mills Road, John B. Parkin Associates, 1955.

In downtown Toronto the Parkin firm attracted notice with another large commission for a headquarters building for the Salvation Army on Albert Street. Here John C. admitted that even with his growing enthusiasm for the ideas of Mies van der Rohe he could not ignore the huge presence of E.J. Lennox's dark red Richardsonian Romanesque City Hall diagonally across the road at the corner of James Street. Mies had to "'give way' to a matter of higher concern." The design had at least to acknowledge the numerous redbrick structures all around the new building, which were owned by the T. Eaton Company. The result featured striking white-glazed brick exterior, strong verticals, and on the south wall small projecting sunshades (the *brises-soleils* so favoured by Le Corbusier) – a design that stood out sharply amidst its surroundings.[43]

With so many big projects on the go, including many schools, the Parkin team became frustrated almost from the outset by the difficulty of finding

5.30
Parkin office,
Don Mills Road.

engineers to manage their work: "We looked very carefully at the engineering firms who were then in existence and found them unaware of the most elemental of architectural criteria, certainly as we saw them. Therefore we started our own engineering departments within a year or two, and by 1949 we were a fully integrated firm consisting of engineers, mechanical engineers, electrical, and interior designers." John C. always claimed that this idea was born in 1944 when he had read a promotional brochure for the firm of Albert Kahn, house architect for the Ford Motor Company and other large corporations. The organizational chart there set forth the various functional departments within the Kahn firm and led him to press to imitate them.[44] Parkin was always defensive about the claim that his firm had simply duplicated the model of the American firm, Skidmore, Owings, and Merrill, which offered a similar range of services. As he remarked in a 1975 interview, "In effect, the often-repeated canard that our firm as modelling on Skidmore, Owings and Merrill is entirely wrong. It was modelled on the organization of Albert Kahn." Yet in the same interview John C. admitted that by 1947 he had been impressed

> through emerging importance of the work of Skidmore and Owing [sic], later Skidmore, Owing [sic] and Merrill. They demonstrated to me that there was nothing mutually exclusive about good design and

good organization, nor between scale and quality in the complexity of contemporary architecture. I found this greatly reassuring for it became clear to me that if we, as younger men, were to prevail in contemporary architecture then we had to have a superlative organization. We had to have at our disposal an organization that would emphasize absolute cost control and absolute commitment to the completion of drawings on time, an absolute commitment to outstandingly professional and responsible people ... The Kahn monograph is rather sentimental to me because that was where it really started, together with the supplementary reinforcement of SOM's early work.[45]

5.31
John C. Parkin meets Le Corbusier, 1957.

So the Parkin firm's readiness to offer more than simply architectural design services had more than one sire.

The extent of Parkin Associates' capabilities in a wide range of specialties was displayed with panache in the mid-1950s by a three-building industrial complex at Islington Avenue and Highway 401 in Etobicoke. Included was a huge 417,000-square-foot mail-order centre for the department store chain Simpson-Sears. Across a rail spur lay a printing building for Electrotypers Limited and a private power plant fuelled by coal, which produced heat and steam for printing operations. The north wall of the power plant featured a five-storey cantilevered staircase, which was intended to provide a focus for the ensemble through the use of different coloured enameled panels at each landing. The building exteriors were brick, painted steel, or smooth concrete into which steel sash windows were set. This array won a silver Massey Medal in 1955 for industrial buildings; the jury noted that "engineering elements, notably in the power plant ... are given convincing architectural meaning ... Areas and surfaces of gargantuan size are handled with complete confidence."[46]

In 1959 British architect Kenneth Wood recorded his impressions of the state of design across Canada.[47] After crossing huge windblown spaces with settlement dispersed along a boring grid of roads, Wood showed a proper degree of lordly distain for the colonies, dismissing Vancouver's "litter of honkytonk boomtown." Toronto's large office towers he condemned for their "crude curtain walls," which, by comparison with the best of New York or Chicago, "have not left the kindergarten stage." But one thing about Toronto did attract favourable comment from Wood:

> Away from the unbelievably crude and ugly synagogues and churches, the brash ostentation of the luxury apartment blocks and the hamfisted flats, away from the boxes with the television aerials sprouting from their roof like weedy cornstalks, in Don Mills there are almost fully glazed banks, offices, industrial buildings and modern courtyard houses and shopping centres, largely the work of one team – John B. Parkin Associates – that have a quality of consistently good design that sets them apart and would do so in any city in any country ... Don Mills will no doubt fall victim in due course to the maniac chaos of commuters, but they [sic] *are* evidence of creative designers who refuse to paddle in the same puddle as the mediocre. The shopping centre, with its covered ways, its well designed furniture, restrained advertising and atmosphere of pedestrian quiet, is an oasis in the desert.

Wood complained that nobody in Canada had bothered to ask him about what was going on in Europe, preferring instead to look inward like other North Americans whose cities were daily getting uglier, more stultifying, boring, and depressing. And he could only conclude sadly that, despite structures like the Don Mills plaza and the Ortho Pharmaceutical plant, these "gems on the dunghill do little to reduce the overall stench."[48]

5.32 (Opposite left)
Salvation Army, Canadian headquarters, Albert Street, John B. Parkin Associates, 1955.

5.33 (Opposite right)
Salvation Army with *brises-soleils*.

5.34 (Left)
Simpson-Sears industrial development, Etobicoke, John B. Parkin Associates, 1955.

In a lecture to the Society of Architectural Historians in 1962 John C. Parkin delivered his assessment of the progress of Modernism in Canada: "I would plead that the immediate postwar period in Canada – perhaps as late as 1952 or 1953 – was not significant in its production of noteworthy examples of contemporary architecture. Those earlier years for my firm (and I suspect for most others in Canada – save those on our Pacific coast) were taken with proselytizing and moulding a previously conservative public taste, rather than in creating lasting architecture. That these were well-spent years, however, may be found in the continuing ascendancy of contemporary architecture today." Parkin argued that one reason for this slowness was the small number of architects ready to take up the battle for Modernism. The Depression of the 1930s had either deterred people from entering the profession or driven them out, so that only a small number of older architects and recent graduates from the postwar era had been available to fight the good fight.[49]

Thirty years after the work of the firm first began to catch people's attention John C. Parkin declared that his Ontario Association of Architects building had "proved pivotal in the acceptance of contemporary architecture in Ontario." The choice of design by the association "gave its official imprint of approval to the movement and thus, symbolically, a respectability to contemporary architecture. The Ortho Pharmaceutical building, completed in 1956, with its clear, classic, contemporary design influenced building not only in Ontario but throughout Canada and the United States. Victory had clearly been won for the progressive modern movement, and contemporary design became the mainstream of Canadian architecture."[50]

III

By the early fifties there was competition for Parkin from other proponents of Modern design in Toronto. In mid-1952 the RAIC *Journal* published sketches of two new projects by the firm of Page and Steele for an office building at 111 Richmond Street West and for the Benvenuto Place apartments, which would stand highly visible on the crest of the escarpment on Avenue Road.[51] Both of these were the work of a young British immigrant named Peter Dickinson who had joined the firm in 1950, his ideas much influenced by the "Picturesque Modernism," which had been developed for the Festival of Britain held in 1951 to celebrate the centennial of the Victorian Great Exhibition.[52]

Called "the most skilled and assured of some four hundred British-trained architects drawn to Canada after the war,"[53] Dickinson was scathing about the office buildings in his adopted city whose small, barred windows and heavily embossed doors below high parapets seemed designed to shield defenders in case of siege by an angry mob. Sometimes he even expressed regret at the disappearance of earlier flourishes: "Gone are the graceful cornices and colonnades that provided shelter for the pigeons and so suited an age of ease and elegance." Of downtown Toronto he wrote, "These are the buildings of modern Europe fifty years ago. They are contemporary inasmuch as Russian Communist building is contemporary." He claimed that one fellow architect had boasted about his buildings being hermetically sealed against air from the outside, another about fluorescent lights that

5.35 (Opposite) Peter Dickinson, c. 1960.

5.36 (Above) Benvenuto, Peter Dickinson, 1955.

provided better illumination than daylight: "Perhaps the next great step forward will be a revival of medieval architecture." The only comfort he could draw was that a few of the newer designs were cautiously following styles that had appeared twenty years earlier in Europe and the United States.

Dickinson grumbled about the lucrative jobs that seemed to keep flowing to a few old-line firms in Toronto: "I feel that nothing can come of our collective or individual efforts if this mutual admiration society continues, in which the man who get the highest commission is regarded as the finest architect." Sometimes he even dismissed the "starkitecture" of the glass and steel towers planned by Mies van der Rohe and others, though some of Dickinson's Toronto designs were in the full International Style with cantilevers, glass curtain walls, and strip windows. But he was congratulatory about John C. Parkin's Miesian design for the new offices of the Ontario Association of Architects, despite the fact that his own more traditional entry in the competition had been rejected. Dickinson predicted that some of his colleagues might have a hard time knowing when construction was finished since the OAA building was sufficiently organic that it looked as though it might sprout at any moment.[54]

The best-known of Dickinson's early buildings was the Benvenuto on the west side of Avenue Road just south of Edmund Avenue. Benvenuto was the brainchild of Leon Yolles of developers Yolles and Rotenberg who had acquired a sizable property on the brow of the escarpment on one of the city's major arteries leading north from downtown. He decided to build a combined apartment house and hotel that was bound to be noticed. Peter Dickinson prepared a design with cantilevered balconies stretching across the entire southerly frontage as well as at the sides and the back, clearly emphasizing the horizontality of the large seven-storey building and the extensive strip windows in the Modern manner.[55]

As the planning of Benvenuto proceeded, new construction methods were being developed that demonstrated the important links between advanced technology and Modern design. The structural engineer for the project was Leon Yolles's son, Morden, who was already exploring the possibilities of using relatively thin flat slabs of reinforced concrete as floor plates. Having studied the work of European engineers like Robert Maillart, the younger Yolles concluded that it was possible to build with flat plates supported by a concrete framework allowing larger bays without requiring the columns to have flared capitals or even thinner, wider drops on their tops to spread the loads.[56] As a shrewd commercial developer Leon Yolles immediately grasped that this method could be used to create more usable room height with less separation between floors while leaving space for ductwork and other services under the plates. But when Morden Yolles approached the city of Toronto Building Department he discovered that its outdated building code did not permit this method. He had to persuade municipal officials to reconsider by using the technique of "moment distribution" to calculate the stresses and strains. Benvenuto was the first Toronto building to use flat plates without either caps or drops where the columns joined the floors, making it a thoroughly Modern structure both internally and externally.[57]

5.37
Benvenuto entrance canopy.

The result was a much-acclaimed design that seemed to float on the top of the Avenue Road hill with curtain walls of cream-coloured brick between the metal-sash windows. In the courtyard to the north were the two entrances to the hotel and the apartments clearly marked out by the gravity-denying cantilevered canopies that became something of a signature for Dickinson. The ensemble, as historian Harold Kalman points out, was "a lively rhythmic composition that appears uncontrolled when contrasted with the severity of a disciplined Parkin composition."[58] The risks of pioneering with Modernism in the Canadian climate were demonstrated, however, by the fact that the flat plates extended out through the brick curtain walls and formed the floors of the balconies; this design meant that thermally conductive material passed through the building envelope to display the internal structure. The effects of this method had been little studied in the 1950s and 1960s but later on the energy costs of such "thermal bridges" rendered them obsolete.[59]

5.38
240 Oriole Road, Peter Dickinson, 1955.

Dickinson followed up the Benvenuto with another apartment house for Yolles and Rotenberg at 240 Oriole Parkway on the irregular corner formed by Oxton Avenue, where he perched an apartment building one storey up in the air on "pilotis" or pillars in approved Corbusian fashion because there was a large sewer running underneath that precluded digging a foundation. The triangular shape of the lot led him to twist the cruciform shape enough so that the windows of the apartments had wide views from its balconies, very much like those at the Benvenuto.[60]

Dickinson was ready to tackle almost any kind of project, and soon after his arrival in Toronto he set to work on 111 Richmond Street West in the downtown also for Yolles and Rotenberg. This building came to be regarded as among the first truly Modern office towers in Toronto with a reinforced concrete frame supported by fifty-six massive columns enclosed by a curtain wall (and newfangled automatic elevators). The fifteen storeys, with the top three set back, had an appearance of lightness as the stone bands formed spandrels under lightweight steel casement windows, which extended around the corners of the building without visible support. On the west side, a short

5.39 (Left)
111 Richmond Street West, Peter Dickinson, 1955.

5.40 (Above)
Wawanesa Insurance, Peter Dickinson, 1957.

distance back from the street was an unpierced masonry wall of green glazed brick that was cantilevered out from the structure, reaching from the second to the twelfth floor, so that it appeared to be floating in space. Dickinson's original plan envisaged twin towers with a public plaza between, which would have been another innovation for Toronto, but that second tower was never constructed in the way the architect originally intended.[61] On Yonge Street at Merton he created a four-storey building for Wawanesa Mutual Insurance with a windowless granite-clad wall cantilevered out at the second floor level facing onto Yonge. The north and south walls had alternating panels of windows and grey brick supported by exposed concrete columns and floor slabs polished and painted white.[62]

Dickinson's biographer reckons that working at whirlwind speed the architect tackled well over a score of projects between 1950 and 1955 in the greater Toronto area plus a number in other parts of Ontario – not all of them realized. Besides a large number of business offices with adjoining plants in the suburbs, he completed several schools. His first institutional design was the Beth Tzedec synagogue at 1700 Bathurst Street to provide a new home for two older Jewish congregations from downtown that were uniting – another job he acquired through Leon Yolles. Inside its yellow brick walls were a variety of different elements like a library and a school fanning out behind an octagonal chapel and a vast sanctuary that could be

5.41 (Above)
Beth Tzedec synagogue,
Peter Dickinson, 1954.

5.42 (Left)
Toronto Teachers' College,
Peter Dickinson, 1955.

expanded to hold 2,600 people.[63] He also took on the Toronto Teachers' College on a small site at 951 Carlaw Avenue in the east end, a steel-framed structure with brick and aluminum curtain walls around an interior court with a reflecting pool, which won a silver Massey Medal for educational buildings in 1955.[64]

One of Dickinson's most eye-catching designs was for the Juvenile Court and detention centre at 311 Jarvis Street. The slightly concave front wall of Kingston limestone had 411 small rectangular windows punched into it with one of the architect's flying canopies over the central doorway. German immigrant Horst Theis, who joined the Page and Steele firm in 1953, remarked of the design, "Nobody in his right mind would do something like this. It is

5.43 (Right)
Toronto Teachers' College, interior.

5.44 (Below)
Juvenile and Family Court,
Peter Dickinson, 1957.

highly impractical from a window cleaning point of view. It looks good and everybody loves it."[65] Unfortunately, the last sentence was quite untrue. It's likely that the juveniles judged and locked away behind this wall weren't too fond of these surroundings. After all, the building looked like a branch of the ministry of truth from which hundreds of eyes were peering out to catch any miscreants. Nevertheless, there can be no doubt that in his first five years Peter Dickinson had made a splash in the Toronto pond and thrust the ideas of Modernism firmly in front of people's noses, as he was to continue to do until his untimely death in 1961 at the age of only thirty-five.

The early 1950s finally saw other architects besides Parkin and Dickinson producing notable Modern buildings. Gordon S. Adamson received a silver Massey Medal in 1952 for an apartment building at 130 Old Forest Hill Road, which featured a long facade with a concave curve resting on pillars at ground level with strip windows and strong horizontals separating the floors. In 1954 Peter Caspari laid out Toronto's first multi-building apartment complex, the three towers of the

5·45
Juvenile and Family Court, interior.

City Park Apartments on Church Street just north of Carlton. The exterior reflected the vocabulary of Modernism with no more decoration than that provided by the strong verticals between the horizontal balconies. Rather than the more common steel framing with curtain walls the European developers allowed Caspari to use a design like the Benvenuto, featuring a reinforced concrete frame bearing the weight of the concrete slab floors as well as the poured concrete walls between the units. Not only did this method eliminate the need for wind bracing in such a tall structure but provided soundproofing, which made the unusually large apartments highly desirable.[66]

5.46
130 Old Forest Hill Road, Gordon S. Adamson, 1952.

5.47
City Park Apartments,
Peter Caspari, 1954.

Even ecclesiastical designs were starting to look different. While Islington United Church might cling to the Gothic Revival, other denominations proved more adventuresome. Parkin Associates drew up a Modern plan for Central Christadelphian (John B. Parkin being a faithful Christadelphian), while Michael Bach's St Peter's Estonian Lutheran and First Unitarian by Richard A. Fisher were equally avant-garde.[67]

5.48
Irving Grossman, 1950.

Nonetheless, private houses in the Modern manner still remained few and far between by the mid-1950s. Dickinson designed a house for Bernard Stainman in North York in 1953 about which not much seems to be known, though a photograph of the facade shows Modern touches.[68] Probably the most strikingly advanced layout in Toronto was created for the Betel family, adventuresome clients who commissioned the youthful Irving Grossman to design a house for them in suburban North York. Grossman was a 1950 graduate in architecture at the University of Toronto who had worked during summers with Rudolf Schindler in California before a stint with the well-known British Modernist firm of Fry, Drew, and Partners. Grossman set up practice in Toronto in 1954 and was retained by the Betels to design their house at 33 York Downs Drive.[69] He produced a layout for the sloping ravine-side lot composed of two interlocking rectangles with garage and kitchen on the street side and a second storey at right angles, obedient to the municipal bylaw that required some part of the house to be at an upper level. The two-storey living-dining room running right through the building stuck out over the front door rather like a television monitor and included an internal balcony and large windows overlooking the wide back lawn.[70] This was the first of a number of notable Modern home designs by Grossman in the Toronto area.

The report of the Massey Medal jury in 1952 suggested that, even by that relatively early date, some Modern details were becoming so prevalent as to be formulaic: Shore and Moffatt got a silver medal for municipal and government structures for its building for the Township of York but the jurors expressed regret that a fine design included V-shaped supports for the projecting entrance canopy, a cliché that could better have been replaced by something more straightforward.[71]

The tide of Modernism only lapped around the shores of the University of Toronto. The central administration remained highly wary about newfangled ideas and kept the faculty of the School of Architecture well away from designing any new buildings.

5.49 (Above)
Betel house, Irving Grossman, 1957.

5.50 (Right)
Betel house, rear.

Nevertheless, in 1950 Victoria College, which was federated with the university but semi-independent, took the decision to commission Eric Arthur and his partner, W.E. Fleury, to draw up a master plan for the redevelopment of their buildings at the northeast corner of the campus. The choice of Arthur's firm was surprising since he was known to have a particular dislike for the Romanesque Revival, and the college's main building was just such a design completed by William Storm in 1892 (see Figure 1.12). Arthur considered the structure with its heavy arches of multicoloured sandstone "a depressing pile," which he lumped together with the nearby Ontario

5.51 (Left) Wymilwood, Fleury and Arthur, 1954.

5.52 (Right) Wymilwood, interior.

legislative building and the Toronto City Hall (see Figure 1.13) as among the "illegitimate children" of H.H. Richardson's more successful works in the United States. Not unexpectedly, therefore, Fleury and Arthur drafted a plan that entailed the demolition and replacement of the despised main building. Though this proposal came to nothing, the architects were allowed to carry out their scheme for a new student union for the college called Wymilwood. This unabashedly Modern structure at the corner of Queen's Park and Charles Street opened in 1953 featuring a flat roof and brick panels between large windows; the folding plate roof over the sunken cafeteria was near the cutting edge for its time. Inside a cantilevered spiral staircase of reinforced concrete wound up a semicircular wall of masonry overhung by a large mobile. The chair of the committee that chose the interior décor recorded that, for the curtains, "happily, a free-flowing indefinite pattern was chosen, after discarding such alternatives as college crests, Canadian symbols, etc." The furniture and other interior decoration reflected heavy borrowing from the latest Scandinavian designs, which had only recently begun to penetrate into specialty shops in Canada.[72]

Victoria College added another Modern building in 1960 with a new library designed by Gordon S. Adamson. He persuaded the college to demolish the house occupied by its president and replace it on the southward-facing slope with a steel-framed block with continuous glazing around its base on three sides below a solid cut stone wall to house the book stacks. The ultimate aim was still to remove the Richardsonian Romanesque main building to create a new quadrangle, though in this regard Arthur's desires were eventually thwarted.[73]

In 1956 when the new magazine *Canadian Architect* prepared a list of twenty-five notable postwar buildings in Toronto that visiting architects might wish to examine, Modern designs predominated heavily. Page and Steele were represented by four of Peter Dickinson's designs (Benvenuto,

5.53 (Left)
Victoria College Library,
Gordon S. Adamson, 1960.

5.54 (Right)
Victoria College Library.

240 Oriole Parkway, 111 Richmond Street West, and Toronto Teachers' College), along with the same number of projects from the office of Parkin Associates (OAA Building, Salvation Army Headquarters, offices for Yardley of Canada, and George Harvey Vocational School on Keele Street). James Murray was recognized not only for his Spaulding house but for the Robert E. Cook building for Anglo Canada Insurance at 76 St Clair Avenue West, which had one of the first glass and aluminum curtain walls in Toronto.[74]

Gordon S. Adamson received recognition for the Crystal Glass and Plastics Plant on Queen's Quay as well as a house for property developer K.W. Peacock at 98 Teddington Park Avenue. Churches included Michael Bach's work for St Peter's Estonian Lutheran, Fleury and Arthur's hall for St Cuthbert's Anglican Church,[75] and Matsui and Yamazake's Toronto Buddhist Church at 918 Bathurst Street. Among the old guard only Marani and Morris were represented by the decidedly old-fashioned office for Crown Life Insurance at 120 Bloor East and the grandstand at the Canadian National Exhibition, along with Mathers and Haldenby's Imperial Oil Building on St Clair West.[76]

By the mid-1950s the Modern was beginning, at long last, to find acceptance among some homeowners. In 1957 *Canadian Homes and Gardens* reported that a couple had chosen Parkin Associates, described as one of the foremost Canadian promoters of the International Style (words not used with any frequency by the magazine previously), to design them a home in Belleville, about one hundred miles east of Toronto. With brick panels separated by unclad steel beams supporting a flat roof, the building revealed its strong horizontals and verticals and even had exposed steel on the interior.[77] James A. Knight used this design to give the magazine's readers a short tutorial on "Why Houses Don't Look Like Caves Anymore." Early Modernists

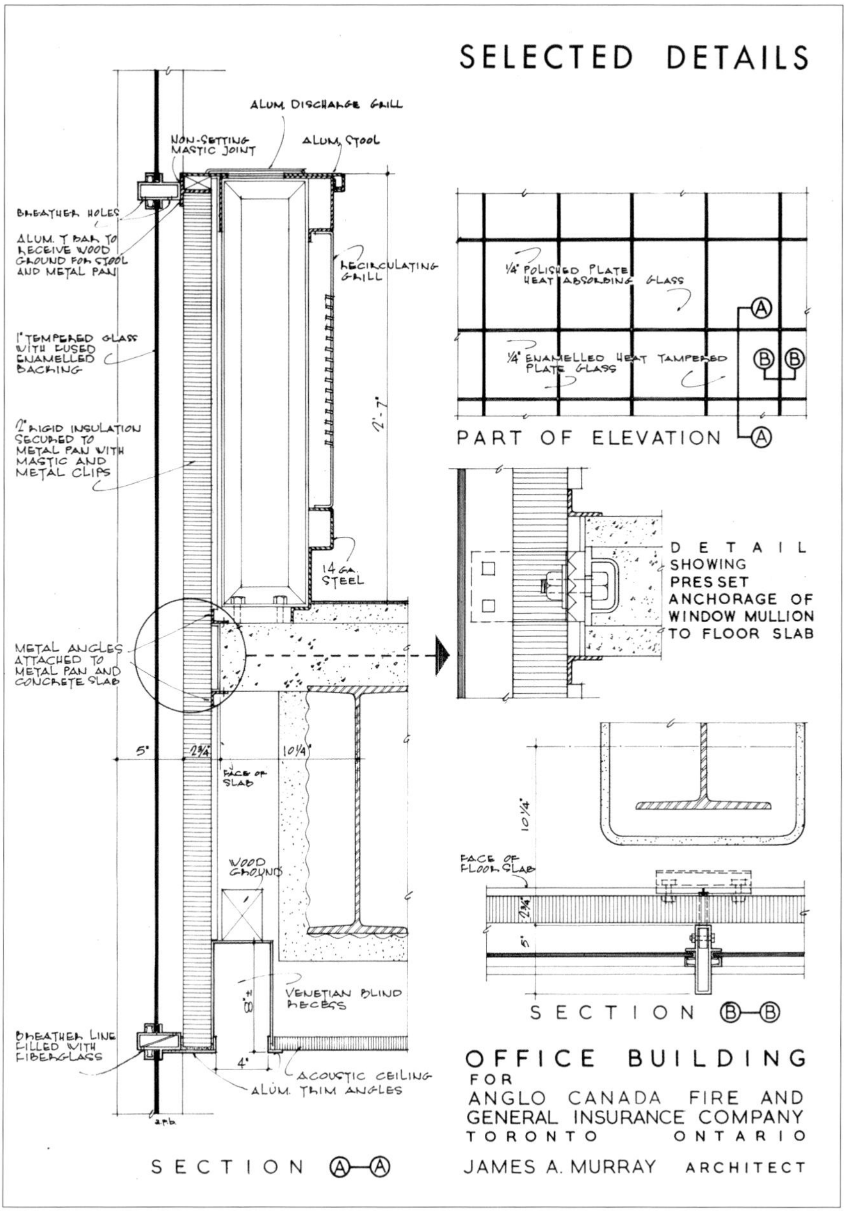

5.55
Anglo Canada Insurance, detail drawings of exterior cladding, James Murray, 1955.

had rejected historical styles, he said, but many people had shunned the less accomplished examples of advanced design employing clichés like round port-hole windows. Sharp corners and flat roofs like those of the Belleville house, which rose abruptly out of its site, were still off-putting even though some features like glass walls below low-pitched overhanging roofs had prolifer-ated. Suburban builders might prefer split-level bungalows but, said Knight, the International Style seemed here to stay whatever its critics might say.[78]

Still, the critics refused to be silenced. In 1950 *Canadian Homes and Gardens* asked "What Is Wrong With the Modern?" The answer was

5.56
"Uncompromising Modern Inside and Out": Belleville house, John B. Parkin Associates, 1957.

that Modernists were too keen to return to nature and cultivate pseudo-primitivism. Architects wanted to let the garden into the living room, filling it up with rubber plants and cactuses; planting beds and pools with trees growing in them would soon penetrate inside. Then the interior decorators would start bringing in driftwood and using fabrics with primitive designs. Wasn't civilization about getting away from nature in the raw making it unwise for people to reverse the process in their homes?[79]

Senior members of the architectural profession still proved dubious about Modernism. In 1953 the chair of the RAIC *Journal*'s editorial board, Earl Morgan, wrote that traditional styles might seem static yet some modernistic designs were no less slavish copies than a Georgian Revival house. What excuse was there for building in California fashion with bare uninsulated panes of glass abutting one another on corners or putting great upswept roofs overhanging western walls in view of the Canadian climate?[80] At the same time the president of the RAIC, R. Scholfield Morris (of Marani and Morris), detected a "turning away" by some thoughtful critics from the exuberances of the postwar period. Freedom from restraint and tradition had finally induced sober second thoughts about the new fads, making people "less willing to accept the philosophies of contemporary prophets without fully understanding them." Designers were again becoming concerned about the restraints imposed by climate and environment, and new methods and materials must be scrutinized for their fitness, beauty, economy, and durability rather than for mere novelty. Architects might be on the verge of rejecting the "shoddiness" of many aspects of present-day existence and reflecting worthwhile things in their designs. "Perhaps now that the Gothic has been vanquished we can devote more of our energies to resisting the Goths."[81]

Another old hand was James Govan who had come to Canada in 1907 to work with John Lyle and later established his own firm that built over fifty hospitals. In 1954 Govan uncorked a splendid dose of Scottish pessimism concerning the hallmarks of the Modern, detailing the foolishness of some designers in ignoring local realities. The present trend was to replace walls with the maximum amount of glass and as little masonry between panes as possible, but the Canadian climate could easily erode narrow strips of masonry. Young architects seemed unworried by heat gain and loss and used glass panels everywhere. Looking around downtown Toronto in 1954 Govan spotted a new federal government building (presumably the Mackenzie Building on Richmond Street East at Toronto) with glass curtain walls on all four sides, where three-quarters of the windows were already covered with paper for protection against the sun. Insulated walls could cause problems if care was not taken to ensure that heat conduction did not allow moisture buildup on the outside. Adding air conditioning, said Govan, might only make matters worse because of the dramatic variations of heat absorption in materials.[82]

Even such an enthusiast for the Modern as Eric Arthur had some quibbles: it was impossible to hang pictures on the walls of new houses. Mies van der Rohe and Philip Johnson might think such decoration unnecessary, but Arthur was not convinced. Moreover, the open plan provided little of the privacy that inhabitants of a two-storey Georgian had enjoyed with separate living, eating, and sleeping areas. Rather incoherently Arthur suggested that perhaps split-level houses and schizophrenia were somehow connected. Then he went on to muse about whether it was any wonder that living in a glass box had led Philip Johnson to remain a bachelor.[83] Such grumbling would no doubt have struck a sympathetic chord in the tract houses of Applewood Acres but couldn't obscure the fact that by the mid-1950s Modern architecture had finally elbowed its way into a small but definite place in the cultural life of Toronto. What would come next?

6

VARIETIES OF MODERNISM 1956–1965

In 1956 the well-known architectural critic Lewis Mumford published an article entitled "The Gift Horse's Mouth," which vehemently condemned the evolution of International Style Modern architecture. Mumford observed that the Museum of Modern Art, which had been responsible for publicizing Modernism in the 1930s, had recently built a new library in the canonical Modern manner, rejecting traditional forms and ornamentation. In his usual iconoclastic fashion, Mumford condemned the new building: "It has very little to say and is content with not saying it." The results, he said, showed all the weakness of the "arid and often flagrantly anti-functional formulas of the International Style – now abandoned, incidentally, for something even worse in Le Corbusier's recent chapel at Ronchamp." All too likely, he predicted, there would be more such buildings to come, reflecting "neither the old nor the new, neither functional usefulness or aesthetic purity, still less an effective synthesis." What was needed was a new architecture that displayed none of the personal idiosyncrasies of Le Corbusier or Frank Lloyd Wright or the formalistic arbitrariness of Mies van der Rohe.[1]

6.1 (Opposite) Toronto International Airport, Terminal 1, John B. Parkin Associates, 1964.

In 1961 Mumford renewed his denunciation in a speech upon receiving a gold medal from the Royal Institute of British Architects. When defending the "absurd constrictions" imposed on residents by his Unité d'habitation in Marseilles, Le Corbusier had proclaimed the need to alter human nature to fit his architectural requirements, while Mies made the same "peremptory demands" without even bothering to defend them. Mumford said that "By practical necessity if not by avowed demand the inhabitants of the great highrise structures that are now marching across the landscape must be trimmed and altered to fit the architectural design." The only comfort that Mumford could draw was that Le Corbusier's chapel at Ronchamp, "however faked and deliberately naïve the elements in its composition," showed that he was gradually awakening to the "sterile bureaucratic images" of the city of the future that had dominated architecture since 1900.[2] Could it be that Modernism had had its day even before it obtained widespread acceptance in a place like Toronto?

The following year John C. Parkin (who was, of course, a fervent promoter of the International Style) recalled that in the years following the Second World War designers of Modern buildings were still very much a minority among architects in Canada. People like him were "doctrinaire in our emulation of the great international masters" since local practitioners had not yet had time to develop distinctive personal philosophies. He distinguished two principal currents in Modernism, one most closely associated with Mies van der Rohe, the other with Frank Lloyd Wright. The latter had followers like Ron Thom, but because Wright was an American, said Parkin, he did not attract so many disciples since Canadians tended to look away from the United States to the wider world. Mies was the outstanding international influence (though of course a long-standing resident of the United States) "because he created a no-nonsense vernacular particularly appropriate in a country of more restricted no-nonsense budgets" and because he demonstrated a relative mastery of technique particularly adaptable for commercial purposes.[3]

There were also other European influences, less geometric, less formalistic, and more humane than Miesian abstractions, particularly associated with Scandinavian architects like the Finn Alvar Aalto who brought into play curvilinear forms. Architectural historian Alan Gowans wrote, "Around 1955 there was a decided change. For whatever deep psychological or sociological reasons, more and more new architects and new buildings appeared whose ideas and principles showed a determination to accept the best going, whatever its source."[4] The authors of a study of Modern Canadian houses built between 1945 and 1985 noted that "Modernism in the 1950s resonated with pleasing and positive connotations of progressiveness and innovations – qualities which seem to explain why an increasing number of Canadian clients seem to have been favourable to commissioning buildings in this idiom." Members of the profession were becoming well-aware of the writings and the works of leading Modernist architects (a familiarity fostered by contemporary advances in photographic reproduction). In practice Canadians were "pragmatic and informal with respect to Modernist theory, adhering to a relatively few Modernist-inspired visual forms rather than an underlying theory." They took seriously the Modernist dictum of designing by modules and were committed as a point of honour to revealing structural systems.[5] What remained in question was the degree to which such principles would affect actual building layouts.

I

In the mid-1950s debate about the place of Modernism on the Toronto scene crystallized over the construction of a new city hall. Almost from the time E.J. Lennox's Richardsonian Romanesque pile opened on Queen Street West at the head of Bay in 1899 there had been complaints that the amount of space occupied by courtrooms was leaving the ever-growing municipal civil service cramped for offices. The City Beautiful plan for revamping the downtown in 1911 included a civic square on Queen to be surrounded by monumental buildings, including a new courthouse and police station. The only building actually constructed at that time was at the northwest corner of the proposed square where the Neoclassical land Registry Office opened in 1917. The shortage of accommodation forced the city to rent ever-larger amounts of space, and a new building was proposed in the 1920s. The revival of the scheme for a civic centre on Queen Street in 1929 included a new municipal building next to the Registry Office, but that plan also came to nothing as economic depression and then war prevented action. As the bureaucracy continued to expand after the Second World War municipal departments came to occupy an entire City Hall Annex on Bay Street just north of Lennox's building

The idea of a civic square refused to die. In 1943 city officials recommended the acquisition of the whole area extending west from Bay along the north side of Queen as far as Osgoode Hall and north to Louisa Street, which ran behind the Registry Office. Four years later the ratepayers approved borrowing $2 million to purchase these lands to create such a square. Properties began to be acquired. Various layouts for a new city hall on the square were suggested during the next few years.[6] In 1952 an advisory committee recommended a plan prepared by Marani and Morris for a Neoclassical structure, which led to public protests from students at the School of Architecture. An angry exchange of correspondence ensued, which Eric Arthur observed showed the "contrasting philosophies of a die-hard architectural minority and the current students."[7]

6.2
The 1955 City Hall proposal that set the stage for an unprecedented international architectural competition, Marani and Morris, Mathers and Haldenby, and Shore and Moffatt.

Finally in 1955, at the city's request, the long-established firms of Marani and Morris, Mathers and Haldenby, and Shore and Moffatt jointly presented the city's executive Board of Control with a design for a similar Neoclassical pavilion housing a new city council chamber to face onto the northern edge of a square. Its colonnaded front would echo the Registry Office to the west, and behind it would be built a new municipal office block that appeared to be a duplicate of Mathers and Haldenby's Imperial Oil building uptown on St Clair Avenue West at Avenue Road (see Figure 5.14). Architecture students at the university again denounced the layout as "a funeral home of vast dimensions" and a "monstrous monument to backwardness." Frank Lloyd Wright was induced to call it "a cliché already dated," and Walter Gropius described it as "a very poor pseudo-modern design unworthy of the city of Toronto." Mayor Nathan Phillips remarked wittily that the model looked like "the Grand Hotel with the longest balcony in the world. All it needs is a swimming pool."[8] He wanted to hold a design competition open to every architect in the world. Nonetheless the city council endorsed the plan and asked the ratepayers to approve an expenditure of $18 million at the 1955 election. A spirited debate ensued, which, according to William Dendy and William Kilbourn, stemmed "less from the design itself than from the dissatisfaction felt by many people in the Toronto arts community at the extremely slow acceptance of Modernism and its forms in Toronto. The design's stripped Classical monumentality and conservative inspiration seemed to typify the 'Old Guard' that dominated painting, architecture and the other arts in the city."[9]

Whether moved by parsimony or by aesthetic sensibilities, the ratepayers turned down this rather dusty scheme by a margin of over four thousand votes out of sixty thousand cast, which left the city stuck with a bill for $96,000 in design fees. Yet the need for additional space for offices was becoming increasingly acute as the staff of the newly created Municipality of Metropolitan Toronto ("Metro") grew alongside the employees of the city proper. But who was to design a new building?

Eric Arthur at the University of Toronto was a strong proponent of architectural competitions for major public projects, an idea he helped persuade the Royal Commission on National Development in the Arts, Letters, and Sciences to endorse in its 1951 report.[10] Juries in such contests could go for the safe but dull choice, but in the RAIC *Journal* Arthur editorialized, "it is fair to assume that the modern jury will not be lacking in courage or foresight. Our only reason for saying so is that we have surely passed the stage when a jury would hide behind a façade of archeology on the grounds that it was safe and tried. Creative design has come to have meaning even to the 'man in the street.'" In 1952 the Toronto chapter of the Ontario Association of Architects (OAA) also suggested that a competition would be the best way to ensure high quality in the layout of the proposed civic square. The OAA soon had a change of heart, and the following year Toronto chapter chair E.C.S. Cox argued that the commission should go to some well-known local architect.[11]

In the spring of 1956 a joint committee of politicians representing both Metro and the city met to consider what to do and concluded that any building should be utilitarian rather than a showpiece, which seemed to guarantee a dull design.[12] This seemed to suit Metro chair Frederick Gardiner, who, after hearing about advanced civic design in Switzerland and Scandinavia, asked why so many people from those countries wanted to emigrate to Canada. Metro was, however, persuaded to buy Lennox's old city hall for $4.5 million to use as a courthouse, and, at the municipal elections in December 1956, Toronto's ratepayers approved a new building budgeted to cost $18 million. Mayor Phillips, with the editorial support of the Toronto *Telegram*, took this as an endorsement for his long-standing desire to hold an international design competition.

The idea led Forsey Page (of Page and Steele) to ask what would happen if the winner were a Chinese Communist, but in January 1957 city council approved a competition and appointed Eric Arthur to be the professional advisor to the jury. Though the director of the National Gallery of Canada told the OAA annual meeting that its members ought to be delighted to take part in such a prestigious contest, the association retreated only grudgingly, arguing (with the endorsement of the RAIC president) that entrants should at least be restricted to Canadian residents. Not, it was emphasized, because of any fears about the superior talent among foreigners. After all, Canadians themselves had been recognized around the world by their fellow professionals: "More than that, many have been commissioned to design buildings abroad and in countries as far off as Pakistan." Rather it was because of possible "psychological reaction" to such competition amongst architects. In addition Canadians understood the unique climate and the construction materials available. And anyway it would cost the locals $3,000 to $5,000 to prepare their entries while foreigners could do so for much less owing to lower labour costs.

In April the *Toronto Star*, which had opposed the idea of a competition all along,[13] discovered that the rules of the International Architectural Union required all competition judges to be professional architects or planners. Weren't such people likely to select a "faddy design" that would make the building look like a 1937 automobile? "Modern" architects were certain to favour a modernistic design, but the judges should not share the same point of view or favour an "eccentric style." In reply, the *Telegram* pointed out that no self-respecting architect would enter a competition without confidence in the integrity of the judges. If a Canadian won, then he would secure a worldwide reputation, while a foreign winner would ensure the city international attention.

6.3 (Above)
Civic Square and New City Hall site from the south-west, 1955, Registry Office centre, the Armouries at left.

6.4 (Right)
Civic Square and New City Hall site from the southeast, with the Registry Office in the distance.

The wrangling continued throughout the early months of 1957. Questions remained about whether the Neoclassical Registry Office should be removed to free the entire area for redevelopment. Would a new street grid be constructed and would other buildings find a place around the civic square? What would happen to the massive Romanesque Revival Armoury building, erected by the federal government in 1891 just to the northwest, with its soaring window arches and crenellated towers of red brick ornamented by grey limestone?[14]

Fortunately Eric Arthur brought what was for him a somewhat uncharacteristic air of "intelligent calm" to his role as professional advisor, and one by one the controversial questions were settled. In July the rules were formally approved. After all the lobbying by the OAA its president grumbled that the city was "insistent that it be open to architects in all parts of the civilized world and this includes Russia." Eight finalists would be selected, each to receive a $7,500 award along with a grant of $25,000 to flesh out the details of an entry. After much debate the OAA Registration Board (chaired by Eric Haldenby) consented that the winner (who would receive a 6 percent commission) could be granted a temporary membership in the association to superintend the job if that winner was not licensed to practise in Ontario.[15]

The nature of the project, announced in the autumn of 1957, was broadly defined. The city hall was not to resemble "just another office building, hardly differentiated from the commercial structures which surround it," but to be designed to suggest "government, continuity of certain democratic traditions and service to the community." Nothing much was said about the civic square except that it should be "a landscaped open space of great beauty serving as a forecourt to the city hall, and as an open space for the pleasure of citizens." A water feature was not mandatory, but careful consideration should be given to its inclusion in view of the heat of the summer season and it might function as a skating rink in winter. A blunt reminder was included that any design must take account of the 1,300-space underground parking garage that had recently been completed beneath the south end of the site so that a tall building could not be erected above it.[16]

The previous controversies meant that public attention was sharply focused upon the jurors. Charles E. ("Ned") Pratt was a 1939 graduate of the University of Toronto who had joined the Vancouver firm of Thompson, Berwick, Pratt, long sympathetic to Modern design in the "West Coast" style; he was already the focus of much attention for his nearly completed headquarters building for BC Hydro in Vancouver, which was probably why he was asked to join the panel.[17] Gordon Stephenson had come from Liverpool University in 1955 to be head of Urban and Regional Planning at the

6.5
New City Hall competition jury, 1958 (*left to right*): Arthur, Pratt, Saarinen, Rogers, Holford, Stephenson.

University of Toronto. Sir William Holford, the well-known town planner, was another Liverpool man who was working on layouts for three different national capitals in Rhodesia, South Africa, and Australia. Ernesto Rogers had been professor of Theory of Architecture at Milan Polytechnic since 1952. Eero Saarinen, son of the distinguished Finnish émigré to the United States, was a Yale graduate who headed his own architectural firm in Detroit. Eric Arthur remained as professional advisor.[18]

The deadline for entries was 18 April 1958, and Arthur's secretary, Mrs Marian Fowler, was soon dealing with all manner of questions. Did the 54.6 inches of annual snowfall in Toronto occur all at once? How was she to decipher a telegram in Polish? Would it be alright for an Indian to pay the cost of shipping his model by sending a bag of rupees since he could not obtain foreign exchange? When it was all over there were 532 entries from people in forty-two different countries. Some were well-known like the American I.M. Pei, others dark horses like a team of Harvard architectural students headed by John Andrews whose instructors had shown little enthusiasm for their activities. One finalist claimed he had spent just fifteen dollars on his entry while some American firms invested as much $10,000.[19]

Laid out (with entrants' names carefully concealed) the models and drawings filled the 32,000 square feet of the Horticultural Building at the Canadian National Exhibition. In their final report the jurors explained the principles of selection that had guided them. A city hall could be similar to other downtown buildings and derive its importance only from its sitting on a large open square, but this seemed too tame. Or it could be so tall as to soar above the surrounding structures, yet this was an expensive and inefficient approach and impossible to maintain indefinitely. A low horizontal building standing detached would contrast with its background, which had a definite appeal. After a day and a half of deliberations the jurors had agreed upon the entries to be eliminated from further consideration.

At that moment, however, as Eric Arthur later revealed, events took an unexpected turn. The absent Eero Saarinen finally showed up in Toronto, and, as the most famous of the judges, made an immediate demand to the other jurors: "Show me your discards."[20] Irritated though they must have been, the others gave way, and Saarinen not only got to see the rejects but persuaded them that at least one was worthy of reconsideration. The eight finalists included five low horizontal structures, and two others featured slab towers in the full International Style. When the jury's final decision was released in September 1958, it turned out that Saarinen had been able to convince a majority of the jury to consider a different notion: that a building highly distinctive in both form and in material from its surroundings might be the best choice.

The winning design submitted by Finnish architect Viljo Rewell was the reject that Saarinen had persuaded the others to reconsider.[21] (After he moved to Toronto the architect changed the spelling of his surname to Revell because the locals persisted in mispronouncing it like "jewel.") Born in 1910 Revell had spent some time in the office of Alvar Aalto and opened his own practice in 1945. Awarded a Fulbright Fellowship in 1954, Revell had come to Mies van der Rohe's base at the Illinois Institute of Technology but, finding the atmosphere too "Miesian," he moved on to the University of California at Berkeley.[22]

Revell represented a new wave of Modernists, distinct from the founding generation, with a particular interest in new materials and techniques of construction such as the use of concrete. His year in North America (where he also became acquainted with Eero Saarinen) had made him conversant with developments there. He much admired Saarinen's design for the parabolic Gateway Arch to stand on the banks of Mississippi River in St Louis, designed in 1948 though not completed until 1965. Revell's own work progressed from early functionalist designs to more free-flowing forms like those favoured by Aalto. Indeed, when the news of his selection for the Toronto job arrived, Aalto wired Revell, "Seldom does a colleague feel so happy over another's victory."[23]

Revell submitted a highly attractive model supported only by a bare minimum of drawings. Asked by a CBC interviewer if the design had taken a long time he replied, "No, it was very fast, it was teamwork, you see."[24] Later it was claimed that the initial concept had come from a fascination with the shadow that a light cast upon the shade of a Luxor fixture, the pattern of which a junior designer doodled as a drawing.[25]

6.6
New City Hall. Viljo Revell reviewing his design model at the Parkin office in Don Mills, 1958.

The distinctive layout featured two curving buildings of unequal height whose glass inner walls cupped a clam-shaped council chamber, so that the central focus was on the public, political functions of the building surrounded by tall office towers for the staff. The jury debated long and hard about whether Revell should win because of serious concerns about whether such a structure could be built within the allotted budget (which was probably one of the reasons why Revell's proposal had originally been rejected until Saarinen intervened). Eventually, at three o'clock in the morning, a three-person majority composed of Pratt, Rogers, and Saarinen carried the day for the Finn.

The majority argued that Revell's design not only made excellent use of the square to the south but also drew attention to Lennox's existing city hall to the east and the open space in front of historic Osgoode Hall to the west. The towers constituted a superb aesthetic statement, while the distinctive shape of the complex would make it a landmark on the city's skyline. Though Revell's original entry was far sparser in detail than the other finalists, all the key elements of the final layout were present: the elevated colonnade and walkway to surround the vast paved square and the reflecting pool at its south edge aligned with the old city hall across Bay Street. The most significant alteration made from Revell's original plan was that the taller tower was moved from the west to the east so that more afternoon sunlight would reach the open space between.[26]

The other two jurors, Holford and Stephenson, were convinced that some of the other finalists had submitted outstanding designs that could be built more economically. They joined in acknowledging the originality of Revell's conception but in their minority report they made some pointed criticisms. The unusual boomerang shape of the two buildings and the circular council chamber almost guaranteed budget overruns. The cost of construction was bound to be high since each of the floors in the towers was cantilevered from the outside walls rather than using simpler framing. Internal circulation was complicated with long corridors on every floor plus the need to navigate from one tower to the other. The curving outside walls of the two towers were windowless from east and west, showing nothing but blank walls, which would hardly welcome future development around a square that was itself rather stark.[27] Yet all the jurors were keen to see the project go ahead, so they left many details to be solved by Eric Arthur as the professional advisor, believing that his influence would make it easier to gain final approval from the city council.[28]

Always ready with a pithy quote, Frank Lloyd Wright glanced at a drawing and declared, "You've got a headmarker for a grave and future generations will look at it and say: 'This marks the spot where Toronto fell.'" Local critics compared the towers to a couple of pieces of broken sewer pipe standing on end. Yet the popular reception to Revell's plan seems to have been enthusiastic: thousands of citizens flocked to Eaton's department store on College Street to look at the model. The press was filled with comment, overwhelmingly favourable, since even those not seduced by the design concluded that the project would give Toronto's cultural development a long-overdue shot in the arm.[29]

One of the archpriests of Modernism, Sigfried Giedion, congratulated the city for holding an international competition and resisting the temptation to restrict entry to local citizens as had been done with the design for the new national capital city at Brasilia.[30] He praised the design for embodying the transformation undergone by Modernism since its birth in the 1920s. New Yorker Thomas Creighton lectured the Ontario Association of Architects about the "New Sensualism": designs like Le Corbusier's Ronchamp, Saarinen's Trans World Air terminal at Idlewild (later renamed Kennedy), and the New City Hall rejected "geometric precision and proportional niceties" and appealed directly to the emotions. Eric Arthur pointed out that a minority of the five hundred entries in the contest were Miesian, and that only one of the finalists had included a transparent curtain wall. Toronto architect Eberhard Zeidler claimed that the austere rectilinear forms and restricted choices of materials common to early Modernism were already being replaced by more exotic shapes like Saarinen's hockey rink at Yale University, whose curving roof suspended from above had earned it the sobriquet, "the Whale." Somewhat immodestly Zeidler made similar claims for his layout for a new church where the roof was formed by overlapping two parabolic arches that created a clerestory at the ridge line of the roof.[31]

Politicians continued to grumble about the likely costs, but eventually the city council voted to ask Revell to prepare preliminary drawings and estimates. To undertake this task the architect moved his family and principal associates on the project to Toronto in 1959.[32] Because the financial viability of the project depended upon the Metro government becoming a tenant of the building, the views of Metro chair Frederick Gardiner could not be ignored. In the spring of 1959 he expressed a personal preference for such *retardaire* designs as Marani and Morris's Bank of Canada on University

Avenue (see Figure 5.12) or the Crown Life building on Bloor Street. The *Canadian Architect* fretted that the whole project might yet be aborted by the "grotesque squabbling" between local politicians.[33] At the end of 1960 the delay continued as Gardiner was still talking in terms of substituting a run-of-the-mill office building costing only five dollars per square foot, even though the city was now on the hook to Revell for thousands of dollars worth of preliminary work.[34]

Finally the logjam broke. Two people seemed to have played key roles: Eric Arthur and John B. Parkin. Arthur, as professional advisor for the competition, had never ceased to press for the winning design. And in 1959 Revell, presumably acting on Arthur's advice, chose John B. Parkin Associates as his local representative; a formal partnership named Revell-Parkin was created to undertake the work. Not only was Parkin a prominent figure whose opinion the politicians respected, but his large firm of engineers provided a guarantee that the layout could be produced successfully despite the fact that the radical design might involve complex problems. Three members of Revell's firm moved with him to Toronto to live in Don Mills; Revell even designed a house for himself but its construction proved too costly and he bought a place instead.

When the architects began detailed work, however, serious problems were quickly revealed. Cost estimates for the new building indicated that it was likely to cost between $30 and $40 million dollars. Confidentially warned of this prediction, Mayor Phillips advised the architects that any proposed outlay over $25 million would have no chance of approval by city council. Revell-Parkin set to work to see if a cost-saving redesign was possible without compromising the fundamental layout of the building. In the end the cost estimates were pared down to a projected $25 million. Early in 1961 the city council at last gave its approval, and 14 August was fixed as the date for bids. Though wavering continued to the end, Mayor Phillips was able to carry council with him, and Anglin Norcross (Ontario) was granted the contract a month later. The city council was so pleased that the costs had come in at $23 million, $2 million less than feared, that they ordered a two additional floors added to each of the towers.[35]

The building that began to rise looked very much like the original sketches, but there were in fact important engineering changes made for both economic and structural reasons.[36] Because the curving towers were of different heights (twenty and twenty-seven storeys respectively) and had slightly different lengths and floor shapes, the wind loads on the building proved difficult to compute. The engineers pointed out that, as designed, the inner faces of the towers were catenary or boomerang shapes with thin sharp edges at either end containing stairs and services, forming the shape of the underside of the wing of an airplane created to lift it aloft. In theory (and perhaps practice) strong winds might generate enough force to strip the curtain wall right off the edge of each floor.

Moreover, there was concern about the design of the floors, which were supposed to be flat slabs cantilevered from the solid back walls to the fully glazed ones on the interior face, leaving a clear open space with the secretarial offices having windows and the executive offices to the rear. Wind forces might cause those floors to deflect dramatically. Unable to develop arithmetical formulas to predict these forces precisely, a model of the building was dispatched to the University of Toronto for wind tunnel tests.

As a result the architects decided to order certain changes that, it was hoped, would be largely imperceptible. With Revell's reluctant assent, the two Parkins, John B. and John C., ordered the redrafting of a substantial number of drawings at a personal cost to them of $90,000. A line of columns was inserted along the centre of each floor to support the sixteen foot long underfloor beams that tapered from thirty-six inches deep at the rear wall down to nine inches at the glass curtain wall. The shape of the towers was altered, their pointed ends blunted; the inner walls would be parallel to the exterior of the round council chamber rather than like an airfoil and the curtain wall could be securely fastened to the floor plate. The structural plan thus came to resemble more closely a conventional office building that had been bent, giving each tower a bulkier silhouette, particularly noticeable on the lower west one, which looked a bit like a squat cylindrical tank once its sharp finlike ends had been shorn off. In addition, a central elevator-service core was inserted in each tower to stiffen it along with the stair-service shafts at the blunt ends of each floor.

In addition, rather than being freestanding, the towers were connected to a central podium at the third-floor level to increase stability, though due to cost cutting the roof of the podium was never really landscaped. Rather than extending further northward to provide more relatively inexpensive office space for future expansion of the municipal staff, the towers were left to stand almost at the podium's northern edge.[37]

Inside the front doors a grand entrance hall lit by a circular skylight under the domed lower side of the council chamber was eliminated. Rather than sitting upon three large concrete supports, the chamber would now rest upon a vast trunk rising tree-like from ground level, emphasized by hollowing out the floor around its base. The chamber itself remained a striking semicircular amphitheatre with sloping seats topped by reception areas around the outside under the upper dome.

The actual materials for construction also required technical innovations. Revell called for the outer walls of the towers to contain vertical strips of yellowish Bottocino marble that would cause the building to sparkle when lit. The $2.5 million contract to produce the four thousand precast concrete panels, each containing four hundred marble strips, was won by the Beer family's Toronto Cast Stone Company. To do the job the Beers had to develop a special precasting machine to turn out the panels within the required eighteen months. Moreover, as construction proceeded the panels were used as the formwork for the eighteen inch thick reinforced concrete structural walls inside that actually supported the towers – something never done on such a large scale before.[38]

Construction got under way under the supervision of the city's property commissioner, Harry H. Rogers, but by the spring of 1963 the structural work was five months behind schedule. It was clear that plans to open the building in 1964 had to be abandoned. As a result the council decided to create the special position of city hall and civic square coordinator to oversee the job and try to manage the unending wrangles between the architects, the contractor, and the subtrades. Most vexing was the need to keep the Registry Office building at the west edge of the site at least partly open until other premises were found and it could be demolished. And Perini Limited, which

6.7
New City Hall rises as the Registry Office falls, 1961.

had been given the contract to construct a huge northerly extension of the underground parking garage under the new building, spent a great deal of energy on blaming delays on other parties.

At first glance the choice of coordinator was somewhat surprising. George Bell was tapped for the job on the grounds that as the city's parks and recreation commissioner he had a great deal of experience in overseeing the letting and completion of contracts. Bell spent the next two and one half years driving the project to completion so that it could open upon the revised schedule in the fall of 1965.

While the building was going up another source of controversy arose. From the outset Revell was convinced that he would be asked to design the interiors and furniture of the public spaces to harmonize with his building, and he hired two Finnish designers to move to Toronto for this purpose. In 1962, however, Revell absented himself to teach at the Massachusetts Institute of Technology, and in 1963 (apparently frustrated with all the obstacles he was encountering in Toronto) he moved back to Finland. He had also fallen seriously ill, and, despite repeated pleas from Eric Arthur and others, insisted that his doctors had advised him against taking the risk of the lengthy trip to Toronto. His reluctance was doubtless reinforced by the fact that in April 1964, the city, anxious to contain costs, took away the furnishing contract from the architects. A separate competition was announced for the decoration of the mayor's office and important public spaces, and plans were made to shift as much well-worn furniture as possible from the old city hall for the offices.[39]

Revell finally did visit Toronto again in the autumn of 1964, though he resigned as a member of the Furnishings Design Committee when his own proposal was rejected. He died in November of that year with the building uncompleted. The furnishings contest, still under way when he died, quickly degenerated into a farce. The conditions of entry had not specified a budget until George Bell issued a "bulletin" in January 1965, fixing the maximum cost at $850,000. Some of the four finalists protested at this retrospective limit, but in the spring of 1965 the committee selected Knoll International as the winner on the grounds that the proposed forms, materials, and colours would best have satisfied Revell. It soon turned out that the Knoll bid had been priced unit by unit, and that the committee had not bothered to tally up its total cost, which was revealed to be more than $1 million. When the other three bids were finally costed, one of them was even higher but the other two met the $850,000 limit.

Eric Arthur, as chair of the Furnishings Design Committee,[40] then announced that only Knoll's designs were acceptable in fulfilling Revell's vision. Local politicians started backing and filling, each suddenly an expert on

6.8
New City Hall, interior, 1965.

modern furniture design. Mayor Philip Givens (who had succeeded Nathan Phillips) demanded the Knoll bid be accepted whatever the cost, but when a motion came before council on 15 April 1965, it was lost on a tie vote of ten to ten. Then one alderman departed and the mayor put a new motion that passed by one vote. In the face of public criticism a group of local architects argued that the choice should always have been made on the basis of aesthetics not cost, but the outcry got so loud that Knoll felt required to reduce its bid to $849,562. Many politicians still favoured the local department store, Simpson's, whose original bid had been lowest at $848,310, but in the end Givens carried the day. *Canadian Architect* pronounced it very curious that city politicians who had been bold enough to sponsor an international design competition found it so hard to accept furnishings that suited Revell's design. The knockabout humour continued when it turned out that Knoll had specified some desks made simply of three massive slabs of precast concrete as legs and a work surface, which later had to have "vanity panels" installed under their tops at the front as mini-skirts became the new order of fashion.[41]

The New City Hall (as it came to be known) was opened with splendid ceremony on 13 September 1965 in the presence of the governor general, the prime minister of Canada, and the premier of Ontario. A throng of citizens viewed the building lit up in a blaze of spotlights amidst much back-patting about Toronto's new sophistication. But just to keep the laughs coming, plans were announced in the spring of 1966 to install in front of the building on Nathan Phillips Square one of Henry Moore's monumental bronze sculp-

6.9
New City Hall, complete, 1968.

tures. Moore and Revell had first met in 1960 and began discussing the installation of a work by the sculptor in front of the new building. One of the architect's clients who had purchased a Moore work for his house in 1961 remembered Revell declaring, "None of my buildings is ready until there's a Henry Moore sculpture in front of it."[42] The architect and the sculptor agreed that "3-Way Piece Number 2" (popularly known as "The Archer") would best compliment the city hall. The Toronto council, however, refused to approve an expenditure of $120,000 for an object that some alderman announced they would not want in their own backyards. In the end Mayor Givens had to turn to a group of local philanthropists to raise the necessary funds privately in order to permit the installation of Moore's work to proceed in October 1966.[43]

Even before the building opened, a cottage industry had developed as architects jostled with one another to get their assessments of Revell's design into print. With the architect hardly cold in his grave in the autumn of 1964, *Canadian Architect* convened a panel discussion where transplanted westerner Ron Thom opined that the building was very important, though he thought that the podium and the colonnade framing the square were deficient. C.F.T. Rounthwaite drew comfort from the fact that the public had accepted a form so radical. Irving Grossman observed that the layout, however irrational, would make a powerful symbol, and Jack Klein declared it ought to have an important impact on the rest of the downtown by breaking up its relentless rectangularity. Prominent Modernist Serge Chermayeff hastened to town to claim that it was too big and looked as though it were made of cardboard: how could any subsequent development on the south side of the square be tied to this ridiculous design?[44]

With the opening at hand in September 1965, another panel of architects was convened at which nothing much of consequence was said, except that it provided a platform for one of the unsuccessful finalists, John Andrews, to air his complaints. Competitions, he said without great subtlety, were only as good as the jury members who judged them. Much grumbling ensued about the fact that the city had forced the designers to site the building at the north edge of the square by installing a huge parking garage underneath the southerly section that could not bear more than the weight of a three-storey building. Irving Grossman again felt compelled to defend Revell's effort to construct a powerful symbol. In a separate report Parkin Associates soberly detailed what had been done to solve the structural problems in the original design. The following month Thom got a chance to reprise his criticisms though he conceded that the square looked as though it should provide a popular gathering place for Torontonians.[45]

In the spring of 1966 architecture professor Douglas Shadbolt from the Nova Scotia Technical College, another unsuccessful entrant in the original competition, provided the RAIC *Journal* with a lengthy analysis based upon a careful study of Revell's sketches and plans dating right back to the beginning. Shadbolt argued that the real problem was that the Revell and Parkin had had to change horses in mid-stream by making major structural changes without undertaking a complete reassessment of the original plan. The rows of columns supporting the floors of the towers and the placing of the council chamber upon a central post rather than integrating it better into the podium had simply been add-ons. Fellow teacher Guy Desbarats expressed admiration for the grandeur of Revell's conception but complained that the Parkin firm had undermined this by weak interior fittings and finishes used in the name of cost-cutting. Still, both men admitted that any danger of imitating the opera house in Sydney, Australia, where eight years of work had seen the budget metastasize from $8 million to $60 million, would likely have been fatal. All that could be said was that the majority of the jury had been over-optimistic in believing that Revell's

scheme could ever be accomplished within the allotted budget, proving the minority report correct.[46]

Yet what the professionals thought mattered very little since the building and in particular the square with its wading pool cum skating rink seemed to have thoroughly captured the admiration of the locals. *Canadian Architect* published a photograph taken during the federal election campaign of 1968 showing the square jammed with people listening to a speech by Prime Minister Pierre Trudeau. The magazine's managing editor Robert Gretton observed that this showed how superbly Revell's layout functioned for such purposes, unlike any other location in the country. Architects might continue to complain about perceived design flaws, such as the "wrongness" of the elevated walkway surrounding the perimeter of the square, but that mattered little now. The striking building and its square had aroused interest in future development across Queen Street to the south and in urban planning in general, whereas a decade earlier "most citizens hardly cared whether it snowed blood oranges or not."[47] At long last Torontonians had a Modern building unlike any other in the world so people could no longer say that they were a bunch of backward provincials.

What remained unsettled was what would be constructed on the south side of Queen Street opposite the New City Hall to complement Revell's layout. To secure control over the design, the city had taken the unusual step in 1964 of expropriating most of the city block from Bay to York facing the civic square as far south as Richmond Street. A string of rather rundown premises along the south side of Queen had thus been removed including

6.10 (Opposite)
The new courthouse complex west of New City Hall, replacing the Armouries, opened in 1966 to plans by Marani, Rounthwaite, and Dick.

6.11 (Above)
New City Hall, complete, between Chinatown and the south side of Queen Street, 1965.

one important cultural institution, the city's only burlesque house. The aim of redevelopment was to ensure a mixture of new uses that would attract people to the area outside of office hours, the principal structure being a new hotel. An overhead walkway would form a link across Queen to the colonnade around the square, and there was even ambitious talk about putting Queen Street underground between Bay and York to expand the open space further southward.

To decide upon a design the city organized an architectural competition in 1968 with the winner gaining the right to lease these lands for ninety-nine years. The jury was composed of C.E. Pratt along with architect John Bland and planner Hans Blumenfeld. Competing designs were submitted for the Hilton hotel chain by Webb Zerafa Menkes (successors to Peter Dickinson Associates) and for the Four Seasons group by John B. Parkin Associates. There was little to choose between the two entries, which were remarkably similar. Both featured fairly low structures sloping back from Queen Street opposite the civic square that would contain retail space and allow pedestrian access through the block to Richmond. And both designs sited their massive hotel towers at the west end of the property near York Street. The jury was divided. Pratt and Bland voted for the Hilton scheme, the former because he thought it would attract more people at nighttime, the latter because he considered the low block across from the square more expertly handled. Blumenfeld favoured the Four Seasons design due to the regular colonnade along the entire Queen Street frontage that unified the complex rather than treating the hotel as a separate structure.[48]

6.12
South side of Queen, competition winner, unbuilt, Webb Zerafa Menkes, 1968.

Local politicians were keen not to impose too many obstacles because of fears that the commercial heart of the downtown was in decline. If they imposed onerous conditions the developers might simply shift their interest to Montreal, which was still basking in the afterglow of Expo '67. As a result the executive Board of Control constituted itself as the deciding authority and began lengthy secret deliberations. In April 1968 they opted for the Hilton group, a decision approved by city council seventeen to five. Early in June, however, city Finance Commissioner William Campbell announced that he did not believe that the backers had sufficient financial resources to carry out the project. The Hilton people threatened to sue the city if it failed to go through with the deal, but the controllers declared the whole competition void and proposed to start all over again. Council, however, voted twelve to ten to accept the very similar layout from the Four Seasons group.[49]

The design by Parkin Associates (which became Searle Wilbee Rowland during this time owing to the withdrawal of John C. Parkin to found his own firm) involved a low three-storey podium opposite the civic square, rising upward to an eleven-storey commercial block to the south. Inside would be 1.5 million square feet of shops, offices, and convention space, roofed by terraced gardens sloping down from south to north to a trendy bar overlooking the civic square with the sky-lit lobby of the hotel below. Automobile access to the hotel (now to be part of the Sheraton chain)[50] would be off Richmond Street, with a huge 1,466-room slab located at the western end of the site so as not to block off the view from the square southward to the downtown core. The entire structure would be supported by prominent prestressed concrete beams, the largest of their kind in North America, lightly sandblasted so as to fit with the exterior of Revell's City Hall. The complex was intended to attract people at all times of the day by linking it to a "plus-fifteen" overhead walkway across Queen Street to the colonnade of the civic square, an elevated pedestrian system which was supposed eventually to extend much further eastward.

6.13
South side of Queen, competition loser, built, John B. Parkin Associates, 1968.

James Acland was not impressed by the huge building completed in 1972. The hotel block was so high that it shadowed the southerly part of the square in winter time (though some people claimed this was a good thing since it helped prevent the ice on the skating rink from melting). The whole design seemed to have been shaped to meet the needs of the big shopping mall, and the spindly columns in the hotel lobby appeared to have aluminum foil glued to them. Acland thought that the developers had "missed the boat" with their "hard and unlovely addition" to the much-admired civic square. He could only warn the new reformist city council under Mayor David Crombie against committing similar mistakes in future. This warning provoked L.A. Oxley to write to *Canadian Architect* to suggest that Acland might be less critical if he accepted the "paeleolithic streaks" that afflicted both politicians and architects and came to terms with the fact that things could have been much worse. In fact, within a few years the overhead walkway across Queen Street was almost never used and the bar overlooking the square had been closed, so that the shopping centre and hotel turned in upon itself like a fortress though the square to the north remained a powerful magnet.[51] Nevertheless Revell's building and square remained an unqualified success in the minds of Torontonians and a triumph for a new variant of Modern architecture.

II

While attention was focused upon the New City Hall there were other important buildings going up in Toronto. The design for Massey College at the University of Toronto followed Revell's City Hall in its move towards a mixture of elements that might be characterized as "reactionary" Modernism.

Massey College was certainly old-fashioned in a variety of ways. First of all, it reflected the vision of a single patron exercising close control over both its design and execution in a fashion rarely seen in Canada by the mid-twentieth century. Vincent Massey, the governor general of Canada, had studied at Balliol College, Oxford before the First World War. He was lovestruck by an idealized Balliol, an infatuation that continued to the end of his life. (He remarked, "The college was what a college ought to be – a community … Nothing is harder to describe than what a college means to you. Its influence is always intangible."[52]) In 1957 he hit upon the idea of creating a college at the University of Toronto exclusively for male graduate students that would not only provide residential accommodation but also suites for selected faculty members who would be designated as senior fellows.

Two years later he took up the matter in earnest, asking the university to consider creating "an institution for graduate students of the greatest promise … to select the best men available and form a distinguished collegiate community."[53] There was considerable criticism of the whole idea of creating something that resembled a watered-down version of All Souls College, Oxford, leading some local wits to dub the project "Half Souls College, Toronto." The university, however, eagerly accepted the offer of a $2 million building and immediately agreed to donate a prime site at the corner of Hoskin Avenue and Devonshire Place near the centre of its campus. The family-controlled Massey Foundation made its desires very clear:

> It is of great importance that [the college] should in its form reflect the life which will go on inside it, and should possess certain qualities – dignity, grace, beauty, warmth. Such a college as we have in mind possesses antecedents in various countries, and whatever their physical forms may be or the date of their erection, they have a character in common. What

we wish is a home for a community of scholars whose life will have intimacy, but at the same time academic dignity.

The building was to contain the rooms for the junior fellows, offices (with fireplaces) for the senior fellows, a common room, a dining hall, a library, a chapel or two, and a master's lodge.[54]

Those who paid attention probably imagined that the resulting design would resemble the Collegiate Gothic of Hart House, the foundation's other great gift to the university overseen by Vincent Massey at the time of the First World War. However the original intention was to have a building designed jointly by two of the six foundation board members, Vincent's son Hart Massey and his nephew Geoffrey, both architects known to be sympathetic to Modernist ideas. Ultimately this notion was abandoned owing to "legal and practical problems." The board could not agree on a design so they decided in February 1960 to hold a private competition and invite just four people to enter. The best-known among them was John C. Parkin, who had already solidified his reputation as Canada's most prominent practitioner of Miesian International Style Modernism. The other three were younger men who would presumably be even more attracted by the opportunity to earn a three thousand dollar fee and secure a commission from a prestigious client. Carmen Corneil was a recent graduate of the University of Toronto who had just returned from two years in Scandinavia, including work in Alvar Aalto's office. Arthur Erickson was a promising talent from British Columbia who was then starting up his own practice.

6.14
Ron Thom, 1963.

Ron Thom was less known, not having attended architectural school but undertaken a four-year apprenticeship and passed the examinations of the Architectural Institute of British Columbia in 1949.[55] He joined the Vancouver firm of Thompson, Berwick, Pratt where he worked on a variety of projects, including a large number of "West Coast" style houses. Thom's work showed the influence not only of the early Frank Lloyd Wright but the Greene brothers and two other Californians, the Modernist émigrés Rudolf Schindler and Richard Neutra. Thom became a registered architect only in 1957, by which time he had attracted attention for his collaboration with his senior partner, Ned Pratt (one of the judges for the Toronto city hall competition), on the much-acclaimed BC Hydro headquarters building.[56]

Vincent Massey remained concerned that "none of the candidates had any experience of college life and it was obviously necessary to convey to these young men what a college really was. Without understanding the conception they could hardly be expected to prepare a building in which Massey College could be housed." The four competitors were therefore summoned to a meeting with Vincent Massey and his son Lionel in February 1960, where "We stipulated that it should be in the form of a quadrangle – that it should be turned inwards, not outwards, excluding the turmoil and clamour of the modern city and giving its residents the quiet and peace in which an academic community should appropriately live." Despite these adjurations, when the entries came in on 30 June, Corneil and Parkin had ignored the demand for a closed quadrangle, leaving some open access to the surrounding streets. Parkin's rigourously Modern design was a banal effort with a central dining hall that looked better suited to a minimum security jail, while Corneil and Erickson both produced "strong modernist statements."[57]

Thom's entry was a curiosity. He submitted a plan for a fully enclosed quadrangle to shut out the noise from traffic on the adjoining streets with a gate at the southeast corner where a covered way led past a porter's lodge. The five "houses" of residence, each with a distinctively decorated staircase entrance, were aligned around the gently sloping site following the approved Oxford model. The other facilities were grouped together in the south wing along Hoskin Avenue. The common room projecting into the quadrangle was to be contained in a small imitation Frank Lloyd Wright house with wide overhanging eaves, behind which rose an upper-level dining hall that looked from the street side like some sort of bastard Oriental temple rendered in brick.[58]

Offered $1,500 to modify his design, Parkin took his $3,000 and withdrew. Erickson and Corneil fiddled around with their entries but showed an unwillingness to drastically modify their original efforts. Thom proved more accommodating and began a quick study of the colleges of Oxford and Cambridge. He removed the Wrightian house and a lot of steeply pitched roofs, though the common room interior remained reminiscent of Wright's early work with brick walls surrounding a raised ceiling and dropped floor. The second-floor dining hall was now clad in a sort of pastiche-Gothic fenestration and roofline; this decoration was visible from outside the college apparently as a bow to the Gothic Revival of Sir Giles Gilbert Scott's new Trinity College chapel down the street. Thom also added a Modernist bell tower with a clock at the southwest corner of the quad composed of many panes of brick arranged at right angles to one another, topped by a pierced stone latticework that supported the bell to tell the hours as in the old world.[59]

Arthur Erickson later complained to Thom's biographer that the two men had compared notes before they mailed off their first-round plans and that in his second revision Thom had "copied" Erickson's designs with just a change in sensibility. Author Douglas Shadbolt concluded that while there were some similarities between the two designs so far as the walls of the quadrangle were concerned, fortunately Thom's window treatments "make this discussion academic if not irrelevant."[60] At the time, however, Erickson seems to have revealed nothing publicly about his complaints.

The Massey Foundation was delighted with what Thom had produced, so delighted in fact that they agreed to let him design all the interior furnishings down to the college's tableware and calligraphy. (This emulation of Wright

COMPETITION

MASSEY COLLEGE

The Massey Foundation recently announced the results of a limited competition for the design of Massey College, a gift by the foundation to the University of Toronto.

Four architects were originally invited to prepare designs: Ronald Thom and Arthur Erickson of Vancouver; John C. Parkin of Toronto; Carmen Corneil of Thorold, Ontario. After this first stage was completed, foundation trustees criticized the designs and asked for various modifications to be incorporated into second stage designs. Only three of the architects proceeded with this second stage, John C. Parkin withdrawing from the competition. The design selected to be built is by Ronald Thom.

The college will be a residence for selected men students engaged in post-graduate studies at the university. It will also house a number of faculty members, visiting teachers and lecturers, and guests of the college. This collegiate community will be headed by a Master of high academic qualifications.

The 300-ft. by 150-ft. site is on a corner adjacent to an existing church, across from the back campus area of the university.

The program included residential accommodation (with a house for the Master), a dining hall — the most important interior space, common rooms, recreational rooms, and a small chapel.

6.15
Drawing of Massey College dining hall, Ron Thom, 1960, built as drawn.

6.16
Massey College, complete, Ron Thom, 1963.

also allowed him to create what Thom's friend, Shadbolt, described as the world's most uncomfortable chairs "however elegant and appropriate" in appearance.) Under the eagle eye of Vincent Massey, who monitored the smallest details, the building was completed by 1963. Thom had produced exactly the kind of elaborate "scenery," which the first master of the college, Robertson Davies, had suggested in a speech to the Royal Architectural Institute of Canada in 1960 was the proper task for architects.

Looking at the results alarmists declared that Thom had set Canadian architecture back fifty years. Writing in *Canadian Architect* University of Toronto professor James Acland denounced the whole idea of the college admitting only male students as a disquieting archaism. Moreover, he said, it seemed foolish to provide such things a parking spot for the master right next to the entrance but not to offer underground parking for any other members. Looking south down the quad transported one back before the First World War while the interiors seemed to date to the Arts and Crafts era. Still, Acland contended, the dining hall was a splendid space and the entire ensemble compounded its annoyances with some delights.[61]

Peter Collins, a British immigrant to Montreal who had begun to write a series of critiques that would ultimately be republished as *Changing Ideals in Modern Architecture* (1965), suggested that Thom had offered a useful challenge to the reigning orthodoxy of Modern architecture. Vincent Massey knew what he wanted and he got it. If, said Collins, Frank Lloyd Wright had created modern masterpieces before 1913, there was nothing wrong in imitating him fifty years on. Critics who complained about load-bearing brick walls with carved limestone trim were ignoring the fact that traditional materials could still be used in certain circumstances. Yet perhaps, suggested Collins, it was wrong to construct a large three-storey building this way if one believed that great designs should be infused with the desire to use the most up-to-date structural systems that the spatial requirements permitted. Still, if the building was not epoch-making, the Massey Foundation had asked for a functional, sturdy, and handsome building, and they had certainly got their wish.[62]

Collins's rather limp article took pains to praise the building as excellent. He carefully excluded any very clear complaints even about the silliness of features such as the spun-sugar pinnacles on the outside of the dining hall. His appraisal pointed up the general feebleness of architectural criticism in Canada to this time, though he was at least trying to provide a reasoned assessment whereas most of his professional confrères jumped away from making critical statements about colleagues like cats facing a stream of boiling water. Indignation was expressed in some quarters when Ron Thom's design failed to win a Massey Medal for architecture (though that might have seemed a bit incestuous).[63]

A few years later Carol Ede agreed that the hall at Massey was an exciting space though she regretted the "pretentious overstatement" of the bell tower.[64] Meanwhile, the college building settled down to become a familiar presence at the University of Toronto; it has been described as the "most loved" modern building campus, in whose design the university's architectural historian was able to detect not only the obvious influence of Frank Lloyd Wright but also, in the walls and clock tower, echoes of the Dutch modernist W.M. Dudok as well as the Dutch de Stijl.[65]

Certainly those who managed to gain entry inside Massey's fortress-like walls of ruddy brick found there a pleasant and comfortable retreat (though one eventually punctuated by the admission of women as full members). This experience could inspire a fair measure of superiority and condescension towards outsiders, even if the institution itself contributed little directly to the academic and intellectual life of the wider university.[66] Looking back after thirty years, architect Brigitte Shim argued that far from setting Canadian architecture back, Thom had simply repudiated the conventional wisdom current in the architectural press of the time. For the insiders he had created a "total environment," extending right down to the salt shakers, that was "both modern and traditional, institutional and domestic, monumental and intimate." And the college had not only enriched lives, but this "significant" building had defined "a rich alternative modern tradition – one with roots in the past as well as its contemporary condition and one that can guide us into the future."[67]

III

Viljo Revell and Ron Thom were two architects responsible for important Modernist buildings in Toronto that would always be associated with their names.[68] In addition, there were two other architects, Peter Dickinson and John C. Parkin, who produced a wide range of work after they settled in the city. In little more than ten years before his untimely death in 1961, Dickinson turned out a flood of designs that reflected a variety of Modernist influences. By contrast Parkin was always seen as a faithful proponent of a particular brand of Modernism, the International Style.

By the mid-1950s Dickinson was producing proposals for Page and Steele at breakneck speed. One of his largest commissions was part of a vast public housing development for the City of Toronto. Dickinson, whose approach to Modernism was always more eclectic than most of his contemporaries in Canada, did not disappoint. He produced a reminder about the agenda of social reform in the formation of Modernism along with an explicit salute to Le Corbusier.

The idea of "slum clearance" within the six-block area of over forty acres in the southeastern part of the city, bounded by Parliament, Gerrard, Dundas, and River Streets, had been raised as early as 1934. In 1947 the ratepayers approved spending $5.9 million on Regent Park, which consisted of two-storey row houses and small three-storey apartment buildings that covered the entire site. There was nothing Modern about the buildings designed by J.E. Hoare, though there were reminders of reformist ideas in the elimination of the internal street layout to create a traffic-free space where children could play. Certainly the promoters were as convinced as their European counterparts had ever been about the value of rehousing

6.17
Blevins Place, 1956, buried beneath the towers of Regent Park South.

in improving family life and reducing problems like juvenile delinquency. One of the prime movers, a professor of social work at the University of Toronto, later wrote, "Most of the persons and families admitted to Regent Park from the deteriorated houses in a slum environment did respond very quickly to the stimulus of the new housing accommodation ... There is little question that the physical and mental health, family welfare and social behaviour of a substantial portion of the individuals and families rehoused in Regent Park have greatly improved."[69]

A second development to the south was celebrated by urban planners as "a bold beginning in the huge task of urban renewal in their battle against blight." Despite some doubts about whether it was wise to concentrate so much public housing in a single area "rather than spreading pockets of sound design dispersed through the blighted areas each acting as a focus for renewal by public and private enterprise," a decision was quickly taken to proceed with Regent Park South on the six city blocks right across Dundas Street. As had been done previously, the site was almost completely cleared and the internal street system eliminated; parking was provided around the perimeter.[70]

Enthusiasts were convinced that Regent Park South would "very probably [be] the most important housing project in Canada." The northern section had received a good deal of criticism from "vested interests," and it was admitted that architecturally the result was "a depressingly ugly argument for slum clearance." Yet blessed with the benefit of experience, more time, and better planning, the southern section was bound to be superior. The continuing demand for affordable housing required higher density to accommodate over seven hundred units on 26.5 acres while still leaving lots of open space. Besides 250 row houses, there would be 480 units in five great fourteen-storey apartment slabs – "the heart" of the development with a "significance for the city out of all proportion to the comparatively few people they house and a major architectural achievement." A variety of housing types within a landscaped area would permit the same high quality of urban design that existed in parts of Europe and the United States.[71]

Page and Steele were awarded the design contract for the towers.[72] Peter Dickinson attempted to deliver upon these high expectations by paying homage to Le Corbusier's Unité d'habitation, constructed in Marseilles between 1947 and 1952. He was not allowed to be quite as radical as Le Corbusier in incorporating shops and social services into the buildings (though he did design a separate recreation centre and a day care that were never built).[73] Nor did he perch his structures up in the air on pilotis. Instead, the first two floors of each tower were constructed as townhouses, each with separate access to the outdoors. The Corbusian influence was clearest in Dickinson's

6.18 (Above)
Regent Park South, Peter Dickinson, 1956.

6.19 (Right)
Regent Park South, apartment interior.

decision to create two- and three-storey apartments with internal staircases. This layout permitted cross-ventilation and saved space by requiring elevator stops and corridors only on every second floor.[74] In case of fire each apartment was provided with a small balcony adjacent to one in the next-door unit, and there was a charmingly Rube-Goldbergian solution to the problem of making sure that occupants of one apartment could gain entrance to their neighbours' place if necessary: a handy little glass-fronted box containing a hammer was mounted on the wall between the balconies that could be used to break the window next door in an emergency.[75]

Dickinson's design provided a good number of large two- and three-bedroom apartments that were attractive to families with children, though mothers high above remained concerned about how to supervise the young when they played outside. As in Marseilles the two-storey units were far from popular with many tenants who joked about falling downstairs inside their own apartments. Critics noted that the windows in living rooms and dining rooms were placed in the corners rather than centred but conceded that keeping costs down necessitated certain sacrifices on layout and materials. The glass and brick infills inside the grid of the exposed concrete frame with its projecting centre section provided "a vibrant pattern" that made the towers less overwhelming. The design received a silver Massey Medal in 1961.[76] Moreover, the conscious attempt to provide a variety of housing forms within one development and even within a single building had a considerable influence on the future design of public housing elsewhere in Toronto.[77]

Dickinson also showed a willingness to adopt advanced technological solutions to design problems as in the creation of a large exhibition space (and theatre) in the Women's Building at the Canadian National Exhibition. The original 1955 model showed six large parabolic arches from which the ceiling would be suspended, but this design was rejected as too costly. Dickinson again turned to the engineering firm of Morden Yolles with whom he had collaborated on the Benvenuto. Roland Bergmann, Yolles's associate, who had received very advanced training in Europe before emigrating to Toronto, developed a folded-plate, accordion-style concrete roof that could support heavy loads over a long span, a system hardly ever tried before in Canada. The roof created large open areas for displays inside; the only other load-bearing elements to counter the downward thrust from the slopes of the plates were four rows of columns resting upon concrete foundation beams post-tensioned with steel ties that transferred the forces to shear walls at either end of the building. Though the exterior, barring the roofline, was not particularly distinguished, it proved an economical and efficient layout for a building that was only used for a few weeks each year.[78]

Dickinson also became involved in an ambitious plan to create a new theatre complex at the corner of Yonge and Front Streets. E.P. Taylor, the creator of Don Mills, controlled the O'Keefe Brewery and decided to finance an O'Keefe Auditorium as a means of calling attention to his beer at a time when opportunities for advertising alcoholic drinks were severely restricted. On an entire block east of Yonge, running all the way from Front down to the Esplanade by the railway viaduct, he proposed to create a very large multipurpose hall that would seat thousands for musical shows, opera, and

6.20 (Above)
CNE Women's Building, Peter Dickinson, 1956. Marani and Morris's Grandstand is visible in the distance.

6.21 (Left)
CNE Women's Building lobby, built as drawn.

ballet. The original plan included an office tower and a hotel around a plaza on land that the brewery already owned just to the north across Front up to Wellington and east to Scott Street; the rental income was intended to help defray the expense of running the big theatre. The project was almost on the scale of Rockefeller Center in New York with its Radio City Music Hall.[79] The supervising architect chosen was Earl Morgan, who worked for the brewery and was related to Taylor by marriage but had a very small firm, and he quickly called in Page and Steele as associates.

Unfortunately for Dickinson, the project was drastically scaled back.[80] In the end only the big theatre (known as the O'Keefe Centre) was constructed, but the architect was able to imprint it with a couple of bold gestures outside and in. He wanted a canopy over the entrance foyer even longer and wider than anything he had yet attempted, a great upward-sloping outthrust extending over fifty feet above the driveway. Once again Morden Yolles created a fine engineering solution using reinforced concrete ribs and slabs. When the house opened in 1960, with the world premier of the musical *Camelot* starring Richard Burton, formally clad theatregoers could disembark from their limousines in the glow of the recessed spotlights overhead. Inside, the challenge was to engineer a large upper balcony retaining unobstructed views of the stage without filling up too much space with structural support. With Bergmann's help, Yolles devised a folded-plate structure spanning the entire 160-foot width of the auditorium without columns by using a reinforced concrete open-box girder under the balcony floor. The result was a wood-panelled interior of impressive sweep, though the acoustics were never equally distinguished.[81]

Dickinson remained popular with developers not only because his designs looked good but because they were economical enough to deliver a high rate of return. For Yolles and Rotenberg he created 561 Avenue Road, the first high-rise apartment tower on the stretch of that street north of St Clair, with the fourteen storeys permitted under the city of Toronto's new zoning code. The architect delivered a stylish design assembled from the motifs he had developed. The projecting centre section was flanked by two equal wings with checkerboard black and white brickwork under the windows. The dramatically projecting balconies on the corners of the building rested upon the exposed underfloor concrete slabs, each surrounded by nicely transparent wired glass panels of the kind used at the Benvenuto. A crisp flat roof with an overhang all around topped off the composition. The developers were sufficiently impressed that they promptly commissioned a smaller-sized twin directly across at 500 Avenue Road.[82]

Yolles and Rotenberg wanted a new luxury hotel on Yonge Street at Wood just north of College. The Westbury would provide bars, restaurants, and

6.22 (Above)
O'Keefe Centre, balcony under construction, Peter Dickinson, 1959.

6.23 (Right)
O'Keefe Centre, Peter Dickinson, 1960.

6.24
561 Avenue Road,
Peter Dickinson,
1956.

sizable air-conditioned rooms for well-off visitors, topped off by a piano bar with tall windows facing south to Lake Ontario. Dickinson rotated the design for the Benvenuto from the horizontal to the vertical to create a sixteen-storey tower. He used the same reinforced concrete frame and ribbed floor slabs engineered by Morden Yolles for 111 Richmond Street to produce sixteen single rooms and four doubles per floor, each with balcony and bathroom. Dickinson's innovation was to set the hotel back atop a two-storey podium that not only provided an impressive entrance but lots of rentable retail space at street level. Visitors were so taken with the sense of sophistication created by lounging around on the white Naugahyde furniture in the Sky Lounge that planning began almost immediately for an extension of the hotel to the north.[83]

Designing, smoking, drinking, and partying, by 1957 Peter Dickinson had decided that Forsey Page and Harland Steele owed him a larger place in their partnership. When they failed to arrive at a satisfactory arrangement he announced in early 1958 that he was leaving. Rather than buying him out the partners agreed to let him take the fees for the Trans-Canada Pipeline office tower that he was designing at 150 Eglinton Avenue East, money that he used to set up Peter Dickinson Associates.[84] Dickinson showed his openness about recently developed materials by facing this building with a new type of precast concrete curtain wall. The Toronto Cast Stone Company (which also provided the cladding for the New City Hall) had joined the Mo-Sai Institute, a consortium of American firms that offered its members the rights to use a patented system of precast panels that had embedded pebbles or crystals that made them resemble mosaics and sparkle when floodlit.[85] Simple and economical when bolted to the framework these panels provided an attractive surface highlighted by the vertical mullions that projected outward from them between each window, creating a play of light and shadow across the south-facing exterior. The only weakness of the Trans-Canada building was that the mullions sprang abruptly out at the cornice over the first floor revealing that they were purely decorative and had no structural purpose.[86]

Dickinson quickly became a keen user of the Mo-Sai technology, which he prescribed for a number of schools as well as for commercial buildings. In 1960 he used the panels on an office building for the Continental Can Company at 790 Bay Street on the southwest corner of College Street. Here

6.25 (Top)
Westbury Hotel, Peter Dickinson, 1956. This photo shows 1950s modernism rising behind 1930s moderne-isms with City Park Apartments, 1954, at centre right (see Figure 5.47)

6.26 (Above left)
Westbury Hotel piano bar.

6.27 (Above right)
Westbury Hotel, Peter Dickinson, 1963, the expansion along Yonge Street, original wing at right.

6.28
Trans-Canada Pipeline building, 150 Eglinton West, Peter Dickinson, 1959.

6.29 (Left)
Continental Can, 790 Bay, Peter Dickinson, 1959.

6.30 (Right)
801 Bay Street, Peter Dickinson, 1959.

he faced a particular problem: the soil conditions were such that a large excavation for an underground parking garage was impossible using the foundation techniques of the time. So Dickinson put in only shallow underpinnings but solved the parking problem by drawing upon the idea of a podium that he had employed for the Westbury Hotel. The ground floor was available for rent to retail outlets and was dignified by black granite facings on the concrete columns inset with vertical strips of stainless steel, another Dickinson trademark. Above the shops was the parking garage concealed behind frosted glass panels with the office block set back on top of the podium.[87]

Diagonally across the intersection on the northeast corner, Dickinson designed another commercial tower at 801 Bay Street. Always conscious of the need to maximize rentable floor area by reducing the size of a building's core he included a space-saving feature that demonstrated why commercial developers liked to work with him, the first use of a "scissor staircase" that permitted two separate flights of steps to crisscross in an X pattern within a single stairwell. In an article describing these three buildings Dickinson provided a statement aimed at publicizing the innovative work being done by his firm in comparison with the old-guard architectural offices: "Significantly, the pace-setters in office building design are more often speculative projects than buildings for individual companies and clients, and it is a sorry state that large national enterprises, who could well be the patrons of virile design, are consistent in commissioning the dullest buildings for themselves."[88]

The sign that Dickinson's firm was ready to compete directly with the oldsters was the commission to create a building for the Prudential Insurance Company of America at a highly visible location on the northwest corner of King and Yonge Streets in the heart of the financial district. At twenty storeys high, it was the tallest structure that Dickinson had yet designed, and the developers, Walter Zwig and Jacob Hendeles, relied upon him to produce the maximum usable space by relying upon a combination of methods he had already hit upon. The podium with its two-storey lobby was dramatized by its stainless steel cladding around the reinforced concrete columns and the marble wall panelling inside, while above was the recessed office tower framed in structural steel that kept column sizes to a minimum. The exterior columns were covered in light-gauge stainless steel and the spandrels were Mo-Sai panels embedded with white quartz that helped to withstand the wind loads. With 350,000 square feet of rentable space the complex was one of the largest in the city.[89]

The other large project that Page and Steele had permitted Dickinson to take with him when he left was a seminary for the Jesuit order at 4325 Bayview Avenue in the northeast corner of the city. Here he laid out a

6.31
Prudential Insurance, King and Yonge Streets, Peter Dickinson, 1961.

Modernist residential block and dining hall running north and south with a half-circular chapel protruding from its west side using Mo-Sai curtain wall. The exterior of this layout was not entirely happy: the west front of the chapel was largely a blank wall with a single big window cut into one side, and at the top was a protruding loop that looked like a handle inviting one to carry off that part of the building that did not seem well connected to the rest. However the Jesuits were apparently very happy with the results, a

6.32 (Left)
Jesuit Seminary, Regis College,
Peter Dickinson, 1961.

6.33 (Below)
Jesuit Seminary, Regis College.

distinct improvement over their noisy, smelly, and dirty nineteenth-century home overlooking the railway yards from 444 Front Street West.[90]

Dickinson took on new commissions at a feverish pace in part because he remained resentful at the fame of John C. Parkin. He aspired to create a full-service engineering and architectural firm like John B. Parkin Associates, and to this end he approached Morden Yolles with the idea of a merger between their two practices. After considering the idea, however, Yolles decided to continue as an independent consulting engineer.[91]

Dickinson's best-known building was built not in Toronto but in Montreal. The Bank of Commerce had recently merged with the Imperial Bank of Canada, and Neil McKinnon who headed the new Canadian Imperial Bank of Commerce decided that he wanted a tower on Dorchester (later René Lévesque) at Peel as tall as the Royal Bank of Canada's new offices at Place Ville Marie. Dickinson won the job by quoting a ridiculously low fee, since he argued that a forty-storey structure was really just two twenty-storey structures (like the Prudential) stacked one atop the other. In fact, the design of such steel-framed skyscrapers in Montreal had always been the province of American firms like I.M. Pei for the Royal Bank or Skidmore, Owings, and Merrill for Canadian Industries Limited. Morden Yolles's plan for a diagonally stiffened core-braced steel frame was questioned by the steel suppliers, Dominion Bridge, who believed that the slender, almost square tower would not be able to resist possible wind lifting. The design had to be reworked at a large cost for additional steel that would have bankrupted both Dickinson and Yolles if the bank had not agreed to pay higher fees. The result was a very striking structure with vertical stainless steel ribs that took its overall blue-grey colour from the slate imbedded in the concrete spandrels under each window.[92] The CIBC building showed that Dickinson could produce a piece of International Style Modernism when it suited him. He made this equally clear when he turned out a small medical office building in Toronto at 250 Lawrence Avenue West near Avenue Road. The white brick panels between the black steel framing members on the sharply-angled and stripped-down structure revealed how versatile he could be.[93]

6.34
Four Seasons Motor Hotel, Jarvis Street, Peter Dickinson, 1961.

6.35
Inn on the Park, Peter Dickinson, 1963.

By the end of 1960 a great deal of friction was developing in Dickinson's office with his long-term associates, Colin Vaughan and Roderick Robbie, expecting to be made partners. When that failed to occur, they left to form their own firm, and Dickinson had to rely on the younger people such as Peter Webb, Boris Zerafa, and René Menkes. Moreover, by mid-1961 Dickinson was ill with cancer, though he remained determined to show that he could still do his stuff. For developer Isadore Sharp, Dickinson had already designed a new kind of building – the Four Seasons Motor Hotel on Jarvis Street at Wellesley, which offered parking and had rooms arrayed around an inner courtyard where guests could relax.

Sharp came to see Dickinson in hospital about a larger hotel that he was planning on a sixteen-acre site at the northeast corner of Eglinton Avenue and Leslie Street. The developer could only finance two hundred rooms to start with but wanted a design that could ultimately be greatly expanded. After thinking about the problem in his bed for a couple of days Dickinson handed over a rough sketch. "This isn't my idea. It's a concept that Frank Lloyd Wright developed," he told Sharp, suggesting that the sections of the hotel should be joined together not at right angles but at 60 or 120 degrees. Additional wings could be added along with a tower block and would ultimately enclose a courtyard. Notable for the angular design, which extended even to the outer walls of the guestrooms that left each with a triangular

6.36
University Avenue, 1959: what design control hadn't wrought. A short drive north up old-school design-controlled University Avenue from Armoury (bottom) to Gerrard (top); the ambition of uniformly ordered stone facades that arose before the First World War remained on the books, abandoned only in the 1970s.

balcony, the Inn on the Park became the cornerstone of Sharp's Four Seasons Hotel chain when completed by Peter Webb after Dickinson's death.[94]

By the time of he died in October 1961, a few days short of his thirty-sixth birthday, Peter Dickinson had certainly gained the attention of the architectural and construction community in the little more than ten years that he spent in Canada. Webb, Zerafa, and Menkes formed a new firm that carried many of his projects to completion. Above all, Dickinson's willingness to adopt what he deemed useful and functional from several different strands of Modernism left a many-faceted legacy of design not only in Toronto but in other places like Ottawa and Montreal.

IV

John C. Parkin gained prominence in the early 1950s through his work on Don Mills. He had a reputation for sticking closely to the abstract brand of Modernism that came to be particularly associated with the name of Mies van der Rohe. This International Style relied upon the regularity of surfaces and the intrinsic elegance of the materials employed, technical perfection, and fine proportions rather than any applied ornament. Mies proclaimed, "Form follows function," "Less is more," and "God is in the details," which became the creeds of this school.

Though John B. Parkin Associates completed hundreds of projects during its first decade, the firm never received a commission to build an office tower in downtown Toronto until 1958 when the Sun Life set out to build on a highly visible site at 200 University Avenue.[95] This was the one street in Toronto subject to design controls imposed more than twenty-five years earlier and intended to feature uniform cornice lines and stone facing materials. Any

6.37
University Avenue, north from Queen Street, 1968.

plan required approval from a committee composed of the city's commissioners of buildings and of planning, plus representatives of the Ontario Association of Architects.

In his preliminary sketches for Sun Life, however, Parkin was faithful to his intellectual heritage in proposing a sleek fourteen-storey International Style tower with a curtain wall composed of a rigourous grid of windows framed by exposed perimeter columns of welded steel clad in anodized aluminum. The location on the bend in University Avenue at the southwest corner of Richmond would make the structure highly visible. With its vertical accents intended to display a combination of strength and lightness, the building would be illuminated

"God is in the details"

Sun Life Building, Toronto.

6.38 (Opposite)
Sun Life, John B. Parkin Associates, 1961.

6.39 (Above)
Sun Life: "God is in the details," in *Canadian Architect*, October 1961.

at night to form a "tower of light," contrasting sharply with the rest of the downtown.[96]

A wrangle broke out with the city's committee: the metal curtain wall was forbidden by the building code, the structure on its slightly irregularly shaped lot was not aligned with the street, and it was taller than permitted under the city's zoning code without a setback on the upper floors.[97] The OAA felt it necessary to send a five-man delegation to the committee that eventually agreed to approve variances on the curtain wall and the alignment. The building would be parallel to Simcoe Street in the rear but set back from University at the southeast corner, a triangular space that Parkin ultimately agreed to fill with a one-storey pavilion housing a bank. The OAA refused to take a position on the matter of setbacks at the top, but Parkin was eventually forced to redesign the top floor as a glassed-in penthouse set back with two service floors for equipment above resting upon it. This change gave the building a somewhat ungainly look as though the topmost floors had been dropped onto it from the sky as against the sleek outline originally proposed.[98]

Canadian Architect took this opportunity to demand that the Toronto chapter of the OAA should show some "awareness of current architectural problems" before presuming to advise the municipal government about buildings designed by its members. The magazine claimed that allowing architects to control layouts proposed by fellow professionals was bad in itself. All OAA members must be considered equally competent to make decisions, since those who sought to control the works of others were not themselves above criticism so the practice was "both unethical and unreasonable." Such lèse-majesté got the chair of the Toronto chapter excited enough that he wrote to explain that the design committee was not seeking control but merely trying to ensure that municipal bylaws were complied with. The architects had supported variances on the Sun Life's curtain wall and the alignment with the street but refused to endorse a building 240 feet high and 130 feet long separated from its southerly neighbour by no more than a six-foot wide space. The commissioners of buildings and of property had endorsed this recommendation to the city council that insisted upon the setback. Editor James Murray shot back that if a bunch of OAA members could decide whether a change in the local bylaws was reasonable or not, then Parkin Associates was in just as good a position to make such a judgment as any other architect.[99] This unseemly row finally faded away leaving behind the one major International Style office building for which John C. Parkin was personally responsible, though with a rather unhappy modification.

The other major job for which Parkin became responsible at this time was the new Toronto airport for the federal government. The firm recruited a staff of hundreds to work on the plan of which the centrepiece was the building

6.40
Toronto International Airport model, John B. Parkin Associates, 1959.

known as Aeroquay No. 1 (later Terminal 1). Here again John C. Parkin produced an International Style classic in which a circular structure contained the arrivals level on the ground floor, the check-in counters and departure lounges on the second floor, and an observation deck and restaurant on the third. Enclosed within that ring was what appeared from a distance to be a higher office block but was actually a huge parking garage reached by a system of tunnels and ramps. (See Figure 6.1.) The master plan envisaged as many as four of these structures as passenger traffic increased, along with a control tower, administration building, and power plant.[100]

6.41 (Above)
Toronto International Airport, John B. Parkin Associates, 1964.

6.42 (Left)
Toronto International Airport, interior.

When the new airport opened in 1964 James Acland greeted it in *Canadian Architect* as stunning and admirable, the central garage a "splendid achievement." An appraisal by Peter Collins was less enthusiastic; Collins noted that distant grandeur evaporated with the maze of ramps in amongst the supporting columns that, however functionally efficient, made arrivals and departures "oppressive and dismal." A particular deficiency was the refusal by the airlines to pay the cost of elevated telescopic gangways (later called "jetways") that would allow passengers to board and disembark directly

6.43
Bata Head Office, Don Mills, John B. Parkin Associates, 1964.

from the lounges, forcing them instead to ride up and down escalators and walk to and from aircraft. The circular form also prohibited any expansion and required the expensive duplication of an entire new building.[101] The result was one of those design achievements best viewed from afar.

One of John C. Parkin's most playful and least severe creations was the headquarters for the Bata shoe empire, opened in 1965. Here one might almost sense the influence of Frank Lloyd Wright, a man otherwise largely antithetical in spirit to Parkin's austerity. Sitting on a grassy rise in Don Mills, surrounded by geometrically precise plantings, three sides of the building were supported around its perimeter by five-branched tree-like columns over which the upper two floors extended. On the fourth side were six windowless boxes containing the services that extended the full height of the building, looking rather as though they had been clipped into place. Broad precast concrete panels formed the upper facade with large recessed windows in between. Inside the ground floor the tree-like columns continued with floor-to-ceiling windows creating a transparent effect, and the outside was lit from the base of the columns at night.[102]

V

Thus a number of commercial and institutional buildings of Modern design had appeared from the mid-1950s onward, but persuading Torontonians to commission houses in the same mould remained a challenge. In 1957 John C. Parkin signalled his arrival as an important figure amongst the city's businessmen by building himself a sternly Modernist house in North York

6.44
John C. Parkin house, 75 Bridle Path, garden view, 1957.

6.45
Crashley house, Old George Place, John B. Parkin Associates, 1965.

at 75 the Bridle Path, a district north of Lawrence Avenue and east of Bayview that had once been the preserve of the hunt club set. Set back one hundred feet from the street, the front of the house showed only a very long white brick wall broken by one doorway. Inside was a courtyard with a pool leading to the living room overlooking a two-acre garden through a back wall entirely of glass. To the left were the bedrooms and to the right, garage, kitchen, and maid's room. Built at a cost of $65,000 the four modules with load-bearing brick walls and a precast concrete roof enclosed 3,600 square feet with provision for another wing to be attached by a glass neck.[103]

Parkin's wife, Jeanne, recalled that he thought the design an act of daring with its colour scheme of black and white. The floors were terrazzo with no carpets allowed, antiques and paintings banned. Nothing was supposed to distract the eye from the design: "John did not believe in bringing the outside in. Only two kinds of plants were allowed: split-leaf philodendron or rubber plants. Those were his signature plants." The architect might sit in his Barcelona chair under a family coat of arms beside a big dictionary on a stand from which he could memorize words for his speeches.[104]

A couple of years later the Parkin firm built a Modernist house half a mile or so to the north at 35 Country Lane for Patrick Brigham, who wanted a semi-rural retreat on the southern edge of E.P. Taylor's Windfields Farm where he could display his art collection. The view from the street was blocked off but, within, the house had a large marble-floored entrance hall that gave onto a central atrium containing an array of tropical plants. Other modular units opening from this atrium included a high-ceilinged living room with a ten-foot tall fireplace giving onto a terrace to the south. The roof was raised over the living room and the hall to permit a clerestory to allow light to flood in. The windows were punched into the white wall surface in approved Modernist fashion.[105]

There were not many unoccupied building lots available in the city of Toronto proper, but some owners and architects sought out vacant land along the edges of the many ravines that could offer sharp changes in grade as well as treed slopes to the rear. In 1959 Douglas Crashley, who was a member of the city Planning Board, retained John B. Parkin Associates to design him a house at 3 Old George Place, off sloping Roxborough Drive, where the land had never been subdivided. The design prepared by John C. Parkin displayed the "elegance, precision, austerity and reticence" that characterized his approach to Modernism. All that was visible from the keyhole shaped cul-de-sac was an expanse of brick that formed the back wall of the garage since the driveway looped around to an unseen drop-off place where an open-sided canopy led to an equally invisible front door set in a

6.46 (Above)
Fraser house, Old George Place, Ron Thom, 1965–67.

6.47 (Below)
Fraser house, ground floor plan.

6.48 (Opposite)
Fraser house, elevations of the house at the brow of the Rosedale Ravine.

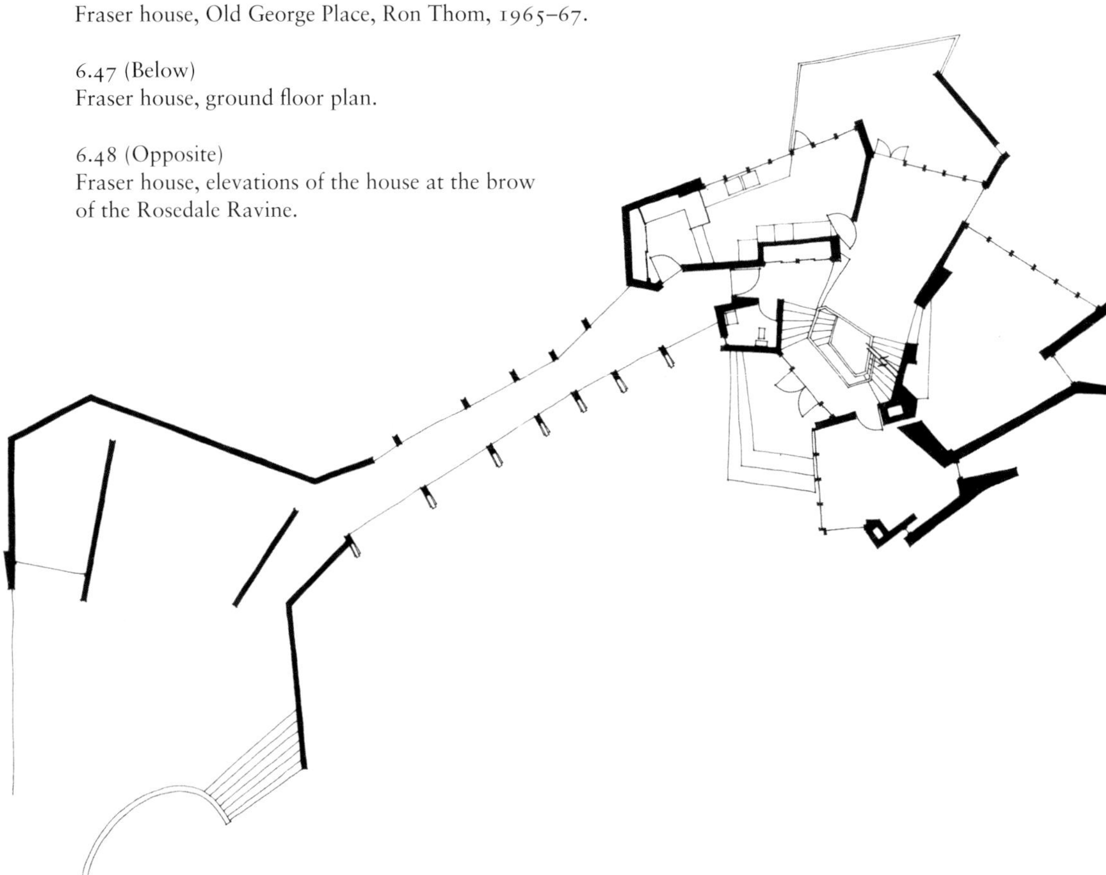

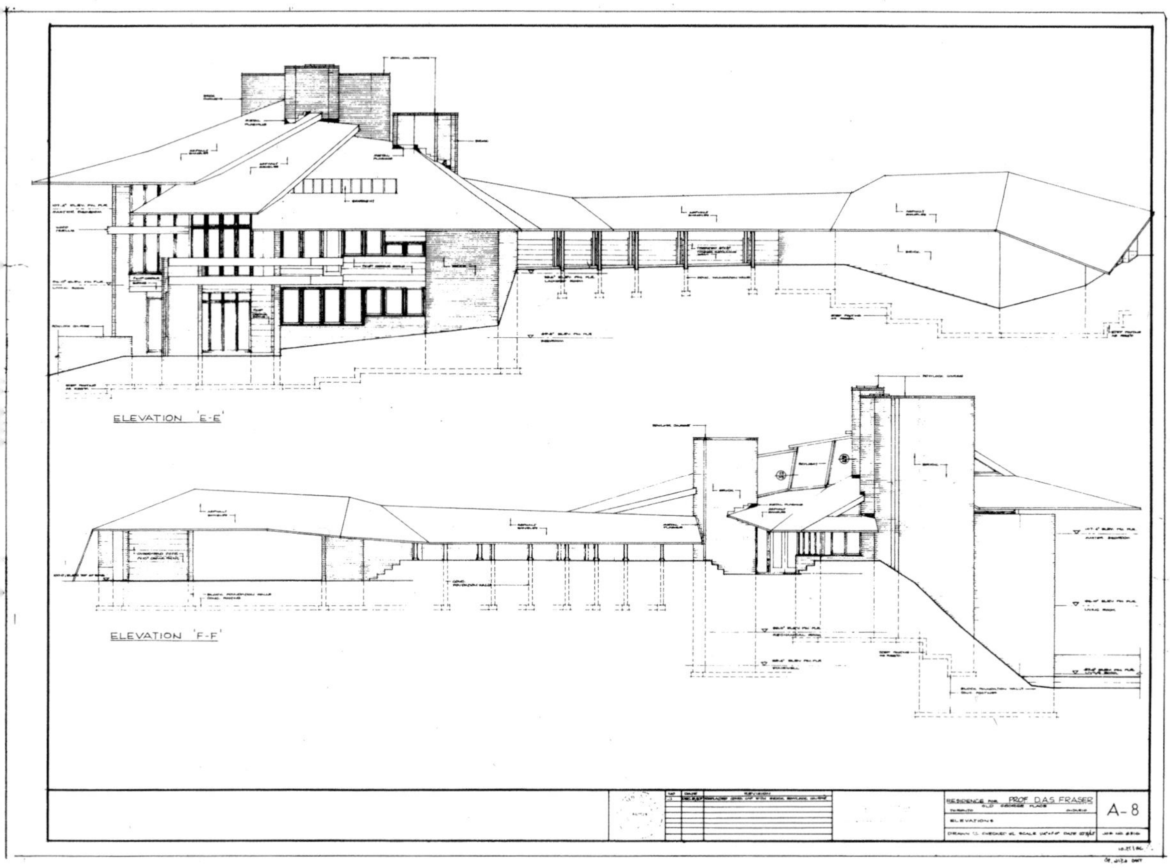

mostly blank brick wall. As one commentator remarked, "Architectural good manners allow only understated and subtle expressions of individuality. Rather than a willful, flamboyant display, good architecture presents a discrete [sic] anonymous public face." This 6,500-square-foot home for a bachelor was arranged in the shape of a T with its stem projecting dramatically out and down into the ravine. The materials employed were brick, stone, metal, and glass, expressing the precision, durability, and permanence often found in large commercial and industrial buildings. The lower floor, overlooking a circular swimming pool built into the slope, had, at Crashley's suggestion, natural stone walls. The strict geometrical patterns and the restraint displayed created a house that "splendidly exemplifies the intentions and accomplishments of a central stream of twentieth century Modernism."[106]

In 1964 a new house for University of Toronto professor Donald Fraser designed by Ron Thom began to rise next door to Crashley's at 4 Old George Place.[107] Thom's design displayed how different was his brand of Modernism from John C. Parkin's. Thom aimed to create a West Coast style house that blended into the landscape in Japanese fashion, all sloping walls and asymmetrical roof shapes with red brick piers and a chimney that would project above the brow of the slope. From the street, little would be visible beyond the garage alongside which the house was approached by a roofed walkway open at the sides. Unlike the simple forms, straight lines, and right angles of the Crashley house, the Fraser layout was a spiral design whose three storeys extended down into the ravine around a central open stairwell with connecting bridges and cantilevered decks.[108]

Peter Dickinson himself bought a steep ravine lot on Beaumont Road in Rosedale where he intended to create a striking home, but city officials refused to grant a building permit despite decades of struggle on the part of his widow, Vera. He did, however, build several homes for his developer clients up in North York. In 1957 he got a commission for a house at 89 the Bridle Path from Burle Yolles, who recalled, "I don't think we wanted a conventional house at all, so we were in a mood to experiment, something that had not been done." Originally there was discussion of a courtyard to be enclosed by a concrete dome engineered by Burle's brother, Morden Yolles, but that proved too expensive. Instead an open plan was developed that brought in light and allowed easy access to the outdoors. On the outside was pale yellow brick, a flat white roofline, and strip windows. Inside, the Yolles wanted exposed wooden beams, which arrived from British Columbia and were erected rough-sawn until the owners got to work with a floor sander afterwards. Burle Yolles expressed content: "It's much more exciting when you have no money and an architect who wants to express himself."[109]

George Montegu Black, a business associate of E.P. Taylor who had built himself a house on Park Lane Circle overlooking the valley of the West Don, acquired about 150 acres of land running east from Park Lane Circle across to the Bridle Path and in the 1950s decided to subdivide into two-acre lots.[110] Developer Walter Zwig discovered that he could buy a lot on the Bridle Path for $15,000, and Dickinson who was working for him on the Prudential building suggested that he design the house. The two went to look at the site, and Zwig claimed that the architect took out his cigarette package and drew a layout, adding, "And when I tell you he drew it, except for the closets, there wasn't a change. And that was the house we built." The structure was light-filled with twelve-foot ceilings, again framed in exposed redwood. Dickinson even designed the furniture. The only thing that Dickinson's design lacked, according to Zwig, was a front door, which the architect never got around to providing. Zwig also alerted his lawyer, Sidney Robins, who bought a lot nearby. Gloria Robins had always wanted a circular dining room table, so Dickinson gave her a round dining room with a skylight at the centre of the house surrounded by curved screens of differing woods and stone.[111]

Isadore Sharp of the Four Seasons hotel group wanted to build in Hogg's Hollow off Yonge Street just north of the city limits, but when Sharp pointed out a design that he and his wife liked, Dickinson told him, "'Well, if you want a mock-Georgian house, you really don't want me. If you want me to do something, let me do something that's in keeping with my style.' So he built me a house that was very modern, very much a different house."[112]

6.49 (Left)
Fogel house,
Irving Grossman, 1959.

6.50 (Below)
Fogel house, interior.

Architect Irving Grossman, who had built a dramatic Modernist house for the Betel family in the mid-1950s (see Chapter 5), continued to work in this idiom; his best-known residential design was his 1959 house for the Fogel family at 100 Sandringham Drive in North York on a similar sloping ravine lot. The garage was placed in front of the house with only a grey brick wall and a doorway facing the street. Looking onto a terraced garden the living-dining room at the rear had a large expanse of glass framed with strict geometry that made it appear to float. Connected at a right angle was a long wing stretching down into the ravine for four bedrooms and a maid's apartment where the slope of the land allowed light to enter the lower floor. For this design Grossman won a gold Massey Medal.[113]

In 1961 Brook and Banz designed a very large flat-roofed bungalow in pale yellow brick at 78 the Bridle Path for drug manufacturer Leslie L. Dan. The central section was flanked by two lower wings with glazed walls projecting at the rear around a courtyard. At the centre was the high ceilinged living-dining room while each of the four bedrooms had a separate courtyard divided from one another by low walls. Extending over the front door and

6.51
J. Posluns house, 32 Park Lane Circle, Jerome Markson, 1964.

6.52
Cleeve Horne's Toronto house/studio, Balmoral Avenue, 1949.

in the courtyards were pergolas constructed of white-painted wood, their supporting columns springing from steel pipes extending five inches above grade to give the effect that these structures were floating.[114]

Jerome Markson, who graduated from the University of Toronto in 1953, was another young architect who built a number of Modernist houses in the Bridle Path area during the early 1960s. He later expressed particular fondness for 32 Park Lane Circle, where in 1961 he laid out a 3,300-square-foot house with a long low sloping roof rising gradually from front to rear before peaking in a kind of saltbox design. "It was one of my favourites; we tried certain things that were important to us." Inside was a series of linked rectangles, some of them sliding alongside one another so the rooms did not simply appear to open out in a row. Each wall of the dining room was of different material: brick, glass, plaster, with an oak ceiling and a slate floor. Markson noted, too, that very fine materials were used: American redwood and bricks as well as copper flashing; the grounds were carefully landscaped to include some sculpture. Forty years on when the building had been demolished to make way for a monster house, Markson observed, "You don't feel very good about it." A place "really belongs to the client. But they're our babies too, if you're very close to what you did, and I was close because they [the clients] were friends."[115]

The most extraordinary residential building in the Toronto region in this period was a weekend home built northeast of the city near the village of Claremont in 1959 for the artists Jean and Cleeve Horne. The Hornes, who already had a Modernist studio attached to their city house, had acquired a 210-acre farm and decided to put up a new house place atop a hill where they might enjoy the sweeping views.[116] On the advice of Eric Arthur they held a design competition and invited six young architects to participate. They did not fancy the winning entry but were attracted to one of the other proposals submitted by Michael Clifford and Kenneth Lawrie, two recent British immigrants who had met while working at Page and Steele and opened their own practice in 1956. The central idea was for a concrete roof with a plastic form that would span the entire space to be enclosed, but nobody seemed to know how to engineer such a thing until Morden Yolles was retained to advise. Yolles had become interested in the thin shells that Europeans such as Pier Luigi Nervi were creating, using reinforced concrete within a rigid frame that was subject to a combination of bending, compression, and shear forces. Nervi designed these rotated structural forms to be self-supporting. Attracted by the idea of such an innovative modern technology, Yolles suggested using a hyperbolic paraboloid for the Horne's roof.[117]

The roof was essentially square in plan but bent downward at two opposing corners that were anchored to the ground while the other two corners were lifted upward, forming a roughly saddle-backed shape. The chief problem with using such a shell lay in anchoring it against the outward thrust transmitted to the foundation at the low corners and in tying down the high corners so as to resist upward forces like wind loads. Here Yolles's associate Roland Bergmann was able to undertake the sophisticated calculations required to ensure such a structure would be stable. The foundation would be laid first, then the roof created, and finally the walls installed underneath.

One deterrent to using such shapes was the complicated and expensive forms normally required to create a curved concrete shell, particularly because of high Canadian labour costs. But Yolles realized that hyperbolic paraboloids were formed by a series of straight lines called generatrices so that by careful planning each section could be formed out of pie-shaped plywood panels into which the reinforcing bars and concrete would be placed. This method avoided the use of highly expensive special forms and made it possible to meet the Hornes' $20,000 budget rather than costing more than three times as much as had been estimated.[118]

The general contractor chosen was a local man, Nils Eriksson, who had some experience in his native Sweden that persuaded the architects and engineers that he could handle the job. But when he began to construct the forty-eight foot square roof he proved dubious that the shell a mere two

6.53
Cleeve Horne country house, Clifford and Lawrie, 1959.

and one-half inches thick that Yolles had specified would be strong enough to span the diagonal distance of sixty feet. Eriksson decided to pour the concrete much deeper in order to strengthen it. Architect Michael Clifford recalled, "We had to rush around and find garden rakes and rake the concrete off, and he was so worried, this guy, because he felt absolutely sure that as soon as the formwork was stripped it would tumble down."[119] The steel I-beams at the edges carried the compressive forces down to big buttresses at the two lower corners, which were anchored to one another by steel rods below the concrete floor, post-tensioned after it was poured. The two high corners were tied down to large concrete deadmen by vertical steel ties running through the framing of the windows.

Into the four triangular spaces under the roof, with eaves overhanging six feet all around, were inserted glass walls that enclosed a space forty-two feet square. To permit the roof to flex due to thermal expansion and contraction, the windows had a highly unconventional system of pins inside a slot along the top edge to allow play in case the roof shape changed by up to half an

HOW CH&G DECORATED THIS REMARKABLE HOUSE

The soaring space of the Hornes' house, a far cry from the usual cube-shaped rooms, makes an incomparable setting for the exciting new furniture chosen by CH&G's Decorating Editor

Toronto artist Cleeve Horne and his wife Jean, who is a sculptor, are shown here in their traditional city home, with sons Robert, 15, Richard, 12, and Arthur, 13.

JUST AS THE CLEEVE HORNES gave the architects a free hand in designing their weekend house, so they gave CH&G a free hand in furnishing it as an experiment for this feature. When we approached them last summer, the Hornes had not decided on their own decorating plans. So before they went ahead, they co-operatively agreed to let our Margit Bennett try her hand at seeing what she could do with such a radically different house. The unique roof creates ever-changing ceiling lines and wall shapes, and with glass all around, there is very little to stand furniture against. "I chose furniture with metal frames and the sculptured look to go with the glass, concrete and sculptured look of the house itself. Conventional upholstered furniture would have looked too bulky for the light structure, and handcrafted Scandinavian furniture would not have suited the geometric concept of the building." Why are there no draperies except in the boys' bedroom? "The house was designed to make the outside truly a part of the inside—and needless screening would have interfered. Besides, the Hornes have no near neighbors to disturb their privacy." ▶

Den is sunk 18 inches below main floor to give more headroom under low corner of roof. Cleeve Horne and his architects designed hooded fireplace with cantilivered hearth. Chair at left is a Bruno Matthsson design; chair at right, an Italian design in black metal, red upholstery, is the Hornes' own. Rug is polar bear skin.

inch due to summer heat or winter cold. However the roof did not deform and since hornets found the slots a handy route into the house they were eventually removed. The ceilings were thirteen feet at the high corners, so the living room had fine views through the glass walls with a raised triangular stone slab at one outside corner for a fireplace (though that, too, was eventually removed because it never worked properly). The large open interior was divided up by freestanding cabinets and closets, and in the two low corners the terrazzo floor was dropped eighteen inches to provide more headroom. The only break in the symmetry of the glass walls was a small brick structure near the centre of one wall that contained an outside door, two bathrooms, and a furnace. In the end, despite the Hornes' concerns, the whole job cost $22,000 or just $12 per square foot.[120] Toronto would see nothing like this for a house with the combination of adventuresome design and advanced technology for years to come, but its existence spoke very clearly about the diverging variety of expressions that Modernism was displaying by the end of the 1950s.

6.54 (Opposite)
Cleeve Horne country house, *Canadian Homes and Gardens*, January 1959.

7

MODERNISM AND BEYOND
1960–1975

The claim has often been made that avant-garde architects in Canada "evinced little interest in the more doctrinaire aspects of Modernism and certainly none of the interest in social reform that characterized European Modernism,"[1] but this does not appear to be correct. One strand of Modernism, typified by the designs of Mies van der Rohe, did eschew a social mission. Instead he produced buildings that became an archetype for commercial towers, acceptable to business leaders in Toronto because they seemed practical and made their city appear increasingly like New York or Chicago.[2] This impression was reinforced by Mies's vast Toronto-Dominion Centre complex, which stood right in the heart of the city's downtown, and by the fact that other designers followed in his footsteps in continuing to turn out office buildings that were pale imitations of the master's model into the twenty-first century.

7.1 (Opposite) Two giants of Toronto modernism: John B. Parkin, standing before the Toronto-Dominion Centre, 1968.

Yet the fact remains that from the 1960s onward some architects continued to debate how Modern designs might promote social amelioration. These discussions revolved around the need to change the look and the layout of the housing in which the vast majority of Canadians resided. The guiding assumption was that changing the built environment would offer a means to the improvement of society. In the 1940s the promoters of slum clearance in Toronto had been firmly convinced that new housing would improve lives, and that conviction survived during the second half of the century.

As the city grew rapidly many architects became persuaded that suburban developments filled with near-identical single-family homes on large lots were not only costly and ugly but produced undesirable social impacts. This conviction was particularly evident in discussions about the construction of new large-scale housing projects during the 1950s and 1960s. The hope was that careful planning of a variety of housing types, including row housing and apartment blocks laid out with due attention to the provision of community facilities, could create a more satisfactory milieu, especially for lower-income families.

Similar notions about the social and educational impact of architectural design also made an impact upon the city's rapidly growing school system. With new buildings being constructed in the suburbs at a frantic pace, was it not possible to devise methods that would produce a better and cheaper result that could also deliver a superior education to children? That train of thought fitted well with the long-standing fascination of Modernists with the machine aesthetic and the promise of prefabrication. Might a system be found to produce standardized components that could be assembled to create schools economically where and when they were needed, buildings that also fitted with current educational philosophy?

Universities, too, began to recognize a role as leaders rather than followers in the field of architectural design. As with schools there were strong pressures for economical methods of construction within the province of Ontario's rapidly growing system of post-secondary institutions. Not only were new universities being created from scratch, but by the 1960s there was developing an interest in using avant-garde architecture to accommodate thousands of additional students. In the 1960s the University of Toronto began to construct its new west campus and finally adopted Modernist design for these buildings. Eventually the university even moved towards the avant-garde by approving a Brutalist design for Scarborough College in the eastern suburbs and then for its new research library right at the centre of the downtown campus.

Moved by the growing use of private automobiles, shopping centres surrounded by acres of parking lots began to spring up in the suburbs of Toronto. However modern the forces propelling those developments, the buildings that housed them were not architecturally distinguished. In the late 1960s, when Eaton's moved to create a huge retail complex around a new downtown department store, the design moved away from the austerity of classic Modernism and adopted the more playful embellishments drawn from historical precedents, which came to be called "Postmodernism." By the mid-1970s Modernism had carved out an important niche in the city's architectural history, but now this orthodoxy faced rivals. Even by that date, however, only a very few Torontonians were prepared to adopt classical Modernism or its successors as a template for residential construction.

I

The apotheosis of International Style Modernism was reached during the 1960s in the Toronto-Dominion Centre.[3] In 1955 the Bank of Toronto merged with the Dominion Bank to form Toronto-Dominion. In 1962 the New York developer William Zeckendorf approached the chair of the bank, Allen Lambert, with a suggestion to build a large tower near the corner of King and Bay Streets that could be used by both the Toronto-Dominion and the recently created Canadian Imperial Bank of Commerce. Lambert was not enthusiastic about sharing space with a much larger rival, but he began to consider the possibility of putting up a new building on the southwest corner of King and Bay where the Bank of Toronto's Renaissance Revival head office had stood since 1913 (see Figure 1.17). Just to the south on Bay was a sales office for the Seagram distillery, which was controlled by the Bronfman family. Leo Kolber, manager of Fairview Corporation, the real estate arm of the Bronfman's Cemp investment trust, agreed to enter into a joint venture with the bank as equal partners to combine these properties and put up an office tower.[4] Though the bank only required about seven floors for its offices, by 1963 the project had grown into a scheme to acquire the entire super-block bounded by King, Bay, Wellington, and York Streets, an objective speedily and secretly achieved, making a large tract of land to accommodate a number of rental office towers.[5]

The partnership agreement left it to the bank to choose the architect, which favoured John B. Parkin Associates while Fairview pressed the case for another Toronto firm, Bregman and Hamann. Both were asked to produce drawings but neither one had ever undertaken such a tall building, and in the end the partners agreed to bring in an experienced American firm. Gordon Bunshaft of Skidmore, Owings, and Merrill, designer of the renowned Lever House on Madison Avenue in New York, produced a scheme utilizing a lightweight curtain wall supported by huge external columns to carry the weight of over fifty storeys. Engineering consultants immediately expressed concerns about what would happen on a Toronto winter day when the south wall expanded in sunlight while the north face lay in chilly shadow. Bunshaft proposed to deal with this problem by placing a stainless steel, piston-like slip joint at the top of the building, but Samuel Bronfman's daughter, Phyllis Lambert, who received a degree in architecture in 1963, dismissed this idea as "a daring and unproved solution." She called it "a ridiculous proposal on many levels" and "problematic" even in a more temperate climate. Worried about any added risk the partners asked the head of the structural engineering department at MIT to assess the problem, and when he also showed reservations Bunshaft was asked to reposition the columns inside the building envelope. When he stuck to his original layout he was dropped. The Parkin firm was then asked to rework its design, which proposed to place the new banking hall out of sight underground.

Lambert, who had persuaded her father to use Mies van der Rohe to design the renowned Seagram building on Madison Avenue in New York, then pushed for him to be interviewed. The bank endorsed the idea in hopes he might produce a design to burnish its corporate reputation in the same way he had done for Seagram's. Having met with Allen Lambert, who was particularly keen to have a highly visible setting for the main branch of his

7.2
Mies van der Rohe in his apartment on East Pearson Street, Chicago, 1964.

bank rather than burying it below grade, Mies delivered a plan involving a freestanding one-storey banking pavilion with a flat clear-span roof and glass walls framed in steel, modelled upon his design for the National Gallery in Berlin. This structure would stand right on the corner of King and Bay replacing the old Bank of Toronto building while nearby would rise two towers, fifty-four and forty-four storeys, set upon an elevated plaza, one tall and slender, the other squatter and squarer, both of which looked very like Mies's much-discussed apartment houses on Lakeshore Drive in Chicago as well as the Seagram building. The steel framework would be painted black on the exterior with the glass curtain walls tinted bronze to appear almost black from a distance. The taller tower would be sited behind the bank to the southwest with the lower one directly to the west facing onto King. Other matching towers could be added to the site later on. When Mies presented a model to the top brass the response was enthusiastic, though Samuel Bronfman insisted on pushing one tower nearer King Street to ensure it secured that mailing address while Allen Lambert also moved the components around. In the end Mies had to tell the businessmen that it was the architect's task to decide the layout, and that they should "take it or leave it."

Leo Kolber reported that the clients remained adamant about only two changes. Despite Mies's resistance the bankers wanted an above-grade connection between the pavilion and the main tower so that people would not be forced to go outside in winter. And both partners insisted upon an entrance to the underground shopping concourse from the plaza itself rather than it being accessible only through the buildings. In the end Mies acceded to these demands, and an entrance to the shops was also provided by a broad flight of steps leading down under the plaza from the north side of Wellington Street to take advantage of the upslope of the land from south to north.[6]

Toronto had never seen a real estate development on such a scale. Questions arose immediately about how financing was to be arranged. The bank initially thought of a conservative plan where 40 percent of the cost would be an equity investment by the partners with the remainder being raised by the sale of long-term bonds. Leo Kolber dismissed that as a model that might suit a manufacturing enterprise but did not fit rental real estate. TD's Richard Thomson then proposed raising the entire cost through issuing debt to be repaid by the flow of rental income, but Kolber argued that the owners ought to show their bona fides by having at least a small investment share. Finally the partners settled upon a split of 95 percent debt to 5 percent equity that would only require each of them to put up about $6 million. The depth of their pockets was sufficient to underpin guarantees of repayment of the bonds and make them saleable, so that the pension fund of J.P. Morgan and Company took the first tranche of thirty-year bonds at 4.85 percent interest with further issues to follow as construction proceeded.[7] With the funds in hand, construction commenced and John B. Parkin Associates was chosen to oversee the job for Mies along with Bregman and Hamann.

Occupants had to be found for 1.25 million square feet of rentable space (the bank needed only about 10 percent of it). Would tenants be willing to pay six dollars per square foot when five dollars was the normal top rate in Toronto? Both the International Nickel Company and the law firm of McCarthy and McCarthy, who were long-time clients of the TD Bank, signed up early on, but the other chartered banks put pressure on their customers not to move into a competitor's real estate. When the big brokerage firm Dominion Securities was being wooed, the Royal Bank urged their client not to act on the grounds that it was planning to erect its own large tower nearby. In the end Dominion Securities was persuaded to take a lease for just seven years so that it would remain free to move (as it ultimately did). Once Abitibi Pulp and Paper, a long-time Royal client, agreed to sign up, however, leases got to be a much easier sell. In fact, as the project gained a sort of cachet, prospective tenants began to seek out space.

7.3
Toronto-Dominion Centre, Mies van der Rohe, 1967: banking pavilion left, Toronto-Dominion Tower right.

The TD tower was scheduled for completion by the end of 1966, when tenants began to move in, with a grand ceremonial opening planned for 1 July 1967, the centennial of Canadian Confederation. By then the big black tower (and its already-rising young relative, the Royal Trust building) had markedly changed the face of Toronto's downtown.[8] Large and dark as they were, Mies's careful balancing of the width and depth of the towers and the rigourous discipline of the verticals and horizontals particularly evident in the banking pavilion diluted any menace. By recessing the ground floors with only a row of pilotis around the perimeter, even these massive blocks seemed to float above the ground.[9]

Naturally the TD Centre had its critics. Some architects mourned the loss of the elegant Bank of Toronto designed in 1913 by Carrère and Hastings of New York.[10] Keen-eyed observers noted that Mies didn't always tell the truth about form rigorously following function, and that sometimes a bit more was adjudged better than less. The vertical mullions running up the face of each tower between the windows were I-beams that had no functional purpose; they were merely attached to the structural framework. This fact was evident because they started their upward journey by springing out unsupported at the cornice line above the first floor of each tower, though they did serve as a pleasing artifice by emphasizing verticality and casting attractive patterns of light and shade on the surrounding smooth surfaces. Perhaps the greatest problem with the entire ensemble turned out to be the vast grey granite plaza shadowed by the towers that created powerful wind gusts, making it inhospitable on all but the sunniest summer days. Pedestrians tended to stick close to the building walls or to go inside and dive down into the subterranean shopping mall so that the large space usually looked empty. Moreover, the edges of the plaza seemed to have little relationship to the surrounding sidewalk, making it hard to tell where one ended and the other began and blurring the streetscape.[11] Well-travelled folk complained that Mies had simply produced copies of designs already constructed elsewhere, though this objection was muted somewhat by the sheer size of the project and by the knowledge that it was the last major work he produced before he died with construction of the later towers still in progress.

Some sophisticates thought that the form was passé even before the development was started. In 1961 Anthony Jackson, executive editor of *Canadian Architect*, wrote that designs like Lever House with its translucent, regular prisms had many disadvantages. Functionalism provided no unavoidable solution to architectural problems. Boring as a symbol, the rectangular simplicity of the International Style made it difficult to create variety and the setback of the freestanding towers on the plaza was antithetical to the canyon-like streets. He suggested that more playful designs like Ron Thom's Massey College only showed that styles changed with the times: "Miesian International Style is no longer avant garde. This obviously is nothing to worry about."[12]

As with the New City Hall everybody seemed to have a view about the TD Centre. Local politician Herbert Orliffe condemned the tower as "four blank walls reaching up into the sky." Here was a classic case of the need for firm municipal design controls. James Murray, editor of *Canadian Architect* and a vociferous critic of the committees dominated by architects so much favoured by the Ontario Association of Architects, disagreed. Why should such bodies have the right to exercise control over the work of fellow-professionals? This provoked Morris Charney to defend controls as essential to modern urban planning. By focusing upon the objectives and principles underlying regional plans, it was possible to concentrate on the content of a design rather than merely arguing about aesthetics. Architects were the right people for such a task since many of them reject "the exaggerated visual taste scene that is architecture today."[13]

Local architects wanted to have their say once the TD Centre was under way. The developers issued a self-congratulatory promotional brochure when the first tower opened, claiming that people who had dismissed it as an example of "modern architectural sterility" could now see that the it "stands in elegant serenity" confounding its critics by contrast with surrounding structures. This effusion proved too much for architect Macy DuBois. He maintained that the TD Centre was "twenty years too late because the lessons it teaches us were taught long ago. It is a building displaying the hand of one of the great architects of the twentieth century, but it is not great architecture." Sigfried Giedion might admire Mies for the way his work linked back to the turn-of-the-century Chicago School and for his sheer staying power, but "what once was a fresh and vital method of attack had now become a style codified and listless." Teaching the "lessons of simplicity" could simply mean ignoring functional problems if they could not be solved. DuBois went on to complain about the interior layouts, particularly the dark low-ceilinged shopping concourse where no natural light was allowed to penetrate. "What Mies is teaching us with this building, he taught us long ago but teach he did." Still, even DuBois pulled his punch at the end, concluding in the next sentence, "For this we shall be grateful."[14]

A great deal of huffing and puffing broke out when it was noticed that Mies was not being given sufficient credit for his work since the billboard at the construction site failed even to mention his name. Robert Gretton, the managing editor of *Canadian Architect*, revealed that when he had raised

the matter with the developers he was sent a load of publicity that also omitted the great architect's name. The Fairview people went so far as to claim that it was against the law even to mention Mies. Gretton complained, "We have … consistently encountered a veil of half-truths and omissions in attempting to present the work done in Canada by international designers." If local architects wanted to claim credit, they had better be ready to submit documentary proof of their role, or in the argot of those times, "Just tell it like it is, man."[15]

Toronto, which was on the verge of overtaking Montreal as Canada's national metropolis, could take pride in the fact that their city had secured a complex of classic Mies buildings before its urban rival. The developers of Westmount Square on St Catherine Street created a miniature TD Centre composed of a twenty-storey office building and two twenty-one-storey apartment towers, but it did not open until some months after the Toronto buildings.

The TD Centre provoked flattery in the form of imitation. In the autumn of 1968 the Canadian Imperial Bank of Commerce announced its intent to build a fifty-seven-storey tower right across Bay Street on the southeast corner of King, designed by American I.M. Pei. This massive slab, twice as long as wide, would overtop the TD Tower by three storeys, its stainless steel skin one-eighth of an inch thick crafted of panels fifty-six by thirteen feet with the windows inset. The panels were attached to the frame by only two bolts to allow them to move independently of the welded steel frame, providing for

(Opposite left to right)
7·4
Toronto-Dominion Centre, banking hall with interior furnishings by Mies van der Rohe.

7·5
Toronto-Dominion Centre, banking hall.

7·6
Toronto-Dominion Centre, banking hall.

7·7
Toronto-Dominion Centre, banking hall.

7.8
Commerce Court under construction, I.M. Pei, 1971.

thermal or other displacement. The steel was sandblasted to give it a silvery finish with matching windows into which a layer of mercury was laminated. Moreover, the new building would be linked to the old 1929 headquarters building of the Bank of Commerce (long Toronto's tallest structure) (see Figure 2.18) to create a new, enclosed Commerce Court. Though little used except in summer, the courtyard was greeted as a more welcoming space than the large windy open spaces around Mies's towers.[16]

James Murray saw little distinctive about Pei's building: "In fact, the tower is yet another box, and (notwithstanding the extra twenty-six feet) will be overshadowed by the exciting and simple strength of the nearby Mies tower. Whereas the Toronto Dominion tower is Mies twenty years too late but with a mature beauty of form, the CIBC tower seems to be just too late."[17] By the time of its completion, however, one injustice had been rectified as the rules of the Ontario Association of Architects were being amended so that the real designer's name could be displayed on billboards and other promotional material.[18]

Commerce Court set off a "bank war" in downtown Toronto as the other chartered banks scrambled to put up towers to show they possessed the same vigour. Next in line in 1975 was the Bank of Montreal, which erected the much taller First Canadian Place right across the street on the northwest corner of King and Bay. Phyllis Lambert, who thought Pei's work for the CIBC was a fine piece, dismissed this thoroughly undistinguished design by Edward Durrell Stone with the local firm of Bregman and Hamann as "an appalling building of no real quality at all." The Royal Bank of Canada had always had its headquarters elsewhere (notionally in Halifax but really in Montreal), but in 1955 it commissioned Peter Dickinson to design a handsome ten-storey Modernist office tower just along King Street.[19] A decade later Marani, Morris, and Allan supplied them with a new building, but in 1976 (fleeing like the Bank of Montreal from the threat of the separatist movement in Quebec) the Royal moved most of its central operations (though not its official head office) to Toronto. Since the four corners of King and Bay were already occupied with bank headquarters, the Royal's new tower was pushed off to the southeast corner of Wellington and Bay. There Webb Zerafa Menkes and Housden (successors to Dickinson) produced for the bank a huge complex composed of two triangular towers linked by

7.9
Royal Bank Plaza, Webb Zerafa Menkes Housden, 1977. Royal Bank Plaza was the last of the big-bank developments of the 1970s but the first to eschew tower height as its signature.

a vast atrium. The zigzag vertical facing of the towers was covered in gold leaf mirror glass with results which Phyllis Lambert rightly dismissed as "so cheesy, so chintzy."[20]

As often, being the first mover generated extra benefits for the Toronto Dominion Bank. Not only did Mies deliver a design that produced much attention, but also Allen Lambert (who had once had doubts about calling the development the TD Centre) must have been delighted not only with the fine rental revenues but the yards of free publicity the project generated. All this from a job for which Mies was paid a fee of just $75,000.[21] The arrival of the TD Centre meant that nobody could ignore the fact that International Style Modernism had finally arrived in Toronto in a big way.

II

Modernism had no equivalent success in the field of residential design. In 1957 James Acland, professor of planning at the University of Toronto, wrote a fierce denunciation of current trends in the field of housing: "Let's admit: The romantic suburban retreat has been among the most costly and disastrous of contemporary mankind's delusions. The wheel has turned full cycle, and suburbanite and exurbanite have all but destroyed the city in their effort to recreate the pattern of a primitive agricultural community." Undistinguished in appearance and expensive to service, the suburban bungalow set amidst a wasteful expanse of lawn cried out for replacement. Something must be done to reverse the exodus of homeowners and persuade them to return to life in the inner city.[22]

In an editorial in *Canadian Architect* the following year James Murray echoed the condemnation of the single-family home on a forty-foot wide suburban lot: "Why is so much of this type of housing so bad?" Murray placed much of the blame upon builders, often little more than glorified carpenters or bricklayers and lacking the ability to produce designs beyond the "incoherent" or "aesthetically petty." Even creating an attractive streetscape was highly impractical when a single subdivision was often the work of so many different hands turning out only a few houses each. Clearly architects must be summoned to the rescue.[23]

In 1958 the Ontario Association of Architects created a Committee on Housing Design, which reported the widely held view that improvements were long overdue. A common criticism was that tract houses were too much alike in appearance. The increasing use of the automobile had led subdivisions to sprawl across the landscape in uneconomical fashion, gobbling up acres of land and requiring expensive services and road construction.[24]

By 1960 the urban areas in Canada were growing by roughly one hundred square miles each year so that one-third of people now lived in houses built since the Second World War. The Royal Architectural Institute of Canada created a blue-ribbon panel to inquire into the "Design of the Residential Environment." Travelling to fifteen cities across the country over a period of eight months, Peter Dobush and his colleagues John C. Parkin and C.E. Pratt listened to five hundred people and received fifty written briefs. The National Council of Women was enlisted to collect information from 1,400 suburban housewives. The overwhelming response was that subdivisions were "monotonous, boring, dull, rubber-stamp," lacking features of interest and good taste and likely to face speedy deterioration. The University Women's Club of Toronto condemned a subdivision dating from 1954 as "ugly, unimaginatively planned, the same plan used for every exposure ... [with] garish colours shouting for attention." What resulted were developments that looked "like slums almost before they were occupied." Concern was focused upon the monotony of suburbia: "These widespread complaints betray a note of aesthetic despair but also strong currents of human compassion." What could be done? The tyranny of the bungalow must be broken by providing a greater variety of housing types like low-rise apartment blocks and townhouses.[25]

Eric Arthur, who had been delivering such jeremiads for a generation, chimed in that the average builder's house "defies all known standards of design; it is riddled with clichés, nooks, and gimmicks; it can be described only as revolting to the person of taste, and yet represents to a large section of the Canadian public all that is desirable in the moderately priced house. That such a state of affairs exists causes us no surprise, but it is nonetheless disturbing." The situation was so serious that Arthur was even forced to reconsider his previous condemnation of the ill-conceived products of the Victorian era: "We once regarded the latter as horrors, but with the perspective of 1961 ... we must revise our standards. What architect would not prefer to live in the most whimsical of Victorian villas, if he had to choose between that and the most popular of contemporary Canadian builders' houses."[26]

Some architects were making efforts to concoct solutions to these problems along lines suggested long ago by the founders of the Modern movement. They believed that large-scale housing developments could be designed at higher densities while offering greater amenities and a better quality of life. Townhouses and apartments facing onto common green spaces could offer an affordable alternative to cookie-cutter bungalows. Pedestrian walkways rather than streets clogged with parked cars would allow children to play safely outdoors.

Henry Fliess had come to Canada from Britain as a German internee at the outbreak of the Second World War and remained to study architecture at the University of Toronto. Upon his graduation in 1946 he started to teach there; he left to join the team that planned Don Mills in 1953 and, with James Murray, designed the row housing called Southill Village in 1957 (see Figure 5.6). At a time when such buildings were considered only a small cut above the slums, Fliess and Murray had the sense to leave a row of trees along the boulevard in the centre of the access road, which helped to mask some rather ugly exteriors, and they also provided proper storage space for household garbage. The results won them a silver Massey Medal for group housing in 1958.[27]

In 1956 Belcourt and Blair designed some terrace housing called Greenbelt Heights Village in Don Mills where two-storey, two-bedroom apartments were stacked on top of single-floor bachelor units. Through traffic was excluded from this inward-looking enclave and North York agreed to waive its requirement for sixty-six foot road allowances. Instead the buildings were reached by twenty foot wide laneways with bumps to limit cars to ten miles per hour. Central heating, garages, and laundry facilities were supplied. *Canadian Architect* declared this project to be "one of the most enlightened pieces of residential planning in Canada," despite the fact that the larger units (which would presumably attract families with children) were placed on top of the smaller ones for singles and couples and were only reachable by exterior flights of steps leading to balconies.[28]

7.10
Greenbelt Heights Village, Belcourt and Blair, 1956.

7.11 (Left)
Yorkwoods Village,
Klein and Sears, 1962.

7.12 (Right)
Don Valley Woods,
Klein and Sears, 1964.

Jack Klein and Henry Sears formed a partnership in 1958 that soon made row housing a specialty.[29] In 1962 they laid out 120 townhouses in Yorkwoods Village, part of a vast development of low- and high-rise buildings totaling 1,700 units on Jane Street south of Finch Avenue at Yorkwoods Gate. Eighty percent of the parking spaces for residents were underground. Soon after, they followed up with about 250 townhouses (as part of eight hundred units in all) in Don Valley Woods at York Mills near Woodbine Avenue. These developments shared many features. The principal aim was to create a pedestrian precinct. Yorkwoods stood on a flat, featureless piece of ground where an effort had to be made to create points of interest, while Don Valley Woods had a sloping site with wooded ravines to the east and south, which permitted the architects to arrange the townhouses in tiers with the roofs of the lower units forming terraces for structures above.[30]

Henry Sears observed that up to the 1950s, in Toronto row housing had been denigrated, despite the existence of some fine examples built in the nineteenth century. To make such layouts acceptable to suburban families with young children, they had to be given sugar-coated titles like "townhouses, garden courts, multiple-family, group housing." He expressed the hope that the success of new designs would interest developers in creating similar projects in the central city. In the same issue of the RAIC *Journal* architect Ian Maclennan, executive director of the Central Mortgage and Housing Corporation, laid out the reasons behind the dissatisfaction with much current suburban development: the monotony of appearance, the land-grabbing sprawl, the lack of community facilities, and the social homogeneity of the occupants, which excluded the old, the young, and the poor. The suburbs had even begun to appear to threaten the vitality of the central city. Maclennan's analysis signalled that the major public lending agency would look with favour at developments with greater density and a wider variety of housing types.[31]

Despite the growing demand for apartment living by the mid-1950s, high-rise towers continued to encounter strong criticism. Social work professor Albert Rose pointed out that before 1958 apartments had never exceeded 30 percent of total dwelling starts in Canada's urban centres, but in that year reached over 36 percent and by the mid-1960s were running at nearly 55 percent. Metro Toronto had reached 50 percent in 1958 and soon expanded to over 60 percent. Still it was widely believed that high-rise buildings were a poor environment for raising children, though research on that point did not sustain such claims.[32]

The editors of *Canadian Architect* followed Rose's article with an analysis of the reasons why so many near-identical apartment blocks of dubious architectural merit were now being built. By the 1960s construction techniques for residential high-rises framed in reinforced concrete had become fairly standardized. Slab towers with about twenty storeys on top of a couple of underground parking levels could be constructed with reinforced eight-inch concrete one-way floor plates and stiffened by vertical shear walls to resist lateral wind forces located at approximately twenty-foot intervals, which also acted as convenient partitions. The speed and economy of such construction methods was increased by the development of flying forms, which permitted cranes to slip them out from a hardened slab and raise them up two storeys for reuse. The most common footprint was the double-loaded slab, but the same methods could be used for smaller point towers and Y-shapes or cruciforms that drastically reduced construction costs but permitted relatively high densities on smaller lots.[33]

The *marxisant* radicals who oversaw the creation of a tower for the residential Rochdale College on the northern edge of the University of Toronto campus at Bloor and St George Streets claimed to provide new models of social and intellectual life. Various modes of communitarian living were offered that would provide radical alternative lifestyles to the morays of modern capitalism. When the experiment was terminated in disarray, however, the building's conversion into residences for the elderly did not prove too great a challenge. The structural forms reflected the grid that rose from the underground parking garage, which made the building much like its despised counterparts elsewhere.

A more interesting variation on the format was devised by architect Gerald Robinson. The Colonnade development on Bloor Street just east of Avenue Road, completed in 1964, provided fifteen retail stores on the ground floor with fifty small boutiques above. This level, which aimed to create the impression of an indoor street, was reached by a striking staircase spiralling one and one-half turns from the street with no central support. Above were 160 apartments. The building also contained a 350-space parking garage as

7.13
The Colonnade,
Gerald Robinson, 1964.

well as office and studio space, a theatre in the round, and even a farmers' market. The framework was of reinforced concrete linked by small exterior columns to allow flexible room layouts.[34]

High-rise apartment construction took off not only in the city proper but in the suburbs. The creation of Metropolitan Toronto permitted the speedy development of an expressway box (composed of Highways 401 and 427, the Gardiner Expressway, and the Don Valley Parkway) that, along with a

7.14
Bathurst and Steeles, looking north, in the 1970s.

program of arterial road construction, greatly facilitated automobile commuting. The development industry was quick to locate apartment complexes along these routes even at the outer edges of the built-up area. In contemporary photographs the cluster of towers located at the intersection of Bathurst Street and Steeles Avenue at the very edge of Metro appear striking on account of the open fields stretching beyond them to the north.[35]

Such developments had clear connections to long-standing ideas of the Modern movement in architecture. Tall towers set in parkland crisscrossed by broad roads harked back to Le Corbusier's *cité radieuse* as well as to the urban utopias of Frank Lloyd Wright. Concentrated developments of affordable housing surrounded by green open space designed for lower-income groups had also been one of the major objectives of the Bauhaus in Europe. The effort to combine such notions became particularly evident in Toronto in the case of several large-scale suburban developments.

In 1955 developer Robert McClintock purchased the lands owned by the Fleming estate east of the intersection of Don Mills Road and Eglinton Avenue East, south of Don Mills. Three hundred and fifty acres were sold in 1958 to Toronto Industrial Leaseholds (TIL), which acquired an additional 250 acres the following year. TIL was affiliated with the developers Webb and Knapp Canada, and together they established Webin Communities. Macklin Hancock drew up a plan for a diversified development on the property rather like his layout for Don Mills, including a residential section at the southeast corner with industrial plants located north of Eglinton and office towers on the south side. Over one hundred acres was to be used by the Canadian Broadcasting Corporation for the construction of a "Radio and Television City," which would allow the network to consolidate operations scattered all over Toronto. The route of the new Don Valley Parkway was shifted further eastward so as not to cut the property in half but to follow the rim of the valley of the East Don River, providing easy access southward to downtown and northward to Highway 401.[36]

In 1959 Modernist architect Irving Grossman was retained to devise a master plan for the residential section of the new Flemingdon Park to house about fifteen thousand people. Here was the rare chance to create a community through comprehensive planning because the developer controlled a large enough area to permit the architect to lay out relatively high density housing while retaining sizable areas of open space. The key was to place road access and parking underground with pedestrian walkways at grade. As Grossman put it, "For myself, the architect, the sight of children at play in the open greens, of people strolling along the landscaped pedestrian malls, while cars move unseen in the garages below is, of course, a source of satisfaction in itself." The unusual opportunity would make this part of Toronto grow "properly," a step towards "the utopia of planned environment" not unlike the Garden City movement that was clearly among its antecedents.[37]

Grossman's design for Block H3 on Vendome Place, overlooking the Don Valley Parkway, was a radical attempt to mix one-, two-, and three-storey elevations along a pedestrian street. Block D3 between Dennis, Rochfort, and Deauville would be a large concentration of "garden homes." Residents would be able to walk up to 1,500 feet along paths encircling a tree-lined square and a sunken garden without encountering any vehicular traffic, which would be routed along the one-way system of underground roads. Future expansion would include the whole gamut of housing types from row houses to tall point blocks. Grossman believed Flemingdon Park would be a distinct improvement over previous planned communities.[38]

THE STREET

7.15
Drawing of pedestrian "street," Flemingdon Park, Irving Grossman, 1961.

Yet, by the time the first units were ready in 1961, Toronto found itself with a glut of rental apartments, and tenants proved unenthusiastic about Flemingdon Park. The leasing executive for Flemingdon Park Management pointed out that many of the housing designs were unusual, and that the row houses were viewed with suspicion or rejected outright on account of their association with slum conditions. Webb and Knapp came under severe financial pressures, but instead of imposing curbs on the "utopian" notions of the architect and planner, the company simply bulled ahead until work ground to a halt early in 1964. At that point 1,400 units surrounded by large open spaces were left standing vacant for a year.[39]

Irving Grossman later conceded that inquiries among residents had produced some surprising results. Architects sometimes acted upon assumptions that did not always prove well-founded. For instance, he believed that people would be less eager to rent housing with balconies that overlooked the Don Valley Parkway, yet discovered that the units facing the expressway were the first to be occupied. Rather than seeking a quieter location fronting on a green space, tenants apparently preferred the noise and lights of cars speeding by. Why, he asked in frustration, when architects were insistent that Modern designs were superior, did 95 percent of homebuyers still prefer the familiar neo-Georgian knockoffs?[40]

In 1964 a syndicate of four developers calling themselves Central Park Estates purchased the rental buildings at Flemingdon Park and announced their intention to develop all the remaining land, but the contracts with Grossman and with Hancock were terminated. By that time it had become clear that the original layout suffered from deficiencies. Particularly serious was the location of the shopping centre at the western boundary off Don Mills Road, which was hard for pedestrians get to. If the shops had been located nearer the middle of the residential area, they might have attracted more custom and seemed less dismal and barren. There were no hardware or clothing stores, and the supermarket was too small. Both residents and passersby used their cars to journey the short distance northward to the Don Mills plaza, which offered a much better choice of retail outlets. By 1967 the second floor of the Flemingdon Park mall had been closed off altogether, and there were a depressing number of empty shopfronts on the lower level.

Equally disturbing were the deficiencies in community facilities. The school was located far from the centre of the residential area in an undistinguished building, yet was soon so overcrowded that a gaggle of portable classrooms was required. Where such planned developments that mixed residential, commercial, and industrial activities had been laid out in Europe following the Second World War, the land was normally publicly owned; whereas in Canada municipalities were not keen to acquire real estate or to finance social and recreational centres. The fact that Flemingdon Park was bought and sold by several different developers in succession only helped to inflate the cost of land, making it more costly for community purposes. The townhouses had such small private outdoor spaces that they proved to be inadequate, but the playgrounds that existed were neither large enough nor properly maintained. A suggestion that a stretch of land under the overhead powerlines of the Ontario Hydro-Electric Power Commission be secured as parkland came to nothing, while a small ravine that crossed the site from north to south that might have been attractive open space was filled with rubbish and abandoned shopping carts. A golf course east of the expressway, originally to be open to Flemingdon Park residents, was sold off and the green fees raised so that few of them could afford to use it. No churches offered to locate in the neighbourhood. Organizations like the YMCA showed no interest in building branches, and financing such structures was made difficult because neither the Central Mortgage and Housing Corporation nor private lending institutions would provide funds for such purposes. When approached to create facilities, the municipal government of North York placed the development far down on the priority list below more conventional subdivisions.

The biggest change at Flemingdon Park occurred at the end of 1966 when all of the row housing was purchased by the Ontario Housing Corporation (OHC) as rent-controlled public accommodation. By that date so many requests for repairs had accumulated that OHC was forced to bring in sixty workers to cope with the problems in more than five hundred units. When surveyed by a group of university students, many of the residents of both public and private housing complained bitterly about poor or non-existent building maintenance. They wanted the dearth of cultural and recreational facilities rectified and the lack of easily accessible shopping remedied. Grossman insisted that he had not been involved in decisions about the location and design of the school or about recent changes to the shopping centre and admitted that maintenance had been neglected, but otherwise defended the principles underlying his master plan.

Undeterred, the new owners pressed ahead with construction of a thousand additional apartments on the vacant lands. When confronted with problems with the existing development, the usual response was to criticize the planners and architects as unrealistic in their original expectations. By 1968 the northern part of Flemingdon Park was complete with the whole project due to be finished by 1972. As the years passed, the neighbourhood would achieve notoriety as a zone for gang activities and drug dealing. When asked what had gone wrong with a development that was once touted as one of the finest integrated rental complexes in North America, the former property manager pointed out that many of the ideas dearest to the hearts of the architect and the planners had ultimately been jettisoned for economic reasons. Yet he defended the plan that at least sought to combine residential, commercial, and industrial activities in one area. While rejecting the notion that the original conception had been flawed, Hans Elte, a professor of planning at the University of Toronto's School of Architecture, was forced to admit that developments like Flemingdon Park were no longer suitable for the late twentieth century, being based on "antiquated" notions that required complete rethinking.[41]

Irving Grossman did not agree. In 1962 his residential plan for Flemingdon Park was used as a case study at a civic design seminar in Stratford, Ontario, where he argued that Canadians needed only to be convinced of the "horrors" of outmoded layouts in order to put an end to public apathy.[42] His layout received an award of merit in a housing design competition.

Smaller projects by other architects reflected similar principles. Henry Fliess created a "maisonette" layout on busy Victoria Park Avenue north of Lawrence at Clintwood Court that provided high-density row housing at between fifteen and twenty units per acre. In the first phase two buildings ran at right angles to the east side of Victoria Park ninety feet apart, each unit having a patio open to the common space between them. Access to the parking lots at the rear was by internal corridors. Jumble in the open areas was reduced by replacing garbage cans with incinerators and banning laundry lines for clothes driers. A sandbox visible from each kitchen window was provided for children to play; they made so much use of the green space that the grass wore off and eventually much of it was asphalted over. A second set of buildings, which opened in 1961 on the west side of Victoria Park, aimed to provide more privacy for the patios by separating them with low brick walls.

7.16
Clintwood Court,
Henry Fliess, 1961.

7.17
Edgeley, Irving Grossman, 1961.

This layout won Fliess an award of merit in a housing design competition in 1962. James Murray of *Canadian Architect* praised Clintwood Court as much better designed than the usual multiple housing, though he did note that the layout produced odd results with some living room windows looking onto major roads, some onto the open spaces, without apparent logic. Large glass windows along the pedestrian walkways seemed to contravene well-established principles concerning privacy. Yet Murray remained enthusiastic about efforts by Modernists to create innovative housing designs: "If it wasn't for those pioneers who set some sort of design against the apathy of the postwar years, people like Grossman wouldn't be able to work today."[43]

Grossman was certainly not discouraged by the problems encountered at Flemingdon Park. He was soon at work designing another large housing project in North York. In 1954 a joint federal-provincial land bank acquired 655 acres of land just south of the Metro boundary at Steeles Avenue between the old concession roads of Keele and Jane Streets. Eventually 475 acres were given to the newly founded York University, and eighty-eight acres to the Metro Toronto Conservation Authority that used the land to resite historic buildings at Black Creek Pioneer Village. The remainder, which ultimately totalled ninety-five acres along Jane Street, was retained for residential use. Metro Toronto wanted to construct public housing along with accommodation for the elderly, and Central Mortgage and Housing Corporation retained Grossman's firm, Environmental Planning Associates, to devise a master plan for this Edgeley development.

Grossman's design called for the Ontario Housing Corporation's public housing to be sited to the north along Jane Street – 455 row houses along with 135 units in a sixteen-storey apartment tower, accessed from exterior balconies rather than by internal corridors. To the south would be 736 privately owned condominiums. As at Flemingdon Park, a major objective was to separate pedestrians from automobiles, though at Edgeley this would be done by keeping cars on the periphery rather than underground. The centrepiece of the project was a broad mall, one thousand feet long, to be surrounded by an elementary school, a high school, two churches, a community centre, and health care facilities alongside a twelve-storey apartment tower with 360 units for the elderly. This open space would be linked to the public housing to the north by a pedestrian bridge over Shoreham Drive so that children need not encounter automobile traffic on the way to school. Public roadways would take up only 9 percent of the ground area versus about 17 percent in a typical development with 14 percent being public open space, as against the requirements of the North York zoning bylaw that called for a minimum of 5 percent of total area plus two and one half acres for each thousand head of population in new subdivisions.[44]

The architect was convinced that the way to avoid the whole development acquiring the stigma attached to public housing was to build the different housing types simultaneously. However, during the first one and a half years while the public housing and accommodation for the elderly were completed, only about 115 condominiums were built, and from the outset the condominium owners had reservations about mixing with tenants in the public housing. Some people argued that, instead of building public housing, it would have been better to provide rent subsidies to the less well-off to permit them to choose where they wished to live.[45]

Grossman's faith in his guiding principles, particularly automobiles being excluded as far as possible and row housing for families with front doors opening onto pedestrian streets, remained undimmed. In a 1973 speech to the Urban Development Institute, a lobby group for apartment developers, he repeated the familiar arguments, claiming that the public now favoured such ideas. Yet he had to admit that not everybody shared his particular enthusiasms since there was now popular pressure to preserve older houses in existing urban neighbourhoods: "This focus has taken even architects by surprise. I have to admit to me this had never been important in my eyes, because I'm convinced that my talents would surely produce more housing that was far more interesting and comfortable than what existed, and that was enough justification to condone demolition in any particular location in the city; architecture was art."[46]

Some of Grossman's fellow Modernists developed a means to combine ideas about both preservation and improvement in the inner city. Alexandra

Park was a working-class neighbourhood southeast of the corner of Bathurst and Dundas Streets where small two-storey frame homes for about 4,400 people were mixed in with some industrial activities like a large bakery.[47] In the late 1950s studies revealed that almost half the houses required replacement, and in the early 1960s the city designated the area for redevelopment. Homeowners began to wonder if the government would follow the slum clearance model and simply demolish practically every structure as with Regent Park, fears that led many homeowners to delay repairs and only hastened deterioration. Eventually in 1966 the city concluded that what was required was not slum clearance but "urban renewal": dilapidated buildings should be demolished and replaced by super-blocks of public housing while the remaining homes would be rehabilitated. A variety of housing types was clearly required to accommodate a large number of children for whom it was agreed front doors at grade and private yards were necessary.

Design of the project was handed over to Webb Zerafa Menkes along with Jerome Markson and Klein and Sears, who were, of course, all keenly interested in Modernist solutions. Surveys revealed that parked automobiles were clogging the roads in the neighbourhood as there were few garages. The architects concluded that the main north–south street, Vanauley, should be replaced by a pedestrian spine with links to east and west where Cameron and Augusta Avenues ran. Blocks of public housing would be placed inside perimeter parking lots providing one space for every two units, so that even people who did not live in the public housing would be forced to pass through it en route to their homes. The centre would be reserved for row housing so that children could roam the entire eighteen acres without encountering a major street. The whole area was to be provided with visual links by using a uniform colour of brick and exterior paint.

When the work was done Jerome Markson pronounced himself particularly well satisfied:

> Much can be said in favour of Alexandra Park. It is probably no exaggeration to term it by international standards an exemplary design solution. So many correct human judgements were made within its concept – keeping the density at a moderate level, housing the families with children in a working relationship to the ground in terms of public, semi-public and private space, maintaining the intimacy and face-to-face nature of the pedestrian street, separating cars and people, respecting human scale and sociability, making the landscape durable, and conserving the existing trees, and above all displaying a perceptive sensitivity of the human urban residential condition.

7.18
Alexandra Park, Webb Zerafa Menkes, Jerome Markson, and Klein and Sears, 1966.

Canadian Architect agreed that the result was a success. Dilapidated houses had been replaced and the non-residential activities removed; the car-clogged streets were gone. The one admitted failure was that insufficient funding was provided for rehabilitating the sound houses. In the end all these old buildings were demolished and replaced by new construction, raising questions about whether it was really possible to combine upgrading and repairs with a public housing development. All in all, however, urban renewal in Alexandra Park had resulted in much of what had been aimed for: "Its shortcomings appear to be due not to faults in planning, but rather to a lack of decisiveness and acumen in carrying it out."[48]

Only later in the 1980s did it become clear that cutting off housing developments like Alexandra Park from the street grid and connecting the units only by footways could engender serious problems. With no cars and only a few people passing along the paths, such dimly lit spaces could become a haven for those seeking quiet locations to carry out illicit activities such as drug dealing. The police did not patrol the lanes on foot, nor could public transit serve them. Large common spaces between buildings were often perceived as a kind of no man's land to which adjoining owners had only a tenuous claim so that they were not well maintained.

Unfortunately, Modern architecture did not prove to have the hoped-for effect of ameliorating social problems and modifying human behaviour. Indeed, by the 1980s, Edgeley and Yorkwoods Village had come to form the northern and southern boundaries of the notorious "Jane–Finch corridor," which Toronto's popular lore associated with drug dealing, racial conflict, gang violence, and not infrequent gunplay and murder. Residence in the area was considered to be a burden to be borne by some of the least fortunate people in Metro Toronto. Such a change in perception marked the culmination of a shift in fashions in urban planning, which had largely turned against the Modernist ideas that had once seemed so appealing.[49]

Meanwhile, architects devoted little attention to the kind of dwellings that most Canadians preferred to inhabit. In 1969 Bruno Freschi observed that the detached single-family house was "not a mainstream architectural problem" and likely to recede even further from attention. Fred Hollingsworth noted that a recent federal government task force had received the clear message that the public favoured such accommodation, but that juries at publications like *Progressive Architecture* had made it plain in recent times that detached single-family houses were unimportant. Rather than being a significant problem or a legitimate concern, such layouts were considered of little interest by the architectural profession. Less than 1 percent of this kind of housing was now designed by architects who considered that its day had passed. Most Canadians refused to accept Modernist layouts, so that its time fled without ever really having arrived in the residential field.[50]

III

During the 1960s Ontario's educational system was expanding by leaps and bounds. Since all schools were intended to perform roughly the same functions, such buildings seemed to offer the chance to experiment with the long-standing dream of prefabrication, particularly if mated with the machine aesthetic of Modern architecture. School boards in the Toronto area, watching as their pupil counts rose inexorably, were particularly attracted to the idea of turning out new buildings on something resembling an assembly line basis. Was it possible to create an attractive and efficient design that could be tailored slightly to particular requirements while bringing rising construction costs under control?

Educational bureaucrats came to believe that one possible solution was large open-plan schools that would utilize team teaching. This idea flowered in California in the early 1960s as the San Carlos School District (SCSD) project supported by the Educational Facilities Laboratory.[51] The Scarborough Board of Education proved particularly interested,[52] and in 1968 Howard V. Walker designed North Bridlewood Public School on Collingsbrook Boulevard near Warden and Finch Avenues, the first open-plan school in Canada built on the SCSD model. When Russell K. Yapp visited North Bridlewood for *Canadian Architect* the following year, he received an upbeat account of how the new design had turned out. The director of the Scarborough school system felt that that teachers liked working together in groups and could assist each other with on-the-job training. The principal thought his staff was more content and student discipline problems fewer than in a conventional school. Some teachers believed that students were happier because they felt greater freedom, which made them more creative, while the teachers liked having their own private offices to retreat to. The atmosphere was more informal and there was more interaction between teachers. One person even suggested that it would be better to open up the interior even further at times: "We need more moveable walls so that we can become one big family," as when everybody at the school was watching the same television program. Students felt that they had more privacy, and having lockers in the hallways meant that personal possessions did not get stolen as often as at conventional schools.

Closer inspection, however, revealed a more critical viewpoint, especially starting from the bottom up. Russell Yapp reported that the pupils liked having greater freedom in the classroom but complained about other students walking around and peering over their shoulders. Sometimes they were distracted by what was being done in the other parts of the large rooms or found it hard to hear due to background noise. The teachers thought there was an urgent need for more small seminar rooms where pupils could go and work on individual problems. The director noticed that when movable partitions were provided the teachers often left them permanently in place so that they might as well be walls. Yapp concluded that the open plan seemed to work for an elementary school but wondered what would happen when the pupils moved on to secondary school where this kind of freedom would not be suitable. All in all, it seemed that those involved were engaged in a kind of Orwellian doublethink where obvious problems were plainly stated but in the end denied and ignored.[53]

The Metropolitan Toronto School Board was responsible for providing capital funding for construction to local boards that staffed and managed the schools. In 1966 the Metro board decided to undertake a formal study to discover if it was possible to develop a system of modular construction that would permit speedy completion with maximum flexibility at a reduced cost. The non-profit Educational Facilities Laboratory supported the idea because it was keen to see such an experiment conducted on open-plan schools in a large metropolitan area with a wide diversity in income levels, preferably where racial tensions were absent. The result was the creation of a formal "Study of Educational Facilities" (SEF), headed by architect Roderick Robbie.[54]

The objective was to develop systems and modules that could be easily and economically combined to produce structures of the required size and shape, while still leaving some leeway to customize buildings to be used as junior or senior public schools. SEF identified ten sub-systems that together accounted for 80 percent of total building costs and invited thirty-two bidders to tender for contracts.[55] In order to encourage contractors to develop and innovate, each of the ten winners would be guaranteed to supply the components for about thirty schools that together would contain up to two million square feet of space. Roughly one-third of these schools were to be completed by July 1970; the entire project was budgeted at $41.7 million with the aim of saving $3.5 million (or 8.4 percent). Some local school boards saw such interference by the Metro board as a threat to local autonomy and participated only minimally. Others, such as Scarborough and North York, faced with skyrocketing enrollment, considered SEF a boon that would lessen their financial burdens and embraced it enthusiastically.

Robbie himself was highly optimistic. By the spring of 1969 technical testing of the components had been completed. Construction of the first SEF building was under way at Roden Public School on Hiawatha Boulevard in Toronto near Dundas Street and Greenwood Avenue. Roden was expected to be ready by February 1970, and another eleven schools were scheduled for completion by the summer. The well-known management consulting firm of Woods Gordon were retained to see that the separate sub-systems arrived at the right moment to speed each job onward. Robbie predicted that once fully developed SEF would deliver significant economies over traditional building methods, so that space would cost $19.10 per square foot or $1.85 less than the current cost in greater Toronto. He also contended that the results would deliver a level of finish and flexibility that was up to one-third superior to conventional construction methods costing the same amount.[56] Nothing could have fitted better with the strain of social reformism that lay within Modern architecture and the faith that windows, walls, and doors could modify human behaviour significantly. (For a list of the SEF schools eventually constructed and their costs, see Appendix A.)

At the end of 1969, even before the first school opened, Alexander Leman gave an enthusiastic endorsement to SEF in *Canadian Architect*.[57] He claimed (without substantiation) that since the Second World War school buildings had become the most radical centres for architectural innovation, a tradition perpetuated by SEF. Why had architects not previously considered the potential of modular systems for all kinds of construction? Was it because they believed that these methods would interfere with their professional autonomy

Eastview Public School addition, designed by SEF staff architects, is the first SEF test project. Exteriors at top show playground entrance and stairwell linking addition to existing school. Above and below: classrooms with partitions in open and closed positions. Right: two views of the classroom areas in use. The furniture, which is temporary, is non-SEF.

by limiting design choices? Certainly some of the initiative would be shifted to sub-system designers, but the project did offer choices and opportunities. Robbie reported to Leman that so far architects and other professionals like engineers had been cooperative or at least were not actively obstructionist. Leman wondered if architects might feel constrained in shaping spaces by a system with only five approved ceiling heights and uniform lighting fixtures. Did the exterior wall designs show enough sensitivity to the need to link inside to outside, a problem that had preoccupied architects for the past half century? And finally would SEF really generate the promised cost savings when it was widely used? Leman did note that questions remained about whether the open-plan layout was more than the latest fad in educational philosophy, but on the whole he was highly positive, applauding Robbie for doing an invaluable service upon which others must build in future.[58]

7.19 (Opposite) SEF (Study of Educational Facilities), Roderick Robbie et al., 1969: "Eastview Public School Addition, designed by SEF staff is the first SEF test project."

Other architects hardly seemed to know what to think. When George Banz was invited by *Canadian Architect* to look into new school layouts in the autumn of 1970, he hemmed and hawed so much that he had to provide a (not very helpful) clarification several months later: "What I tried to express was my concern with the tendency of architects to continue putting their traditional prerogative to [sic] artistic expression ahead of a growing obligation to serve social needs. If, as architects, we continue to view school design as a vehicle for personal aggrandizement, we should not be surprised if school boards turn to the type of barracks architecture exemplified by Toronto's SEF project in an attempt to provide a viable teaching and learning environment that is unencumbered by our dreams of professional glory."[59]

When the construction program was completed Roy Brown, who had spent seven years working with Irving Grossman and now taught part time at the School of Architecture at the University of Toronto, enthusiastically endorsed SEF in the autumn of 1971. He had to begin, however, with the admission that the first twenty-two public schools had cost more than traditional buildings as had happened so often before with prefabrication schemes. Architects seemed to have little interest in SEF since the systems ruled out much of the artistic licence usually offered them. What criticism there had been within the profession to date had largely focused upon the external appearance of the bland concrete walls broken only by narrow window slots. Yet this was like judging a car by kicking the tires without bothering to look beneath the hood. Brown remonstrated with the "old guard" for fulminating against the lack of surface variation and reentrant corners.

The more Brown wrote, however, the more confused he became. He admitted that SCSD had rejected uniform exteriors (which accounted for only about 6 percent of costs) on the grounds that site, topography, neighbourhood, and microclimate varied too greatly. Why, he asked, should the

Toronto area be filled up with near-identical school buildings in order to emulate Los Angeles, where people had to lock their car doors on the freeways? SEF schools showed little sensitivity to ethnic, class, or income divisions in different areas. Yet they were based upon the ideas of people such as Marshall McLuhan who claimed that existing schools were actually hostile to learning, a viewpoint that Brown seemed to share. He got himself so wound up that he concluded with a diatribe against Board of Education bureaucrats who locked up their schools after hours so that his wife was unable to use them to teach her dance classes. The two sensible points his article made – that SEF schools were relatively expensive to build and ignored their sites – were drowned in this conjugation of silliness.[60]

Gradually, however, opinion within the profession hardened. In February 1972 the cover of *Canadian Architect* showed a Rubik's cube that read, "SEF IS A BAD BOY." Inside was an edited version of a report by a six-member committee of the Ontario Association of Architects created to assess the project.[61] The conclusions were damning. Between 1966 and 1968 construction costs in the greater Toronto area were rising by 5 percent annually so SEF had been forced at the outset to allow its suppliers an escalation clause for their prices. The result was that the cost of the sub-systems, however innovative, rose steadily by an average of 22 percent during the life of the experiment while other educational construction costs had almost stagnated. The management consultants at Woods Gordon had drawn up the construction schedule, but the sub-system producers organized delivery for their own convenience, and once buildings were off the schedule it became very difficult to recover. Participating architects were forced to wade through reams of paperwork to solve problems and disliked their lack of freedom in dealing with aesthetic issues. Claims that the final product would yield at least 25 percent more value than conventional methods in terms of better finish or greater flexibility did not appear justified; the results were either no better in quality or else that quality had been paid for. While the experiment might have been a remarkable one, the committee expressed the hope that the concrete walls and gun slot windows would disappear from future school buildings. Robert Gretton of *Canadian Architect* observed that SEF schools produced an assault upon the aesthetic sensibilities of both users and the public for which there was "no excuse." He added the wounding comment that, "Many of the individual schools have exteriors very similar to European biological warfare laboratories circa 1943."[62]

Roderick Robbie, who had had moved on to other things,[63] declined to meet with the OAA committee, simply styling its report "naïve, cunning and myopic." SEF, he said, had been intended to create buildings for users rather than for architects. No longer would they be a caste of "priests" or a "self-appointed elite of architectural taste-makers." Evidence of the utopian element in SEF was that Robbie had to concede to those who complained about the unpleasant appearance of the buildings that he had anticipated the development of a strippable plastic exterior paint that would allow the students to personalize the outside of their school and change it year by year in negotiation with the surrounding neighbourhood. The fact that this key component had failed to materialize was not, of course, his fault.

He said he had deliberately drafted the sub-system bidding documents in order to encourage something truly innovative. Here was an opportunity to emerge as a leader in linking quality designs and flexibility at lower cost. Nobody much had paid attention in the United States (which he claimed was undergoing a social crisis) but Ontario had led the way towards world standards in open-system building. Sub-system suppliers had to be guaranteed large orders to induce them to bid and turning back now would quickly surrender any advantage to American competitors (despite the supposed social crisis there). The chance to persuade the construction industry to adopt new methods would be squandered and old habits would live on. As for Ontario's architects, they had deliberately sought to discredit SEF, and the decision to give wide circulation to this report would only ensure that Canada never achieved a predominant position as the first mover. Criticisms of the appearance of the new schools showed that aesthetic preferences were simply determined by economically available solutions, and the complainers had just failed to notice that traditional tastemakers were already being replaced.

Because Robbie had by then been succeeded as SEF's director by P.D.J. Trion, it fell to the latter to make a rather feeble effort to defend the details of the program. Yet Trion refused to take up the criticisms one by one on grounds that to do so would only draw attention to them and instead simply restated the project's objectives. After much rehashing of old documents, Trion insisted that SEF had only been two weeks behind schedule when it ended in mid-1971. In any event, he said, speed of construction was not as important to a board of education as to a private client. The flexibility of the design was already evident in the significant alterations that some of the schools had already undergone with little fuss or expense. Like Robbie he insisted that the real source of the hostility towards SEF arose from the resistance of architects to any restraints on their freedom of design. Users were happy, the techniques were being widely adopted elsewhere, and a bright future lay ahead.[64]

A group of architecture students from the University of British Columbia weighed in to support SEF on the grounds that the role of the architect in society needed fundamental rethinking. Most architects had no familiarity with construction using sub-systems. The OAA contented itself with a brief reply to them, stating that their committee's task had been to deal with "facts, not theories" so they had focused on SEF and not on general questions about new construction methods. The students should beware of being led astray by "tired old donkeys" like discussions of threats to the place of the architect in society and should concentrate upon how well this kind of system building had worked in the real world.[65]

The children and teachers who spent their days within the twenty-eight SEF school buildings had their own views. Though many of them were positive about their new surroundings, they continued to register a number of common complaints: the large open spaces could be noisy and distracting; the lack of large window openings was a persistent cause of discontent. When researchers from the Metro Toronto School Board came around in 1975, the students in the junior public schools (from kindergarten to grade six) were quite clear: "One thing is that we don't have enough windows; that's about it." Their teachers agreed: "Not enough windows. Windows are very important and children should be kept in touch with the natural environment much more. Too many cement blocks to look at. Visually stagnating." And the exterior appearances got even less enthusiastic reviews. Said one student, "I don't like the outside of it because of the windows. It looks like a jail." Another added, "It has a very cold appearance. I don't think the outside matches the inside. The inside is quite nice. Our school looks like it has just been stuck here."[66]

With its planned school program completed, SEF seemed to be headed towards decent obscurity but it gained one last hurrah. The provincial government wanted to create a new post-secondary community college at the corner of Davenport Road and Walmer Road on the edge of downtown

7.20
George Brown College, Casa Loma Campus, Fairfield and DuBois, 1971.

7.21
Chapel Glen under construction, Boigon and Heinonen, 1972.

Toronto. In 1970 architects Robert Fairfield and Macy DuBois were asked to come up with a design for 350,000 square feet linking together some existing buildings to new structures and using system-built components on the SEF model. In the end many of the SEF systems were found to be unsatisfactory for the college's needs,[67] though the layout did consist of seventy-two-foot-square bays with precast concrete framing. The SEF-style heating and cooling system was adopted, though it required a minimum of window area so that classrooms had little or no exterior light. In an assessment of George Brown College, Ron Thom argued that overall the SEF model had been a mixed blessing: it had exposed inefficiencies in existing construction practices, but most of the energy expended had gone to trying to persuade system contractors to accept it. Making satisfactory interfaces between the systems was difficult and expensive and, except for the very largest projects, had little appeal to contractors who could not be forced to standardize their methods.[68]

System building certainly aroused little enthusiasm in Toronto, where it was tried only for a few public sector projects. In 1971 a group of developers did form a consortium called Modular Precast to construct the Chapel Glen public housing complex for the Ontario Housing Corporation at the southeast corner of Flemingdon Park.[69] First came three twenty-six-storey apartment towers at the northeast corner of Gateway Boulevard and Grenoble Drive, built using the Wates system, which had been developed in Britain, in which floor slabs, shear walls, stairs, and exterior cladding were all precast in concrete and delivered in units that weighed up to six tons. Eight apartments could be assembled every four days or at about the same speed as conventional methods. Costs were slightly higher than anticipated owing to the need for workers to learn new techniques and the cold winter weather, and savings were lower than expected due to stagnating prices for conventional construction.

The architects, Boigon and Heinonen, professed to find the Wates system satisfactory though their plans and layouts were fixed in advance by the slab sizes. One advantage for the architects was that once the design had been agreed upon it could not easily be changed. There was no pressure for constant adjustments due to price fluctuations, but the developers had to bear the risks of fixing layouts a year in advance of completion. The components were pronounced well-produced, smoothly finished, and carefully aligned, but the rooms in each unit were arranged in the usual rigid sequence. Despite the supposed flexibility of the systems approach, advanced technological methods were being used to turn out a standardized, old-fashioned layout.[70]

In 1973 *Canadian Architect* observed that large precast modular buildings systems had "about as much chance of obtaining a reasonable level of architectural quality as pigs have of flying." The magazine noted that Moshe Safdie's much admired Habitat in Montreal might seem to be an exception, but, in fact, the scheme had had to be reengineered when it turned out that the load-bearing walls required reinforcement so that the units were not really mass produced.[71] Unfortunately, projects like Toronto's SEF schools "show the low level to which such systems usually aspire."[72] As so often before, Modernist dreams concerning prefabrication proved unattainable.

IV

Plans to greatly expand the Ontario university system began to take shape in the 1950s. Whole new institutions were conjured into existence by the provincial government. For instance, architect Ron Thom designed a much-admired campus for Trent University on the banks of the Otonabee River in Peterborough.[73] The University of Toronto, however, remained highly conservative. Mathers and Haldenby continued to be the architects of choice, and in 1954 turned out a design for a residential hall named after Sir Daniel Wilson on St George Street south of Harbord in the same Georgian Revival style that the firm had adopted for Whitney Hall just to the north in 1931. In 1951 the firm designed a home for the university's Canadiana museum on Queen's Park Crescent. The architectural historian of the university provided this guarded assessment: "This small but monumental building finally commands our attention because it is so fascinatingly transitional in terms of style. It marks a mid-twentieth century period in Canada when modernism was, for the most part, in the crevices and still far from full-blown." In fact, the building looked like a miniature version of the chateau-style hotels erected across the country by the railways during the early twentieth century. Seven years later Mathers and Haldenby produced a bookstore and offices for the university press that stood at the northwest corner of the Front Campus, just next to the Sir Daniel Wilson residence. This building was virtually

7.22 (Left)
University of Toronto, Canadiana Building, east front facing the Legislative Building, Mathers and Haldenby, 1951.

7.23 (Below)
University of Toronto, Canadiana Building, view from southwest with the link to the original University Library spanning the traces of Taddle Creek.

indistinguishable from the Canadiana museum, though it lacked the statues of historical figures jutting out from its front wall.[74]

Architect Ruth Cawker, writing in the late 1980s about the impact of Modernist ideas on the design of the university's buildings, observed,

> Although more than a dozen new structures were built on the original campus in the decade following World War II, any visitor to the university would have formed an impression of stone colleges – in the manner of Cambridge or Oxford – clustered picturesquely in a park, a park too close to its wilderness state, however, to evoke the cultivated gentility of Oxbridge or the Ivy League. The picturesque hybrid of English architecture and Canadian landscape, captured so evocatively by William Notman in turn-of-the-century photographs of mist-shrouded dreaming spires, changed only subtly as new buildings invaded the old campus.[75]

By the mid-1950s the university had decided to expand westward to Spadina Avenue between Bloor and College Streets, acquiring thirty-three acres of housing. Academic buildings would be located on the west side of St George Street as near to the existing campus as possible with more residences and athletic buildings beyond, totalling two million new square feet in all. The buildings would be limited in size to about eight or ten storeys, with heavily used lecture theatres located near ground level because universities, such as Pittsburgh, had encountered severe internal congestion problems with taller towers. In the university's master plan nothing more specific was said about the matter of architectural form, except (with the unstated aim of placating the provincial government) that "all buildings on the west campus would be simple and economical in construction and maintenance" in contrast to the "varying degrees of aesthetic luxury" of older ones. To create more quiet, green, open space, it was hoped that the city could be persuaded to close up most of the existing street grid, though this ultimately proved impossible.[76]

In 1957 the university began to plan a very large new building to concentrate the offices of departments in the humanities and social sciences, which were scattered all over the campus. The design was handed to the committed Modernists at John B. Parkin Associates. In the words of the firm, "Since the building, to some extent, is a precedent for the remaining buildings that form part of the west campus, the question of height was extremely important."[77] John C. Parkin produced a layout for a six-storey slab tower at right angles to St George Street south of Harbord so as not to tower over the low neo-Georgian residence buildings to the east. The office section was linked to a rectangular two-storey block of lecture halls and seminar rooms by a spacious glazed entrance hall, and the whole structure was raised up on a podium.

7.24
University of Toronto, Sidney Smith Hall, John B. Parkin Associates, 1961.

Laid out in the full International Style, this "uncompromisingly modern" building, named Sidney Smith Hall after a former president of the university, had a concrete framework clad in precast concrete, brick, and stone, which made it a "trailblazer" on the campus.[78] With its sealed windows, the air circulation was abominable, and the maze of hallways made classrooms difficult to find, while the professors did not even have individual telephones in their offices but had to lean into niches in the concrete block corridor walls to discuss their business. Still, nobody could plausibly claim that the layout was luxurious. During the 1960s buildings of a similar sort were erected nearby for Zoology, Chemistry, and Physics. None of these was of particular architectural distinction, and the four buildings suffered from the fact that each was the product of a different firm of architects working without any overarching plan.[79]

The most distinguished building on the new part of the campus was produced by the firm of Fairfield and Dubois, which in 1959 was given the task of designing the first new residential college for undergraduates, given the inspired name, New College.[80] Macy DuBois had come to Toronto from

7.25
University of Toronto, New College, Fairfield and DuBois, 1964.

Harvard as part of the team assembled by John Andrews for the New City Hall competition. In an attempt to neutralize the effect of the street grid, DuBois created a design for the first phase of the college that presented a right-angled facade at the southwest corner of Classic and Huron Streets. On the side facing inwards onto a green space the building had an interesting sinuous shape that reflected the influence on DuBois of Finnish Modernist Alvar Aalto. At ground level this frontage had square concrete columns supporting the four upper storeys faced in brick with a strip of ribbon windows at the top featuring concrete fins. Inside, the university insisted upon the residence rooms opening off corridors, so DuBois relied upon the curving floor plan to avoid vistas down long narrow hallways.

The university was sufficiently pleased with this building, completed in 1964, that it promptly commissioned DuBois to design a second phase of New College to cover the remainder of the city block bounded by Willcocks Street and Spadina Avenue. Since the latter was supposed to carry the traffic flooding up and down from the planned Spadina Expressway to the north, DuBois created another rectangular facade at that corner with no windows facing westward onto Spadina. Inside, there was another curvilinear facade so that the two blocks enclosed an S-shaped courtyard. Though he observed that architects rarely had the opportunity to build a new structure right next to a previous design, DuBois made few changes, except to replace the square columns supporting the second floor (which he deemed "clunky") by round ones and to eliminate the concrete fins at the top level. True to the Modernist mission of social engineering, DuBois had decided not to provide any common spaces on the residence floors of the first phase to encourage all of the students to intermingle in the larger public areas, but, since the second phase was to be occupied by female students, he did provide common rooms there "because of the women's hair in curlers problem." New College was the most attractive and successful building design on the new west campus, though the architect complained that the landscaping of the courtyard by the university had not been satisfactorily done.[81]

The other great project for this part of the campus was intended to be a student centre. In 1965 John Andrews was retained to study the matter and recommended building at the corner of Russell and St George Streets but nothing happened. In 1971 the student government asked the School of Architecture to create a task force to consider the issue further. Headed by Professor Douglas Engel, this body produced a document entitled "The Campus as the Campus Centre," which is worth noting only because it incorporated a great number of fleetingly fashionable notions that were common among both faculty and students of that era.[82] Three so-called principles were formulated: that the campus should be "educational terrain"; that the university ought to be "a network of enlightenment"; and that it ought to have a community image. All this heavy thinking led to the conclusion that a campus centre was not required. Instead, small structures should be permitted along St George Street, replacing the broad sidewalks and "useless lawns," and new east–west pedestrian routes should be created, preferably walkways through the buildings at the first floor level owing to the winter climate. No more was heard of these ideas.[83]

Meanwhile, the provincial government had concluded that the greater Toronto area required a second university to meet the growing demand for post-secondary places. The new institution, to be called York University, was founded under the wing of the University of Toronto, taking in its first students in 1960. Two years later the province gave York 475 acres adjoining the Edgeley development on Keele Street south of Steeles Avenue in the northwestern corner of the city, on which to create a campus designed ultimately to serve fifteen thousand students. A consortium called University Planners, Architects and Consulting Engineers (UPACE) was created to draft the plan by Gordon S. Adamson Associates, John B. Parkin Associates, and Shore and Moffatt and Partners with Professor Thomas Howarth of the University of Toronto as consultant. Here, too, the results showed a good bit of confused thinking, since it was concluded that what was wanted was "an essentially pedestrian campus" despite the fact that up to three-quarters of the students would be commuters arriving by private automobile. The solution was a ring road around a central core of academic buildings from which

7.26 (Above)
York University, Founders College, UPACE (Gordon S. Adamson and Associates, John B. Parkin Associates, Shore and Moffatt and Partners), 1968.

7.27 (Right)
York University, Vanier College, UPACE, 1968.

all but service traffic was banned. Along this road would be situated clusters of residence buildings with acres of parking lots beyond. The lengthy walk from the parking lot to the classroom and back thus became a defining characteristic of a York education, especially in wintertime.

The most notable building was the humanities and social sciences building (named after York's first president Murray Ross). Designed by the Adamson firm for UPACE to sit upon a three-storey podium, this huge six-storey slab had a massive concrete frame of exposed rough-cast piers infilled by precast concrete panels with integrated glazing. From the east, a huge ramp (cut off from any automobile traffic) led up from the university's main driveway

7.28 (Above)
York University, Scott Library, UPACE, 1971.

7.29 (Left)
York University, Ross Humanities Building, UPACE, 1968.

through an opening in the Ross Building to a vast windswept expanse of concrete bordered on its western side by the main university library. When it opened in 1968, it was noted that this central location would "with its central arch recall Italian architecture of the late thirties" – a polite description for a piece of post-fascistic kitsch.[84]

7.30
Central Technical School, Arts Centre, Fairfield and DuBois, 1963.

The 1960s were a time when new architectural fashions appeared to challenge classic Modernism, the most muscular contender being Brutalism. This term was coined by the British architects Alison and Peter Smithson, referring to *beton brut* or raw concrete bearing the markings of the forming boards, a material often used by Le Corbusier following the Second World War. Macy DuBois had studied at Harvard with J.L. Sert, who supervised the construction in *beton brut* of that university's Carpenter Center for the Visual Arts Center, Le Corbusier's only North American building. After losing the City Hall competition, both DuBois and John Andrews had joined John B. Parkin Associates, aware that the firm had "created an aura for modern architecture" in Canada. John C. Parkin told DuBois, "I'm sorry, we can't do exposed concrete here in Canada. It just won't work because of our climate." Fired by the Parkin firm, DuBois thought about the many poured concrete bridges exposed to the elements and remained keen to use the material. However, the University of Toronto mandated the brick exterior for New College that he attached to a concrete framework as a skin. When offered the chance to design a new Arts Centre at Toronto's Central Technical School on Harbord Street near Bathurst, DuBois was able to display his interest in building in concrete using Brutalist ideas for the first time in the city.

The Arts Centre was placed behind the school's main Gothic Revival pile in a separate building at the northern edge of the property facing onto

Lennox Street. DuBois sought to create as much north-lit space as possible by cantilevering the two floors of studios outward from the central core, each half-covered by downward sloping glass ceilings. In true Brutalist fashion the exterior finish showed the imprint of the forming materials, while the interior was concrete block for toughness and graffiti-resistance. Looking back after forty-five years, DuBois's only regret about the building, for which he won a Massey Medal, was that he had not designed a better system of flashing and gutters to shed the water running down the sloping skylights, which left stains on the concrete exterior.[85]

7.31
Central Technical School, Arts Centre, interior. The artistic squiggles were cropping instructions for publication purposes in 1963.

That problem was indeed to recur with other buildings in Toronto. Engineer Morden Yolles often complained about the poor quality finish of much exposed poured concrete, contending that unskilled labour working to tight deadlines produced an inferior product, especially in school and university buildings: "The making of good architectural concrete is a hand-crafted operation."[86] George Baird, later dean of architecture at the University of Toronto, argued, like John C. Parkin, that cast-in-place concrete was not a very satisfactory finish for the climate of a city where sunlight rarely shone directly upon exterior walls or was absent altogether for long periods in the winter. Moreover, Brutalist buildings were often constructed with shadowy undercrofts like Le Corbusier's Carpenter Center, whose rain and snow stained walls looked so "dank" that Baird found it "difficult to love unreservedly." Baird believed that precast concrete cladding with its finer finishes was a more satisfactory material for Toronto, once remarking "somewhat ironically" that sophisticated structures like Mount Sinai Hospital on University Avenue were, if not masterpieces, highly satisfactory, and provided the city with "some of the best second-rate architecture in the world."[87]

Having dabbled in the world of Modern architecture with buildings such as Sidney Smith Hall and New College, the University of Toronto finally screwed up enough courage to commission a truly radical experiment in Scarborough College. Despite the fact that the new York University was already under construction, it was decided that more university places were needed in the greater Toronto area, and in 1962 the University of Toronto was persuaded to expand by creating an entirely new campus in the eastern suburbs to accommodate 1,500 students with the potential to expand to five thousand. A two-hundred-acre property was purchased on the north side of the valley of Highland Creek near the intersection of Military Trail and Ellesmere Road, and a planning team assembled, composed of planner Michael Hugo-Brunt, landscape architect Michael Hough, and architect John Andrews, who, like his classmate Macy DuBois, had been fired by Parkin and set up his own firm. Hough analyzed the site carefully for means to control the erosion of the slopes and concluded that construction should be confined to a thirty-nine-acre area right along the edge of the river valley.[88]

With construction supposed to start in the summer of 1963 so that the college would be ready to open in just two years, time was short. Watching the steady rise of enrollment figures, provincial bureaucrats and university administrators became convinced that there must be a means to extract more productivity than that possible from having students take notes while listening to a live lecturer. (After all, as an English humourist once observed, the lecture was the least efficient way to communicate information except for sneezing in Morse code.) Technology seemed to provide the answer. A zoologist at the university named William Beckel was already experimenting with taping lectures and delivering them to groups of students via closed-circuit television. Scarborough College would therefore be fully equipped with television facilities like a production studio and feeds to every classroom.

John Andrews sited the science wing to the west with a humanities wing to the east arranged in a V-shape linked by a central meeting space. Each wing would be pyramidal in form mirroring the slope down towards the valley floor. Near the east end of the humanities wing stood a huge three-piped chimney stack, for some reminiscent of Italian Futurism, to others more like part of the Atlantic Wall erected by Nazi Germany to repel an Allied invasion. Inside were lecture halls of varying sizes and laboratories for groups of twenty, all equipped with large screens or television monitors. As a bow to the local climate, "pedestrian streets" would run the length of each building on various floors so that people need not venture outside during winter.

7.32
Scarborough College, John Andrews, 1965.

7·33
Scarborough College, interior.

Construction was to take a mere two years, less than half the time normally allotted to such a project, so a critical path schedule was developed to provide a timeline for sequential tendering as the work progressed. Poured concrete was the obvious construction material because it permitted much more flexibility than steel framing. In fact, the footings were made 10 percent oversize because their exact loads had not yet been calculated by the engineers. Flying buttresses were added later during construction to the sloping facade of the science wing because of fears that the beams were not wide enough to withstand the forces without buckling. The marks of the forming boards were left to show both inside and out according to Brutalist fashion.[89]

Architects then and later waxed enthusiastic about Andrews's creation. In 1966 Raymond Affleck of Montreal called it a significant "happening," and the following year James Acland proclaimed it one of the crucial new experiments in Canadian architecture along with Safdie's Habitat.[90] In the early twenty-first century George Baird described it as an "amazing icon," still one of the few "internationally consequential" buildings in Toronto. He argued that it avoided the deficiencies of other cast-in-place structures because it could be viewed from the valley side in a "natural" landscape where the facades "describe" what the building faced. Moreover, it avoided the damp dark undercrofts often employed in Brutalist design. Baird was particularly enthusiastic about the astonishing "plastic effects" of combining poured concrete with more colourful quarry tiles and wood panelling on the inside, so that the interior spatial system was "visually charged." The University of Toronto's architectural guide (also by a former dean of architecture) remarked upon the bold megastructure of forms "highly sculptural and masterful in their composition," a "giant educational machine charging through the landscape."[91]

People compelled to use the buildings were decidedly less enthusiastic. In a 1967 paper entitled "Educational Needs and Architectural Solutions" delivered at Scarborough College, David Abbey scandalized the architectural community by calling it "one of the most expensive government-supported fallout shelters in North America." Adding (perhaps unnecessarily) that, "I do not feel neutral towards this building," Abbey pointed out that while it was extremely difficult to pick up an architectural journal anywhere in the world that did not praise Scarborough, it was equally hard to find a single student who felt any enthusiasm for the place. He reserved particular scorn for the sky-lit four-storey central meeting place between the two wings, "which a significant proportion of the students refuse to cross because of their discomfort with the large open space within which they report feelings of inadequacy and of being under scrutiny from above." Such lèse-majesté almost caused the editors of *Canadian Architect* to explode over the attention paid to the comments of an "iconoclast anxious to create a newsworthy stir."[92]

The passage of time did not engender more sympathetic feelings. In 1971 Carol Ede recorded Andrews's insistence that architects should rid themselves of concerns about "exterior aesthetics" and instead pursue the "people-oriented, problem-oriented" approach that he had used. While some might call Scarborough an architectural triumph, wrote Ede, "By others, and especially by some students, it has been called inhuman." Forty years on Paolo Scrivano dismissed Scarborough as "out-of-scale and hard to reach," a paradigm of the alienating effects of Brutalism. Despite its initially enthusiastic reception from other architects, he noted that even when it was being built the style had created much controversy and was soon to lose its cutting-edge reputation. The author of the University of Toronto's guidebook had to concede that the buildings were "not universally loved."[93]

In defence of Andrews, it should be added that events overtook his design almost as soon as it was created. Students never favoured the system of lectures piped to them by closed-circuit television (something also tried at York University), demanding contact with human instructors. Many professors were equally unenthusiastic about handing over their lectures to the university to replay at will since they regarded these as their own intellectual property. So resistance to these technological innovations existed from the first. Even more damaging was a dramatic change in the curriculum of the University of Toronto that occurred at almost the same time. The long-standing distinction between courses offered only to General students seeking a three-year degree, and those for Honour students pursuing a four-degree in a specific discipline, was dropped. As a result the small courses offered to Honour students in the upper years began to disappear and more large lecture courses were offered.[94] No amount of architectural genius could overcome the effects of that combination of human preference and bureaucratic change.

The University of Toronto's other experiment with Brutalism was its new library. By the early 1960s an expansion of the university's main library was sorely needed. President Claude Bissell was keen to have a monumental building to reflect the kind of research university that he hoped to create. Bissell worked to persuade the provincial government to fund a vast structure that would sit upon the three-acre city block bounded by St George, Harbord, and Huron Streets, and Sussex Avenue once the existing houses had been acquired or expropriated. He eventually secured support from the province by promising to provide a central research library for the entire Ontario university system, including study space for visiting faculty. The New York architectural firm of Warner, Burn, Toan, and Lunde, which had designed libraries at both Cornell and Brown, was retained to produce a layout.

The result was a triangular fourteen-storey tower that sat right in the centre of the rectangle of open space bounded by the street grid. Lower wings, attached by a raised podium to the northeast and southeast corners of the main block, housed a school of library science and a rare book room. The upper floors of the tower were cantilevered outward and clad in precast concrete panels into which were let narrow vertical strips of glazing to provide the tiny windows for each of the one thousand lockable study-carrels arranged upon nine floors surrounding six levels of book stacks. At several

7.34
University of Toronto, Robarts Library, Warner, Burn, Toan, and Lunde, 1974.

points there protruded from the facade service ducts that rose the entire height of the building beyond the roofline. The southeastern corner of the rare book room, overlooking the corner of Harbord and St George, sported another towering stack with a great flanged top that seemed designed to provide a lookout over the rest of the campus.

In the book that helped to define Brutalism as a distinct architectural style, the British critic Reyner Banham observed that one of its defining features was the sensory effects that such buildings created in observers, often a feeling of unease.[95] That being so, the library named after Ontario Premier John Robarts that opened in 1974 at a cost of $42 million certainly achieved the desired effect. Students promptly nicknamed it "Fort Book" for its protruding gun emplacements, and members of the architectural profession unleashed a torrent of criticism about virtually every aspect of the design. Robert Gretton of *Canadian Architect* recounted the history of the building whose scale, he declared, "rams home" the "sterility of our restless, anomic society" in a way reminiscent of George Orwell's *1984*. He rejected the very notion of "constructive" criticism in this case as the kind of limp evasion worthy of Richard Nixon, who that very month had been forced to resign as US president over the Watergate affair. Ron Thom, over whose Massey College layout the library now loomed from the west, delivered a particularly fine diatribe that opened with the declaration that the building represented "everything in architecture that is arrogant and wrong." Hard as it was to know where to start on "this illustrated dictionary of architectural miseries," Thom chose its clumsy placement, a triangle within a square, surrounded by a flat green space that simply collided with the foundation walls though not without creating some of those dark undercrofts that seemed to plague Brutalist buildings. Why make the tower so tall and out of scale with its neighbourhood when it occupied only a portion of its site, so that it appeared to retreat from the approaching visitor while at the same time being threatening due to the overhang a hundred feet above? The main entranceway was an "arrogant" staircase of twenty steps set at a confusing angle that led up to the podium level between the main building and the rare book room. All in all, said Thom, the Robarts Library was "one of those buildings that were it not for its extreme cost should be taken down and done over again."

James Acland continued in the same vein with a swing at the "nameless genius" from New York who had hit upon a layout that paid no attention to its setting in Toronto. The outside appearance was "particularly horrid" with the concrete projections looming above. How, he asked, would the planners of the rest of that part of the campus cope with such a structure in future? Perhaps it would simply be best to leave the area vacant like the field of fire surrounding a fortress. L.S. Langmead pointed out that the interior

7·35
Sears Canada (Simpson-Sears), Jarvis Street, Maxwell Miller, 1971.

layout was equally unsatisfactory since users had to ride an escalator up several flights before even reaching the catalogue, the circulation desk, and the entry to the stacks. Inside, the stacks were large, noisy, uncarpeted spaces where study was made difficult by the racket from the mechanized conveyor system for retrieving books. (That system was soon mothballed when student demonstrations led the university to abandon the policy of closing the stacks to undergraduates.) The triangular stack floors were so confusing that even with colour-coding of the shelves it was difficult to find one's way to a particular section.[96]

Thirty-five years on, the university's architectural historian was forced to admit that "scathing reviews appear even today." All he could manage in defence of the Robarts Library was the rather lame excuse that, "Perhaps its monumentality and slightly spooky 'otherness' are the causes. It stands alone, proud and aloof, serving as a harsh reminder of our minuscule place in the grand scheme of things – something we would generally prefer to forget."[97]

Brutalism aroused little enthusiasm as a building style outside of the university system.[98] The only notable example of such a commercial building in Toronto was the headquarters for the department store chain Sears Canada on the west side of Jarvis Street north of Dundas. Designed in 1971 by the company's chief architect, Maxwell Miller of Boston, this consisted of a square box around a reinforced concrete core sharply cantilevered outward several floors above grade and clad in dark red brick veneer. The oppressive nature of this top-heavy mass was emphasized by window separations with pointed end piers that give it a menacing heft.[99]

In the residential field, architecture professor Ants Elken commissioned his fellow Estonian Taivo Kapsi to design him a house in Ardwold Gate

7.36
Elken house, 95 Ardwold Gate, Taivo Kapsi, 1968.

composed of box-like forms of poured-in-place concrete showing the form marks of rough-cut lumber. Along with an overhanging second floor wing above a courtyard, the structure was cantilevered out over the steep slope of ravine at the rear.[100] For most Torontonians, Brutalism was too strong a dose to stomach.

V

The shopping centre was definitely a response to an important contemporary phenomenon – the increasing use of the private automobile. In the 1950s and '60s such malls gobbled up hundreds of acres of suburban land around Toronto. One early example, John C. Parkin's design for the Don Mills centre, suggested the possibilities for creating such developments using the language of Modern architecture. Yet Don Mills proved exceptional. The other centres that followed across the greater Toronto area were thoroughly undistinguished in design – from the outside huddles of buildings surrounded by acres of treeless asphalt parking lots, on the interior a riot of conflicting colours and signs.

Not surprisingly the T. Eaton Company, operators of Canada's leading department store chain, became interested in the idea of a suburban shopping centre at an early date. In 1953 a feasibility study was commissioned,

7.37 (Above left)
Yorkdale Shopping Centre, Simpson's store, John B. Parkin Associates, 1964.

7.38 (Above right)
Yorkdale Shopping Centre, Eaton's store, John Graham Associates (Seattle), 1964.

7.39 (Left)
Yorkdale Shopping Centre, interior court at Simpson's, John Graham Associates (Seattle), 1964.

and two years later Eaton's purchased ninety-nine acres of land on the south side of the planned intercity expressway (Highway 401) east of Dufferin Street. Nothing was done, however. Webb and Knapp Canada (the developers of Flemingdon Park) bought the land in 1960 and formed Trizec Corporation to create the Yorkdale shopping centre. Trizec followed the pattern developed in the United States of seeking a department store as an anchor tenant for one end of the mall, preferably with a similar anchor at the other end to encourage foot traffic between the two. Eaton's agreed to occupy a 366,000- square-foot store at the eastern end of Yorkdale with Simpson's taking 285,000 square feet at the western end, leaving another 576,000 square feet for other merchants, which made Yorkdale the largest indoor shopping mall in the world when it opened. Access roads to the 6,500 parking spaces were constructed from both Highway 401 and the city's planned north–south Spadina Expressway to the east by a highly complex system of ramps and bridges.

The centre was an immediate success, and in 1962 a Dominion Stores supermarket was constructed south of Eaton's, creating an L-shape. A cinema was also added to draw in more visitors. Ninety merchants took up spaces along the mall, mostly selling shoes and clothing, though other products like housewares and liquor were ultimately offered. The exterior of the long building was undistinguished with no identifiable main entrance, and in fact the most heavily used route became the door to the grocery store at the southeast corner. The only architectural feature to stand out was the facade of the Simpson's store, designed by John B. Parkin Associates, which featured large projecting columns separating ribbed white precast concrete panels without windows, a design bold enough to attract a few glances from the cars speeding past on Highway 401.[101]

Architects were not impressed with the results. Donovan Pinker complained that however pleasing such a centre might be to its financial backers, it merely fragmented the urban community by offering only a narrow range of retail services. Even more vehement was Ron Thom who complained that, with the exception of the Simpson's store, the exterior of Yorkdale was an "architectural salad" that left the shoppers searching for a way in amidst a jumble of colours, materials, and textures. Once inside, the forty-foot-wide mall had a ceiling only sixteen feet high, and the variations in size and labelling of the shopfronts created a visual jumble. The fittings were as shoddy as the building, and there were no dramatic spaces, except for a double-height courtyard outside Simpson's. Thom's emphatic (if rather murky) conclusion about Yorkdale was that, "*It is a gigantic compendium of follies, and it fails disastrously to answer up to the complex sociological conditions implicit in any such place, particularly one of this size.*"[102]

None of the other shopping centres constructed in Toronto's suburbs during the 1960s and 1970s created much debate.[103] However, when Eaton's attempted to duplicate the success of Yorkdale by building a huge new office and commercial centre around its downtown store, a great deal of controversy resulted.[104] As early as 1958 city planners had approached the company with the suggestion that it redevelop its extensive land holdings. The idea was that Project Viking would encompass the entire area north of Queen from Bay to Yonge as far up as Dundas Street. Eaton's explored joint ventures with several partners but eventually decided to go it alone.[105] The opening of the New City Hall revived the debate about whether to demolish the old one (owned since 1961 by Metro Toronto). Critics were quick to point out that Viljo Revell's layout for the civic square had been careful to respect the vista to the east across Bay Street towards the 1899 building. In the autumn of 1965 Eaton's approached the city with a proposal to demolish the old building, leaving only the tall slender tower at the head of Bay Street with the cenotaph in front of it. *Canadian Architect* remarked upon the strangeness of a city bold enough to stage the international competition won by Revell now wanting to turn around and raze the familiar Romanesque Revival pile.[106]

The city requested more detailed plans, which were produced by the internationally known firm of Skidmore, Owings, and Merrill in the spring of 1966. The proposed Eaton Centre included a new seven-storey flagship store at the corner of Queen and Yonge with a huge shopping mall attached – at two million square feet, it would be the largest retail complex in the world. On the rest of the 22.5-acre site would be a sixty-nine-storey office and apartment building north of the store at the centre of the development, twin fifty-seven-storey office towers, one at Bay and Dundas and the other looming over the old City Hall tower, with a doughnut-shaped twenty-storey hotel and convention space and a smaller thirty-two-storey office tower at Yonge and Dundas. The towers would be geometrical Miesian structures, and all the minor streets would be closed to create a vast open plaza, aligned due east of the New City Hall. The whole project would cost $260 million. The building designs were Modernist if undistinguished, looking as one local politician put it, like "a collection of cereal boxes."[107]

When asked by *Canadian Architect* to comment upon this plan, architects enthusiastically seized the opportunity to make their views known.[108] Eric Arthur, no fan of Romanesque Revival, said that he would be the last person to call for the retention of the old building if he didn't think that it could be put to good use but that it would make an excellent adult education centre. Having only recently come around to the views of urban preservationists, he now insisted that the building, its tower, and the war memorial in front were of such symbolic importance that to remove them would be "an act of philistinism unequalled in this century in Toronto if not in Canada." Mandel Sprachman thought that historic public buildings should continue to flank Nathan Phillips Square both east and west, helping to protect the city's investment in Revell's design. To tear down a structure of architectural and historical interest for a soon-to-be obsolete commercial complex was foolish. If it was decided to sell the old city hall at some future time, there would be more money to be made, so architectural, historical, and financial considerations all counselled preservation.

Jack Klein raged that even debating the question would be humourous if it were not so tragic. The humour lay in the fact that the developers were only interested in making money "versus the outraged cries of the wounded persons of lately found sensitivity." The tragedy was that the preservationists had waited so long to weigh in while the discussions about the New City Hall had been going on. People should have been thinking about redevelopment all around the square for ages. James Acland observed that it was paradoxical that developers should be proposing to demolish one of only three buildings in Canada mentioned in Sir Banister Fletcher's *History of Architecture on the Comparative Method*, long a bible for students and practitioners alike.[109] There were plenty of uses to which the old city hall could be converted, including roofing over its central courtyard as an auditorium.

Not surprisingly, a couple of prominent architects who worked closely with developers disagreed. Sidney Bregman recalled that when he was at architectural school none of his teachers had considered the old City Hall historically significant though Eric Arthur might have changed his mind since. Better to get on with the task of revitalizing the downtown core and raising real estate assessments. John B. Parkin called for careful appraisal of all significant structures but wondered about how many Torontonians really cared about a building that was after all just a copy of Richardson's Allegheny County Courthouse in Pittsburgh. Personally he could see little reason for keeping a building of "questionable architectural worth" when Skidmore, Owings, and Merrill had produced a design that made "more competent" use of the area.

The infighting even attracted attention in Montreal. Peering southwest down Highway 401, a couple of architects there disagreed about what Torontonians ought to do. Raymond Affleck professed to find the idea of demolition mystifying. Cities were organisms that grew through time and space, and there surely was a better way to respond to change than tearing down such a fine Victorian landmark. To the contrary, Peter Collins claimed that the local ratepayers had settled the whole matter in the mid-1940s when they voted to acquire the lands for a civic square and a new city hall. The idea of conversion was just a silly insult to Revell since no work of architecture could have "aesthetic values divorced from the purpose it was originally designed to serve" – a pretty silly claim in itself. Keeping dead specimens around rather than affording them a decent burial was "repulsive."

Toronto architect Jack Diamond, who, as a new editor, was trying to breath some life into the Royal Architectural Institute of Canada's journal, asked what guarantee there was that the completed development would look anything like the preliminary plans, which he dismissed as a mere "snow job." Why demolish the old building in order to hand over control of twenty acres of valuable downtown land to Eaton's for private profit? He followed up that condemnation the next month by claiming that the huge towers sprouting from an empty wasteland without regard for human needs were the work of kitsch-mongers like Minoru Yamasaki, whose plan for the twin towers of the World Trade Center in New York City he called among the ugliest designs in the world.[110] Enough of a row occurred that the Institute's Committee on the Preservation of Historic Buildings even roused itself to condemn the destruction of the old city hall.[111]

Despite a determined campaign by the preservationists, in June 1966 Metro Toronto council agreed in principle by a vote of sixteen to five to sell the old city hall to Eaton's. By that time the developers did not even propose to keep the tower. Councillors then started to waver about whether Eaton's could be relied upon to carry out its plans and decided to lease the old city hall site rather than selling it. But agreement could not be reached upon the rental, and in May 1967, to great surprise, Eaton's suddenly announced that it was calling the whole thing off. Why this decision was taken was never entirely clear but it seems likely that the developers concluded that they could not fill eleven million square feet of space at the very time that the Toronto Dominion Centre had just finished leasing one-tenth of that area well to the south on King Street.

Soon afterwards, Leo Kolber of Fairview Corporation (which had partnered with the bank on the TD Centre) was approached by Eaton's about joining in building a much scaled-down shopping mall on the land it owned north of a new department store at Queen and Yonge.[112] Kolber expressed interest but laid down a couple of conditions. He wanted nothing to do with the controversial idea of tearing down the old city hall. And he demanded that Eaton's shift its store right to the northern end of the site at Dundas Street so that it would act as an anchor to the shopping centre. The mall would run all the way south to Queen and connect by a bridge with the existing Simpson's department store on the south side of the street, generating the traffic that he believed to be essential to success. The Eaton family resisted both conditions but, because they needed the money to be realized from selling the land, eventually gave way. The Eaton Centre would be a joint venture with Fairview having a 60 percent interest, Eaton's and the TD Bank each getting 20 percent.

The greatest obstacles remained several parcels of land that the developers did not control. One was the headquarters building of the Salvation Army on the west side of the site at Albert Street, a much-admired Modernist design by John C. Parkin, but in the end it was decided to build around it. Even more controversial was Holy Trinity Anglican church, a small building designed in 1846 by Henry Bowyer Lane that stood some distance north of the Salvation Army.[113] The original plan was to move the church to a new site but the preservationists, emboldened by their success in saving the old city hall, made a great fuss and gained support from local politicians. To persuade the council to close off the small street leading west from Yonge Street to Trinity Square (cutting right across the proposed mall site) the developers eventually had to agree to leave Holy Trinity intact. Too high a price was asked for a parcel on the northwest corner of Queen and Yonge owned by McMaster University, so it was left. On Yonge Street was a piece of land that had been given to the University of Toronto on condition that it never be sold to Eaton's; the university, however, was happy to sell and in the end the courts were persuaded to lift the restriction.

Who would design the huge mall building? Early on Fairview retained Victor Gruen Associates, an American firm that had worked on other malls for the company, and at another point it was announced that Bregman and Hamann had drawn up a plan for two million square feet of space to cost $200 million.[114] In the end Fairview's choice was swayed by Phyllis Lambert, who thought that suburban shopping centres were undistinguished.[115] With Mies van der Rohe dead she had become impressed with the work of Toronto architect Eberhard Zeidler. He had recently designed Ontario Place, an amusement park built for the government of Ontario in its effort to replicate some of the excitement that Expo '67 had generated for Montreal. South of the Canadian National Exhibition grounds, Ontario Place took the form of a series of pods slung by cables from poles rising out of sunken caissons in Lake Ontario and linked together by bridges. Critics dismissed the design as looking like a cluster of brightly lit oil rigs, and James Acland referred to it as the kind of "baroque folly" that politicians used to bedazzle voters. Zeidler admitted that he was seeking freedom from "outdated formalism,"[116] and Ontario Place certainly possessed none of the austerity of classical Modernism, a first venture towards Postmodernism.

7.40
Ontario Place, Zeidler and Strong, 1971.

The practical-minded developers at Fairview had originally envisaged a string of shopfronts along the mall with a large parking garage overhead but by 1972 Zeidler and Lambert agreed upon a towering glass-roofed structure. The design was a knockoff of the famous Galleria Vittorio Emanuele II of 1877 connecting the opera house and the Piazza Duomo in Milan. Here was a sign for Torontonians of Post-modernism's interest in taking over and repurposing historical motifs. The galleria was supposed to re-energize commerce in Toronto's downtown by encouraging pedestrian traffic. The original idea was to continue the mall right through the Eaton's store at the north end as far as Dundas Street but the department store owners refused to agree, which put an end to the idea of a continuous pedestrian street. The Eaton family even resisted the name Eaton Centre, ignoring the advertising value the TD Centre had demonstrated. More importantly

7.41
Eaton Centre, Zeidler Partnership and Bregman and Hamman, 1977. The first phase is complete, and the original Eaton's store at left awaits demolition.

7.42
Eaton Centre, interior.

7·43
Eaton Centre, interior.

from a public point of view, Metro Toronto's traffic engineers insisted that the building be set back ten feet from Yonge Street to permit its eventual widening, and Fairview rejected Zeidler's plan to permit entry into all the retail outlets from the street. The result was that, rather than re-energizing downtown commerce, the Eaton Centre drained all the life out of the long block on Yonge from Queen to Dundas by diverting people indoors.

The first phase of the project, including the new Eaton store and the northerly half of the mall as far down as Albert Street, opened to great fanfare in early 1977. In *Canadian Architect* Henry Sears greeted the event with guarded enthusiasm, noting the crowds thronging the mall, but he was critical of the heavy, awkward exterior of the department store with its dull beige panels. Along Dundas the circular parking garage and twenty-six-storey office tower at Bay seemed to him a jumble, and the Eaton Centre a collection of buildings rather than any sort of entity. For its part Fairview remained convinced that Eaton's failure to allow the galleria to pass right through its store would be detrimental, though Leo Kolber later argued that the amount of customer traffic generated by the mall allowed the family-owned store to stay in business for a couple more decades before it slid into bankruptcy.[117]

The southerly part of the multilevel mall opened in 1979, providing a connection both at street level and by a first-floor bridge to the Simpson's store across Queen Street. Fairview celebrated this event by purchasing from artist Michael Snow a huge mobile called "Flight Stop," which consisted of a large flock of Canada geese coming in to land, each one suspended separately from the soaring glass roof. The operators celebrated the fact that the Eaton Centre had become a tourist destination in its own right. Toronto's Postmodern moment really arrived when Snow's geese were equipped with red Christmas bows around their necks, but the decorations were removed when the artist sued for defacement of his work.

VI

By the 1970s it was clear that some Toronto architects were leaving the age of classic Modernism behind. Some Postmodernists continued to display an interest in the use of historical details or motifs. Others aimed to use new materials and technologies in a manner not previously envisaged. Form no longer needed to follow function. Among the most adventuresome designers was Barton Myers, who came to Canada to form a partnership with A.J. Diamond in 1968. Myers developed a particular fondness for steel as a construction material because of the precision with which it could be bent and shaped and the large range of finishes that had become available.

He soon acquired land at 19 Berryman Street off Davenport Road at the head of Bay Street in the Annex, where he wanted to create a home for his family principally using steel. The lot was only twenty-five feet wide and the structure occupied almost its entire width with a garage and entrance doorway right at the street line. The concrete block side walls formed two cubes separated by a courtyard, the entire structure roofed, at the suggestion of engineer Morden Yolles, by rigid steel frames with exposed web joists to bear the lateral forces. The service ducts for air circulation, water, and lighting were exposed, and the twenty-by-forty-foot courtyard with a second floor deck linking the two cubes was topped like a greenhouse with corrugated fibreglass supported by the steel trusswork. The challenge, of course, was to control heat loss and gain through the roof so that an elaborate system of insulated blankets that could be opened and closed as needed was required. The house, built at a cost of $25,000, secured much attention for Myers, who said, "It was one of the first modern houses in downtown Toronto. It was really a pioneer work in that sense."[118]

7.44 (Opposite) Myers house, 19 Berryman Street, Barton Myers, 1972.

Despite the problems of climate control created by using steel and glass, Myers was retained by Larry and Mary Wolf to build them something similar at 51 Roxborough Drive off Mount Pleasant Road in Rosedale. On a

Myers Residence, Toronto

Architects: A. J. Diamond & Barton Myers

This house for partner Barton Myers and his family attempts to prove the feasibility of infilling on vacant properties to maintain and reinforce the urban fabric, and offers an economic alternative to renovation in older urban areas. The site was a vacant, narrow lot, 25 ft. x 125 ft. in Yorkville Village. The City waived the normal 20 ft. street setback on this project and granted permission to maintain the existing building line.

The concept is that of a court house but with the courtyard covered by a 40 ft. x 20 ft. standard greenhouse roof. The court separates the house into two units, connected at the upper level by a bridge. At the ground floor level the garage and entry are at the front and living and kitchen at the rear. Upstairs are two bedrooms, bath and study at the front and master bedroom and bath at the rear. Two roof decks which serve as outdoor gardens and platforms for cleaning the greenhouse roof are reached by ladders from the bedroom areas. Expansion will occur within the volume and a future studio will be built among the greenhouse trusses. The total area, including courtyard and garage, is 2,400 sq.ft.

The house is constructed of structural steel frame, open web steel joist and ribbed metal deck with concrete topping. Concrete block, insulation and drywall for fire separation form the side walls but all other partitions are steel stud and drywall, giving complete flexibility to the interior arrangements. The structural steel frame provides lateral reinforcement and becomes the glazing frame with the plate glass clipped directly to the structure. The environmental systems—air, water and lighting—are frankly exposed.

The consultants were M. S. Yolles & Associates, structural and G. Granek & Associates, mechanical. The general contractors were McMullen & Warnock Ltd.

7·45
Wolf house, 51 Roxborough Drive, Barton Myers, 1976.

lot of fifty by 150 feet backing onto a gently sloping ravine, this freestanding house would be thirty feet wide. Because of poor soil conditions, the weight of the structure had to be reduced so that the sidewalls were steel-stud with aluminum siding on the exterior. The floor plan was the same as Myers own house, but with glass walls at front and rear for the two cubes separated by an unroofed central courtyard facing west. The architect admitted that in

Toronto's climate a building composed almost entirely of glass and steel was highly energy inefficient, requiring a heavily layered system of blinds and wool curtains to control heat loss and gain. With these coverings drawn back, the building did allow for "spectacular" views right through it from front to back and out into the treed ravine beyond.[119]

These two steel houses seem to mark a good point at which to end the story of the arrival and spread of Modern architecture in Toronto as the austerity and formalism of its classic period began to be eroded by new ideas about decoration and ornamentation, often executed through the use of unusual materials. Brutalism and Postmodernism now jostled for places near centre stage, though uninspired imitations of Mies van der Rohe's skyscrapers held their place due to economy and efficiency. Toronto had been given a modern look.

7.46
Wolf house.

CONCLUSION

8.1 (Opposite)
The '70s skyline from the south.

What were the influences that made Toronto modern? First there was the American example. News from Chicago about the Columbian Exhibition of 1893 and its aftermath sparked a coalition of architects, artists, and businessmen to form a City Beautiful movement that sought the redesign of the city's street layout and fuelled the demand for monumental new buildings like the Union Station. Toronto architects kept in touch with the latest fashions south of the border where the Classical Revival was becoming dominant. For instance, John Lyle was fortunate enough to be able to attend Yale University and (following a stay at the Beaux-Arts in Paris) to join the prominent New York firm of Carrère and Hastings where he worked on the design of that city's great public library. On his return to Toronto in 1905 he became the consulting architect to the Civic Improvement Committee and developed a plan that included not only the new station but a grand avenue that would lead to a civic square north of Queen Street surrounded by noble public buildings.

Architects worked to keep abreast of developments in the United States, though most of them had to rely upon pictures and articles in journals. A few others were fortunate enough to go and study south of the border, such as John C. Parkin whose stay at Harvard in the mid-1940s included study with Walter Gropius and Marcel Breuer. At the same time, there was a small flow of practitioners northward from the United States, such as John Andrews and Macy DuBois, who were attracted to Toronto by the competition for the New City Hall in 1958, and later arrivals like Barton Myers who produced his radical steel houses in the 1970s.

The flow of ideas across the Atlantic was also important. Like good colonial subjects, the planners of the Civic Guild first sought advice from British experts when developing a new street plan after the disastrous fire of 1904.[1] The appointment of Eric Arthur, trained at the University of Liverpool, to the faculty of the architecture school at the University of Toronto in 1923 ultimately had an enormous impact: his growing appreciation of the Modern movement during the 1930s led him to familiarize a generation of students with these ideas, which he also promoted to the wider profession through his long-running editorship of the *Royal Architectural Institute of Canada Journal*. Peter Dickinson, who had trained at the Architectural Association in London, arrived in 1950 becoming the most notable of a sizable group of British immigrants who found work in Toronto following the Second World War.

Continental Europe was also important. In the late 1920s the innovations of the moderne found a receptive audience amongst interior designers and some architects. Slower to be accepted were the principles advanced by Le Corbusier and others associated with the Modern movement. Held back by the Depression and then war, it was only around 1950 that some clients were persuaded to adopt these radical ideas. Finn Viljo Revell's victory in the competition to design Toronto's New City Hall led to the creation of a notable building, which earned broad popular acclaim. And the creation of the Toronto-Dominion Centre by Mies van der Rohe, a German émigré to the United States, made a similar impact and exercised an important influence upon the design of commercial towers that continued for years to come. Engineers like Morden Yolles (assisted by his European-trained associate Roland Bergmann) paid careful attention to new designs that used reinforced concrete promoted by people such as Robert Maillart and Pier Luigi Nervi.

Developments in other North American cities were always of interest to Torontonians; after all, they aspired to have their hometown take its place among the continent's important metropolises. New York's skyscrapers were never far from the minds of local boosters, who noted the visual impact of the canyons of downtown Manhattan as well as the importance of practical modern conveniences like high-speed elevators and mechanical ventilation. No Toronto building could ever claim the title of tallest in the world, but the shadow cast by the United States was clear behind the endless touting of a series of local towers as the tallest in the British Empire. Montreal, of course, attracted particularly close scrutiny as Canada's economic metropolis. Especially disturbing to knowledgeable Torontonians was the belief that Montrealers were more receptive to modern architectural ideas, since they wished to appear just as progressive as their neighbours in Quebec.

The European founders of the Modern movement were convinced that new designs might permit the alleviation of social problems, particularly through the provision of desirable low-cost housing amidst green, open spaces yet near to workplaces. The members of the Bauhaus had, of course, been deeply involved with such projects. No comparable institution developed in North America but some Toronto architects and urban planners came to share these concerns. At Harvard, Walter Gropius taught Macklin Hancock, who was responsible for devising the plan for Don Mills; Hancock was also influenced by the noted British town planner William Holford. Irving Grossman was responsible for the design of developments like Toronto's Flemingdon Park where row housing and apartment buildings were intermixed around pedestrian precincts in which children might play free from the danger of passing cars.

In one area, however, Torontonians did strongly resist the precepts of the Modern movement. With the exception of a few highly venturesome clients, single-family homebuyers remained unimpressed by avant-garde layouts. In this rejection, however, Toronto was little different from other places in North America. Writing about the "Comfortable House" in the 1980s, Canadian architectural historian Alan Gowans observed that the ideas of Modernism made only a negligible impact upon such housing. By eliminating all ornament as unscientific and backward-looking, said Gowans, the Modernists had created a kind of reverse mirror image of the Picturesque in which lightness was emphasized over mass and straight lines over curves, which produced designs that were unappealing to most North Americans. "Despite control of all the public relations in the art world," Gowans wrote, "Modernists were never able to produce a house that the average middle-class or even upper-middle-class American would buy, much less one for the working class." What was distinctive about the North American house was the way in which it continued to mix together details from the past so that it evoked no particular previous epoch but spoke instead of the confidence and prosperity of the present.[2]

With that exception, modernist ideas did eventually gain widespread acceptance. The functional innovations that appeared in the years before the First World War were quickly received with general enthusiasm. Who, after all, would not favour amenities like central heating and gas or electric lighting if they could afford them, especially when such innovations remained wrapped in the comfortable cloak of traditional architecture? But broader schemes of civic improvements proved a harder sell to property owners and local politicians who focused sharply upon the mill rate at election time.[3] A few projects like the Bloor Street viaduct got approved, but the wider ambitions of the Civic Guild largely failed to gain acceptance. A recession starting in 1913, followed by the outbreak of war a year later, finally squelched more ambitious proposals such as the construction of a north–south subway under Yonge Street, which had to wait until the 1940s.

After peace returned in the 1920s, the most celebrated building in Toronto was the university's Collegiate Gothic Hart House. Yet the ideas of moderne design emanating from Europe in the latter years of that decade found a warmer reception, since these styles involved no radical shifts in the layouts of either commercial or residential buildings. Elements of the moderne could be smoothly blended with a Stripped Classicism. Some of the conservatism about modern design that persisted until after the Second World War may be put down to the fact the city possessed no star architects to help persuade

Torontonians to be more open-minded, as did Frank Lloyd Wright in Chicago. At the same time extravagant display remained generally frowned upon, and there were doubtless many in Toronto who viewed the 1924 takeover of Sir Henry Pellatt's Casa Loma due to unpaid city taxes as no more than just retribution for excess.

When the idea of a new street layout for the downtown was revived in the late 1920s, a majority of municipal voters still proved unenthusiastic. Even the comprehensive zoning bylaw and land use plan developed in the late 1930s and early 1940s met resistance from property owners who were fearful of interference with their private rights. It took until the 1950s for such statutory regulations to be imposed; by that time the rising use of private automobiles had also created popular support for a system of expressways to eliminate congestion and serve commuters. The spread of publicity about Modern architecture and an influx of new practitioners persuaded people that dramatic buildings could help Toronto project a more positive image to the wider world, a notion that the New City Hall seemed to confirm.

In the 1960s Modern designs began to carry all before them. In addition to Viljo Revell's New City Hall, new institutional buildings at the University of Toronto such as Massey College, Sidney Smith Hall, and New College, capped off by the Robarts Library and John Andrews's essay in Brutalism at Scarborough College, which gained worldwide acclaim from architects. And the enthusiasm of the pioneers of the Modern movement for the machine-made and the prefabricated found its echo in the SEF program of primary school construction, completed in the early 1970s.

By that time, however, challenges to the gospel of the Modern movement were beginning. Torontonians would continue to see features of the Modernism such as the glass curtain wall used in new buildings, particularly for commercial office space and apartment towers, but by the seventies Postmodernists were reviving an interest in historically derived details. For some architects the dogma that "less is more" was beginning to be replaced with the complaint that "less is a bore." By that time, however, the impress of modernism over the previous eighty years had thoroughly transformed the city in both architecture and design.

8.2
Toronto transformed, 1971.

Municipality	School	Address	Gross Area (sq.ft.)	Cost (sq.ft.)
Etobicoke	Melody Village	520 Silverstone Dr	60,585	25.96
	Albion Heights	45 Lynmount Rd	57,499	22.05
North York	Denlow Blvd.	-	48,276	25.58
	Ranchdale Cres.	60 Ranchdale Cr	51,972	22.72
	Don Valley	3100 Don Mills Rd	72,750	25.06
	Pleasantview	175 Brian Dr	87,510	22.73
	Hillmount	245 McNicoll Ave	34,275	23.90
	Firgrove	270 Firgrove Cr	43,414	23.66
	Windfields	385 Banbury Rd	82,031	24.40
Scarborough	Brooks Road	85 Keeler Blvd	45,744	21.89
	Cedar Drive	21 Gatesview Ave	45,744	22.15
	Iroquois	265 Chartland Bl S	45.744	21.95
	Beverly Glen	85 Beverly Glen Bl	53,859	23.03
	Charles Gordon	25 Marcos Bl	72,675	23.75
	Sir A. Mackenzie	33 Heather Rd	50,752	23.58
	Henry Kelsey	1200 Huntingwood	74,480	23.93
Toronto	Howard	30 Marmaduke St	57,695	23.57
	Roden	151 Hiawatha Bl	80,587	21.05

APPENDIX A
STUDY OF EDUCATIONAL FACILITIES BUILDINGS

Municipality	School	Address (sq.ft.)	Gross Area	Cost (sq.ft.)
York	George Syme	69 Pritchard Ave	74,884	23.57
	Arlington	501 Arlington Ave	83,949	24.10
	Administration	-	33,341	27.66
Total First SEF Building System: 21 Buildings			1,257,722	23.57

Municipality	School	Address (sq.ft.)	Gross Area	Cost (sq.ft.)
East York	R.H. McGregor	555 Mortimer Ave	69,504	20.68
	Administration	-	35,374	22.59
Toronto	Withrow	25 Bain Ave	71,108	21.47
York	Humewood	15 Cherrywood Ave	64,678	23.56
Total 1B SEF Building System: 4 Buildings			240,664	21.97
Etobicoke	John D. Parker	202 Mt Olive Dr	33,832	17.73
Metro	William J. McCordic	45 Balfour Ave	33,749	19.41
Scarborough	Brookmill Bl	25 Brookmill Bl.	34,932	19.38
	Chester Bl.	Chester Le Bl	34,932	19.29
	Brimwood Bl	151 Brimwood Bl	34,932	19.28
Total Second SEF Building System: 5 Buildings			172,377	19.02
Total All SEF Building Systems: 30 Buildings			1,670,813	22.87

Source: "E6: Academic Evaluation: A Report on SEF Open Plan Schools," (typescript, Metropolitan Toronto School Board, 1975), 268, http://www.eric.ed.gov.80/Ericdocs25ol/content_storage_01/0000019b/80/31/0a.pdf.

I have made significant efforts to identify, credit appropriately, and obtain publication rights from copyright holders of illustrations in this book. Notice of any errors or admissions will be gratefully received and required corrections made in any subsequent editions.

Each entry in the list contains information about its subject, the architect concerned (where relevant), the date of buildings, the name of the photographer (if known), and the repository or source from which the image has been taken. Dating buildings can, however, be problematic, and often the only information available concerns the date on which a particular picture was published.

ABBREVIATIONS

CA	Courtesy of *Canadian Architect*
CAA, UC	Courtesy of Canadian Architectural Archives, University of Calgary
CTA	City of Toronto Archives
Panda	Panda Fonds, Canadian Architectural Archives, University of Calgary
RAIC	Courtesy of Royal Architectural Institute of Canada
RAIC Journal	*Royal Architectural Institute of Canada Journal*

ILLUSTRATIONS

0.1 "Toronto's New Skyline," *Construction*, March 1930, 78.

0.2 Presenting the New City Hall, 1958, *Canadian Architect*, July 1962, 6, CA.

1.1 Waterfront ambitions, 1912, *Construction*, December 1912, 68.

1.2 Civic topography, 1915, *Report to the Civic Transportation Committee on Radial Railway Entrances and Rapid Transit for the City of Toronto* (1915), vol. 2, Plans, Map 3, Map and Data Library, University of Toronto.

1.3 Extent of the fire, 1904, Library and Archives Canada, e008222106.

1.4 After the fire, 1904, CTA, Fonds 1408, item 0015.

1.5 Toronto fire ruins, April 1904, Galbraith, *Construction*, February 1908, 23.

1.6 Guild of Civic Art Fonds, "Plan of Improvements to the City of Toronto, 1908," Baldwin Room, Toronto Public Library.

1.7 Bird's-eye view of proposed Toronto waterfront, 1905, *Canadian Architect and Builder*, February 1906.

1.8 John Lyle, c. 1926. Courtesy of Glenn McArthur and Norah Harris.

1.9 Civic Improvement Commission, "Plan Showing Proposed Federal and Municipal Squares and Federal Avenue," 1912, *Construction*, June 1911, 52.

1.10 Toronto Harbour Commissioners' plan, 1912, Map and Data Library, University of Toronto.

1.11 Prince Edward viaduct over the Don valley, c. 1920, CTA, Fonds 1244, item 2473.

1.12 Victoria College, W.G. Storm, 1892, *Art Work on Toronto*, W.H. Carre, 1898, plate 3.

1.13 City Hall, E.J. Lennox, 1899, *Fifty Glimpses of Toronto*, McLeod and Simpson, 1901.

1.14 Confederation Life Building, Knox, Elliot, and Jarvis, 1891, *Art Work on Toronto*, W.H. Carre, 1898, plate 17.

1.15 Temple Building, George W. Gouinlock, 1895, *Fifty Glimpses of Toronto*, McLeod and Simpson, 1901.

1.16 Central Public Library, Wickson and Gregg and A.H. Chapman, 1909, CTA, Fonds 1231, item 0722.

1.17 Bank of Toronto, Carrère and Hastings, 1913, *Construction*, September 1913, 328.

1.18 Chorley Park, F.R. Heakes, 1915, *Construction*, January 1916, 37.

1.19 View northwest from the City Hall clock tower, 1925, CTA, Fonds 1548, series 0393, item 19978.

1.20 Convocation Hall, University of Toronto, c. 1930, Darling and Pearson, 1906, *Toronto: An Illustrated Tour*, 1930.

1.21 Hart House, University of Toronto, Sproatt and Rolph, 1919, *Construction*, May 1920, 140.

1.22 Flavelle House, Darling and Pearson, 1902, 49795-3, Panda, CAA, UC.

1.23 Ardwold, Wickson and Gregg, 1911, CTA, Fonds 1244, item 0316.

1.24 Casa Loma, E.J. Lennox, 1913, 67041-8k, Panda, CAA, UC.

1.25 Reconstructed warehouses on Bay Street, 1905, *Canadian Architect and Builder*, July 1905.

1.26 Robert Simpson Company's Mail Order Building, N. Max Dunning and Burke, Horwood and White, *Construction*, January 1918, 1.

1.27 Robert Simpson Company's Mail Order Building, conveyor and parcel chute, *Construction*, January 1918, 7.
1.28 Yonge Street, 1919, CTA, series 0372, subseries 0041, item 0080.
1.29 The old Union Station, Thomas Seaton Scott, 1873, and Strickland and Symons, 1895, *Fifty Glimpses of Toronto*, McLeod and Simpson, 1901.
1.30 Atlas: City of Toronto, 1910, Library and Archives Canada, e010757077.
1.31 North Toronto Station, Darling and Pearson, 1916, *Construction*, April 1917, 120.
1.32 Drawing of the proposed Union Station, Ross and Macdonald, Hugh G. Jones, and John M. Lyle, 1914, *Construction*, May 1914, 199.

2.1 Central Motor Apartments, Toronto, Wickson and Gregg, 1925, *Construction*, March 1925, 91.
2.2 Eric Arthur, 1923, Collection of Alec Keefer.
2.3 Bronze entrance doors, Dominion Bank, John Lyle, 1929, *RAIC Journal*, March 1932, 67, RAIC.
2.4 Breay-Nash automobile showroom, Earle L. Sheppard, 1927, *Construction*, July 1927, 219.
2.5 Automotive Building, CNE, D.E. Kertland, 1929, *RAIC Journal*, November 1929, 401, RAIC.
2.6 Donalda Farms, Wickson and Gregg, 1919, *Canadian Homes and Gardens*, May 1929, 23.
2.7 Ashley-Crippen house, A.E. LePage and B. Kelly, 1922, *Construction*, October 1922, 323.
2.8 Ashley-Crippen house, interior, A.E. LePage and B. Kelly, 1922, *Construction*, October 1922, 324.
2.9 Gerald Larkin house, George, Moorhouse, and King, 1926, *Canadian Homes and Gardens*, April 1929, 21.
2.10 University Club, Mathers and Haldenby and F. Hilton Wilkes, *RAIC Journal*, April 1930, 133, RAIC.
2.11 Metropolitan Building, William F. Sparling, 1925, *Construction*, July 1925, 222.
2.12 Sterling Tower, Chapman and Oxley, 1928, *Toronto: An Illustrated Tour*, 1930.
2.13 *Toronto Star* Building, Chapman and Oxley, 1929, *RAIC Journal*, April 1929, 147, RAIC.
2.14 Concourse Building, Baldwin and Greene, 1929, *Construction*, May 1929, 138.
2.15 Concourse Building, entrance, Baldwin and Greene, artwork by J.E.H. MacDonald, 1929, CTA, Fonds 1244, item 2495.
2.16 Victory Building, 1936, Baldwin and Greene, 1938, CTA, series 0372, subseries 0001, item 1410.
2.17 Canada Permanent Building, F. Hilton Wilkes and Mackenzie Waters, 1930, *Construction*, March 1930, 74.
2.18 Bank of Commerce, York and Sawyer with Darling and Pearson, 1930, *RAIC Journal*, December 1931, 414, RAIC.
2.19 Eaton's College Street store, Ross and Macdonald, 1930, Archives of Ontario, www.archives.gov.on.ca/english/online-exhibits/architecture/big/517_7_eatons.aspx. Accessed 29 May 2012.

2.20 Eaton's College Street, elevator arcade, interiors by Jacques and Natasha Carlu, 1930, *Construction*, November 1930, 365.

2.21 Eaton's College Street, dining room, interiors by Jacques and Natasha Carlu, 1930, *Construction*, November 1930, 367.

2.22 Advisory City Planning Commission, "Suggested Improvements to the Street System," from the *Report of the Advisory City Planning Commission with Recommendations for the Improvement of the Central Business Section of the City of Toronto*, 1929, Map and Data Library, University of Toronto.

2.23 Beginning of demolition south of Queen Street, 1930, CTA, Fonds 1244, item 10092.

2.24 Ford Motor Company, Danforth assembly plant, c. 1933, Albert Kahn, 1923, Collection of the author.

2.25 Ford assembly plant, Toronto, Ontario, interior, Albert Kahn, 1923, Photograph by W.A. Young, 1 October 1923, Collection of the author.

3.1 Toronto Hydro-Electric Commission head office, 1933, *Construction*, July 1933, 84.

3.2 "The Canadian House of Today," René Cera, 1929, *Canadian Homes and Gardens*, June 1929, 17.

3.3 Drawing of Lawren Harris house, Alexandra Biriukova, 1931, *Canadian Homes and Gardens*, April 1931, 40.

3.4 J.S. McLean house, Eric Arthur, 1933, *Construction*, May 1933, 56.

3.5 William Lyon Somerville, *Construction*, March 1936, 39.

3.6 "Small House of Tomorrow," W.L. Somerville, 1931, *Canadian Homes and Gardens*, June 1931, 17.

3.7 Mrs Peter Larkin's house, George, Moorhouse, and King, 1932, *Canadian Homes and Gardens*, February 1932, 17.

3.8 Glendon Hall (E.R. Wood house), Molesworth, West, and Secord, 1927, *Construction*, January 1927, 4.

3.9 Penryn, Mathers, and Haldenby, 1934, *Canadian Homes and Gardens*, January 1934, 19.

3.10 Graydon Hall, George and Moorhouse, 1936, *Canadian Homes and Gardens*, September 1938, 18.

3.11 Toronto Stock Exchange, George and Moorhouse, 1937, RAIC *Journal*, April 1937, 58, RAIC.

3.12 Toronto Stock Exchange, east wall of trading floor, Charles Comfort's murals, RAIC *Journal*, April 1937, 60, RAIC.

3.13 Toronto Stock Exchange, members' dining room, interior by S.H. Maw, 1937, RAIC *Journal*, April 1937, 63 RAIC.

3.14 Toronto Stock Exchange, management committee room, interior by S.H. Maw, 1937, RAIC *Journal*, April 1937, 65, RAIC.

3.15 Customs House (Dominion Public Building), first phase, Department of Public Works, Chief Architect's Branch, 1931, CTA, Fonds 1548, series 0393, item 23456.

3.16 Postal Station K, Murray Brown, 1937, RAIC *Journal*, September 1937, 183, RAIC.

3.17 City Delivery Building, Charles B. Dolphin, 1939–40, 541132-2, Panda, CAA, UC.

3.18 William Wright Building, Mathers and Haldenby, 1937, *RAIC Journal*, August 1938, 175, RAIC.

3.19 Staunton Wallpaper Factory, Mathers and Haldenby, 1937, *RAIC Journal*, August 1937, 163, RAIC.

3.20 Drawing of Garden Court, Page and Steele, 1941, *Canadian Homes and Gardens*, January 1944, 25.

4.1 Toronto waterfront, 1957, 57362-20, Panda, CAA, UC.

4.2 "Post-war conditions encourage a search for new focus," panel five of UNESCO photomontage, *RAIC Journal*, March 1947, 88, RAIC.

4.3 Hawke House, Eric Arthur, 1944, *Canadian Homes and Gardens*, November 1944, 13.

4.4 "Sun House," Gordon S. Adamson, 1944, *Canadian Homes and Gardens*, November 1944, 16.

4.5 "Suggested Yonge Street Improvement with War Memorial," Murray Brown, 1922, *Construction*, February 1922, 64.

4.6 "Yorkville Area Redevelopment Model," City Planning Board, 1944, Toronto Planning Board, Map and Data Library, University of Toronto.

4.7 TTC Adelaide Coach Terminal, John B. Parkin Associates, 1947, 47645-6, Panda, CAA, UC.

4.8 TTC Adelaide Coach Terminal, John B. Parkin Associates, 1947, 47645-3, Panda, CAA, UC.

4.9 TTC subway, full-scale station mock-up, John B. Parkin Associates, 1948, 48160-17, Panda, CAA, UC.

4.10 TTC subway, newsstand mock-up, John B. Parkin Associates, 1948, 48160-18, Panda, CAA, UC.

4.11 TTC subway, Davisville station, John B. Parkin Associates, 1954, 54413-2, Panda, CAA, UC.

4.12 "Planning," *Canadian Homes and Gardens*, January–February 1944, 24.

4.13 Model of Thorncrest Village, Town Planning Consultants Limited, 1945, *Canadian Homes and Gardens*, April 1945, 33.

4.14 Sunnylea School, John B. Parkin Associates, 1946, 4634-4, Panda, CAA, UC.

4.15 Leaside High School, S.B. Coon and Son, 1946, 54654-2, Panda, CAA, UC.

4.16 Centennial Road School, Murray Brown and Elton, 1946, Photographic Arts, *RAIC Journal*, October 1947, 352, RAIC.

4.17 G.H. Locke Library, Beck and Eadie, 1949, 52736-5, Panda, CAA, UC.

4.18 University of Toronto Mechanical Engineering Building, Allward and Gouinlock, 1948, Warner Bros., *RAIC Journal*, June 1949, 188, RAIC.

4.19 University of Toronto Bookstore, James Murray, 1948, 50523-2, Panda, CAA, UC.

4.20 Maclean-Hunter Publishing Company, Allward and Gouinlock, 1948, Rice and Bell, *RAIC Journal*, June 1949, 192, RAIC.

4.21 CNE Grandstand, Marani and Morris, 1948, 48513-4, Panda, CAA, UC.

4.22 Bank of Nova Scotia, Mathers and Haldenby, 1951, Ralph Greenhill and Bob Howard, *RAIC Journal*, November 1951, 323, RAIC.

4.23 Bank of Nova Scotia murals, Jacobine Jones, 1951, Ralph Greenhill and Bob Howard, RAIC *Journal*, November 1951, 329, RAIC.

4.24 Bank of Montreal, Chapman and Oxley and Marani and Morris, 1951, 51205-1, Panda, CAA, UC.

4.25 Royal Bank of Canada, Islington Avenue, E.C.S. Cox, 1950, 50588-3, Panda, CAA, UC.

4.26 Bank of Toronto, Warden Avenue, Casewin Ltd., 1954, 54512-9, Panda, CAA, UC.

4.27 Bank of Nova Scotia, Yonge Street at St Clair Avenue, Murray Brown and Elton, 1957, 571334-3, Panda, CAA, UC.

4.28 Thematic spread by E.C.S. Cox and Gordon S. Adamson, Panda Associates and Rapid, Grip and Batten Ltd, RAIC *Journal*, August 1947, 266-7, RAIC.

4.29 "How New is Modern?" C.R. Worsley, *Canadian Homes and Gardens*, January 1948, 16.

5.1 Canadian Bank of Commerce, C.B. McLean, 1954, 54436-25, Panda, CAA, UC.

5.2 Applewood Acres, 1954, *Canadian Homes and Gardens*, May 1955, 26.

5.3 Don Mills underway, 1954. Reproduced from Nancy Byrtus, Mark Fram, and Michael McClelland, eds., *East/West: A Guide To Where People Live in Downtown Toronto* (Toronto: Coach House, 2000).

5.4 The builders of Don Mills, c. 1954, Ryerson University Library and Archives, *Canadian Architect* Magazine Image Collection, 2009.002.2092.001, CA.

5.5 Don Mills houses under construction, 1953, 53864-10, Panda, CAA, UC.

5.6 Southill Village, James Murray and Henry Fliess, 1957, Neil Newton, *Canadian Architect*, February 1957, 24, CA.

5.7 Schutte house, James Murray, 1950, Mac-Gill, RAIC *Journal*, December 1950, 398, RAIC.

5.8 Diagram of split levels of Schutte house, James Murray, 1950, RAIC *Journal*, December 1950, 399, RAIC.

5.9 Spaulding house, James Murray, 1952, RAIC *Journal*, November 1952, 327, RAIC.

5.10 Spaulding house, James Murray, 1952, RAIC *Journal*, November 1952, 327, RAIC.

5.11 Pickard house, Harry Seidler, 1953, *Canadian Homes and Gardens*, August 1953, 14.

5.12 Bank of Canada, Marani and Morris, 1958, 58432-1, Panda Associates, CAA, UC.

5.13 US Consulate, Mathers and Haldenby, 1951, 51364-3, Panda Associates, 1951, CAA, UC.

5.14 Imperial Oil Head Office, Mathers and Haldenby, 1957, 57785-24A, Panda, CAA, UC.

5.15 Imperial Oil building lobby, interior by John B. Parkin Associates, 1957, 57785-17, Panda, CAA, UC.

5.16 John B. and John C. Parkin with R.E. Moore, RAIC *Journal*, September 1947, 335, RAIC.

5.17 "Family Helicopter," John C. Parkin, RAIC *Journal*, July 1947, 247, RAIC.

5.18 Entry for CMHC's first small house design competition, John C. Parkin, 1947, in *67 Homes for Canadians:*

Attractive House Plans Designed Especially for Canadian Requirements, Including Prize Winners of the Canadian Small House Competition (Ottawa: CMHC, 1947), 92.

5.19 Ontario Association of Architects building, John B. Parkin Associates, 1957, 57885-1, Panda, CAA, UC.

5.20 Ontario Association of Architects building, interior, John B. Parkin Associates 1957, 57885-2, Panda, CAA, UC.

5.21 Don Mills Shopping Centre, John B. Parkin Associates, 1955, 55943-1, Panda, CAA, UC.

5.22 Don Mills Shopping Centre, John B. Parkin Associates, 1955, 55943-19, Panda, CAA, UC.

5.23 Don Mills banks: Bank of Nova Scotia, John B. Parkin Associates, 1957, 57880-4, Panda, CAA, UC.

5.24 Don Mills banks: Bank of Montreal, John B. Parkin Associates, 1957, 68113-1, Panda, CAA, UC.

5.25 Ortho Pharmaceutical Head Office, John B. Parkin Associates, 1955, 56360-1, Panda, CAA, UC.

5.26 Offices of Sproatt and Rolph, 1919, *Construction*, March 1919, 73.

5.27 Offices of Mathers and Haldenby, 1948, 48566-1, Panda, CAA, UC.

5.28 Offices of John B. Parkin Associates, 1966, 66414-6, Panda, CAA, UC.

5.29 Parkin office, Don Mills Road, John B. Parkin Associates, 1955, 551149-2, Panda, CAA, UC.

5.30 Parkin office, Don Mills Road, John B. Parkin Associates, 1955, 551149-7, Panda, CAA, UC.

5.31 John C. Parkin meets Le Corbusier, 1957, 57805-1, Panda, CAA, UC.

5.32 Salvation Army, Canadian headquarters, 1955, 551134-1, Panda, CAA, UC.

5.33 Salvation Army, John B. Parkin Associates, 1957, Brian Shawcroft, *Canadian Architect*, May 1957, 42, CA.

5.34 Simpson-Sears industrial development, Etobicoke, John B. Parkin Associates, 1955, 55544-6, Panda, CAA, UC.

5.35 Peter Dickinson, c. 1960, Herb Nott and Co. Reproduced from John Martins-Manteiga, *Peter Dickinson* (Toronto: Dominion Modern, 2010), 5, courtesy of Dominion Modern.

5.36 Benvenuto, Peter Dickinson, 1955, 55300-1, Panda, CAA, UC.

5.37 Benvenuto entrance, Peter Dickinson, 1955, 551012-3, Panda, CAA, UC.

5.38 240 Oriole Road, Peter Dickinson, 1955, 56093-1, Panda, CAA, UC.

5.39 111 Richmond Street West, Peter Dickinson, 1955, 55243-5, Panda, CAA, UC.

5.40 Wawanesa Insurance, Peter Dickinson, 1957, 571328-2, Panda, CAA, UC.

5.41 Beth Tzedec synagogue, Peter Dickinson, 1954, 54376-16, Panda, CAA, UC.

5.42 Toronto Teachers' College, Peter Dickinson, 1955, 551127-15, Panda, CAA, UC.

5.43 Toronto Teachers' College, interior, Peter Dickinson, 1955, 551127-3, Panda, CAA, UC.

5.44 Juvenile and Family Court, Peter Dickinson, 1957, 571075-4, Panda, CAA, UC.

5.45 Juvenile and Family Court, interior, Peter Dickinson, 1957, 571075-1, Panda, CAA, UC.

5.46 130 Old Forest Hill Road, Gordon S. Adamson, 1952, 52809-2, Panda, CAA, UC.

5.47 City Park Apartments, Peter Caspari, 1954, 561002-2, Panda, CAA, UC.
5.48 Irving Grossman, *RAIC Journal*, October 1950, 363, RAIC.
5.49 Betel house, Irving Grossman, 1957, Arthur James, *Canadian Architect*, June 1958, 51, CA.
5.50 Betel house, rear, Irving Grossman, 1957, Arthur James, *Canadian Architect*, June 1958, 54, CA.
5.51 Wymilwood, Fleury and Arthur, 1954, *RAIC Journal*, February 1954, 44, RAIC.
5.52 Wymilwood, interior, Fleury and Arthur, 1954, *RAIC Journal*, February 1954, 45, RAIC.
5.53 Victoria College Library, Gordon S. Adamson, 1960, Arthur Coughtry, *Canadian Architect*, January 1962, 35, CA.
5.54 Victoria College Library, Gordon S. Adamson, 1960, Arthur Coughtry, *Canadian Architect*, January 1962, 37, CA.
5.55 Drawings of exterior cladding for Anglo Canada Fire and General Insurance Company, James Murray, 1955, *RAIC Journal*, May 1955, 163, RAIC.
5.56 House in Belleville, John B. Parkin Associates, 1957 *Canadian Homes and Gardens*, January 1957, 24.

6.1 Toronto International Airport, Terminal 1, John B. Parkin Associates, 1964, 64040-12, Panda, CAA, UC.
6.2 City Hall proposal, Marani and Morris, Mathers and Haldenby, and Shore and Moffatt, 1955, City of Toronto Archives, CTA, Series 1188.
6.3 Civic Square and New City Hall site from the southwest, 1959, 591161-9, Panda, CAA, UC.
6.4 Civic Square and New City Hall site from the southeast, 1959, Ryerson University Library and Archives, *Canadian Architect* Magazine Image Collection, 2009.002.2130.005, CA.
6.5 New City Hall competition jury, left to right: Arthur, Pratt, Saarinen, Rogers, Holford, Stephenson, 1958, 58504-2, Panda, CAA, UC.
6.6 Viljo Revell reviewing his design model of New City Hall, 1958. Photo by Herb Nott used with permission of NORR architects. Reproduced from John Martins Manteigo, *Mean City: From Architecture to Design: How Toronto Went Boom* (Toronto: Dominion Modern, 2005), 54.
6.7 New City Hall under construction and demolition of Registry Office, 1961, 61881-207, Panda, CAA, UC.
6.8 New City Hall, interior, c. 1965, Viljo Revell, Ryerson University Library and Archives, *Canadian Architect* Magazine Image Collection, 2009.002.2318.037, CA.
6.9 New City Hall, complete, Viljo Revell, 1968, 68677-1, Panda, CAA, UC.
6.10 The new courthouse complex west of New City Hall, Marani, Rounthwaite and Dick, 1966, 66744-1, Panda Associates, CAA, UC.
6.11 New City Hall and surrounds, 1965, *Canadian Architect*, October 1965, 55 CA.
6.12 South side of Queen, competition winner, Webb Zerafa Menkes, *Canadian Architect*, May 1968, 42, CA.

6.13 South side of Queen, competition loser, John B. Parkin Associates, *Canadian Architect*, May 1968, 47, CA.
6.14 Ron Thom, 1963, Trent University Archives, http://www.trentu.ca/admin/library/archives/zthome.htm.
6.15 Sketch of Massey College dining hall, Ron Thom, 1960, *Canadian Architect*, December 1960, 38-9, CA.
6.16 Massey College, Ron Thom, 1963, Peter Varley, RAIC *Journal*, November 1964, 64, RAIC.
6.17 Blevins Place, c. 1955, Ryerson University Library and Archives, *Canadian Architect* Magazine Image Collection, 2009.002.2064.004, CA.
6.18 Regent Park South, Peter Dickinson, 1956, Ryerson University Library and Archives, *Canadian Architect* Magazine Image Collection, 2009.002.2134.011, CA.
6.19 Regent Park South, apartment interior, 1956, Ryerson University Library and Archives, *Canadian Architect* Magazine Image Collection, 2009.002.2134.002, CA.
6.20 CNE Women's Building: Marani and Morris's Grandstand in the distance, Peter Dickinson, 1956, 571325-3, Panda, CAA, UC.
6.21 "Perspective of Theatre Foyer," CNE Women's Building, Peter Dickinson, 1956, 56616-1, Panda, CAA, UC.
6.22 O'Keefe Centre, balcony under construction, Peter Dickinson, 1959, 59078-59a, Panda, CAA, UC.
6.23 O'Keefe Centre, Peter Dickinson, 1960, 61709-4, Panda, CAA, UC.
6.24 561 Avenue Road, Peter Dickinson, 1957, 571277-16, Panda Associates, 1957, CAA, UC.
6.25 Westbury Hotel, Peter Dickinson, 1956, 56623-2, Panda Associates, CAA, UC.
6.26 Westbury Hotel piano bar, Peter Dickinson, 1957, 57682-28, Panda, CAA, UC.
6.27 Westbury Hotel expansion, Peter Dickinson, 1963, 63581-2w, Panda, CAA, UC.
6.28 Trans-Canada Pipeline building, Peter Dickinson, 1959, 59936-1, Panda, CAA UC.
6.29 Continental Can, Peter Dickinson, 1959, 59351-1, Panda, CAA, UC.
6.30 801 Bay Street, Peter Dickinson, 1959, 59263-1, Panda, CAA, UC.
6.31 Prudential Insurance, Peter Dickinson, 1961, 61123-1, Panda, CAA, UC.
6.32 Jesuit Seminary, Regis College, Peter Dickinson, 1961, *Canadian Architect*, May 1962, 39, CA.
6.33 Jesuit Seminary, Regis College, Peter Dickinson, 1961, 61775-1, Panda, CAA, UC.
6.34 Four Seasons Motor Hotel, Peter Dickinson, 1961, *Canadian Architect*, November 1961, 57, CA.
6.35 Inn on the Park, Peter Dickinson, 1963, 63423-1, Panda, CAA, UC.
6.36 A drive up University Avenue, 1959, Ryerson University Library and Archives, *Canadian Architect* Magazine Image Collection, 2009.002.2165, CA.
6.37 University Avenue, north from Queen Street, 1968, 68372-3, Panda, CAA, UC.
6.38 Sun Life, John B. Parkin Associates, 1961, 61147-25, Panda, CAA, UC.

6.39 "God is in the details," Sun Life, John B. Parkin Associates, 1961, *Canadian Architect*, October 1961, 66, CA.
6.40 Toronto International Airport model, John B. Parkin Associates, 1959, 59681-1, Panda, CAA, UC.
6.41 Toronto International Airport, John B. Parkin Associates, 1964, 64040-206, Panda, CAA, UC.
6.42 Toronto International Airport, John B. Parkin Associates, 1964, 64040-96, Panda, CAA, UC.
6.43 Bata Head Office, John B. Parkin Associates, 1964, 641003-1, Panda, CAA, UC.
6.44 John C. Parkin house, garden view, John B. Parkin Associates, 1957, 581100-1, Panda, CAA, UC.
6.45 Crashley house, John B. Parkin Associates, 1965, CAA, UC.
6.46 Fraser house, Ron Thom, 1965–67. Courtesy of Carol Moore Ede.
6.47 Fraser house, ground floor plan, Ron Thom, 1965–67, THO 6516, CAA, UC.
6.48 Fraser house, elevations, Ron Thom, 1965–67, THO 6516, CAA, UC.
6.49 Fogel house, Irving Grossman, 1959, Morley Markson, *Canadian Architect*, August 1960, 48, CA.
6.50 Fogel house, rear, Irving Grossman, 1959, Morley Markson, *Canadian Architect*, August 1960, 50, CA.
6.51 J. Posluns house, Jerome Markson, 1964, Ryerson University Library and Archives, *Canadian Architect* Magazine Image Collection, 2009.002.1085.001, CA.
6.52 Cleeve Horne's house/studio, 1949, 52800-1, Panda, CAA, UC.
6.53 Cleeve Horne country house, Clifford and Lawrie, 1959, *Canadian Homes and Gardens*, January 1959, 14.
6.54 Cleeve Horne country house, Clifford and Lawrie, 1959, *Canadian Homes and Gardens*, January 1959, 17.

7.1 John B. Parkin at the Toronto-Dominion Centre, 1968, 68169-6, Panda, CAA, UC.
7.2 Mies van der Rohe, 1964, Werner Blaser, Whitney Museum of American Art.
7.3 Toronto-Dominion Centre: banking hall left, Toronto-Dominion Tower right, Ludwig Mies van der Rohe, 1967, 68854-23, Panda, CAA, UC.
7.4 Toronto-Dominion Centre: banking hall with interior by Ludwig Mies van der Rohe, 1967, 68854-17, Panda Associates, CAA, UC.
7.5 Toronto-Dominion Centre: banking hall with interior by Ludwig Mies van der Rohe, 1967, 68854-20, Panda, CAA, UC.
7.6 Toronto-Dominion Centre: banking hall with interior by Ludwig Mies van der Rohe, 1967, 68854-31, Panda, CAA, UC.
7.7 Toronto-Dominion Centre: banking hall with interior by Ludwig Mies van der Rohe, 1967, 68854-22, Panda, CAA, UC.
7.8 Commerce Court under construction, I.M. Pei, 1971, 71229-8c, Panda, CAA, UC.
7.9 Royal Bank Plaza, Webb Zerafa Menkes Housden, 1977, Arthur James, *Canadian Architect*, April 1977, 43, CA.

7.10 Greenbelt Heights Village, Belcourt and Blair, 1956, 56885-3, Panda, CAA, UC.

7.11 Yorkwoods Village, Klein and Sears, 1962, Roger Jowett, RAIC *Journal*, August 1964, 50, RAIC.

7.12 Don Valley Woods, Klein and Sears, 1964, Roger Jowett, RAIC *Journal*, August 1964, 42, RAIC.

7.13 The Colonnade, Gerald Robinson, 1964, Ryerson University Library and Archives, *Canadian Architect* Magazine Image Collection, 2009.002.854.001, *CA*.

7.14 Bathurst and Steeles in the 1970s. Reproduced from Michael McClelland and Graeme Stewart, *Concrete Toronto: A Guide to Concrete Architecture from the Fifties to the Seventies* (Toronto: Coach House, 2007), 215.

7.15 Drawing of "The Street," Flemingdon Park, Irving Grossman, 1961, *Canadian Architect*, May 1961, 50, *CA*.

7.16 Clintwood Court, Henry Fliess, 1961, Neil Newton, RAIC *Journal*, October 1961, 48, RAIC.

7.17 Edgeley, Irving Grossman, 1961, *Canadian Architect*, June 1961, 37, *CA*.

7.18 Alexandra Park, Webb Zerafa Menkes, Jerome Markson, and Klein and Sears, 1966, Roger Jowett, Ryerson University Library and Archives, *Canadian Architect* Magazine Image Collection, 2009.002.841.001, *CA*.

7.19 Study of Educational Facilities (SEF), Roderick Robbie et al., 1969, Arthur James, *Canadian Architect*, December 1969, 49, *CA*.

7.20 George Brown College, Casa Loma Campus, Fairfield and DuBois, 1971, Ryerson University Library and Archives, *Canadian Architect* Magazine Image Collection, 2009.002.769.001, *CA*.

7.21 Chapel Glen under construction, Boigon and Heinonen, 1972, Michel Proulx, *Canadian Architect*, January 1972, 51, *CA*.

7.22 University of Toronto, Canadiana Building, Mathers and Haldenby, 1951, 51530-3, Panda, CAA, UC.

7.23 University of Toronto, Canadiana Building from southwest, Mathers and Haldenby, 1951, 51530-2, Panda Associates, CAA, UC.

7.24 University of Toronto, Sidney Smith Hall, John B. Parkin Associates, 1961, 611041-34, Panda, CAA, UC.

7.25 University of Toronto, New College, Fairfield and DuBois, 1964, Roger Jowett, *Canadian Architect*, December 1965, 51, *CA*.

7.26 York University, Founders College, UPACE (Gordon S. Adamson and Associates; John B. Parkin and Associates; Shore and Moffat and Associates), 1968, Panda Associates, Ryerson University Library and Archives, *Canadian Architect* Magazine Image Collection, 2009.002.1359.002, *CA*.

7.27 York University, Vanier College, UPACE (Gordon S. Adamson and Associates; John B. Parkin and Associates; Shore and Moffat and Associates), 1968, Panda Associates, *Canadian Architect*, August 1968, 38, *CA*.

7.28 York University, Scott Library, UPACE (Gordon S. Adamson and Associates; John B. Parkin and Associates; Shore and Moffat and Associates), 1971, 71489-10, Panda, CAA, UC.

7.29 York University, Ross Humanities Building, UPACE (Gordon S. Adamson and Associates; John B. Parkin and Associates; Shore and Moffat and Associates), 1968, Ryerson University Library and Archives, *Canadian Architect* Magazine Image Collection, 2009.002.1362.005, *CA*.

7.30 Central Technical School, Arts Centre, Fairfield and DuBois, 1963, 63416-56, Panda, CAA, UC.

7.31 Central Technical School, Arts Centre, interior, Fairfield and DuBois, 1963, 63416-25, Panda, CAA, UC.

7.32 Scarborough College, John Andrews, 1965, 67985-2k, Panda, CAA, UC.

7.33 Scarborough College, John Andrews, 1965, John Reeves, *Canadian Architect*, May 1966, 51, *CA*.

7.34 University of Toronto, Robarts Library, Warner, Burn, Toan, and Lunde, 1974, 74256-3c, Panda, CAA, UC.

7.35 Sears Canada (Simpson-Sears), Maxwell Miller, 1971, Simon Pulsifer, 2005, used under the Creative Commons Attribution-Share Alike 3.0 Unported license, http://commons.wikimedia.org/wiki/File:Sears_Canada_Building.JPG.

7.36 95 Ardwold Gate, Taivo Kapsi, 1968, John Fulker, *Canadian Architect*, April 1968, 45, *CA*.

7.37 Yorkdale Shopping Centre (Simpson's store), John B. Parkin Associates, 1964, A. Martin, *RAIC Journal*, June 1964, 46, RAIC.

7.38 Yorkdale Shopping Centre (Eaton's Store), John Graham Consultants (Seattle), 1964, A. Martin, *RAIC Journal*, June 1964, 46, RAIC.

7.39 Yorkdale Shopping Centre, interior court at Simpson's, John Graham Consultants (Seattle), 1964, 64536-9, Panda, CAA, UC.

7.40 Ontario Place, Craig, Zeidler and Strong, 1971, Hiro Nakashima, *Canadian Architect*, June 1971, 38, *CA*.

7.41 Eaton Centre, Bregman and Hamann and the Zeidler Partnership, 1977, Arthur James, Ryerson University Library and Archives, *Canadian Architect* Magazine Image Collection, 2009.002.3190.028, *CA*.

7.42 Eaton Centre, interior, Bregman and Hamann and the Zeidler Partnership, 1977, Arthur James, *Canadian Architect*, May 1977, 45, *CA*.

7.43 Eaton Centre, interior, Bregman and Hamann and the Zeidler Partnership, 1977, Arthur James, *Canadian Architect*, May 1977, 46, *CA*.

7.44 Myers residence, Toronto, Barton Myers, 1972, Karl Sliva, *Canadian Architect*, February 1972, 46, *CA*.

7.45 Wolf house, Barton Myers, 1976, John Fulker, *Canadian Architect*, October 1976, cover, *CA*.

7.46 Wolf house, Barton Myers, 1976, John Fulker, *Canadian Architect*, October 1976, 31, *CA*.

8.1 The 1970s skyline, Ryerson University Library and Archives, *Canadian Architect* Magazine Image Collection, 2009.002.3199.011, *CA*.

8.2 Toronto transformed, 1971, 71628-8, Panda, CAA, UC.

A NOTE ON SOURCES

This book is based primarily upon printed sources such as professional journals such as *Canadian Architect* and popular magazines such as *Canadian Homes and Gardens*. I have not sought to make use of the archival collections of records of architectural firms for several reasons. First of all, such sources are spotty so that some important practitioners have not left records; where records do exist, they often consist exclusively of plans and drawings, which are valuable but often require much information to place them in context. Instead, for illustrative purposes, I have used black and white photographs (and a few drawings) that are contemporary with the opening of the buildings being discussed. Colour photographs do exist for some projects following the Second World War, but I decided not to try to include them as it would not be possible to place them in the text alongside the relevant written text as has been done with the other pictures.

Unfortunately, there are not many books and articles on the architecture of twentieth-century Toronto. I have made use of works like Tim Morawetz's study of Art Deco and John Martins Manteiga's monograph on Peter Dickinson where they are relevant. However, the published material did not seem extensive enough to justify occupying space in an already long book with a separate bibliography. I have cited the publications used in the notes, and I am grateful to the authors for the information they provided.

NOTES

INTRODUCTION

1 Rupert Brooke, *Letters from America* (New York: McClelland, Goodchild and Stewart, 1916), 83–4.
2 Useful and important as some of these studies may be, even to mention a work can be interpreted as meaning that one has joined a particular school or pack whether one wants to or not.
3 I have not relied on interviews with architects because only a few who are mentioned in the book are available and I wished to emphasize contemporary reactions. I have made use of secondary material where it seemed valuable.
4 Municipal ratepayers then had to approve the city's major capital spending plans by referendum. For a study of projects (public and private) that never materialized, see Mark Osbaldeston, *Unbuilt Toronto: A History of the City That Might Have Been* (Toronto: Dundurn, 2008) and *Unbuilt Toronto 2: More of the City That Might Have Been* (Toronto: Dundurn, 2011).
5 S. Henbest Capper, "The American Tall Building," *Canadian Architect and Builder* [hereafter *CAB*], 11, no. 1 (1898): 5.
6 "The Electric Lighting Plant, Temple Building, Toronto," *CAB*, 11, no. 1 (1898): 7. For bringing to my attention this illustrated article, like many others referred to in this book, I owe my thanks to Mark Fram.
7 Capper, "The American Tall Building," 6.
8 The other contemporary term for these innovations was *l'art moderne*, which I have also avoided except in a few quotations.
9 The book and the catalogue of the show by Hitchcock, Johnson, and Alfred H. Barr of MOMA entitled *Modern Architects* (New York: W.W. Norton, 1932).
10 Sigfried Giedion, *Space, Time and Architecture*, 1st ed. (Cambridge, MA: Harvard University Press, 1941), 668. Giedion's book stemmed from his Charles Eliot Norton Lectures at Harvard in 1938–39 and was revised and reprinted many times afterwards.
11 Jane Jacobs, *The Death and Life of Great American Cities* (New York: Random House, 1961). Jacobs's influence in Toronto increased following her move to the city's Annex neighbourhood during the 1960s.
12 The city had only created a formal land use plan in 1950 and imposed a comprehensive zoning bylaw a few years later, after prolonged debate.
13 The exception that demonstrates this rule is Figure 7.35, the Brutalist Sears Canada building on Jarvis Street, for which no contemporary picture was found. A few other pictures taken after a lapse of some time, such as Figures 1.20 and 2.24, were used because they seemed much better than any period images.
14 The exception is Figure 2.25, which depicts the Ford Motor Company's assembly plant at Bloor Street West and Victoria Park Avenue, where the photographer, W.A. Young, noted the exact date of 1 October 1923 on the print.

CHAPTER ONE

1 These events are chronicled in Christopher Armstrong and H.V. Nelles, *The Revenge of the Methodist Bicycle Company: Sunday Streetcars and Municipal Reform in Toronto, 1888–1897* (Toronto: Peter Martin Associates, 1977).
2 Patricia Petersen, "The Evolution of the Board of Control," in *Forging a Consensus: Historical Essays on Toronto*, ed. Victor L. Russell (Toronto: University of Toronto Press, 1984), 188–90.
3 See the splendid bird's-eye map from 1893 reproduced in Derek Hayes, *Historical Atlas of Toronto* (Vancouver: Douglas and McIntyre, 2008), 108–9.
4 See Jon A. Peterson, *The Birth of City Planning in the United States, 1840–1917* (Baltimore: Johns Hopkins University Press, 2003), esp. Preface and Chapters 1 and 2.
5 Carl Smith, *The Plan of Chicago: Daniel Burnham and the Remaking of the American City* (Chicago: University of Chicago Press, 2006), 19.
6 On the evolution of the architectural profession, see Kelly Crossman, *Architecture in Transition: From Art to Practice, 1885–1906* (Montreal and Kingston: McGill-Queen's University Press, 1987) and Geoffrey Simmins, *Ontario Association of Architects: A Centennial History, 1889–1989* (Toronto: Ontario Association of Architects, 1989), esp. Introduction and Chapters 1 and 2.
7 See the verbatim report of the OAA convention proceedings in *Canadian Architect and Builder* 8, no. 2 (1895).
8 College Avenue was laid out in 1829 as a tree-lined ceremonial way north from Queen Street to the proposed King's College (the east–west street crossing its northern end then

known as Yonge Street Avenue, later College Street), but was eventually redesigned as a dual carriageway with a central boulevard up to the new Ontario legislature (opened in 1893), which lay just east of the University of Toronto campus, and the street was renamed University Avenue. See William Dendy, *Lost Toronto* (Toronto: Oxford University Press, 1978), 136–7.

9 "The History of the O.A.A., 1895–1900," [by Hynes?] n.d. [c. 1946] quoting Aylesworth's report, J.P. Hynes Papers, Thomas Fisher Rare Bookroom, University of Toronto Library.

10 The original executive of the Guild of Civic Art was composed of bank executive Edmund Walker, lawyers E.F.B. Johnston and Bernard McEvoy, University of Toronto Professor James Mavor, artists Lucius O'Brien and George Reid, and architect W.A. Langton. See "Historical," 27 July 1912, prepared by its secretary Frederick L. Riggs, Guild of Civic Arts Papers, box 1, Baldwin Room, Toronto Public Library (hereafter GCA, BR, TPL).

11 Minutebook (hereafter MB), 1897–1911 [which actually contains records dating up to 1914], Minutes of Directors, 21 May 1897, GCA, BR, TPL; *Globe (Toronto)*, 20 March 1897.

12 Report of Ontario Association of Architects Annual Meeting (hereafter OAA, AM), *Canadian Architect and Builder* 11, no. 1 (1898): 18.

13 Minutes of Advisory Board, 14 January 1898, MB, 1897–1911, GCA, BR, TPL; "Guild of Civic Art," "Report of the Guild of Civic Art," n.d. [c. 1903] typescript, Subject files, vol. 27A, Sir Edmund Walker Papers, Thomas Fisher Rare Bookroom, University of Toronto Library. P.G. Mackintosh makes the point that the Guild and Reid in particular were convinced of the role of artwork in improving the lives of city-dwellers. See Mackintosh, "'The Development of Higher Urban Life' and the Geographic Imagination: Beauty, Art and Moral Environmentalism in Toronto, 1900–20," *Journal of Historical Geography* 31 (2005): 688–722.

14 "Historical," 27 July 1912, prepared by Frederick Riggs, box 1, GCA, BR, TPL.

15 J.M.S. Careless, *Toronto to 1918: An Illustrated History* (Toronto: Lorimer and Company, 1984), 125 and Tables 1, 4, 10, 12.

16 Peterson, *Birth of City Planning in the United States*, 81–5.

17 See Lucy Lawliss, Caroline Loughlin, and Lauren Meier, eds., *The Master List of Design Projects of the Olmsted Firm, 1857–1979*, 2nd ed. (Washington, DC: National Association for Olmsted Parks and National Park Service, 2008), including Nancy Pollock-Elwand, "The Olmsted Firm in Canada," 15–17.

18 Peterson, *Birth of City Planning*, Chapters 1 to 3; William H. Wilson, *The City Beautiful Movement* (Baltimore: Johns Hopkins University Press, 1989), Introduction and Chapters 1 to 3.

19 Simmins, *Ontario Association of Architects*, Chapter 4.

20 The Olmsted firm became well known to prominent Torontonians as the client list of its papers at the Library of Congress includes names such as H.S. Janes, Henry Pellatt, and Frederick Nicholls, among others.

21 Minutes of the Advisory Board, 11 February, 28 April, 6 May, 5 June 1901, and clippings from 22 May 1901 reporting on meeting of previous day, MB, 1897–1911, GCA, BR, TPL; Ontario Association of Architects, *Proceedings*, "Proceedings of the Annual Meeting," (hereafter OAA *Proceedings*, AM), 1902, Report of the Toronto Chapter, 34.

22 A brief account of Howard's ideas for a "garden city" can be found in John Sewell, *The Shape of the City: Struggles with Modern Planning* (Toronto: University of Toronto Press, 1993), 22–7.

23 W.A. Langton, "City Planning," address to the Central Ontario School of Art, 20 March 1902, reprinted in OAA *Proceedings*, AM, 1903.

24 Ibid.

25 See Jacob Spelt, *Toronto* (Toronto: Collier-Macmillan 1973) 4–11 for a brief account of the topography of the site and a relief map.

26 See map 7.53, "Plan of York ... by Lieut. Phillpotts, Royal Engineers," 1818, reproduced in Louis R. Gentilcore and C. Grant Head, *Ontario's History in Maps* (Toronto: University of Toronto Press, 1984), 252.

27 *Canadian Architect and Builder* qtd. in James Lemon, "Plans for Early 20th-Century Toronto: Lost in Management," *Urban History Review* 18, no. 1 (1989): 12.

28 See Frederick W. Armstrong, "The Second Great Fire, 1904," reprinted in Armstrong, *A City in the Making: Progress, People and Perils in Victorian Toronto* (Toronto: Dundurn Press, 1988), 296–327.

29 Much was made of the fact that Baltimore, which had suffered a similar disastrous fire earlier that same year, swiftly undertook a vigourous reconstruction programme.

30 *Globe*, 17 January 1906; "Description of Plan of Improvements for the City of Toronto," n.d., box 1, GCA, BR, TPL. This "Description of Plan" lists as president Sir Henry Pellatt who held office in 1905–06, though the document appears to have been revised slightly afterwards.

31 The coloured originals of the map and the bird's-eye view do not seem to have survived but were reprinted in black and white in *Canadian Architect and Builder* 19, no. 2 (1906).

32 Toronto Guild of Civic Art, *Report on a Comprehensive Plan for Systematic Civic Improvements in Toronto* (n.p., 1909).

33 *Report of the Civic Improvement Committee for the City of Toronto* (n.p., 28 December 1911).

34 On Lyle see Geoffrey Hunt, *John M. Lyle: Toward a Canadian Architecture/Créer une architecture canadienne* (Kingston, ON: Agnes Etherington Art Centre, Queen's University, 1982) and Glenn McArthur, *A Progressive Traditionalist: John M. Lyle, Architect* (Toronto: Coach House, 2009), 58–9.

35 Roy Merrens, "Port Authorities as Land Developers: The Case of the Toronto Harbour Commissioners and Their Outer Harbour Project, 1912–1968," *Urban History Review* 12, no. 2 (1988), 94–5. The 1912 plan is actually labeled as for the Harbor [sic] Commission.

36 See Hayes, *Historical Atlas of Toronto*, 124–5.

37 Jacobs and Davies Inc., "Report on Transit to the Mayor of the City of Toronto," 25 August 1910, Reports, box 2, City of Toronto Archives (hereafter CTA).

38 Christopher Armstrong and H.V. Nelles, "The Rise of Civic Populism in Toronto, 1870–1920," in *Forging a Consensus*, 226–7.

39 The virtues of the plan continued to be rehearsed by the Civic Guild. See Address by C.H. Mitchell on "Town Planning and Civic Improvement," January 1913 and address by CG secretary [Riggs] to Young People's Society, n.d. [1913], box 1, GCA, BR, TPL.

40 Mark Osbaldeston, *Unbuilt Toronto: A History of the City That Might Have Been* (Toronto: Dundurn Press, 2008), 114–20; Steve Mackinnon, Karen Teeple, and Michele Dale, eds., *Toronto's Visual Legacy: Official City Photography from 1856 to the Present* (Toronto: Lorimer, 2009), 110–17.

41 There were several waterworks and sewage projects undertaken in this period, but planning advocates paid little attention to these services. See, for example, Mackinnon, Teeple, and Dale, *Toronto's Visual Legacy*, 106–7.

42 For a map outlining the city's expansion, see J.M.S. Careless, *Toronto to 1918: An Illustrated History* (Toronto: Lorimer, 1984), 125.

43 For a general history of Toronto architecture up to 1900 see Eric Arthur, *Toronto: No Mean City*, 3rd ed., revised by Stephen A. Otto (Toronto: University of Toronto Press, 1986), Chapter 5, "Romanesque and Cast Iron." A more extensive list of Romanesque Revival buildings is contained in Douglas Richardson et al., "Romanesque Toronto: A Photographic Exhibition of Late Nineteenth Century Architecture" (typescript: Department of Fine Art, University of Toronto, 1971).

44 The Ontario legislature, the old City Hall, and Confederation Life are pictured and discussed in William Dendy and William Kilbourn, *Toronto Observed: Its Architecture, Patrons, and History* (Toronto: Oxford University Press, 1986), 134–6, 148–50, 124–5, along with residences like the Gooderham house (129–32), while the demolished Temple Building appears in Dendy, *Lost Toronto*, 102–3, along with such other vanished Romanesque Revival buildings as the Board of Trade (6–7), the Bank of Commerce (94–5), Broadway Tabernacle (132–3), the Armouries (138–9), and Upper Canada College (188–9).

45 Dendy and Kilbourn, *Toronto Observed*, 143–5. In *No Mean City*, Arthur states that the Board of Trade building (1889) was the first Toronto structure with an all-steel frame, but its collapse during construction led the architects to retain load-bearing masonry piers between the windows (184). See also Angela Carr, *Toronto Architect Edmund Burke: Redefining Canadian Architecture* (Montreal and Kingston: McGill-Queen's University Press, 1995), Chapter 6.

46 College Street then ended at a T-intersection at Yonge but there was hope that a southward jog could be created to link up with Carlton Street, creating a new crosstown route.

47 Dendy and Kilbourn, *Toronto Observed*, 164–7.

48 Dendy, *Lost Toronto*, 98–9.

49 Ibid., 176–9.
50 "Sinaiticus," "An Appreciation," *Construction* 20, no. 5 (1927). In 1923, when he had just been elected president of the Ontario Association of Architects, Cobb decided to decamp to California where he settled in the greener pastures of Hollywood; see *Construction* 15, no. 10 (1923).
51 Dendy, *Lost Toronto*, 150–1.
52 Martin L. Friedland, *The University of Toronto: A History* (Toronto: University of Toronto Press, 2002), 186–94; Larry Wayne Richards, *University of Toronto: The Campus Guide* (New York: Princeton Architectural Press, 2009), 71–2.
53 Friedland, *University of Toronto*, 194–6; Richards, *University of Toronto*, 66–7.
54 Friedland, *University of Toronto*, 196; Richards, *University of Toronto*, 69–70.
55 Beginning in the 1890s, Princeton University, then Boston College, and later Yale University, adopted Collegiate Gothic as their characteristic architectural style.
56 Richards, *University of Toronto*, 64–5.
57 Ibid., 84.
58 Massey himself attended the non-sectarian University College.
59 Vincent Massey, *What's Past Is Prologue: The Memoirs of Vincent Massey* (Toronto: Macmillan, 1963), 24.
60 Ibid., 42; Richards, *University of Toronto*, 82–3.
61 Massey, *What's Past Is Prologue*, 24–5.
62 Dendy and Kilbourn, *Toronto Observed*, 196.
63 See Edward R. Ford, *The Details of Modern Architecture*, vol. 1 (Cambridge MA: MIT Press, 1990), 45–7. The most striking use of Collegiate Gothic purely for external decoration was surely the extraordinary building by James Gamble Rogers for Davenport College at Yale University, where the street front was Gothic in deference to his building across the road while the inner face of the college was Federal to match the remainder of the quadrangle.
64 Harold Kalman, *A History of Canadian Architecture*, vol. 2 (Toronto: Oxford University Press, 1994), 706–9; Dendy and Kilbourn, *Toronto Observed*, 194–8; Richards, *University of Toronto*, 53–7. After the Second World War, a cloister was added, linking Soldiers' Tower to University College physically and providing space to record the names of university members killed in that conflict.
65 When the History Department of the University of Toronto occupied the house in the 1950s, one Flavelle descendant was at a loss to understand from a faculty member where his small office (complete with a window) was until she realized that he was quartered in the former linen closet.
66 Dendy and Kilbourn, *Toronto Observed*, 172–4; Richards, *University of Toronto*, 129–30.
67 Dendy, *Lost Toronto*, 185–7. The house was demolished in 1936 and the land subdivided along a short street running east from Spadina Road named Ardwold Gate.
68 Dendy and Kilbourn, *Toronto Observed*, 178–82.
69 Dendy and Kilbourn, *Toronto Observed*, 175–7; Annmarie Adams, "Eden Smith and the Canadian Domestic Revival," *Urban History Review/Revue d'histoire urbaine* 21, no. 2 (1993): 104–15; Carolyn Neal, "Eden Smith, Architect, 1858–1949" (Toronto: Architectural Conservancy of Ontario, 1976).
70 See Smith's 1914 design for multiple housing at Riverdale Court on Bain Avenue in Dendy and Kilbourn, *Toronto Observed*, 183–5.
71 Reyner Banham, *A Concrete Atlantis: U.S. Industrial Building and European Modern Architecture* (Cambridge, MA: MIT Press, 1986), 83–101.
72 On changing construction methods, see Betsy H. Bradley, *The Works: Industrial Architecture of the United States* (New York: Oxford University Press, 1999), Chapter 6.
73 Bylaw #4408, passed 6 July 1904; James Hull, "Science in the City: Reforming the Toronto Building Code," paper delivered to the Canadian Historical Association conference, York University, Toronto, May 2006.
74 Robert G. Hill, "Reinforced Concrete in Toronto: An Early History," in *Concrete Toronto: A Guidebook to Concrete Architecture from the Fifties to the Seventies*, eds. Michael McClelland and Graeme Stewart (Toronto: E.R.A. Architects and Coach House Books, 2007), 68–9.
75 Dendy and Kilbourn, *Toronto Observed*, 168–9.
76 *Construction* 7, no. 12 (1914).
77 Bylaws #6368, 6369, 24 February 1913; *Construction* 8, no. 7 (1915); Dendy and Kilbourn, *Toronto Observed*, 170–1.
78 *Construction*, 6, no. 3 (1913).
79 TPL, BR, GCA, Box 1, "1st Report on Toronto and Proposed Improvements Sent July 4th,

1907" by A.W. Bentham to Sir Ashton Webb, Westminster, England

80 Dendy, *Lost Toronto*, 16–18.

81 See the photographs of the Esplanade to the east and west taken in 1894 and the panoramic view of the York Street bridge in 1897 in Mackinnon, Teeple, and Dale, *Toronto's Visual Legacy*, 62–5, 83; Dendy and Kilbourn, *Toronto Observed*, 211.

82 See Robert McMann, "'... A Kind of Monument to a Time When the World Ran on Steel Rails': Union Station Railways and the City," 27–9, and Ron Haggart, "'Are They Going to Give Us a New Station Or Not?': The Politics of Union Station," 15–16, in *The Open Gate: Toronto Union Station*, ed. Richard Bebout (Toronto: Peter Martin Associates, 1972).

83 Dendy and Kilbourn, suggest that the tower resembled the Campanile of Saint Mark's in Venice that had collapsed in 1902, subsequently rebuilt and often imitated (*Toronto Observed*, 192–3).

84 McArthur, *Lyle*, 66–70; Douglas Richardson, "'A Blessed Sense of Civic Excess': The Architecture of Union Station," in *Open Gate*, 67–94. See also Dendy and Kilbourn, *Toronto Observed*, 209–13.

85 McMann, "A Kind of Monument," in *Open Gate*, 32–41.

86 Richardson, "Blessed Sense of Civic Excess," in *Open Gate*, 81–9.

87 The extension of Bay Street north of Queen (then called Terauley) up to Bloor was begun and completed after a delay during the war, and Dundas (then Agnes) was linked up east and west to form a continuous thoroughfare.

88 For a graphic demonstration of "The Emergence of Corporate Toronto" between 1890 and 1914 showing the scale and scope of changes in downtown land use, see Donald Kerr and Deryck W. Holdsworth, eds., *Historical Atlas of Canada, Volume III, Addressing the Twentieth Century, 1891–1961* (Toronto: University of Toronto Press, 1990), Plate 15 by Holdsworth and Gunter Gad.

CHAPTER TWO

1 See Christopher Armstrong, *Blue Skies and Boiler Rooms: Buying and Selling Securities in Canada, 1870–1940* (Toronto: University of Toronto Press, 1997), Chapter 7.

2 Editorial, Royal Architectural Institute of Canada, *Royal Architectural Institute of Canada Journal* (hereafter RAIC *Journal*) 1, no. 1 (1924).

3 See Christina Cameron, *Index of Houses Featured in Canadian Homes and Gardens from 1925 to 1944* (Ottawa: Parks Canada, 1980) and Hodgins's editorial in *Canadian Homes and Gardens* (hereafter CHG) 2, no. 1 (1925). The Group of Seven's J.E.H. MacDonald supplied the cover designs for several of the early issues.

4 Alcide Chausseé, "The Secretary's Page," RAIC *Journal*, 2, no. 4 (1925).

5 "The RAIC and OAA Joint Meeting," *Construction* 12, no. 10 (1919).

6 Margaret Kentgens-Craig, *The Bauhaus and America, First Contacts, 1919–1936* (Cambridge, MA: MIT Press, 1999), 38.

7 Reyner Banham, *A Concrete Atlantis: U.S. Industrial Buildings and European Modern Architecture, 1900–1925* (Cambridge, MA: MIT Press, 1986), 215, 173.

8 J.H.R. Webster, "The Act of Decorating," *Construction* 15, no. 2 (1922).

9 G.H. Macdonald, "Evolution of Architecture," a paper prepared for the Society of McGill Graduates and read before the Alberta Association of Architects and reprinted in *Construction* 14, no. 2 (1921).

10 See A.S. Mathers, "Thirty-five Years of Practice," RAIC *Journal* 32, no. 12 (1955).

11 Obituary for Berrington, *Construction* 16, no. 4 (1923).

12 The following paragraphs are based mainly upon Angela Carr, "Legacy of an Architectural Conscience" and Alec Keefer, "Eric Arthur's Career: An Overview," in *Eric Ross Arthur: Conservation in Context*, ed. Alec Keefer (Toronto: Toronto Regional Architectural Conservancy, 2001).

13 *Construction* 26, no. 2 (1933): 37.

14 Virginia Wright, *Modern Furniture in Canada, 1920 to 1970* (Toronto: University of Toronto Press, 1997), 4.

15 Melville S. Mann, "The Modern Trend in Architectural Design," reprinted from "The Blue Bell," *Construction* 23, no. 12 (1930).

16 "The Garage as an Element in Domestic Design," *Construction* 17, no. 6 (1924). This article also mentions three new architect-designed houses with built-in garages.

17 Charles Reilly, "Some Impressions of Canadian Towns, II – Toronto," RAIC *Journal* 1, no. 3 (1924).

18 John Lyle, "Sproatt and Rolph – An Appreciation," *RAIC Journal* 2, no. 4 (1925).

19 John Lyle, "Canadian Architecture" address to dinner in honour of Sproatt and Rolph," *RAIC Journal* 4, no. 2 (1927); Massey, "Remarks on Architecture" to the RAIC luncheon, *RAIC Journal* 1, no. 4 (1924); Arthur, "Toronto Chapter O.A.A. Architectural Exhibition," *RAIC Journal* 3, no. 2 (1926). Professor Reilly from Liverpool also declared Hart House a "pleasing Gothic structure," the latest and "most interesting" building at the university, and Professor Percy Nobbs from McGill praised the "fine selective taste" in Gothic models to produce a notable building which had received great popular acclaim; see Reilly, "Some Impressions of Canadian Towns, II – Toronto," *RAIC Journal* 1, no. 3 (1924); Nobbs, "Architecture in Canada" speech to Royal Institute of British Architects, *RAIC Journal* 1, no. 3 (1924).

20 Percy Nobbs, "Architecture in Canada," read before the RIBA, London, 2 January 1924, reprinted in *RAIC Journal* 1, no. 3 (1924).

21 In fact, John Lyle's original design had included such features that were eliminated in the pursuit of economy.

22 S. Lewis Milligan, "Poetry of Architecture," *RAIC Journal*, 1, no. 4 (1924). Milligan got so overwrought by the offence caused to his soul by seeing church spires in Quebec clad in cast iron that he burst out with an abominable poem composed after a recent trip to the Rocky Mountains: "Look where the level prairies leap/ In godlike grandeur to the skies."

23 Letter from Lyle to editor, n.d., *Construction* 3, no. 3 (1926). See also Glenn McArthur, *A Progressive Traditionalist: John M. Lyle, Architect* (Toronto: Coach House, 2009), 125–7; Geoffrey Hunt, *John M. Lyle: Toward a Canadian Architecture/Créer une architecture canadienne* (Kingston, ON: Agnes Etherington Art Centre, Queen's University, 1982); Boyde Beck, *Art in Architecture: Toronto Landmarks, 1920–1940* (Toronto: City of Toronto Archives, 1987), 15–18.

24 "Architectural and Allied Arts Show," *Saturday Night (Toronto)*, 5 February 1927, and "Canada's Architectural Movement," *Saturday Night (Toronto)*, 27 March 1927.

25 *Toronto Star*, 29 March 1927. The members of the group were named in *Saturday Night* (27 March 1927) as Lyle, Mackenzie Waters, W.L. Somerville, A.S. Mathers, Eric W. Haldenby, Bruce H. Wright, and C.B. Cleveland.

26 In fact, a conventional Beaux Arts design completed in 1906 as described in Chapter 1, and Larry Wayne Richards, *University of Toronto: The Campus Guide* (New York: Princeton Architectural Press, 2009), 66–7.

27 *Toronto Star*, 29 March 1927.

28 Lyle, "Canadian Decorative Forms," address to the RAIC convention with illustrations, 19 February 1932, *RAIC Journal* 9, no. 3 (1932)

29 McArthur, *Lyle*, 133–45; William Dendy and William Kilbourn, *Toronto Observed: Its Architecture, Patrons and History* (Toronto: Oxford University Press, 1986), 224–5.

30 Lyle was not alone; in 1927 James Blomfield, an architectural decorator and stained glass maker, argued that there was no need for the designer to cling to classical Greek devices like acanthus leaves: "Let him derive inspiration from the common burdock of the roadside, from the flower and leaf of the native water lily, the sculptural flowerhead, seedpod and leafage of the great milkweed, or any other of a dozen types of native flora which will suggest formal shape and bulk for the required purpose." And why palm fronds, asked Blomfield, when one could use the pine, spruce, cedar, tamarack, hemlock, or fir "whose dark and nobly standing strength give our native landscape such an aspect of pure power?" James Blomfield, "Native Floral and Arboreal Themes in Architectural Decoration," *Construction* 20, no. 12 (1927).

31 That is, Corinthian capitals on pillars.

32 "Correspondence," Arthur to editor, n.d., *RAIC Journal* 11, no. 1 (1934); Fleury, "From Our 'Foreign Correspondent,'" *RAIC Journal* 15, no. 2 (1938); Hunt, *John M. Lyle*, 60.

33 "Toronto Chapter Exhibition," *Construction* 24, no. 2 (1931); Katharine Clive, "The Canadian Galatea Comes to Life, The Development of a National Movement in Art and Decoration," Parts 1 and 2, *CHG* 8, nos. 1 and 2 (1931).

34 "Correspondence," "Evolution" to editor, n.d., *RAIC Journal* 11, no. 3 (1934).

35 Sandra Cohen-Rose, *Northern Deco: Art Deco Architecture in Montreal* (Montreal: Corona, 1996), 11–33.

36 McArthur, *Lyle*, 132–3; "Address by John M. Lyle" to RAIC Luncheon, February, 1929, *RAIC Journal* 6, no. 4 (1929).

37 Ann Elizabeth Wilson, "Spring Fabrics and What To Do with Them," CHG 3, no. 4 (1926).
38 Mary-Etta Macpherson, "Wanted: A Name," CHG 5, no. 11 (1928).
39 Minerva Wilson, "New Fads versus Old Traditions," CHG 5, no. 2 (1928).
40 Herbert Hodgins's editorials, CHG 5, nos. 3 and 4 (1928).
41 Editorial, CHG 7, no. 12 (1930). Macpherson had now become associate editor.
42 For an expansive catalogue of surviving structures, see Tim Morawetz, *Art Deco Architecture in Toronto: A Guide to the City's Buildings from the Roaring Twenties and the Depression* (Toronto: Glue Inc., 2009).
43 Eric Arthur, "Toronto Chapter O.A.A. Architectural Exhibition," RAIC *Journal* 3, no. 2 (1926).
44 *Construction* 20, nos. 5 and 7 (1927).
45 Eric Arthur, "Toronto Chapter Architectural Exhibit," RAIC *Journal* 6, no. 3 (1929). Brown (1884–1945) was born in Scotland, studied at University College, Dundee, and the Royal Academy in London before emigrating in 1914 when he joined Charles Cobb's office for two years, then set up his own practice.
46 The jury consisted of City Architect J.J. Woolnough, Canadian National Exhibition (CNE) vice-president Samuel Harris, CNE director T.A. Russell, CNE planning commission chair G.T. Irving, OAA president W.L. Somerville, Auto Manufacturers' Association secretary S.W. Hobart, and Mayor Samuel McBride.
47 Harold Kalman, *A History of Canadian Architecture*, vol. 2 (Toronto: Oxford University Press, 1994), 759–60; Morawetz, *Art Deco in Toronto*, 67–9; "Awards in the Competition for an Automotive Building for the Canadian National Exhibition, Toronto," RAIC *Journal* 6, no. 1 (1929); H.H.K., "The Automotive Building, Canadian National Exhibition, Toronto," RAIC Journal 6, no. 11 (1929); "Canada Permanent Building, Toronto," *Construction* 23, no. 3 (1930).
48 For a discussion of Brown, including his design for the Belsize Theatre, see "Sinaiticus," "An Appreciation," *Construction* 20, no. 5 (1927). "Toronto Chapter Exhibition" (*Construction* 24, no. 2 [1931]) notes that Brown's design for the Capitol Theatre in Sudbury, Ontario was ultra-modern and highly impressionistic; Morawetz, *Art Deco in Toronto* devotes an entire section to movie houses (119–31).
49 "Sinaiticus," "Two Smaller 'Modern' Buildings," *Construction* 22, no. 12 (1929).
50 "Sinaiticus," "Traditionalism in the Twentieth Century," *Construction* 22, no. 6 (1929). This article also names other new "Tudor" buildings, including Oxford University Press on University Avenue and the Paterson Building on Richmond Street West, which housed stockbrokers, both by Sproatt and Rolph.
51 McArthur, *Lyle*, 132–3; "Address by John Lyle" [to RAIC lunch, February, 1929], RAIC *Journal* 6, no. 4 (1929).
52 W.S. Maxwell, "Exhibition of Drawings, Decorations and Sculpture Representing the Work of Canadian and American Universities and Schools," RAIC *Journal* 7, no. 3 (1930).
53 Carlu, "Tradition and Modernism," RAIC *Journal* 8, no. 5 (1931); Blake, "The New Interest in Architecture," ibid.
54 "Residential Work in Canada," *Construction* 11, no. 6 (1918).
55 Liz Lundell, *The Estates of Old Toronto* (Erin, ON: Boston Mills Press, 1997), 144–7, 149.
56 For a discussion of several of Brown's homes in North Toronto, see "Residential Work in Canada," *Construction* 17, no. 9 (1924).
57 W.L. Somerville, "The Formal City House" CHG 4, no. 6 (1927); "Suiting the Texture to the Style," CHG 5, no. 8 (1928); W.L. Somerville, "Recent Domestic Architecture in the Province of Ontario," RAIC *Journal* 5, no. 7 (1928); W.L. Somerville, "First Aid for Home Builders," CHG 8, no. 8 (1931).
58 "Stucco and Hollow Tile Houses," *Construction* 15, no. 10 (1922).The discovery of the description of this unusual building I owe to Mark Fram.
59 "The Bulletin Board," CHG 12, no. 4 (1935).
60 "Small Homes and Their Plans," CHG 4, no. 6 (1927).
61 "The Old Mill on the Humber and Home Smith and Co. Office" and James Blomfield, "Building with the Landscape" (quoted), *Construction* 22, no. 8 (1929).
62 Dendy and Kilbourn, *Toronto Observed*, 237; Kalman, *Canadian Architecture*, vol. 2, 747; Eric Arthur, "Toronto Chapter Architectural Exhibit," RAIC *Journal* 6, no. 3, (1929).
63 Fletcher's *A History of Architecture on the Comparative Method* first appeared in 1896, and subsequent additions were heavily relied upon by the profession.
64 Mary-Etta Macpherson, "The Progress of Canadian Architecture," CHG 6, no. 4 (1929);

Eric Arthur, "Toronto Chapter Architectural Exhibit," *RAIC Journal* 6, no. 3 (1929).

65 "Proceedings of the 22nd General Annual Meeting of RAIC," *RAIC Journal* 6, no. 3 (1929); "Architecture in Review: Impressions from the Third Biennial Architectural Exhibition at the Art Gallery of Ontario," *CHG* 8, no. 3 (1931). Though unsigned the latter article seems unmistakably to bear the stamp of Eric Arthur's style.

66 "Designs Submitted in a Competition for a Club House for the University Club of Toronto," *RAIC Journal* 5, no. 2 (1928).

67 Walter Moorhouse, "Building Height Limitations in Downtown Districts," *RAIC Journal* 1, no. 2 (1924); Report of OAA Toronto chapter secretary I. Markus. The other members of the committee besides Moorhouse were John Pearson and F.H. Marani.

68 Moorhouse, "Building Height Limitation," *RAIC Journal* 1, no. 4 (1924); *Construction* 17, no. 9 (1924).

69 *Toronto Star* qtd. in editorial on "The Skyscraper Problem" and "The Metropolitan Building," *Construction* 18, no. 7 (1925).

70 Editorial on "The Problem of the Skyscraper," *RAIC Journal* 5, no. 1 (1928). See also *Construction* 20, no. 11 (November 1927), which listed a great many new development proposals.

71 "Sinaiticus," "Canada Permanent Building, Toronto," *Construction* 23, no. 3 (1930). There was, however, no opportunity for the Torontonians, architects or otherwise, to see how the European avant-garde might have handled a skyscraper in practice, since neither Gropius, Le Corbusier, nor any of the others was ever actually commissioned to construct one at this time.

72 New York City's 1916 zoning law mandated setbacks and lot coverage limits for skyscrapers.

73 *Construction* 18, no. 9 (1925); "The Sterling Tower," *Construction* 22, no. 1 (1929).

74 William Dendy, *Lost Toronto* (Toronto: Oxford University Press, 1978), 142–5; Morawetz, *Art Deco in Toronto*, 24–5; "The Toronto Star Building," *RAIC Journal* 6, no. 4 (1929); "Sinaiticus," "The Star Building," *Construction* 22, no. 5 (1929).

75 Dendy and Kilbourn, *Toronto Observed*, 217; Morawetz, *Art Deco in Toronto*, 9–12.

76 Dendy and Kilbourn, *Toronto Observed*, 214; Morawetz, *Art Deco in Toronto*, 15–17; "Sinaiticus," "Canada Permanent Building, Toronto" *Construction* 23, no. 4 (1930); "Sinaiticus," "Thoughts Inspired by Toronto's Centennial Year," *Construction* 27, no. 2 (1934).

77 "Sinaiticus," "The Canadian Bank of Commerce, Toronto," *Construction* 24, no. 1 (1931); Dendy and Kilbourn, *Toronto Observed*, 222; Morawetz, *Art Deco in Toronto*, 18.

78 Kalman, *Canadian Architecture*, vol. 2, 768–70; "The Proposed Eaton Store Building in Toronto," *RAIC Journal* 5, no. 12 (1928).

79 "Sinaiticus," "Eaton's College Street Store," *Construction* 23, no. 11 (1930); Dendy, *Lost Toronto*, 46–9. Except for the seven-storey structure fronting on Yonge and College, the rest of the development was postponed owing to the Depression and was never completed, though an Eaton's store operated there until 1976.

80 Mary-Etta Macpherson, "The Smart Generation Furnishes a House," *CHG* 7, no. 6 (1930). The bedroom décor was the choice of my mother, Mrs. C.H.A. Armstrong.

81 John Lyle, "Monumental Architecture and Town Planning," *Construction* 14, no. 5 (1921); *Construction* 19, no. 5 (1926).

82 Bankrupt during the war, the Grand Trunk had been folded along with other depressed lines into the CNR.

83 Premier Howard Ferguson qtd. in "Annual Banquet of the RAIC," *RAIC Journal* 4, no. 4 (1927).

84 "Business and Beauty" in *Construction* 19, no. 7 (1926) lists the Ontario Realtors Board, the Toronto Convention and Tourists Association, and the past president of the Guild of Civic Arts as supporting a new street plan.

85 James Blomfield, "A City's Need," *Construction* 21, no. 3 (1928); S.G. Curry, "Toronto's Traffic Problem: With Suggestions for Its Solution," *Construction* 21, no. 5 (1928).

86 *Globe*, 9 February 1928.

87 Besides McBride the commission consisted of J.H. Gundy, stockbroker and president of North American Life Insurance; Thomas Bradshaw, former city finance commissioner and vice-president of North American Life; E.L. Cousens of the Toronto Harbour Commission; businessmen J. Allan Ross and H.H. Williams; R. Home Smith, whose development company held large acreage along the Humber River; and W.S.B. Armstrong as secretary (later replaced by Norman D. Wilson). The first

meeting was held on 1 June 1928. See *Globe*, 15 May, 31 May 1928.

88 Editorial, RAIC *Journal* 5, no. 6 (1928). Wilson, a later addition, was an engineer.

89 S.G. Curry, "A Further Study of Toronto's Traffic Problems," *Construction* 21, no. 9 (1928); James Blomfield, "Planning for To-morrow," *Construction* 21, no. 10 (1928).

90 Advisory City Planning Commission, *Report of the Advisory City Planning Commission* (Toronto, 1929), City of Toronto Archives, Toronto Public Library. For a brief account and illustrations, see Derek Hayes, *Historical Atlas of Toronto* (Toronto: Douglas and McIntyre, 2008), 138–40 and Dendy, *Lost Toronto*, 144–7.

91 See "Plan of the Central Area of the City of Toronto Showing Suggested Improvements to the Street System" and "Map of Toronto Area Showing Streets of Greater Width Than 66 Ft. Now Opened or Assured for the Traffic Requirements of the Future" in *Report of the Advisory City Planning Commission.*

92 *Globe*, editorials, 1 January 1929 and 15 February 1929.

93 *Report of the Civic Department Heads Re the Advisory City Planning Commission Report for the Improvement of the City of Toronto* (Toronto, 1929). The committee included the commissioners of finance, assessment, parks, streets, works, the city clerk, city solicitor, city auditor, city architect, the fire chief and the medical officer of health; *Globe*, 5 November, editorial 6 November, editorial 28 November, editorial 4 December 1929.

94 *Globe*, editorial 28 November 1929; 3, 12, 14 December 1929, 2 January 1930.

95 Rosalyn Berger, "History of Planning Organization in Toronto" (typescript, 23 February 1959), RG 32, box 78, City of Toronto Archives (hereafter CTA).

96 LeMay to Commissioner of Works, 8 December 1930 [marked "Not sent"]; draft of above letter, n.d. [marked "Original not sent out"]; leMay to Horrace L. Brittain, Bureau of Municipal Research, 10 December 1930, box 143182-4, Tracy leMay Papers, CTA.

97 Copies of bylaw of 2 November 1931, as slightly amended on 6 March 1933, box 143183-2, Tracy leMay Papers, CTA.

98 Various designs of roof trusses developed in the United States during the nineteenth century are illustrated and discussed in Betsy Hunter Bradley, *The Works: The Industrial Architecture of the United States* (New York: Oxford University Press, 1999), 182.

99 "New Structural Shop Required for Munitions Work," *Contract Record and Engineering Review* (hereafter *Contract Record*) 32, no. 42 (October 16, 1918).

100 "Three Quarters of a Million Dollars Worth of Buildings in Four Months," *Contract Record* 36, no. 52 (December 29, 1922).

101 Gerald T. Bloomfield, "Albert Kahn and Canadian Industrial Architecture," *Society for the Study of Architecture in Canada Bulletin* 10, no. 4 (1985). Bloomfield and others give the date of the opening of the Toronto assembly plant as 1916, but a loose leaf binder entitled "Properties and Buildings, Domestic and Overseas," which was once in the Ford of Canada archives, Oakville, ON, contains a whiteprint plan of the Toronto site, on which somebody has noted, "Bldg opened, Feby, 1915; See Ford Times."

102 Whiteprint of "Plan of Building, Toronto," in loose leaf binder entitled "Properties and Buildings, Domestic and Overseas," Ford of Canada Archives, Oakville, ON.

103 Grant Hildebrand, *Designing for Industry: The Architecture of Albert Kahn* (Cambridge, MA: MIT Press, 1974), 92.

104 See the Babcock-Wilcox and Goldie-McCulloch Limited advertisement in *Contract Record* 37, no. 52 (December 26, 1923).

105 See the advertisement by the Canadian Des Moines Steel Company, which describes the system as "the safest, surest and most economical," because "the water is always ready, independent of the accidents which afflict any community's water works system" and guaranteed reduced insurance rates, in *Contract Record* 37, no. 52 (December 26, 1923).

106 The Model T came only in black because all other paint colours were then subject to severe fading until General Motors developed a new variety of coloured paints.

107 These black and white prints each numbered, dated and labelled "Ford Assembly Plant, Toronto, Ontario, Albert Kahn, Arch." were in an envelope in the Ford of Canada archives, Oakville, Ontario, labelled "Construction Scenes, FOC Plant of Toronto," and are stamped on the back, "W.A. Young, Photographer and Picture Framing, 725 Danforth Ave., Toronto."

108 For a discussion and illustration of the Pond truss and its glazing and ventilation, see

Bradley, *The Works*, 196–8. In Toronto Kahn actually made the design more complicated by separating the two sides of the central M with a space, which allowed the construction railway to run right through the building as long as required before it was covered over with roofing and central *A* ventilator.

109 On the windows and shutters, see the advertisement for the A.B. Ormsby Company, Canadian distributors of Lupton windows, in *Contract Record* 37, no. 52 (December 26, 1923).

110 See advertisement for George R. Knight of Montreal in *Contract Record* 37, no. 52 (December 26, 1923).

111 This decorative brick and stone treatment was carried around the corner from the north to the west side of the building, which was visible from Danforth, but was not used on the other two sides.

112 At his Highland Park plant Ford had insisted on having four smokestacks to carry a huge "FORD" sign even though only two of the stacks were functional; see Lindy Biggs, *The Rational Factory: Architecture, Technology and Work in America's Age of Mass Production* (Baltimore: Johns Hopkins University Press, 1996), 103.

113 Bradley, *The Works*, 196.

114 A.S. Mathers, "Thirty-Five Years of Practice," RAIC *Journal* 32, no. 12 (1955).

115 Advertisement in *Telegram (Toronto)*, 20 April 1923.

116 W. Hawkins Ferry, *The Legacy of Albert Kahn* (Detroit: Wayne State University Press, 1987), 16, 21–2.

117 Terry Smith, *Making the Modern: Industry, Art and Design in America* (Chicago: University of Chicago Press, 1993), 92; Bradley, *The Works*, 257.

CHAPTER THREE

1 In the case of the United States, see Margaret Kentgens-Craig, *The Bauhaus and America, First Contacts, 1919–1936* (Cambridge, MA: MIT Press, 1999), Chapter 2.

2 Le Corbusier, *Towards a New Architecture*, trans. Frederick Etchells (London: John Rodker, 1927).

3 Martin Baldwin, review of *Towards a New Architecture* by Le Corbusier, RAIC *Journal* 6, no. 11 (1929).

4 Philip J. Turner, review of *Modern Architecture* by Bruno Taut, RAIC *Journal* 7, no. 5 (1930).

5 Henry-Russell Hitchcock and Philip Johnson, *The International Style: Architecture Since 1922* (New York: W.W. Norton, 1932); Museum of Modern Art, *Modern Architects* (New York: W.W. Norton, 1932). Neither the book nor the exhibition attracted any notice in the RAIC *Journal*.

6 Elizabeth Mock, "Built in the U.S.A – Since 1932," in *Built in the U.S.A., 1932–1944*, ed. Elizabeth Mock (New York: Museum of Modern Art 1944), 10.

7 Mary-Etta Macpherson, "The Canadian House of Today," *CHG* 6, no. 6 (1929).

8 Herbert Hodgins, Editorial, *CHG* 6, no. 10 (1929).

9 Tim Morawetz, *Art Deco Architecture in Toronto: A Guide to the City's Buildings from the Roaring Twenties and the Depression* (Toronto: Glue Inc., 2009), 115; William Dendy and William Kilbourn, *Toronto Observed: Its Architecture, Patrons and History* (Toronto: Oxford University Press, 1986), 245; "A Canadian Artist's Modern Home," *CHG* 8, no. 4 (1931). The house is at 2 Ava Crescent.

10 Biriukova's exact contribution to the design is unclear, since the plans for the house submitted to the city were actually signed by architect Douglas Kertland and some features resembled the work he had done on the CNE's Automotive Building in 1929 (see Chapter 2). Kertland was obviously sympathetic to Biriukova since he sponsored her registration as one of the first women architects in Ontario along with Harris and F.H. Marani. See Geoffrey Simmins, *Ontario Association of Architects: A Centennial History, 1889–1989* (Toronto: Ontario Association of Architects, 1989), 105–13.

11 The only other private residence pictured in Morawetz, *Art Deco in Toronto* (116) is a white stucco house by an unknown architect at 170 Strathearn Road dating from about 1938; the house has a rounded cornice and balcony, reminiscent of the streamlined contours for ocean liners right down to a porthole window. RAIC *Journal* 18, no. 6 (1941) also includes a photograph of "House of Mr. J.P. Martin, Armour Heights, Ontario, Paul Meschino, Architect," which shows a flat-roofed building on Armour Boulevard overlooking the valley of the West Don River; the

house has corner windows and a large full-height window protruding into the garden alongside a door, but no further information is given. The house appears to have been demolished to make way for Highway 401.

12 Hugh G. Jones, "The Architect's Place in the History of the Royal Canadian Academy," Part II, *RAIC Journal* 12, no. 12 (1935). On Cormier and his house, see Adele Freedman, *Sight Lines: Looking at Architecture and Design in Canada* (Toronto: Oxford University Press, 1990), 113–17, 123–6; and Harold Kalman, *A History of Canadian Architecture*, vol. 2 (Toronto: Oxford University Press, 1994), 776–8. Cormier was also the designer of the Stripped Classical Supreme Court building in Ottawa (which he was compelled to cap with a chateau-style roof) and of the University of Montreal, both of which find echoes in Carr Hall at St Michael's College at the University of Toronto, which he designed in the early 1950s. On Carr Hall, see Morawetz, *Art Deco in Toronto*, 94. The Pine Avenue house was ultimately acquired by Pierre Elliott Trudeau.

13 Eric Arthur, "A Review of the RAIC Exhibition," *RAIC Journal* 9, no. 12 (1932); "The RAIC Exhibition in Montreal," *RAIC Journal* 10, no. 12 (1933).

14 Steven Bell, "The McLean House," in *Eric Ross Arthur, Conservation in Context,* ed. Alec Keefer (Toronto: Toronto Regional Architectural Conservancy 2001), 108–22; Eric Arthur, "A Review of the RAIC Exhibition," *RAIC Journal* 9, no. 12 (1932).

15 "A House Designed for Modern Living," *CHG* 7, no. 8 (1930). See also "Winning Designs in the T. Eaton Co.'s Ideal Ontario Home Competition," *Construction* 23, no. 8 (1930). The *Construction* article complained of the design, while very modern and distinctive, saying, "it is a pity that Mr. Forbes rather fell down on his elevation."

16 "Modernizing in the 16th Century French Style," "Simplicity in the Colonial Spirit," "With an Old-World Spaciousness," "A Circular Hall for Diversion," *CHG* 7, no. 9, (1930).

17 Melville S. Mann, "The Modern Trend in Architectural Design," reprinted from "The Blue Bell," *Construction* 23, no. 12 (1930).

18 "Some House?" *Construction* 23, no. 7 (1930). The article calls the house's creator R. Buckmaster [sic] Fuller.

19 Percy Nobbs, "Present Tendencies Affecting Architecture in Canada," Part 1, "The Inheritance," *RAIC Journal* 7, no. 7 (1930); Part 2, "Modernity," *RAIC Journal* 7, no. 9 (1930); Part 3, "Adverse Influences," *RAIC Journal* 7, no. 11 (1930).

20 Editorial, *RAIC Journal* 7, no. 6 (1930).

21 Herbert Hodgins, "We Observe ...," *CHG* 8, no. 11 (1931); "Hodgins, "The Bulletin Board," *CHG* 11, no. 1–2 (1934).

22 Ruth M. Horne, "The French Furniture Styles, I: 16th Century," *CHG* 9, no. 1 (1932).

23 Hodgins, "We Observe ...," *CHG* 8, no. 12 (1931); Somerville, "A Georgian House to Cost $10,000," *CHG* 9, no. 1 (1932).

24 John Lyle, "Canadian Decorative Forms," speech to RAIC convention, 19 February 1932 in *RAIC Journal* 9, no. 3 (1932).

25 "Notes from the Architects' Show," and "Fashioned of Enduring Stone," *CHG* 10, no. 3 (1933).

26 Eric Arthur, "The RAIC Exhibition in Montreal," *RAIC Journal* 10, no. 12 (1933). Arthur was part of a jury with Percy Nobbs and J.O. Marchand of Montreal that declined to award a RAIC prize to Allward's design in the autumn of 1933.

27 Lyle to editor, n.d., *RAIC Journal* 11, no. 2 (1934).

28 "The Bulletin Board," *CHG* 11, no. 6–7 (1934); "Sinaiticus," "Thoughts Inspired by Toronto's Centennial Year," *Construction* 27, no. 4 (1934).

29 "Whither the Small House," *CHG* 10, no. 8 (1933).

30 "A Steel-Built House," *CHG* 13, no. 1–2 (January–February, 1936); Feature on the house "as modern as tomorrow," *CHG* 13, no. 8–9 (1936); Advertisement by Dominion Oilcloth and Linoleum, Montreal, *CHG* 13, no. 1–2 (1936); Advertisement by Piggott Construction, *CHG* 13, no. 6–7 (1936).

31 B. Evan Parry, "New Materials: New Methods," *CHG* 13, no. 1–2 (1936).

32 Percy Nobbs, "Recent Architecture in Canada," *RAIC Journal* 13, no. 9 (1936); Robin Montgomery to editor, n.d., *RAIC Journal* 13, no. 11 (1936).

33 "Build Now!" *CHG*, 13, no. 3 (1936).

34 Eric Venne, "The Modern Trend in Domestic Architecture" *RAIC Journal* 12, no. 7 (1935).

35 Milton Osborne, "The Modern and Traditional Interpretations of Architecture," *RAIC Journal* 13, no. 4 (1936).

36 H.H. Madill, "If I Were Building a House of My Own This Year, I'd Choose the Modern Style," CHG 14, no. 1–2 (1937). This issue of CHG also included B. Evan Parry's "I'd Follow Traditional Lines," a rather feeble plea not to abandon the spirit of the past but to adopt his proposed English cottage design.

37 Mackenzie Waters, "The New Architecture, Synopses of Radio Broadcasts," RAIC *Journal* 13, no. 3 (1936). Waters lived up to his word with a modernistic design for a resort on a steep rocky site at a lake north of Toronto using a prefabricated frame of steel pipe for a curving restaurant and verandah overlooking the water; see "The Deck, Elgin House, Lake Joseph, Muskoka," RAIC *Journal* 16, no. 7 (1939).

38 Eleanor Stephens, "Chasing Backgrounds," CHG 13, no. 3 (1936).

39 W.L. Somerville, "Why Modern? An Architect Speaks Out," CHG 15, no. 1–2 (1938).

40 R.S. Morris, "The Flat Roof," CHG 15, no. 1–2 (1938).

41 Kent Barker, "Commentary on RAIC Student Competition," RAIC *Journal* 14, no. 4 (1937); "Awards in the T. Eaton Company Architectural Competition for House Design," RAIC *Journal* 13, no. 7 (1936); "Small Houses to Cost $7,500: Two First Prize Modern Designs," CHG 13, no. 8–9 (1936). The other prizewinner was also a modernist design by F. Hilton Wilkes and Richard Fisher.

42 Alec Keefer, "Eric Arthur's Career: An Overview," in *Eric Ross Arthur*, 56.

43 Architect A.S. Mathers recollected that it was John Lyle with the help of Mackenzie Waters who helped rescue the journal from deficits and insolvency during the late 1930s and to install a new format and typography and make it sound financially with Arthur as editor; see Mathers, "Thirty-Five Years of Practice," RAIC *Journal* 32, no. 12 (1955).

44 Eric Arthur, "Review of the Sixth Biennial Toronto Chapter Exhibition," RAIC *Journal* 14, no. 2 (1937).

45 "Circumspice," "We See Ourselves as Others See Us," RAIC *Journal* 14, no. 9 (1937).

46 Eric Arthur, "Editorial Note," RAIC *Journal* 15, no. 1 (1938). "Chu Chin Chow" was a First World War-vintage musical review.

47 Eric Arthur, "Editorial"; Neutra, "Time and the Individual in Architecture"; RAIC *Journal* 15, no. 7 (1938).

48 Eric Arthur, "Editorial," RAIC *Journal* 15, no. 5 (1938).

49 A.H. Gregg, "New Styles and Old," CHG 15, no. 6 (1938).

50 Anthony Adamson, "Lion Among Sheep," RAIC *Journal* 15, no. 11 (1938).

51 RAIC *Journal* 15, no. 6 (1938).

52 Humphrey Carver, review of *An Introduction to Modern Architecture* by J.M. Richards, RAIC *Journal* 17, no. 10 (1940).

53 Peter W. Moore, "Zoning and Neighbourhood Change in the Annex in Toronto, 1900–1970," PhD diss., University of Toronto, 1978), 129–36, 142–3, and map, figure 4.1, 137.

54 Richard Dennis, "Interpreting the Apartment House: Modernity and Metropolitanism in Toronto, 1900–1930," *Journal of Historical Geography* 20, no. 3 (1994): 306.

55 On Lawrence Park, see Derek Hayes, "The Garden Suburb," in *Historical Atlas of Toronto* (Vancouver: Douglas and McIntyre, 2008), 114–17.

56 Moore, "Zoning and Neighbourhood Change," 138–48.

57 City of Toronto, *Report of the Lieutenant-Governor's Committee on Housing Conditions in Toronto* (Toronto, 1934), 13.

58 Chaired by Bruce the committee included two professors from the University of Toronto's Department of Social Science, E.J. Urwick and H.H. Cassidy; businessman J.J. Gibson; chair of the Council of the Federation for Community Service, Mrs. Beryl Plumptre; and Professor H. Wasteneys from the University Settlement house.

59 Albert Rose, *Regent Park, A Study in Slum Clearance* (Toronto: University of Toronto Press, 1958), 103–5, 126–30, 153–8; Kenneth H. Rogers, *Street Gangs in Toronto* (Toronto: Ryerson Press, 1945).

60 Lewis Duncan, *Report on Housing for the City of Toronto*, 23 June 1942, box 143176–7, Tracy leMay Papers, CTA.

61 Rosalyn Berger, "History of Planning Organization in Toronto," (typescript, 23 February 1959), box 78, RG 32, CTA.

62 Moore, "Zoning and Neigbourhood Change," 151–6.

63 Remarks by leMay to public meeting at Jarvis Collegiate, 16 September 1941, box 143184-1, leMay Papers, CTA.

64 Remarks by leMay to public meeting at Harbord Collegiate, 7 October 1941, box 143184-1, leMay Papers, CTA.

65 Remarks by leMay to public meeting at Malvern Collegiate, 3 October 1941, box 143184-1, leMay Papers, CTA.

66 Remarks by leMay to public meeting at Jarvis Collegiate, 16 September 1941, box 143184-1, leMay Papers, CTA.

67 LeMay and Bland qtd. in Peter W. Moore, "Zoning and Planning: The Toronto Experience, 1904–1970," in *The Usable Urban Past: Planning and Politics in the Modern Canadian City*, eds. Alan F.J. Artibise and Gilbert A. Stelter (Toronto: Macmillan, 1979), 329–30.

68 *Report of Independent Committee on Zoning*, 10 September 1942, box 143176-7, leMay Papers, CTA.

69 Ibid.

70 "A Georgian Mansion" *CHG* 9, no. 2 (1932); "A Late Georgian Style for Canadian Needs," *CHG* 8, no. 4 (1931).

71 Dendy and Kilbourn, *Toronto Observed*, 229–31, 233, 235.

72 Ibid., 231–5; Liz Lundell, *The Estates of Old Toronto* (Erin, ON: Boston Mills Press, 1997), 154, 160. Frank Wood ran the brokerage firm of Baillie, Wood, and Croft, and Perry the Assurance Securities Corporation.

73 Lundell, *The Estates of Old Toronto*, 163–7. The Eglinton Hunt kept its hounds at Graydon Hall until 1950.

74 Dendy and Kilbourn, *Toronto Observed*, 228; Morawetz, *Art Deco in Toronto*, 20–3; Christopher Armstrong, *Blue Skies and Boiler Rooms: Buying and Selling Securities in Canada, 1870–1940* (Toronto: University of Toronto Press, 1997), 229.

75 The building was actually built in two separate and unconnected sections: the west wing and projecting central pavilion with its six Ionic columns dating from 1929 to 1931; and the east wing added in 1934–35. See Janet Wright, *Crown Assets, The Architecture of the Department of Public Works, 1867–1967* (Toronto: University of Toronto Press, 1997), 163–5.

76 Ibid. 177, 181. Figure 3.16 shows a curiosity of the building completed in 1937 in the monogram "ER" over the door, representing its construction during the brief reign of Edward VIII.

77 Wright, *Crown Assets*, 181–2, plate 6.20 and coloured plate (unpaginated) show these details; Morawetz, *Art Deco in Toronto*, 81–3.

78 E. Boyde Beck, *Art in Architecture: Toronto Landmarks, 1920–1940* (Toronto: City Clerk's Department, 1988), 28.

79 Beck, *Toronto Landmarks*, 31.

80 In the 1920s the development of Ancroft Place in south Rosedale off Sherbourne Street had grouped houses (but not apartments) around a kind of close, a layout that had proven popular with residents.

81 "Garden Court Apartments, Leaside, Ontario, Forsey Page and Steele, Architects," *RAIC Journal* 16, no. 11 (1939); H.H. Madill, "Massey Medals for Architecture," *RAIC Journal* 28, no. 2 (1951); "Garden Court Apartments, Toronto (1939–41, An Editorial Comment," and Harold G. Peppiat to editor, *Canadian Architect* 3, nos. 6–7 (1958); Dendy and Kilbourn, *Toronto Observed*, 246–8; Kalman, *History of Canadian Architecture*, vol. 2, 774–5; Morawetz, *Art Deco in Toronto*, 111–13.

CHAPTER FOUR

1 Aid to Britain from the United States was vitally important, but the Roosevelt administration was constrained by the extent of anti-war sentiment and legislation like the Neutrality Act until the Japanese attack on Pearl Harbour in December 1941 and the declaration of war on the United States by the Nazi regime.

2 The ideas propagated by the Congrès internationaux d'architecture moderne (CIAM), which had held a number of meetings before the Second World War, had been brought to Canada from Britain by people connected to MARG who helped to found ARGs in Montreal, Toronto, Vancouver, and Ottawa. See H. Peter Oberlander, "Twenty Years of Architectural Growth, 1928–1948," *RAIC Journal* 25, no. 6 (1948).

3 John Layng, "Tomorrow's Work," *RAIC Journal* 19, no. 1 (1942).

4 "Provincial Page" (Ontario) by Gladstone Evans, *RAIC Journal* 19, no. 1 (1942); Eric Arthur, "Editorial," *RAIC Journal* 20, no. 7 (1943).

5 "Canadian Architecture Shown at the United National Educational, Scientific and Cultural Organization in Paris," *RAIC Journal* 24, no. 3 (1947).

6 CHG 20, no. 9–10 (1943) is the first issue of the magazine that openly anticipates an Allied victory and includes Perry's article and "Prefabrication Contributes to Progress." See also "Glass In Your Postwar Home" and "Accent on Plastics," CHG 20, no. 9–10 (1943).

7 "Six Opinions of Prefabrication," CHG 21, no. 1–2 (1944).

8 "Looking Forward," "Urban Modern," and "A Home in Bayview, Ontario," CHG 21, no. 11 (1944).

9 "Invitation to Sunlight," "Heating the Sun House," CHG 21, no. 11 (1944).

10 W.L. Somerville, "A 'Help-less' House for a Family of Four," CHG 22, no. 2 (1945); Frances C. Steinhoff, "Our Garden Editor Landscapes," CHG 22, no. 3 (1945).

11 The list included stables, laundries, butcher shops, stores, factories, blacksmiths, dog kennels, veterinary hospitals, plumbers, machine shops, theatres, private hospitals, public dancehalls, undertakers, tents, junk shops, junkyards, second-hand shops, builders' yards where coal, coke, or other fuel was stored, slaughterhouses, and the sale of goods on private lands.

12 Box 143184-1, Tracy LeMay Papers, CTA contains verbatim transcripts of the meetings, including the one at Oakwood Collegiate Institute, 14 October 1941, which is quoted here.

13 Report of the Independent Committee on Zoning, 10 September 1942, box 143176-7, Tracy leMay Papers, CTA.

14 J.P. Maher to A.G. Partridge, n.d. [July 1942], box 143186-2, Tracy leMay Papers, CTA.

15 City Planning Board, *Second Annual Report*, 31 December 1943. Chair A.G. Partridge, president of Goodyear Tire, was joined by Board of Trade General Manager F.D. Tolchard, C.J. Woolsey, Toronto and District Labour Council, TTC chair W.C. McBrien, architecture professor E.R. Arthur, along with Alderman D.M. Fleming and leMay plus Art Gallery of Toronto Director Martin Baldwin as executive secretary, while the Advisory Technical Committee included engineers A.E.K. Bunnell and S.R. Frost, architect A.S. Mathers, planning consultant E.G. Faludi and landscape architect H.B. Dunnington Grubb along with a Civic Officials Committee consisting of department heads.

16 leMay to Walter Blucher, executive director of ASPO, 2 June 1943, box 143182-5, leMay Papers, CTA. Blucher replied on 10 June that he could not name a single US city with a master plan that met his ideals by dealing with all aspects of community development, though Cincinnati had had a plan since 1925 while Detroit and Cleveland were only in the preparatory stages.

17 The following paragraphs are based upon City Planning Board, *Second Annual Report*, 31 December 1943, of which a condensed version was published as City Planning Board of Toronto, *The Master Plan for the City of Toronto and Its Environs*, 31 December 1943.

18 RAIC *Journal* 21, no. 6 (1944), on which the following paragraphs are based. Adamson had written extensively on the subject and Faludi had played an important role in devising the master plan.

19 79,460 votes for and 8,592 against; *Globe and Mail*, 2 January 1946. For a thorough analysis of the construction of Toronto's early subway lines, see Jay Young, "Searching for a Better Way: Subway Life and Metropolitan Growth in Toronto, 1942–1978" (PhD diss., York University, 2012).

20 Rhodri Windsor Liscombe, "Modes of Modernizing: The Acquisition of Modernist Design in Canada," *Society for the Study of Architecture in Canada Bulletin* 18, no. 3 (1994): 63.

21 Memorandum from leMay, "Alternative Proposals for New Housing," 11 October 1945, box 143181-1, leMay Papers, CTA.

22 Albert Rose, *Regent Park: A Study in Slum Clearance* (Toronto: University of Toronto Press, 1958), 46–73.

23 John Dakin, *Toronto Planning: A Planning Review of the Legal and Jurisdictional Contexts from 1912 to 1970* ([Toronto]: Department of Urban and Regional Planning, University of Toronto, 1974), 14–25.

24 LeMay chaired an advisory committee on the new legislation composed of two architects, two planners, and two surveyors; surprisingly, it was the architects who opposed direct design controls on the grounds that however good in theory, they always proved highly controversial in practice. See Minutes of the Professional Associations Committee, January–February 1946, box 143182-1, leMay Papers, CTA.

25 Eugene Faludi, "Designing New Canadian Communities: Theory and Practice," *Journal of the American Institute of Planners* (hereafter *JAIP*), 16, no. 3 (1950), 71–3. On Faludi see also John Sewell, *The Shape of the City:*

Toronto Struggles with Modern Planning (Toronto: University of Toronto Press, 1993), 55–64.
26 Eugene Faludi, "Communities Must Lose Their 'Topsy' Mentality"; "This Is a Planned Community"; CHG, 22, no. 3–4 (1945); Faludi, "Designing New Canadian Communities: Theory and Practice," JAIP 16, no. 3 (1950), 73–6.
27 Faludi, "Designing New Canadian Communities," 77–9.
28 Toronto City Planning Board, "Notice of Public Meetings," 1 December 1 1947, 19, 21, 25, 27, box 143182-3, leMay Papers, CTA; text of address by leMay to meetings, November 1947; *Report of the City of Toronto Planning Board*, 16 December 1947 (mimeo).
29 leMay to S.R. Frost, 15 October 1948, box 143182-3, leMay Papers, CTA. Frost was a member of the voluntary Independent Committee on Zoning active in 1940–41.
30 Toronto City Planning Board, *Third Report and Official Plan*, 21 June 1949 as amended 21 March 1950, including Maher to Mayor Hiram McCallum, 1 September 1949.
31 Bureau of Municipal Affairs, "Civic Affairs," 30 September 1949 (mimeo), box 143182-5, leMay Papers, CTA.
32 City Solicitor W.G. Angus to Property Committee chair Frank Nash, 14 September 1950, box 134182-6, leMay Papers, CTA.
33 Maher and leMay to Property Committee, 18 June 1951, quoted in City of Toronto Planning Board, "Extract from 4th Report," 1 January 1952, box 143184-3, leMay Papers, CTA.
34 Two new sub-zones were created: R.1A for areas where aging large houses were being converted to flats and permitting their replacement by new types of multiple housing that would not affect the character of a neighbourhood deleteriously, and R.4A, which allowed institutions and non-profit organizations to construct offices on or near major arteries or shopping areas that would be less attractive to apartment developers than other R.4 areas.
35 *Globe and Mail*, 6 November 1951.
36 Board of Trade president J. Gerald Godsoe and general manager F.D. Tolchard to Property Committee, 11 December 1951, box 143184-3, leMay Papers, CTA.
37 leMay to secretary of Winnipeg Zoning Board, 11 December 1952, box 143184-3, leMay Papers, CTA.
38 The new bylaw halved the requirement that developers provide one off-street parking space for each unit in multiple residential building to one space per two units, and in R.1A areas new multiple dwellings were now permitted to cover 35 percent of lot area (versus the proposed 25 percent) and the front yard setback was reduced to twenty feet (from twenty-five feet).
39 leMay to Board of Trade general manager F.D. Tolchard, 7 January 1952; leMay to Lawrence Orton, New York Planning Commission, 6 November 1952; "Notes on the Toronto Zoning Bylaw," Toronto Planning Board newsletter, 22 April 1953, box 143184-3, leMay Papers, CTA.
40 "Toronto Zoning Bylaw," Decision on Toronto bylaw 18642 amended by 18878, by W.J. Moore and R.C. Rowland, 25 January 1954, L.R. Cumming office files, box 7, Ontario Municipal Board records, RG-37-01-02, Archives of Ontario.
41 See Dakin, *Toronto Planning*, 31–3.
42 "The Provincial Page" (Ontario) by Barker, RAIC *Journal* 22, no 7 (1945); Walker, "The Architect and the Post-War World, An Address Given at the Fifty-Sixth Annual Meeting of the O.A.A.," RAIC *Journal* 23, no. 2 (1946). Walker was a New York architect who had edited the US journal *Pencil Points*.
43 John Caulfield Smith, "A Case For Modern," CHG 23, no. 5 (1946).
44 "Object Lesson in Today's Architecture," CHG 23, no. 11 (1946).
45 Eric Arthur, "Editorial," RAIC *Journal* 29, no. 5 (1952).
46 See Rhodri Windsor Liscombe, *The New Spirit: Modern Architecture in Vancouver, 1938–1963* (Vancouver: Douglas and McIntyre, 1997), 26.
47 Eric Arthur, "Editorial," RAIC *Journal* 24, no. 6 (1947).
48 John B. Parkin, "Post-War Planning of Schools," RAIC *Journal* 19, no. 9 (1942); Parkin, "Tomorrow's Schools"; RAIC *Journal* 20, no. 7 (1943); Parkin, "Sunnylea Schooh, Toronto, Ontario," RAIC *Journal* 21, no. 11 (1944).
49 Eric Arthur "Editorial," RAIC *Journal* 24, no. 10 (1947).
50 The jury consisted of RAIC president J. Roxborough Smith, Ottawa architect J.W. Balharrie, and Harvard Dean Joseph Hudnut.
51 H.H. Madill, "Massey Medals for Architecture," RAIC *Journal* 28, no. 2 (1951).

52 Eric Arthur, "Editorial," RAIC *Journal* 24, no. 2 (1947).
53 Larry Wayne Richards, *University of Toronto: The Campus Guide* (New York: Princeton Architectural Press, 2009), 49–50, 70–1, 111–12, 180–2. The only notable departure from the Georgian was Darling and Pearson's 1925 Gothic block on Hoskin Avenue for the Anglican-affiliated Trinity College, an institution once separate from the secular University of Toronto with its own 1851 Gothic building on Queen Street West; Trinity federated with the university in 1904 but only moved into a new home on the main campus twenty years later.
54 Rhodri Windsor Liscombe argues that between the wars Arthur had "almost single-handedly infiltrated Modernist ideas into the University of Toronto School of Architecture," and in addition to familiarizing students with current periodicals had used a series of books extending from Johnson and Hitchcock's *The International Style* (1932) to Sigfried Giedion's *Space, Time and Architecture* (1941), the latter becoming particularly influential in Canadian architectural schools. See Windsor Liscombe, *The New Spirit*, 30–1.
55 Eric Arthur, "Editorial," RAIC *Journal* 17, no. 9 (1940) and 27, no. 4 (1950).
56 S.J. White, "University of Toronto Exhibition, 'Architecture and You'," RAIC *Journal* 25, no. 5 (1948).
57 Martin L. Friedland, Introduction to *University of Toronto: The Campus Guide* by Richards, 27–8; Eric Arthur, "University of Toronto Master Plan," RAIC *Journal* 30, no. 10 (1953). Not until the late 1950s was Arthur's own architectural firm commissioned to produce the rather pallid Women's Athletic Building (1959) on Harbord Street at Huron; see Richards, *University of Toronto*, 171–2.
58 The building was demolished in the 1960s to make way for a new Medical Sciences Building.
59 Eric Arthur, "Editorial," RAIC *Journal* 30, no. 10 (1953).
60 Fisher, "Mechanical [Engineering] Building, University of Toronto, RAIC *Journal* 26, no. 6 (1949); Richards, *University of Toronto*, 75–6; see also Marc Baraness, "Building Modern Ideas," in *Toronto Modern: Architecture 1945–1965*, 2nd ed., ed. Bureau of Architecture and Urbanism (Toronto: Coach House Press, 2002), 21–2, 46–9.
61 See Janet Wright, *Crown Assets: The Architecture of the Department of Public Works, 1867–1867* (Toronto: University of Toronto Press, 1997), 185–6. These buildings are discussed in the previous chapter.
62 Campbell Merrett, "News from the Institute" (Quebec), RAIC *Journal* 25, no. 7 (1948).
63 Eric Arthur, "Editorial," RAIC *Journal* 25, no. 7 (1948); Arthur, "University of Toronto Master Plan," RAIC *Journal* 30, no. 10 (1953).
64 The building is neither indicated on the map nor mentioned in the entry for the one-time university observatory next to which it once stood. See Richards, *University of Toronto*, 51–2.
65 Harold Kalman, *A History of Canadian Architecture*, vol. 2 (Toronto: Oxford University Press, 1994), 782–3; Tim Morawetz, *Art Deco Architecture in Toronto: A Guide to the City's Buildings from the Roaring Twenties and the Depression* (Toronto: Glue Inc., 2009), 26–7.
66 Boyde Beck, *Art in Architecture, Toronto Landmarks, 1920–1940* (Toronto: City of Toronto Archives, 1987), 31. These buildings are discussed in the previous chapter.
67 A.S. Mathers, "Housing and Building Construction," RAIC *Journal* 17, no. 5 (1940).
68 "Standard Chemical Company Limited, Toronto, Ontario," RAIC *Journal* 25, no. 6 (1948); Allward and Gouinlock, "Maclean-Hunter Publishing Company Limited, Toronto," RAIC *Journal* 26, no. 6 (1949).
69 M.F. Allan, "The Canadian National Exhibition Grandstand," RAIC *Journal* 28, no. 6 (1949); Clare D. Carruthers, "Structural Features for the Canadian National Exhibition Grandstand," ibid.; John Martins-Manteiga, *Mean City: From Architecture to Design: How Toronto Went Boom!* (Toronto: Dominion Modern, 2005), 68–71.
70 The Parkin firm also won silver medals for ecclesiastical buildings for Toronto's Central Christadelphian Church and for Humber Memorial Hospital in the suburb of Weston.
71 RAIC *Journal* 31, no. 6 (1954) contains photos and plans of other plants in the Toronto with designs displaying modernist flourishes: Taylor Instrument Companies, North York, (Parkin Associates), Lucas Rotax, Scarborough (Howard D. Chapman), Canada Packers, St Clair Avenue East, Toronto (Fleury and Arthur), Westeel Products, Toronto (Shore and Moffatt), Diamond T Trucks, Weston (Wilson and Newton), Rushton and Hornby Limited, Toronto (Wilson and Newton), Inglis-English

Electric Company, Scarborough (Allward and Gouinlock), Hunter Rose and Company, North York (Richard A. Fisher).

72 H.H. Madill, "Massey Medals for Architecture," RAIC *Journal* 28, no. 2 (1951).

73 Glenn McArthur, *A Progressive Traditionalist: John M. Lyle, Architect* (Toronto: Coach House, 2009), 162–7,192–5; William Dendy and William Kilbourn, *Toronto Observed: Its Architecture, Patrons and History* (Toronto: Oxford University Press, 1986), 252–3; A.S. Mathers, "The Bank of Nova Scotia Building," RAIC *Journal* 28, no. 11 (1951).

74 "Bank of Montreal, Toronto, Ontario, Chapman, Oxley and Facey [and] Marani and Morris, Architects, E.R. Blatherwick, Associate Architect," RAIC *Journal* 23, no. 3 (1946); R. Scholfield Morris, "Bank of Montreal Building, Toronto," and Cleeve Horne, " – And Sculpture," RAIC *Journal* 26, no. 11 (1949).

75 Stephen Vickers, "The Architecture in Sculpture," RAIC *Journal* 26, no. 1 (1949).

76 Kent Barker, "News from the Institute" (Ontario), RAIC *Journal* 26, no. 3 (1949).

77 Kalman, *Canadian Architecture*, 705.

78 Bureau of Architecture and Urbanism, *Toronto Modern: Architecture 1945–1965*.

79 Kelly Crossman, "The Meaning of White," in *Winnipeg Modern Architecture, 1945–1975*, ed. Serena Keshavjee (Winnipeg: University of Manitoba Press, 2006), 131, 136–7, 143.

80 Alan Gowans, *Looking at Architecture in Canada* (Toronto: Oxford University Press, 1958), 164–8.

81 Sydney Cooper "Are Canadians Too Conservative to Live in Modern Houses?" CHG 24, no. 10 (1947).

82 "Residential Interiors," RAIC *Journal* 24, no. 8 (1947). Work featured in these pictures was by Toronto architects, including Eric Arthur himself (with his partner W.E. Fleury), E.C.S. Cox, Gordon S. Adamson, Cameron, Murray and Fairfield, and Harry Seidler.

83 John Caulfield Smith, "Your Future Home Today," CHG 24, no. 4 (1947).

84 CHG 25, no. 1 (1948).

85 Eric Arthur, "Editorial," RAIC *Journal* 24, no. 4 (1947); 28, no. 6 (1951); 27, no. 2 (1950).

CHAPTER FIVE

1 James Lemon, *Toronto Since 1918: An Illustrated History* (Toronto: Lorimer, 1985), Tables 1 and 2.

2 When designing for himself a demonstration Trend House in Toronto for the British Columbia timber industry, Eric Arthur was forced to use a masonry ground floor clad in wood.

3 Frank Morgitsu, "What Stands Between You and a Better House?" CHG 31, no. 4 (1954).

4 Frank Morgitsu, "Why More Canadians Should Have 'Modern' Houses," CHG 31 no. 9 (1954).

5 Stanley Fillmore, "250 Acres of Homes," CHG 32, no. 5 (1955).

6 Faludi set up the firm in 1944 in partnership with architect Anthony Adamson.

7 H.J.A Reitsma, "North York: The Development of a Suburb" (MA thesis, University of Toronto, 1962), 43.

8 The following paragraphs are based mainly upon John Sewell, *The Shape of the City: Toronto Struggles with Modern Planning* (Toronto: University of Toronto Press, 1993), 80–95, and Valerio Rynnimeri, "A Plan for Don Mills: Design and Creation of the Canadian Corporate Suburb" (MA thesis, University of Guelph, 1997); see also Bureau of Architecture and Urbanism, *Toronto Modern Architecture 1945–1965*, 2nd ed. (Toronto: Coach House, 2002), 50–3.

9 See Donald Kerr and Deryck W. Holdsworth, *Historical Atlas of Canada*, vol. 3, *Addressing the Twentieth Century, 1891–1961* (Toronto: University of Toronto Press, 1990), Plate 60.

10 CMHC, "Housing Design," RAIC *Journal* 29, no. 9 (1952).

11 Industrial purchasers would be required to begin construction within three years or allow the developers to re-acquire the lands for the original price.

12 Richard W. White, *Urban Infrastructure and Urban Growth in the Toronto Region, 1950s to 1990s* (Toronto: Neptis Foundation, 2003 [CD version]), 11–13.

13 Bridges on Eglinton were built between 1954 and 1956.

14 "Toronto City Planning Board," 15 December 1945, box 143180-7, leMay Papers, CTA. This roadway was originally to link up to Mount Pleasant Road near Merton Street at the eastern edge of the city.

15 E.P. Taylor did consider approaching the American developer William Zeckendorf to become a partner but, perhaps fortunately, decided against the idea; Zeckendorf subsequently went bankrupt.

16 Sara Bowser, "The Architect and the Merchant Builder," *Canadian Architect*, Third issue, March 1956.

17 Remarks by A.L. McClaskey to "Panel on Housing," RAIC *Journal*, 34, no. 7 (1957); "Fighting Words about City Architecture," *Canadian Architect* 2, no. 9 (1957) reporting on the 11 June program of the show *Fighting Words*, where naval architect Grant Whatmough's remarks provoked general consternation.

18 "Row Housing, Don Mills, Ontario, Associate Architects, James A. Murray and Henry Fliess," RAIC *Journal* 34, no. 4 (1957); W.S. Goulding, "Terrace Houses in Ontario: An Urban Tradition Revived," RAIC *Journal* 34, no. 10 (1957); "Massey Medals for Architecture, 1958," RAIC *Journal* 35, no. 12 (1958).

19 "Canadian Housing Design Council 1958 Awards, Report of the National Jury," RAIC *Journal* 35, no. 6 (1958) records that nine awards were given out – two to Murray for 18 Ballyronan Road and 12 Plateau Crescent in Don Mills, as well as 54 Broadleaf Road, designed by Norman R. Stone.

20 Murray V. Jones, "Don Mills – A Partial Answer," *Canadian Architect* 2, no. 9 (1957); Sewell, *Shape of the City*, 96.

21 On the creation of Metro see Timothy Colton, *Big Daddy: Frederick G. Gardiner and the Building of Metropolitan Toronto* (Toronto: University of Toronto Press, 1980), chapter 3, 52–73. Each of the thirteen constituent municipalities would have its own elected council while Metro council was composed of the mayors and reeves plus eleven indirectly chosen members of the city council, who together elected the chair.

22 White, *Urban Infrastructure and Urban Growth in the Toronto Region*, 13–18.

23 "House of Mr. W.P. Schutte, Port Credit, Ontario, James A. Murray, Architect," RAIC *Journal* 27, no. 12 (1950); H.H. Madill, "Massey Medals for Architecture," RAIC *Journal* 28, no. 2 (1951).

24 "House of Mrs. M.H. Spaulding, Toronto, Ontario, James A. Murray, Architect," RAIC *Journal* 29, no. 11 (1952).

25 "Give Yourself Elegance When the Children Grow Up," *CHG* 30, no. 8 (1953).

26 Eric Arthur, "Editorial," RAIC *Journal* 28, no. 5 (1951).

27 Eric Arthur, "Editorial," RAIC *Journal* 29, no. 5 (1952).

28 Eric Arthur, "Editorial," RAIC *Journal* 31, no. 5 (1954).

29 "U.S. Consulate General Building, Toronto, Ontario, Mathers and Haldenby, Architects," *ibid.* 29, no. 8 (1952); "Bank of Canada, Toronto, Architects, Marani and Morris," and "Imperial Oil Ltd., Toronto, Architects, Mathers and Haldenby," ibid. 32, no. 6 (1955)

30 For this and other information on John C. Parkin, I am much indebted to Linda Fraser, Michael McMordie, and Geoffrey Simmins, who permitted me to see an advance proof of their book, *John C. Parkin, Archives and Photography: Reflections on the Practice and Presentation of Modern Architecture* (Calgary: University of Calgary Press, 2012), particularly "John C. Parkin in Conversation with Michael McMordie," which consists of the transcript of a 1975 interview by McMordie that was subsequently heavily annotated by Parkin. The original of this interview on tape and the transcript are in the Canadian Architectural Archives, University of Calgary.

31 McMordie, "John C. Parkin in Conversation."

32 Ibid.

33 "Parkin Collection," RAIC *Journal* 24, no. 7 (1947); Central Mortgage and Housing Corporation, *67 Homes for Canadians: Attractive Plans Designed Especially for Canadian Requirements, Including Prize Winners of the Canadian Small House Competition* (Ottawa: CMHC, 1947), 92.

34 McMordie, "John C. Parkin in Conversation."

35 Ibid.

36 Harold Kalman, *A History of Canadian Architecture*, vol. 2 (Toronto: Oxford University Press, 1994), 798–9; Geoffrey Simmins, *Ontario Association of Architects: A Centennial History, 1889–1989* (Toronto: OAA, 1989), 129–31; "OAA Headquarters Building," RAIC *Journal* 28, no. 5 (1951); "The Massey Medals for Architecture, 1955," RAIC *Journal* 32, no. 12 (1955). In a sign of the times the location was applauded in the RAIC *Journal* for the fact that "a ravine road skirting the park will take care of parking."

37 Local boosters argue over where the first of such centres was created with claims being made for both Park Royal in West Vancouver and Norgate in Montreal; see Rhodri Windsor Liscombe, *The New Spirit: Modern Architecture in Vancouver, 1938–1963* (Vancouver: Douglas and McIntyre, 1997), 159.

38 "Convenience Centre, Don Mills, Ontario, Architects and Engineers, John B. Parkin Associates," RAIC *Journal* 33, no. 2 (1956).

39 "Two Branch Banks, Don Mills, Ont.," *Canadian Architect* 2, no. 10 (1957).

40 "The Massey Medals for Architecture, 1955," RAIC *Journal* 32, no. 12 (1955).

41 "Ortho Pharmaceutical Corporation (Canada) Ltd., Don Mills, Ontario, Architects and Engineers, John B. Parkin Associates," RAIC *Journal* 32, no. 10 (1955); "Factory and Offices for Ortho Pharmaceutical, *Canadian Architect*, Seventh Issue, July 1956; W.P. Abrahamson to editor (quoted), *Canadian Architect* 2, no. 6 (1957); "Plant and Offices for Ortho Pharmaceutical (Canada) Ltd.," in *Toronto Modern Architecture*, 56–9.

42 "Office of John B. Parkin Associates, Don Mills, Ontario, Architects and Engineers, John B. Parkin Associates," RAIC *Journal* 33, no. 1 (1956). John C. Parkin wrote an obituary for the building when it was torn down in 1978, noting that the property had originally been intended for Ortho, who rejected it because the site was unsuitable for the two-storey building they wanted, and that at a later date the frame had been painted black; see Parkin, "1500 Don Mills Road," *Canadian Architect* 23, no. 5 (1978).

43 McMordie, "John C. Parkin in Conversation"; Detlef Mertins, "Mountain of Lights," in *Toronto Modern Architecture*, 13–14; "National Headquarters, Salvation Army in Canada and Bermuda, Toronto, John B. Parkin Associates, Architects," RAIC *Journal* 30, no. 9 (1953).

44 George Nelson, *Industrial Architecture of Albert Kahn, Inc.* (New York: Architectural Book Publishing 1939)

45 McMordie, "John C. Parkin in Conversation." See also McMordie, "John B. Parkin Associates and Albert Kahn Inc.: An Industrial View of Architecture," *Society for the Study of Architecture in Canada Bulletin*, 20, no. 1 (1999): 16–23 (reprinted in Fraser, McMordie, and Simmins, *John C. Parkin, Archives and Photography*) where McMordie nonetheless writes, "Asked in 1975 about models for the Parkin practice, at its peak in the 1960s the largest and most influential in Canada, John C. Parkin … dismissed the powerful and distinguished U.S. contemporary Skidmore, Owings and Merrill as a source of inspiration. Rather, he said, Albert Kahn's was the formative influence."

46 "Simpson-Sears Industrial Development, Etobicoke, Ontario, Architects and Engineers, John B. Parkin Associates," RAIC *Journal* 33, no. 2 (1956); "The Massey Medals for Architecture, 1955," RAIC *Journal* 32, no. 12 (1955). The Massey jury was composed of McGill University's John Bland, Gordon S. Adamson, Lawrence B. Anderson, and A.J.C. Paine.

47 Wood came as the winner of the British Columbia Lumber Manufacturers Association competition for timber frame houses.

48 Kenneth Wood, "Canada's Architectural Development: A View from Another World," *Canadian Architect* 4, no. 2 (1959).

49 John C. Parkin, "Architecture in Canada Since 1945: An Appraisal," RAIC *Journal* 39, no. 1 (1962).

50 John C. Parkin, "Modern Architecture in Ontario," in *Modern Canadian Architecture*, ed. Leon Whiteson (Edmonton: Hurtig, 1983), 122. Edmund Parkin retired from the firm in 1964 and John B. left and moved to Los Angeles in 1970, whereupon John C. became head of the reorganized Parkin Associates; see John C. Parkin, "1500 Don Mills Road," *Canadian Architect* 23, no. 5 (1978).

51 Page and Steele, "Richmond Street Office Building, Toronto, Ontario," "The Benvenuto, Toronto, Ontario," RAIC *Journal* 29, no. 6 (1952).

52 Dickinson was given a full biography in 2010 by John Martins-Manteiga, *Peter Dickinson* (Toronto: Dominion Modern, 2010), which also includes a catalogue of his projects, including uncompleted works.

53 Adele Freedman, "Introduction: West Coast Modernism and Points East," in *New Spirit*, 12. See also Freedman's essay on Dickinson's career in *Sight Lines: Looking at Architecture and Design in Canada* (Toronto: Oxford University Press, 1990), 1–31.

54 Martins-Manteiga, *Dickinson*, 58, includes a small sketch of the OAA entry; Dickinson, "News from the Institute" (Ontario), RAIC *Journal* 35, no. 5 (1954).

55 Martins-Manteiga, *Dickinson*, 116–17, reproduces a signed sketch of the project dating from 1951; Bureau of Architecture and Urbanism, *Toronto Modern Architecture*, 60–1.

56 Morden Yolles believed that the British American Oil Company building on the northwest corner of Bay and College Street, which he helped his father construct in 1950, was the first flat plate structure in Canada though the

columns had drops and the exterior was more Stripped Classical than Modern in design; see "Morden Yolles: Building In Concrete, Interview with Morden Yolles" by E.R.A. Architects, in *Concrete Toronto: A Guidebook to Concrete Architecture from the Fifties to the Seventies*, eds. Michael McClelland and Graeme Stewart (Toronto: Coach House Books, 2007), 300–1, and for a photograph of the BA Oil building, see Martins-Manteiga, *Dickinson*, 49; however, Kalman, *Canadian Architecture*, vol. 2, 805, states that flat-plate construction was used in apartment buildings in Vancouver's West End designed by engineers Read Jones Christofferson from 1949 on.

57 Martins-Maneiga, *Dickinson*, 116; Beth Kapusta and John McMinn, *Yolles: A Canadian Engineering Legacy* (Vancouver: Douglas and McIntyre, 2002), 39–40, 59. A flexible internal layout that alternated twenty-three-foot bays for living rooms and kitchens and sixteen-foot bays for bedrooms made it possible to expand one- or two-bedroom units as needed, and Morden Yolles used nine-inch thick slabs for the larger bays and 6.5 inches for the smaller ones, which saved considerable concrete; see "Interview with Morden Yolles" in *Concrete Toronto*, 302.

58 "Benvenuto Place Apartments, Toronto, Architects, Page and Steele," RAIC *Journal*, 33, no. 1 (1956); see also "Benvenuto Place," in *Toronto Modern*, 60–1, Martins-Manteiga, *Dickinson*, 118–21 for interior and exterior photographs, and Kalman, *Canadian Architecture*, vol. 2, 805–6.

59 Kapusta and McMinn, *Yolles*, 53–4

60 Martins-Manteiga, *Dickinson*, 144–5.

61 "Richmond Street Office Building, Toronto, Architects, Page and Steele," RAIC *Journal* 32, no. 5 (1955). 111 Richmond Street won an honourable mention for a 1955 Massey Medal in the office building category; see also Martins-Manteiga, *Dickinson*, 55, 122–5.

62 "Wawanesa Mutual Insurance Co., Toronto, Architects, Page and Steele," RAIC *Journal* 33, no. 5 (1956); Martins-Manteiga, *Dickinson*, 140–3. This building was marred somewhat by having the company name rather tackily displayed at the second floor level facing south onto Merton.

63 Martins-Manteiga, *Dickinson*, 126–9.

64 "Toronto Teacher's College, Toronto, Ontario, Architects, Page and Steele," RAIC *Journal* 33, no. 2 (1956); "The Massey Medals for Architecture, 1955," RAIC *Journal* 32, no. 12 (1955).

65 Martins-Manteiga, *Dickinson*, 150–4.

66 W. Sefton, "Cutting Construction Costs with New Techniques," RAIC *Journal* 32, no. 12 (1955); Patricia McHugh, *Toronto Architecture: A City Guide*, 2nd ed. (Toronto: McClelland and Stewart, 1989), 174. The building also provided some salutary lessons in the deficiencies of one hallmark of Modernism in Toronto's climate when the white-painted exterior plaster cladding eventually deteriorated badly and ultimately had to be removed.

67 "Islington United Church, Islington, Ontario," by Bruce Brown and Bisley; "First Unitarian Church, Toronto, Ontario," by Fisher; "Central Christadelphian Church, Toronto, Ontario," by Parkin Associates; RAIC *Journal* 29, no. 7 (1952). The same issue also illustrated additions to existing buildings with some Modern influences: "Sunday School Addition to Manor Road United Church, Toronto, Ontario" by W.J. McBain and Kent Barker, and "Parish Hall for St. Cuthbert's Anglican Church, Toronto, Ontario," by Fleury and Arthur; see also Peter and Douglas Richardson, *Canadian Churches: An Architectural History* (Toronto: Firefly, 2007), 186, 274–6, 278.

68 Martins-Manteiga, *Dickinson*, 80, reproduces a contemporary photograph of the (now demolished) house but gives no more details; he refers to the owner as "Stainman" at 12, 80, and 283 using "Staiman" at 82.

69 See City of North York Planning Department, Urban Design Division, *North York's Modernist Architecture* (Toronto: City of North York, 1997; reprinted with additional contributions by ERA Architects Inc., 2009), at page 7 in 1997 edition. There is some confusion about exactly when the Betel house was commissioned and completed, as the entry for the house in this publication gives the date of 1953 while the unpaginated "Inventory of Modernist Architecture" after page 24 lists the house under the category of "Housing – Private Residence" but gives 1957 as the date. The latter date for the completion of the house seems probable since the Toronto Public Library's Architectural Index for Ontario (available at http://archindont.torontopubliclibrary.ca/) records that Grossman only set up in practice in Toronto in 1954.

70 "The Betel House, Toronto," *Canadian Architect* 3, no. 6 (1958).

71 "The Massey Medals for Architecture, 1952," RAIC *Journal* 30, no. 1 (1953).
72 Eric Arthur, "The Master Plan and the Building," and Mary Rowell Jackman, "Wymilwood, A Students' Union for Victoria College," RAIC *Journal* 31, no. 2 (1954); Larry Wayne Richards, *University of Toronto: The Campus Guide* (New York: Princeton Architectural Press, 2009), 88–90. Mary Rowell Jackman claimed no special expertise as a decorator but admitted in the notes on contributors to the journal that, as a housewife of twenty years, she leapt at the chance to oversee the interiors the building at a college with which her family had a long, intimate connection.
73 "Victoria University Quadrangle" and "Victoria University Library, Toronto," *Canadian Architect* 7, no. 1 (1962).
74 Built in 1954 for Anglo Canada Insurance this has been described as "a veritable textbook of Modern innovations"; see Detlef Mertins, "Mountain of Lights," in *Toronto Modern*, 14–15, 54–5.
75 Arthur and his partner were also recognized for Wymilwood at Victoria College and Arthur's own Trend house for the BC lumber industry.
76 The rest of the list was comprised of G.A. Robb's Shell Tower at the CNE, Brennan and Whale's School of Nursing for St Joseph's Hospital, 1830 Queen West, Elken and Becksted's Seaway Hotel at 894 Lakeshore Boulevard, plus Shore and Moffatt's offices for Canadian Hanson and Van Winkle, 2 Silver Avenue, along with the various TTC subway stations; see *Canadian Architecture*, Fifth Issue, May 1956.
77 "Uncompromising Modern Inside and Out," *CHG* 34, no. 1 (1957).
78 James A. Knight, "Why Houses Don't Look Like Caves Anymore," *CHG* 34, no. 11 (1957).
79 "What is Wrong with the Modern?" *CHG* 27, no. 11 (1950).
80 Earl Morgan, "Editorial," RAIC *Journal* 30, no. 12 (December 1953). The editorial board's chair customarily wrote the year-end editorial. Morgan designed a modernistic plant for Standard Chemical (see Chapter 4). But his criticisms had a point as John C. Parkin's small house design in *67 Homes for Canadians* called for the glazing to be set directly into the wooden window frames.
81 R. Scholfield Morris, "Editorial," RAIC *Journal* 31, no. 1 (1954).
82 James Govan, "Canadian Exterior Wall Problems," RAIC *Journal* 31, no. 10 (1954).
83 Eric Arthur, "Editorial, " RAIC *Journal* 32, no. 3 (1955). Evidently Arthur was unaware of Johnson's homosexuality, hard to miss as it was.

CHAPTER SIX

1 Lewis Mumford, "The Gift Horse's Mouth," reprinted from the *New Yorker* in RAIC *Journal* 34 no. 5 (1957).
2 Lewis Mumford, "Acceptance Speech on Recipt of RIBA Gold Medal, 1961," RAIC *Journal* 38, no. 8 (1961).
3 John C. Parkin, "Architecture in Canada Since 1945: An Appraisal," RAIC *Journal* 39, no. 1 (1962).
4 Alan Gowans, "Twentieth-Century Canadian Architecture as Cultural Expression," *Journal of Canadian Studies* 1, no. 1 (1966): 26.
5 Graham Livesey, Michael McMordie, and Geoffrey Simmins, eds., *Twelve Modern Houses, 1945–1985* (Calgary, AB: University of Calgary and Aris Press, 1995), 2.
6 The proposals are discussed and illustrated in Mark Osbaldeston, *Unbuilt Toronto: A History of the City That Might Have Been* (Toronto: Dundurn Press, 2008), 84–91.
7 Eric Arthur, "Editorial," RAIC *Journal* 30, no. 3 (1953).
8 Wright, Gropius, and Phillips qtd. in "City Hall and Civic Centre," *Canadian Architecture*, Fourth Issue (1956).
9 Osbaldeston, *Unbuilt Toronto*, 90–1; William Dendy and William Kilbourn, *Toronto Observed: Its Architecture, Patrons and History* (Toronto: Oxford University Press, 1986), 267.
10 Edna Hudson, "Arthur's Competitions," in *Eric Ross Arthur: Conservation in Context*, ed. Alec Keefer (Toronto: Toronto Region Architectural Conservancy, 2001), 151.
11 Geoffrey Simmins, *Ontario Association of Architects: A Centennial History, 1889–1989* (Toronto: OAA, 1989), 141–2.
12 The following paragraphs are based on "The Toronto Press," RAIC *Journal* 33, no. 4 (1956); OAA president George Y. Masson to Phillips, reprinted in RAIC *Journal* 34, no. 2 (1957); Sara Bowser, "How to Buy a Work of Art," *Canadian Architect* 4, no. 4 (April 1959).

13 The *Globe and Mail* was also dismissive, once suggesting simply hiring Le Corbusier or Eero Saarinen to design a new city hall.
14 See William Dendy, *Lost Toronto* (Toronto: Oxford University Press, 1978), 138–9. The Armoury building was ultimately demolished in 1963 to make way for a not very distinguished Modernist courthouse extension facing onto University Avenue.
15 E.C.S. Cox, "Institute News, Annual meeting of the O.A.A., President's Report," RAIC *Journal* 35, no. 3 (1958); Sara Bowser, "How to Buy a Work of Art," *Canadian Architect*, 4, no. 4 (1959); Simmins, *Ontario Association of Architects*, 144.
16 Osbaldeston, *Unbuilt Toronto*, 92–3.
17 Douglas Shadbolt, *Ron Thom: The Shaping of an Architect* (Vancouver: Douglas and McIntyre, 1995), 40.
18 "Toronto City Hall and Square Competition," "The Jury," RAIC *Journal* 35, no. 10 (1958).
19 "Odds and Ends," *Canadian Architect* no. 6 (1958); Sara Bowser, "How to Buy a Work of Art," *Canadian Architect* 4, no. 4 (1959).
20 Eero Saarinen qtd. in Robert Fulford, *Accidental City: The Transformation of Toronto* (Toronto: Macfarlane, Walter, and Ross, 1995), 6. For an account of the design contest, see Fulford, *Accidental City*, 3–9.
21 Besides Rewell the finalists were Canadian David E. Horne, Australian student John Andrews from Harvard, John Nielson and Halldor Gunnlogson of Denmark, along with I.M. Pei, Frank Mikutowski, William B. Hayward, and Perkins and Will, all Americans.
22 See Tuula Revell, "Viljo Revell, Biography," in *Viljo Revell: "It Was Teamwork, You See,"* by Tuula Revell et al. (Helsinki: Didrichsen, 2009), 231–43.
23 Susanna Santala, "Viljo Revell and Changing Modernism"; Lauri Pukonen, "Viljo Revell and the New Building Technology," and Revell, "Biography," 238, in *Viljo Revell.*
24 Revell, "Biography," 241.
25 "Odds and Ends," *Canadian Architect* 7, no. 10 (1962).
26 "Toronto City Hall and Square Competition," "Majority Report," RAIC *Journal* 35, no. 10 (1958); Osbaldeston, *Unbuilt Toronto*, 94–7. Municipal civil servants have always complained that this alteration left people working inside the windows of the east tower roasting on hot, sunny afternoons. See also Bureau of Architecture and Urbanism, *Toronto Modern Architecture 1945–1965*, (Toronto: Coach House, 2002), 78–83.
27 "Toronto City Hall and Square Competition," "Minority Report," RAIC *Journal* 35, no. 10 (1958).
28 Gordon Stephenson to the editor, RAIC *Journal* 43, no. 8 (1966). By 1966 Stephenson had moved from Toronto to the University of Western Australia where he could observe at first hand the saga of the controversial Sydney Opera House, which by then was four times over budget.
29 "Odds and Ends," *Canadian Architect* no. 10 (1958); Sara Bowser, "How to Buy a Work of Art," *Canadian Architect* 4, no. 4 (1959).
30 Some people professed to discern a resemblance between the design and Oscar Niemeyer's Brazilian Congress building.
31 Eric Arthur, "Editorial," RAIC *Journal* 37, no. 3 (1960); Eberhard Zeidler, "West Ellesmere United Church and Christian Education Centre, Scarborough, Ont., Architects, Zeidler and Craig," RAIC *Journal* 37, no. 10 (1960).
32 Revell, "Biography," 241.
33 "Reflections on Monumentality" and Sara Bowser, "How to Buy a Work of Art," *Canadian Architect* 4, no. 4 (1959).
34 "Odds and Ends," *Canadian Architect* 5, no. 12 (1960).
35 "Toronto City Hall, Architects and Engineers, Viljo Revell in association with John B. Parkin Associates," RAIC *Journal* 38, no. 5 (1961); "Odds and Ends," *Canadian Architect* 6, no. 8 (1961) and 6, no. 10 (1961).
36 The following paragraphs are based upon Michael McMordie, "John C. Parkin in Conversation with Michael McMordie," in *John C. Parkin, Archives and Photography: Reflections on the Practice and Presentation of Modern Architecture* by Linda Fraser, Michael McMordie, and Geoffrey Simmins (Calgary, AB: University of Calgary Press, 2013); Douglas Shadbolt, "Toronto City Hall, Structure and Materials, A Lesson in Design," RAIC *Journal* 43, no. 3 (1966); Ronald Mar, "Design in Concrete and Architectonic Form in Viljo Revell's Toronto City Hall," in *Concrete Toronto: A Guidebook to Concrete Architecture from the Fifties to the Seventies*, ed. Michael McClelland and Graeme Stewart (Toronto: Coach House, 2007), 78–80.
37 "Toronto City Hall and Civic Square, Ontario," *Canadian Architect* 10 (1965); McMordie, "John C. Parkin in Conversation."

38 Elizabeth Hulse, "Beer Precast," in *Concrete Toronto*, 290.

39 Revell, "Biography," 242; "Progress Report: Toronto City Hall," *Canadian Architect* 9, no. 12 (1964).

40 The committee also included interior decorators Robin Bush and Budd Sugarman and architects Howard Chapman and John Mar.

41 Robert Gretton, managing editor of *Canadian Architect*, captured this wrangle splendidly in "The Great Furniture Debate" (10, no. 6 [1965]); see also Marsha Kelman, "City Hall's Concrete Furniture," in *Concrete Toronto*, 82–7, which includes plans of the desks.

42 Revell, "Biography," 242.

43 "Odds and Ends," *Canadian Architect* 11, no. 4 (1966); Anita Aarons, "A Current of Events – Toronto," RAIC *Journal* 43, no. 5 (1966); Dendy and Kilbourn, *Toronto Observed*, 269. John C. Parkin claimed to have set this fundraising in motion when an anonymous donor telephoned him the day after council voted down the funds for the sculpture and offered to donate $20,000. Parkin telephoned the mayor, who took up the cause, and in the end Moore was persuaded to lower his price to $100,000 on condition that he could make a second copy of the work, which was installed outside Mies van der Rohe's new National Gallery in Berlin; see McMordie, "John C. Parkin in Conversation."

44 "Progress Report: Toronto City Hall," *Canadian Architect* 9, no. 12 (1964); "Odds and Ends," *Canadian Architect* 10, no. 5 (1965).

45 "Panel Discussion on the Civic Design Aspects of the City Hall," and "John B. Parkin Associates, The Architect's Statement on the Competition and Construction and the Structural Solution," RAIC *Journal* 42, no. 9 (1965); Ron Thom, "Toronto City Hall: A Critique," *Canadian Architect* 10, no. 10 (1965).

46 Douglas Shadbolt, "Toronto City Hall" and Guy Desbarats, "L'education et l'architecture symbolique," RAIC *Journal* 43, no. 3 (1966).

47 Robert Gretton, "Comment," *Canadian Architect* 13, no. 8 (1968).

48 "Hotel and City: Winning Entry for South Side of Queen St., Toronto," *Canadian Architect* 13, no. 5 (1968); "[Jury] Report on the South Side of Queen Street, Toronto," *Canadian Architect* 13, no. 7 (1968).

49 "Perspective," *Canadian Architect* 13, no. 7 (1968).

50 In his book *Four Seasons: The Story of a Business Philosophy* (Toronto: Viking Canada, 2009), Isadore Sharp explains how he persuaded the conglomerate ITT (which had acquired the Sheraton chain) to agree to give him a 49 percent interest in the hotel for $3.5 million (65–70).

51 "Four Seasons Sheraton Hotel, Toronto" and James Acland, "Four Seasons Hotel – A Critique," *Canadian Architect* 18, no. 5 (1972); "Voice," L.A. Oxley, *Canadian Architecture* 18, no. 7; Michael McClelland, "The Sheraton Centre," in *Concrete Toronto*, 112.

52 Vincent Massey, *What's Past Is Prologue: The Memoirs of Vincent Massey* (Toronto: Macmillan, 1963), 26, 34.

53 The proposal is quoted in Shadbolt, *Thom*, 58–9.

54 Dendy and Kilbourn, *Toronto Observed* (quoted), 272–3; Massey, *Past Is Prologue*, 527–31.

55 Arthur Erickson and Geoffrey Massey shared a silver Massey Medal in 1958 in the category of residential architect for a 1,200-square-foot house in West Vancouver; see RAIC *Journal* 35, no. 12 (1958). Geoffrey Massey recommended Erickson and Thom, and Hart Massey, Parkin and Corneil; see Shadbolt, *Thom*, 61.

56 Shadbolt, *Thom*, Chapters 4 to 8.

57 Massey is quoted in Shadbolt, *Thom*, 61–2, where the four plans are reproduced at 63; "Massey College," *Canadian Architect* 5, no. 12 (December 1960) also reproduces all the entries.

58 See Thom's original drawings in Shadbolt, *Thom*, 64–6.

59 Shadbolt, *Thom*, 67–83; Bureau of Architecture and Urbanism, *Toronto Modern*, 68–71.

60 Shadbolt, *Thom*, 80–3. A comparison of the drawings, however, make Erickson's complaints reasonably plausible.

61 Ron Thom, "Massey College," and James Acland "Critique," *Canadian Architect* 8, no. 10 (1963).

62 R.J. Thom, "Architect's Statement," and Peter Collins, "An Appraisal," RAIC *Journal* 40, no. 10 (1963). Collins added that Thom had specified concrete spandrel panels but had been convinced by the contractor that carved limestone was actually cheaper, which might have led him to wonder if that pointed to something inherently wrong in the design.

63 "Massey Medal Awards 1964," in the "Critique" section of the *Canadian Architect* 9, no.

12 (1964), declared that the omission of Massey College from the medal winners was "a travesty of judgement," especially since it was a rare example of a single designer being allowed to produce everything from landscaping to furniture.

64 Carol M. Ede, *Canadian Architecture 1960/70* (Toronto: Burns and MacEachern, 1971), 10–23.

65 Larry Wayne Richards, *University of Toronto: The Campus Guide* (New York: Princeton Architectural Press, 2009), 116–8.

66 John Polanyi's Nobel Gold Medal for Chemistry may hang in the private dining room but the work for which it was awarded occurred somewhere else.

67 Brigitte Shim, writing in the 1993 anniversary edition of the in-house publication, "The Massey Bull," is quoted by Shadbolt, *Thom*, 83–4.

68 Revell designed nothing else in Toronto besides the New City Hall, while Thom set up his own office in Toronto in 1970 and worked on a number of commercial and industrial projects there before his death in 1986.

69 Albert Rose, *Regent Park: A Study in Slum Clearance* (Toronto: University of Toronto Press, 1958). Figure 1 (after p. 98) shows the layout and the quotation is from page 221.

70 "Regent Park South Project, Toronto, Ontario, Architects for the High Rise Buildings, Page and Steele, Architects for the Row Housing, J.E. Hoare, Jr.," RAIC *Journal* 34, no. 4 (1957).

71 "Apartments: Regent Park South, Toronto," *Canadian Architect* 4, no. 9 (1959).

72 Ian MacLennan, chief architect of Central Mortgage and Housing Corporation (which oversaw the financing) made the choice and specified the height of the towers, while J.E. Hoare of the Toronto Housing Authority, who had designed the original Regent Park buildings, handled the row housing.

73 John Martins-Manteiga, *Peter Dickinson* (Toronto: Toronto Modern, 2010), 180–3.

74 Another Toronto imitation of Le Corbusier was the prominent Modernist Irving Grossman's design for the 244-unit Somerset Apartments on Finch Avenue for Morden Yolles and his brother Burle; the Somerset Apartments also had two-storey layouts and skip-stop elevators, which yielded more rentable space than conventional designs. See Beth Kapusta and John McMinn, *Yolles: A Canadian Engineering Legacy* (Vancouver: Douglas and McIntyre, 2002), 76.

75 John Sewell, *The Shape of the City: Toronto Struggles with Modern Planning* (Toronto: University of Toronto Press, 1993), 106–12.

76 Anthony Jackson, "Criticism," *Canadian Architect* 4, no. 9 (1959); "1961 Massey Medals for Architecture," RAIC *Journal* 38 no. 11 (1961).

77 Sewell, *Shape of the City*, 112.

78 Martins-Manteiga, *Dickinson*, 146–9; Kapusta and McMinn, *Yolles*, 60.

79 See Osbaldeston, *Unbuilt Toronto*, 217.

80 See Martins-Manteiga, *Dickinson* for a drawing of the never-built office-hotel complex (67). Dickinson maintained his interest in creating a larger complex in that area, urging developer Walter Zwig to buy a property just to the north where in 1956 he designed a handsome ten-storey office tower at 55 Yonge Street; see Martins-Manteiga, *Dickinson*, 136–7.

81 Martins-Manteiga, *Dickinson*, 61–7, 166–73; Bureau of Architecture and Urbanism, *Toronto Modern Architecture 1945–1965*, 64–7.

82 Martins-Manteiga, *Dickinson*, 154–5.

83 Ibid., 159–61. Soon afterwards Dickinson also began planning an extension for Yolles and Rotenerg's Park Plaza Hotel at the corner of Bloor and Avenue Road, where he clad the east and west walls with pink glazed brick and linked it to the original 1930s building with the Empress Room, a space for holding large events behind a forecourt that had a circular ramp to underground parking; see Martins-Manteiga, *Dickinson*, 174–9.

84 Ibid., 68–75.

85 Elizabeth Hulse, *The Beers: Canada's First Family in Precast Concrete* (Toronto: Coach House, 2002), 73.

86 Martins-Manteiga, *Dickinson*, 162–5.

87 Ibid., 199–201 and 87, which has a photograph of the panels being bolted into place.

88 Peter Dickinson Associates, "Three Toronto Office Buildings," *Canadian Architect* 5, no. 3 (1960).

89 Martins-Manteiga, *Dickinson*, 202–7; Bureau of Architecture and Urbanism, *Toronto Modern Architecture 1945–1965*, 16.

90 Martins-Manteiga, *Dickinson*, 73–5, 208–11; "Project: Jesuit Seminary, Toronto, Architects, Peter Dickinson Associates," RAIC *Journal* 36, no. 6 (1959); "Regis College, Willowdale,

Ont.," *Canadian Architect*, 7, no. 5 (1962). Dickinson then designed a new building for the Toronto *Telegram* on the Front Street site, ultimately acquired by the *Globe and Mail* when the *Telegram* folded; see Martins-Manteiga, 222–4.

91 Kapusta and McMinn, *Yolles*, 53–5.

92 Arthur Boyd, "The Skyscraper, *Canadian Architect* 7, no. 6 (1962); Peter Collins, "The Canadian Imperial Bank of Commerce: An Appraisal," RAIC *Journal* 39, no. 10 (1962). The bank ended its contract with Dickinson when the building was two-thirds clad and turned over the project to Clifford and Lawrie who had worked for the Imperial Bank; see Martins-Manteiga, *Dickinson*, 93–7, 108, 254–75, and Kapusta and McMinn, *Yolles*, 93–5.

93 Martins-Manteiga, *Dickinson*, 216–17.

94 Ibid., 107–8, 228–31; Sharp, *Four Seasons*, 46.

95 The Parkin firm was identified with institutional and industrial work, and John C. expressed regret that he never designed an apartment building at a time when Peter Dickinson was turning out apartments and commercial towers for developers; see Adele Freedman, *Sight Lines: Looking at Architecture and Design in Canada* (Toronto: Oxford University Press, 1990), 14.

96 "Sun Life Building, Toronto, Ontario, John B. Parkin Associates," RAIC *Journal* 35, no. 11 (1958); "The Sun Life Building, Architects and Engineers, John B. Parkin Associates," RAIC *Journal* 38, no. 9 (1961).

97 Maximum density permitted for office towers was twelve times lot size.

98 "The Sun Life Building, Architects and Engineers, John B. Parkin Associates," RAIC *Journal* 38, no. 9 (1961); "Sun Life Building, Toronto," *Canadian Architect* 6, no. 10 (1961); see also John Martins-Manteiga, *Mean City: From Architecture to Design: How Toronto Went Boom* (Toronto: Dominion Modern, 2005), 32–9; and Bureau of Architecture and Urbanism, *Toronto Modern Architecture 1945–1965*, 17–18.

99 "Editor's Note" and James B. Craig to editor, *Canadian Architect* 7, no. 2 (1962).

100 "Toronto Airport Terminal Buildings, John B. Parkin Associates," RAIC *Journal* 35, no. 6 (1958).

101 "Toronto International Airport," James Acland, "Critique," *Canadian Architect* 9, no. 2 (1964); Peter Collins, "Three New International Air Terminals, An Appraisal," RAIC *Journal* 41, no. 2 (1964); see also Martins-Manteiga, *Mean City*, 46–53.

102 *North York's Modernist Architecture* (Toronto: Corporation of the City of North York, 1997, 2009 ed., reprinted with additional material by E.R.A. Architects), 16; John Martins-Manteiga, ed., *Endangered Species: Aedificium Novum Extinctum* (Toronto: Dominion Modern, 2007), 34–5.

103 Sara Bowser, "Shoemakers' Children," *Canadian Architect* 3, no. 4 (1958).

104 Freedman, *Sight Lines*, 93–5.

105 *North York's Modernist Architecture*, 17.

106 Michael McMordie quoted regarding design by John B. Parkin Associates for Douglas Crashley, Old George Place, Toronto, 1959–60, in *Twelve Modern Houses*, 28–31; see also City of Toronto, Heritage Preservation Services, Report regarding 3 Old George Place, Refusal of Alterations to a Designated Heritage Property, 3 September 2008, www.Toronto.ca/legdocs/mmis/2008.

107 Crashley, who had sold the property to Fraser, imposed a covenant on his title that forbade any alterations to the new house without approval, presumably to ensure that nothing that he did not approve of was done to the adjoining building, which was largely concealed from next door by the contours and plantings; see Ontario, Ministry of Culture and Communications, Conservation Review Board, City of Toronto – Intention to Designate 4 Old George Place (The Fraser House) Toronto, Ontario, 14 May 1991, http://www.crb.gov.on.ca/stellent/idcplg/webdav/Contribution%20Folders/crb/english/toronto_oldgeorge4.pdf.

108 Michael McMordie regarding the design in *Twelve Modern Houses*, 44–5. Shadbolt, *Thom*, provides a plan and states that most of the detailed design work was done by Thom's associate Paul Merrick (134–5). The architects also provided the built-in furniture and light fixtures; see also Ede, *Canadian Architecture 1960/70*, 254–9.

109 Martins-Manteiga, *Dickinson*, 82–3.

110 Peter C. Newman, *The Establishment Man: A Portrait of Power* (Toronto: McClelland and Stewart, 1982), 30.

111 Martins-Manteiga, *Dickinson*, 82–3.

112 Ibid., 83–4.

113 See Bureau of Architecture and Urbanism,

Toronto Modern Architecture, 62–3; Jose-Castel Branco, "The Fogel House," in *Endangered Species*, 60–5. Grossman's obituary in the *Globe and Mail* (14 September 1995) also listed him as responsible for the Berman house (1956) and the Klamer house (1958) in the Modernist style.

114 *North York's Modernist Architecture*, 11.

115 Dave LeBlanc, "Ghosts of the Bridle Path," *Globe and Mail*, 6 June 2003; see also *Ontario Homes and Living* (December1964); *North York's Modern Architecture*, "Inventory of Modern Architecture" also lists Markson as responsible for the following "Private Residences": 167 Valley Road (1955); 32 Saintfield Avenue (1961); 53 Montressor Drive (1962); 23 Park Lane Circle (1964, client, J. Posluns); 63 The Bridle Path (1967, client, W. Posluns); 17 Forest Wood Road (1970).

116 The farm was in Pickering, south half of lot 16, 8th concession, 1940.

117 *CHG* 36, no. 1 (1959); Dave LeBlanc, "Where the Future Enfolds," *Globe and Mail*, 8 August 2003.

118 "Interview – Morden Yolles: Building in Concrete," in *Concrete Toronto*, 303–4; Kapusta and McMinn, *Yolles*, 44.

119 Clifford qtd. in LeBlanc, "Where the Future Enfolds."

120 Kapusta and McMinn, *Yolles*, 44.

CHAPTER SEVEN

1 See Graham Livesey, Michael McMordie, and Geoffrey Simmins, eds., *Twelve Modern Houses, 1945–1985* (Calgary: University of Calgary and Aris Press, 1995), 2.

2 Interview with Vincent Tovell, "Documenting a Cultural Explosion," in *Concrete Toronto: A Guidebook to Concrete Architecture from the Fifties to the Seventies*, by Michael McClelland and Graeme Stewart (Toronto: Coach House, 2007), 61. Tovell produced the CBC television show *Explorations* in the mid-1960s.

3 The following paragraphs are based mainly upon Daniel Stoffman, *The Cadillac Fairview Story* (Toronto: Cadillac Fairview, 2004), 30–53.

4 Cemp was named after Charles, Edward, Minda and Phyllis, Samuel Bronfman's four children, and it proved fairly easy to persuade TD to enter the joint venture because Cemp had a higher net worth than the bank.

5 The CIBC managed to get hold of a property at the corner of King and York and another holdout remained at Bay and Wellington, so the development did not encompass the entire super-block.

6 Bureau of Architecture and Urbanism, *Toronto Modern Architecture 1945–1965*, (Toronto: Coach House, 2002), 72–7.

7 The path was also smoothed by the fact that after Fairview discovered that downtown real assessments in Toronto varied widely, Bernard Ghert, an expert on this subject, was hired to persuade the city to cut the tax rate from a projected $2.45 per square foot to just $1.45. See Stoffman, *Cadillac Fairview*, 42.

8 See the striking photograph reproduced in John Martins-Manteiga, *Mean City: From Architecture to Design: How Toronto Went Boom* (Toronto: Dominion Modern, 2005), 64.

9 Ultimately there were two more identical structures added, the smaller Commercial Union tower at the corner of Wellington and York and the mid-size IBM tower across the road on the south side of Wellington (whose location made it much less a part of the ensemble). Later still another tower was added on Bay Street south of the banking pavilion, which straddled the preserved premises of the old Toronto Stock Exchange in an infelicitous manner.

10 "Odds and Ends," *Canadian Architect* 10, no. 11 (1965). One person reported that he had urged Parkin Associates to keep the old building in 1962 but that John C. Parkin had replied only that they would weigh all the factors concerned before making a decision; see D. Warrilow to editor, *Canadian Architect* 10, no. 12 (1965).

11 William Dendy and William Kilbourn, *Toronto Observed: Its Architecture, Patrons and History* (Toronto: Oxford University Press, 1986), 278.

12 Anthony Jackson, "The International Style," *Canadian Architect* 6, no. 10 (1961).

13 James Murray, "Editorial," *Canadian Architect* 12, no. 2, (1967); "Dissent," Morris Charney to editor, *Canadian Architect* 12, no. 9 (1967). Murray's editorial was rather unusual as he normally confined himself to expressing brief opinions in the "Odds and Ends" department.

14 "Toronto Dominion Centre," and Macy DuBois, "Toronto Dominion Centre: A Critique," *Canadian Architect* 12, no. 11 (1967).

15 "Perspective," John Kryton to editor and Gretton's response in *Canadian Architect* 14, no. 1 (1969). Fuel was added to the wrangle over the failure to advertise Mies's role as designer in Toronto because Quebec architect Kryton complained that *Canadian Architect* had failed to give his firm due credit for the creation of Westmount Square.
16 "Commerce Court Toronto" and Alastair Grant, "Commerce Court, Critique 1: The Design," *Canadian Architect* 18, no. 3 (1973).
17 Dendy and Kilbourn, *Toronto Observed*, 280–1; Murray qtd. in "Perspective," *Canadian Architect* 13, no. 9 (1968).
18 Alastair Grant, "Commerce Court, Critique 1: The Design," *Canadian Architect* 18, no. 3 (1973).
19 John Martins-Manteiga, *Peter Dickinson* (Toronto: Toronto Modern, 2010), 285.
20 Dendy and Kilbourn, *Toronto Observed*, 282–5; Lambert qtd. in Stoffman, *Cadillac Fairview*, 51. In 1988 the Bank of Nova Scotia replaced its old head office on the northeast corner of King and Bay with a new tower to the east.
21 Stoffman, *Cadillac Fairview*, 51.
22 James Acland, "The Future of the Town House," *Canadian Architect* 2, no. 6 (1957).
23 James Murray, "Editorial," "Three Clients," *Canadian Architect* 3, no. 8 (1958).
24 "Ontario Association of Architects, Report of the Committee on Housing Design- 1957," RAIC *Journal* 35, no. 6 (1958).
25 Peter Dobush (chair), John C. Parkin, and C.E. Pratt, "Report of the RAIC Committee of Inquiry into the Design of the Residential Environment," RAIC *Journal* 37, no. 5 (1960); RAIC *Journal* 37, no. 7 (1960). On the criticisms of suburban society and a defence of its virtues see, S.D. Clark, *The Suburban Society* (Toronto: University of Toronto Press, 1966), chapters 5 to 7.
26 Eric Arthur, "Editorial," RAIC *Journal* 38, no. 10 (1961).
27 "Row Housing, Don Mills, Ontario, Associate Architects, James A. Murray and Henry Fliess," RAIC *Journal* 34, no. 4 (1957); "Massey Medals for Architecture, 1958," RAIC *Journal* 35, no. 12 (1958).
28 "Row Housing, Don Mills, Ont.," *Canadian Architect* 3, no. 6 (1958).
29 "Housing by Jack Klein and Henry Sears," *Canadian Architect* 6, no. 12 (1961); "Oakdale Manor, North York, Ont.," *Canadian Architect* 7, no. 9 (1962).
30 Jack Klein and Henry Sears, "Multiple Family Housing, Don Valley Woods, Yorkwoods," *Canadian Architect* 9, no. 8 (1964); "Don Valley Woods – Phase II, Ontario," *Canadian Architect* 11, no. 8 (August, 1966); "Don Valley Woods/Phase I, Toronto, Architects, Jack Klein and Henry Sears," and "Yorkwoods Village/Phase I, Toronto, Architects, Jack Klein and Henry Sears," RAIC *Journal* 41, no. 8 (1964). Klein and Sears won a Massey Medal in the Centennial Competition in 1967 for Phase II of Don Valley Woods; see "Massey Medals for Architecture, Centennial Competition, 1967," *Architecture Canada* 44, no. 6 (1967).
31 Henry Sears, "Housing in Metro" and Ian Maclennan, "The Architecture of Urban and Suburban Development," RAIC *Journal* 41, no. 8 (1964).
32 Albert Rose, "High-Rise Habitat: The Great Controversy," *Canadian Architect* 10, no. 3 (1965). Such beliefs proved very persistent as, a decade later, a survey of 570 Toronto residents about apartment living revealed that two-thirds of the respondents believed that high-rises were suitable for the young, the childless, and the old but were not desirable places for raising children; see Frederick Schindeler, "High-Rise Living; Fact and Fiction," *Canadian Architect* 19, no. 4 (1974).
33 Peter Barnard, "The Shear Wall-Slab Building," *Canadian Architect* 11, no. 3 (1966). See also E.R.A. interview "Morden Yolles: Building in Concrete," in *Concrete Toronto*, 300–11; Ivan Saleff, "The Age of Modern High-Rise Construction," in *Concrete Toronto*, 218–19; and Lewis Poplak, "The Flying Form and Development in Toronto," in *Concrete Toronto*, 220–1.
34 "The Colonnade, Toronto," *Canadian Architect* 9, no. 4 (1964).
35 Graeme Stewart, "Toronto's Modern Suburbs and the Concrete High-Rise," in *Concrete Toronto*, 212–15.
36 "Housing at Flemingdon Park, Ont.," *Canadian Architect* 6, no. 5 (1961).
37 Grossman qtd. in "Flemingdon Park, A Planned Community, Architect, Irving Grossman," RAIC *Journal* 38, no. 10 (1961).
38 Ibid.
39 T.E. Osborne, "A Developer's View," *Canadian Architect* 12, no. 4 (1967).
40 Howard V. Jones, "Flemingdon Park Revisited," *Canadian Architect* 12, no. 4 (1967).

Jones was the graphic designer of the magazine who interviewed Grossman.

41 Osborne, "A Developer's View" and Hans Elte, "Flemingdon: The Rise and Fall of an Essay in Better Living," *Canadian Architect* 12, no. 4 (1967).

42 A.J. Dakin, "Civic Design, Have We Done the Basic Thinking?," *RAIC Journal* 39, no. 9 (1962). The answer to that question seemed to be negative, though the discussion generated little beyond hot air.

43 "Odds and Ends," *Canadian Architect* 7, no. 12 (1962); "Maisonette Project, Toronto, and Clintwood Maisonette Project, Architect, Henry Fliess, Toronto," *RAIC Journal* 38, no. 10 (1961).

44 "Edgeley Housing Project, North York, Ont.," *Canadian Architect* 12, no. 11 (1967); "Rehabilitation: 2. Toronto Edgeley in the Village," *Canadian Architect* 16, no. 8 (1971).

45 Grossman, "Edgeley Housing," *Canadian Architect* 16, no. 8 (1971).

46 "Voice," "Open Letter to Developers" by Irving Grossman, *Canadian Architect* 18, no. 11 (1973).

47 The following paragraphs are based upon "Urban Renewal: Alexandra Park, Toronto," and Jack Klein, "1 – Alexandra Park: The Problem Stated," *Canadian Architect* 14, no. 9 (1969).

48 Markson qtd. in Klein, "1 – Alexandra Park," *Canadian Architect* 14, no. 9 (1969); "2 – Alexandra Park: Comment," *Canadian Architect* 14, no. 9 (1969).

49 John Sewell, *The Shape of the City: Toronto Struggles with Modern Planning* (Toronto: University of Toronto Press, 1993), 129.

50 Bruno Freschi, "The House as Architecture" and Fred Hollingsworth, "The Professional Gap," *Canadian Architect* 14, no. 3 (1969).

51 On SCSD, see http://archone.tamu.edu/CRS/engine/archive_files/efl/6000.0810.pdf (accessed September 2013). Educational Facilities Laboratories was a non-profit organization set up by the Ford Foundation to help in solving educational problems in Canada and the United States.

52 Scarborough's population rose from 139,744 in 1961 to 217,286 by 1971 and to 387,149 by 1976.

53 Russell Yapp, "Feedback: North Bridlewood Revisited," *Canadian Architect* 14, no. 12 (1969).

54 SEF was a joint venture with the Ontario provincial Department of Education and EFL. Robbie's official title was technical director with Hugh J. Vallery as academic director and a staff of twenty-two academic, technical, and administrative personnel.

55 These categories were defined as structural framing, exterior walls, roofing, plumbing, ceilings and lighting, carpeting and gymnasium flooring, atmosphere (i.e., heating-cooling), electrical-electronic connections, interior space dividers, and furnishings.

56 "Perspective," "Progress," *Canadian Architect* 14, no. 5 (1969); Alexander Leman, "SEF: Boon or Bane? A Progress Report," *Canadian Architect* 14, no. 12 (1969).

57 Various SEF-type systems, like lighting, had already given tests in an addition to Eastview Public School in Scarborough.

58 Alexander Leman, "SEF: Boon or Bane? A Progress Report," *Canadian Architect* 14, no. 12 (1969).

59 "Student Village" and George Banz, "Critique," *Canadian Architect* 15, no. 10 (1970); "Perspective," "Letters," Banz to editor, *Canadian Architect* 15, no. 12 (1970).

60 Roy Brown, "SEF: Did Educators Subvert the System?," *Canadian Architect* 16, no. 4 (1971).

61 The committee consisted of Howard V. Walker (chair), Ronald M. Glaister, W.T. Pentland, George A. Robb, John N. Shaw, and Alan Wilcox.

62 "SEF – A Critical Evaluation," *Canadian Architect* 17, no. 2 (1972).

63 Robbie would be much in the news later on when he designed the vastly expensive retractable roof on the Skydome, Toronto's huge new multipurpose stadium (later renamed the Rogers Centre).

64 Roderick Robbie and P.D.J. Trion, "Voice" *Canadian Architect* 17, no. 2 (1972).

65 Messrs. Hayne, Yamashita and Armstrong to the editor with a reply from the OAA committee, *Canadian Architect* no. 6 (1972).

66 "E6: Academic Evaluation: A Report on SEF Open Plan Schools" (typescript, Metropolitan Toronto School Board, 1975), 268; see http://www.eric.ed.gov.80/Ericdocs250l/content_storage_01/0000019b/80/31/9a.pdf, quotations from 64, 69 (accessed September 2011).

67 For instance, suspended ceilings were undesirable, so the steel roofing system could not be used.

68 "George Brown College of Applied Arts and Technology, Toronto"; Macy DuBois, "1: Architectural Concepts"; Morden Yolles, "2, Structural Aspects," Thom, "4, Critique," *Canadian Architect* 19, no. 3 (1974).
69 Modular Precast was jointly owned by Belmont Construction, Cadillac Development, Greenwin Construction, Heathcliffe Developments, and Meridian Building Group.
70 Ernest Annau, "System: Chapel Glen, Don Mills, Ont.," *Canadian Architect* 17, no. 1 (1972).
71 Hans Elte, "Habitat 67: The Critical Eye," *Canadian Architect* 12, no. 10 (1967).
72 "Perspective," "Progress," *Canadian Architect* 18, no. 10 (1973).
73 Douglas Shadbolt, *Ron Thom: The Shaping of an Architect* (Vancouver: Douglas and McIntyre, 1995), 85–109.
74 Larry Wayne Richards, *University of Toronto: The Campus Guide* (New York: Princeton Architectural Press 2009), 60–1, 63.
75 Ruth Cawker, "Modern Lessons," in *Toronto Modern*, 27.
76 Claude Bissell, "University of Toronto Expansion Program – A Reflection of Academic Policy and Ideals" and Howard Chapman, "The Campus Development Plan," RAIC *Journal* 37, no. 1 (1960).
77 "Arts Building, University of Toronto," *Canadian Architect* 7, no. 1 (1962).
78 Richards, *University of Toronto*, 158–9.
79 Eric Arthur noted that he and Walter Gropius had discussed the fact that designers of adjoining university buildings often seemed to ignore what surrounded their work; see Arthur, "Editorial," RAIC *Journal* 38, no. 11 (1961). Sidney Smith Hall, the Lash Miller Chemical Building, and the McLennan Physical Laboratories each had the misfortune to be surrounded by a dank, gloomy moat intended to allow natural light into the basement level.
80 The four existing colleges were three denominational Christian foundations – Victoria (Methodist, later United Church of Canada), St Michael's (Roman Catholic), and Trinity (Anglican) – each of which also awarded their own theological degrees, along with the religiously neutral University College (which, of course, attracted many Jewish students).
81 DuBois qtd. in "Phase I: New College, University of Toronto," *Canadian Architect* 10, no. 12 (1965); "New College II, University of Toronto," *Canadian Architect* 15, no. 5 (1970); Interview with DuBois by Mary Lou Lobsinger and Larry Richards, "Designing in Toronto: Designing in Concrete," in *Concrete Toronto*, 100–2; Richards, *University of Toronto*, 173.
82 The other members of the task force were P. Cravit, K. Harvey, B. Kuwabara, P. Ortved, and D. Thom.
83 "The Campus Centre"; Douglas Engel, "Part I: A Campus Centre for the Campus"; "Part II: The Campus as Campus Centre," *Canadian Architect* 17, no. 3 (1972).
84 "York University, Toronto," *Canadian Architect* 13, no. 8 (1968). See also "The Campus in Canada," "York University," *Canadian Architect* 9, no. 3 (1964); "Perspective," "Projects," *Canadian Architect* 13, no. 1 (1968); "Central Square Complex, York University," *Canadian Architect* 17, no. 10 (1972); "Three University Studies," "York University, Toronto, University Planners, Architects and Consulting Engineers, Gordon S. Adamson, Architects, John B. Parkin Associates, Architects and Engineers, Shore and Moffatt and Partners, Architects and Engineers," RAIC *Journal* 41, no. 7 (1964); Sewell, *Shape of the City*, 129–33; Philip Beeseley, "Ross Social Sciences and Humanities Building, York University," in *Concrete Toronto*, 264–6.
85 "Central Technical School Art Centre Toronto," *Canadian Architect* 8, no. 7 (1963); Peter Collins, "Central Technical School Art Centre, Architects, Robert Fairfield Associates, An Appraisal," RAIC *Journal* 40, no. 8 (1963); Interview with DuBois by Mary Lou Lobsinger, "Designing in Toronto: Designing in Concrete," in *Concrete Toronto*, 89–99.
86 Morden Yolles, "A Critical Examination of Architectural Concrete," *Canadian Architect Yearbook*, December 1966.
87 George Baird, "On *Concrete Toronto*," in *Concrete Toronto*, 48.
88 Paolo Scivano, "Scarborough College's Brutalist Dreams," in *Concrete Toronto*, 334–6.
89 "Scarborough College Is Concrete," Andrews interview with Vincent Tovell for CBC's "Explorations," (c. 1965), reprinted in *Concrete Toronto*, 328; "Scarborough College, Ontario"; John Andrews, "The Design Concept"; Raymond Affleck, "Comments" *Canadian Architect* 11, no. 5 (1966). Affleck's article seems to contain the first mention in the magazine of Brutalism as devised in Britain.

90 Affleck, "Comments," *Canadian Architect* 11, no. 5 (1966); Acland, "1967: Myth and Reality," *Canadian Architect Yearbook*, December 1967.

91 George Baird, "On *Concrete Toronto*," in *Concrete Toronto*, 48; Richards, *University of Toronto*, 194–6.

92 David Abbey, "Educational Needs and Architectural Solutions," *Canadian Architect* 12, no. 10 (1967). Abbey was a staff member of the Ontario Institute for Studies in Education who delivered his remarks at a symposium on "Education and Architecture in the Twentieth Century"; in its "Comments" section, the magazine promised a full discussion of Scarborough College in its December edition, but this was not forthcoming.

93 Carol Ede, *Canadian Architecture 1960/70* (Toronto: Burns and MacEachern, 1971), 24; Scrivano, "Scarborough College's Brutalist Dreams," in *Concrete Toronto*, 334–9; Richards, *University of Toronto*, 195.

94 Scrivano, "Scarborough College's Brutalist Dreams," in *Concrete Toronto*, 339.

95 Reyner Banham, *The New Brutalism: Ethic or Aesthetic?* (New York: Reinhold, 1966).

96 See Robert Gretton, "John P. Robarts Research Library, University of Toronto"; Ronald Thom, "Protest 1: A Lesson for All"; James Acland, "Protest 2: A Brain Factory"; L.S. Landmead, "Critique; No Room for Change," *Canadian Architect* 19, no. 8 (1974).

97 Richards, *University of Toronto*, 160–2; see also Mary Lou Lobsinger, "John P. Robarts Library," in *Concrete Toronto*, 164–73. One reason that the library aroused little enthusiasm in the wider Ontario academic community was that the University of Toronto reneged on its promise to grant special user privileges to faculty members from other universities, followed up in 2009 by imposing upon them a charge to use what had been sold as a central research library for the entire system.

98 The Ross Building at York University (see Figure 7.29) was often described as another example of Brutalism.

99 Jeff Hayes, "Sears Canada Headquarters," in *Concrete Toronto*, 122. This building is one of the few in this book where a photograph taken near the time of construction has not been found.

100 Ants Elken, "House on [95] Ardwold Gate," *Canadian Architect* 13, no. 4 (1968).

101 Michael Hugo-Brunt, "Yorkdale Shopping Centre, A Study," RAIC *Journal* 41, no. 6 (1964); "Yorkdale Shopping Centre, Toronto" and "Robert Simpson Store, Yorkdale," *Canadian Architect* 9, no. 6 (1964). See also Veronica Madonna, "Yorkdale Shopping Centre," in *Concrete Toronto*, where the detailed design for Simpson's store is ascribed to John Andrews (256–7).

102 Pinker, "Critique Two," *Canadian Architect* 9, no. 6 (1964); Thom, "Critique One," *Canadian Architect* 9, no. 6 (1964) (emphasis in original). Another serious problem arrived with the opening of the Spadina subway line along the route of the expressway as automobile commuters to downtown were drawn to use the hundreds of free parking spaces, eventually forcing Yorkdale to keep its lots closed until nine thirty each morning.

103 The exception was Sherway Plaza at the junction of the Queen Elizabeth Way and Highway 427 on the southwest corner of Metro Toronto, which was strongly resisted by suburban Toronto Township to the west on the grounds that it would draw away many customers from local stores there.

104 The following paragraphs are based upon Mark Osbaldeston, *Unbuilt Toronto: A History of the City That Might Have Been* (Toronto: Dundurn Press, 2008), 31–8.

105 Eaton's explored a joint venture first with Webb and Knapp Canada, who got into financial difficulties, then with E.P. Taylor

106 "Odds and Ends," *Canadian Architect* 10, no. 10 (1965).

107 Osbaldeston, *Unbuilt Toronto*, 37. See also the photographs in Osbaldeston, *Unbuilt Toronto*, 33–6.

108 See "Odds and Ends," *Canadian Architect* 11, no. 2 (1966) for the views of Eric Arthur, Mandel Sprachman, Sidney Bregman, John B. Parkin, Jack Klein, E.H. Zeidler, James Acland, Basil Capes, G.S. Abraham, and from Montreal Peter Collins and R.T. Affleck.

109 This claim produced a rejoinder from the Honorary Secretary of the Banister Fletcher Centennial Committee (Canadian Branch), pointing out that Fletcher had never made this claim himself but that it had been inserted into the seventeenth edition of his book by editor Frank Jenkins only after his death; see M. Anderson to editor, *Canadian Architect* 11 no. 4 (1966).

110 A.J.D[iamond], "Review," RAIC *Journal* 43, nos. 4 and 5 (1966). Diamond's attack upon Yamasaki followed from an article in *Harper's* in May 1966 where Wolf von Eckhardt charged the designer of the twin towers with "urbanicide."

111 Fred W. Price, RAIC executive director, "Communiqué," *Architecture Canada* [formerly RAIC *Journal*] 44, no. 1 (1967).

112 The following paragraphs are based upon Stoffman, *Cadillac Fairview*, 61–3.

113 See Eric Arthur, *Toronto, No Mean City*, 3rd ed., rev. by Stephen A. Otto (Toronto: University of Toronto Press, 1986), 89–90.

114 "Perspective," "Projects," *Canadian Architect* 16, no. 5 (1971).

115 The following paragraphs are based upon Stoffman, *Cadillac Fairview*, 63–71.

116 Eberhard Zeidler, "Ontario Place: Needs for a New Society," James Acland, "Ontario Place: An Excess of Hubris," *Canadian Architect* 16, no. 6 (1971), and the complaints in "Voice" by Zeidler, "Ontario Place: An Excess of Political Bias," *Canadian Architect* 16, no. 8 (1971).

117 "Toronto Eaton Centre: Phase 1" and Sears, "Toronto Eaton Centre," *Canadian Architect* 22, no. 5 (1977); Stoffman, *Cadillac Fairview*, 71.

118 "Myers Residence, Toronto," *Canadian Architect* 17, no. 2 (1972); Myers, "Introduction: 3 Steel Houses," in *3 Steel Houses: Barton Myers*, Kurt G.F. Helfrich et al. (Mulgrave, AU: Images Publishing, 2005), 17–19; Myers qtd. in Suzanne Myers, "Myers Residence, Toronto, An Interview with Barton Myers," in *3 Steel* Houses, 23, 22–30.

119 Barton Myers, "Wolf Residence, Toronto," *Canadian Architect* 21, no. 10 (1976); Suzanne Myers, "Wolf Residence, Toronto: An Interview with Barton Myers," in *3 Steel Houses*, 56, 54–60.

CONCLUSION

1 A.W. Bentham to Sir Ashton Webb, Westminster, England, "Report on Toronto and Proposed Improvements Sent July 4th, 1907," box 1, GCA, BR, TPL.

2 Alan Gowans, *The Comfortable House: North American Suburban Architecture, 1890–1930* (Cambridge, MA: MIT Press, 1986), 102–4, 106. He added sourly that even dedicated Modernists proved reluctant to live in their machines, so that Sigfried Giedion refused to move into his International Style house in Zurich perched on pilotis with strip windows but resided next door in a Biedermeier-style building, while Philip Johnson did not really live in his Glass House in Connecticut but up the hill in an eighteenth century farmhouse.

3 Municipal taxes were calculated in thousands of assessed values, and keeping that mill rate down was a major preoccupation.

INDEX